COALITION THEORIES AND CABINET FORMATIONS

Progress in
Mathematical Social Sciences

COALITION THEORIES AND CABINET FORMATIONS

A study of formal theories of coalition formation applied to nine European parliaments after 1918

ABRAM DE SWAAN

University of Amsterdam

With a preface by Anatol Rapoport

 Elsevier Scientific Publishing Company

Amsterdam · London · New York 1973

For the U.S.A. and Canada
JOSSEY-BASS INC. PUBLISHERS
615 MONTGOMERY STREET
SAN FRANCISCO, CALIF. 94111, U.S.A.

For all other areas:
ELSEVIER SCIENTIFIC PUBLISHING COMPANY
335 JAN VAN GALENSTRAAT
P.O. BOX 211, AMSTERDAM, THE NETHERLANDS

With 115 Tables

Library of Congress Card Number: 73-83396

ISBN 0-444-41144-5

Printed in The Netherlands

Progress in Mathematical Social Sciences

Other books included in this series

Lee M. Wiggins
Panel Analysis — Latent Probability Models for Attitude and
Behavior Processes

Raymond Boudon
Mathematical Structures of Social Mobility

J.K. Lindsey
Inferences from Sociological Survey Data — a Unified Approach

For Hennie and Carrie
in remembrance of
Meyer de Swaan

Author's Foreword

This book has evolved in the course of seven years. It has taken shape in periods of intensive work and perhaps also at times when work was laid aside.

Rather than bring all those who have influenced me and this research under the common denominator of gratitude, I prefer to recall how the late S. Kleerekoper showed me that passion and science go together. I salute Lucas van der Land who guided my steps towards the university, and Hans Daudt who, through our differences, provoked me into reflection and perseverance. In my two American years on a Harkness Fund Fellowship, Martha English and John Fox helped me often. That was also the period in which Emilie de Swaan-Nord shared my life around this work. Michael Leiserson, distant friend and kindred spirit, represents American friends, "politicos" and politicologists.

Nico Frijda emerged as a friend in need and remained a friend in times of joy. Rob Mokken was responsible for the removal of many errors from this book and the insertion of many effective touches. Hans Daalder followed the progress of the work from a distance with close attention, many times pointing out to me the error of my ways.

W.F. van Leeuwen taught me something about the "theory of changes", which made me invest more in the work yet treat it as a game. Ellen Ombre helped to give the finishing touch.

There is, however, one person whom I would like to thank: my teacher of Dutch, who wrote at the bottom of my school essay on the quantification of world misery: Formulitis!

Preface

Before the theory of games appeared on the scientific horizon, the mathematically oriented social scientist had two types of tools at his disposal. One was classical analysis, as it developed in conjunction with theoretical physics. The other was probability theory.

By their nature, the tools of analysis directed the social scientist's attention to deterministic processes. A solution of a system of ordinary differential equations presents itself as a set of functions of a single independent variable, usually interpreted as time, while the dependent variables may be any quantities of interest. Once the initial values of these quantities are given or assumed, the time courses of the variables are typically determined. This sort of mathematics suits the physical scientist, who studies phenomena subject to deterministic "laws". Whether such "laws" operate in human affairs (with which the social scientist is concerned) is a subject of philosophical disputes. Whether they do or not, it seems feasible to search for social phenomena that can be reasonably described by deterministic mathematical models, for instance, phenomena that are resultants of massively summed effects, which in their totality are quasi-deterministic. Thereby mathematical theories of social phenomena are directed into certain channels. Deterministic models have been developed in macro-economics. As an example of models relevant to political science, one might cite the quasi-mechanical models of arms races advanced by Lewis F. Richardson, where time courses of armament budgets appeared as solutions of a system of differential equations.

Probabilistic models represent attempts to capture the basic indeterminacy in phenomena involving human behavior. Whether one assumes such indeterminacy to be inherent in such phenomena or whether it is simply a reflection of our ignorance of the underlying "laws", is again a metaphysical question of little practical importance. That indeterminacy must often be taken into account is obvious, since no empirically verified theory remotely approaching the deterministic theories of physical science has ever been advanced in any social science.

A stochastic process is a typical example of a probabilistic model. The object of investigation is a system with a repertoire of specified "states." In the course of its history, the system passes through a sequence of states, the transitions from state to state being governed by assumed probabilities. The derived consequences of such assumptions relate to the probability of finding the system in a specified state at a specified time. In particular, these probabilities may take on asymptotic values. Thus, in a large *population* of such systems, each governed by identical probabilistic laws, one can expect to see a steady state distribution of the systems in the various states. Models of this sort are encountered in mathematical demography, statistical linguistics, stochastic learning theory, and other areas of social or behavioral science, where the object of investigation can be supposed to consist of a large number of essentially "identical" units. Probabilistic models in social science are analogous to those of statistical mechanics. In both approaches, deterministic features of the macro-system emerge from indeterministic features of the constituent micro-systems by virtue of the law of large numbers.

It can and has been argued that neither the deterministic nor the probabilistic models capture the purposeful, goal-directed, "rational" aspects of human behavior. Again the ontological status of these aspects is not (or should not be) the issue. One may be convinced that every human action is in the last analysis determined by combinations of physico-chemical events. This conviction, however, is no help in designing testable theories of human behavior. On the other hand, *something* can be said about the behavior of human beings on the basis of assumptions concerning their purposes, desires, or interests. In particular, if an actor's preference order of a set of alternatives is known and if he can choose among courses of action, each leading with certainty to one of the alternatives, the actor's choice can be predicted on the assumption that he is "rational." At any rate, the prediction can be taken as a definition of "rational decision" in the simplest conceivable decision situation.

The definition of rational decision can be extended to situations where outcomes are determined by actions only probabilistically. The theory of applied statistical decision rests on this definition. It is usually presented as a normative rather than a descriptive theory; for it seems to prescribe "rational" courses of action. However, if "rationality" *is* attributed to the actor, clearly the theory can be interpreted as a descriptive one, purporting to predict what a "rational" actor will do in decision situations where risk or uncertainty are involved. It is important to note that the theory presupposes more than an actor's given order of preferences for outcomes. The preferences must usually be given on the so called interval scale, where once the zero point and the unit have been chosen, the outcomes are characterized by numerical (not merely ordinal) utilities.

The theory of games is essentially an extension of the theory of rational decision to situations where two or more "rational actors" are involved. Outcomes are determined by the joint (either independent or coordinated) choices of the several actors. The actors' utilities of the outcomes are, in general, different. A rational actor (or "player") is one who has complete information about how the joint decisions determine the outcomes and also about the utilities attached to the outcomes by every player. A rational player assumes that every other player is also rational.

Viewed as a normative theory, the theory of games would be expected to prescribe decisions to "rational players" with the view of maximizing their respective utilities ("payoffs") under the constraints of the situation. Viewed as a descriptive theory, the theory of games would be expected to predict such decisions on the basis of assuming rationality of the players.

It would seem that the format of game theoretic models is ideally suited to the ways of thinking of the mathematically oriented political scientist. For decisions in situations involving conflicts of interest appear to be central to political behavior. The assumption of rationality underlying these models, although of questionable validity as in any situation involving human affairs, is not a serious handicap for two reasons. First, the political scientist may be interested in a normative theory and so in singling out rational decisions, perhaps with the view of recommending them to policy makers or other political actors. Second, predictions based on assumptions of rationality can be taken as a base line for descriptive theory: it is interesting to see to what extent actual political behavior deviates from "rationality" (as defined) and in what direction. If the deviations are systematic, possibly alternative or additional assumptions can serve to develop a "realistic" descriptive theory of political behavior.

On closer examination, game-theoretic formulations of rational decisions in conflict situations are seen to be beset with serious difficulties. If is found that definitive, unambiguous prescriptions of rational decision can be made only in the context of so called two-person constant-sum games, where there are only two players with diametrically opposed interests. In more general situations, ambiguities arise because decisions that are "individually rational" are not necessarily "collectively rational," as demonstrated in the simplest example of the now well known Prisoner's Dilemma game.

Nevertheless, what may have been an embarrassment for a prescriptive theory can be viewed as an instructive broadening of the conceptual repertoire. For the analysis of rational decisions in general conflict situations perforce turns the attention of the investigator to the dialectic opposition between individual and collective rationality, which might be viewed as a central problem in political science.

The theme is further generalized in the theory of the cooperative N-person game. In this model of conflict, the payoffs of the individual players are assumed to be additive, so that it makes sense to speak of the joint payoff of several players. It is shown in the theory of the two-person game that a player can, by a properly chosen strategy guarantee himself a certain minimum payoff regardless of how the other plays. The same is true in a game with more than two players if a player is conceived as pitted against all the others. Further, it stands to reason that if two or more players can coordinate their strategy choices, they can get jointly at least as much as if they played "every man for himself". Thus, a subset of the N players, by joining in a coalition, that is, by coordinating their strategies, can guarantee for themselves a certain minimum joint payoff, called the value of the game to the coalition. The function that specifies the value of the game to every possible coalition is called the characteristic function of the game.

The theory of the cooperative N-person game in characteristic function form disregards the question of *how* each coalition can get its value, assuming simply that they can. The central questions now become the following: (1) Which coalitions will, in fact, form? (2) How will a coalition apportion the joint payoff among themselves?

It will be readily recognized that these questions are also central to a theory purporting to describe certain forms of political behavior. As an example, one might take a presidential nominating convention in the United States. The delegates to the convention usually vote in well defined blocks, each in support of one of several candidates. An absolute majority of votes is required to nominate a candidate. Assuming, as is generally the case, that no candidate initially commands an absolute majority, a coalition must form to effect a nomination. And so it does. Thus, the first question as to which coalition will form is answered empirically. The second question is more difficult to answer empirically, since the werewithals of payoff (e.g., patronage, appointments among the political supporters of a successful candidate, etc.) are not directly observable. Still, if, on the basis of certain interpretations of observed results, the utilities to the members of a winning coalition could be established or assumed, the question of apportionment could also be answered empirically. Thereby it would be possible to compare this form of political behavior with the prescriptions (or predictions) of a mathematical theory, and so the mathematical method of theory construction with its impressive deductive power could be extended to situations where human actors are guided in their behavior by considerations involving goals, purposes, values, or interests.

Before examining the feasibility of relating theory to observations, it is instructive to examine more closely the sort of predictions or prescriptions that are involved in the theory of the cooperative N-person game. In a class of games called "simple", the characteristic function assumes only two values, which, without loss of generality, can be taken to be 0 and 1. That is to say, some coalitions are "winning coalitions": they can appropriate the "prize" represented by the unit of payoff. All the remaining coalitions are "losing". They cannot appropriate the prize. The theory of the cooperative N-person game, which assumes both individual and collective rationality, predicts that a winning coalition will indeed form. But it says nothing about which of several winning coalitions will form. Instead, attention is turned to the question of apportionments.

An apportionment of the prize among all the N players (some possibly getting 0) is called an imputation. In its early formulations, the theory sought to single out imputations characterized by some sort of "stability", that is reflecting the relative bargaining power of the players, the object of bargaining being to get as large a share of the prize as possible by the use of threats (to leave a coalition), promises (to join a coalition) or offers to others to entice them to join a coalition. (In a simple game the power of the players is reflected roughly in how many coalitions they can turn into winning coalitions by joining them.)

Thus, the main emphasis in game theory has been mostly on payoff apportionments. The political scientist, however, is more interested in the determinants of coalition formation, if only because the coalition structure of a political body is much more directly observable than payoff apportionments, whatever may be subsumed under this term. Nevertheless, to apply the apparatus of game theory to political events the political scientist must either know or assume something about the stakes of the political game, that is, the werewithal of payoffs. In simple games, where there is only one prize, it can be defined as the unit of payoff. However, in ignorance of what portions of that prize are worth, special assumptions must be made with regard to the division of the prize among the members of a winning coalition.

Depending on such assumptions, hypotheses suggest themselves with regard to coalition formation. Suppose, for example, that the prize is the power to make decisions, e.g., pass legislation, make appointments, etc. If the benefits are to be apportioned among the members of the winning coalition that has actually formed, it stands to reason that it will be to the advantage of the winning coalition to consist of as few members as possible in order to maximize the *per capita* benefits. This common sense consideration leads to the so called minimum winning coalition hypothesis. However, the term "minimal" is not precise. In the context of a political coalition, it may mean comprising the fewest requisite number of members; or it may mean comprising the fewest requisite number of votes. (Political actors, such as delegations, parties, etc. generally command unequal numbers of votes.)

Aside from this ambiguity the political scientist, striving to construct a "realistic" theory of coalition formation, is obliged to consider specifically political factors. There is the well known band waggon effect, where, once the formation of a particular winning coalition is imminent, its erstwhile opponents are eager to join it. Although the benefits to the minimal winning coalition may be thereby diluted, there may be political reasons for allowing the larger coalition to form, for instance to give the impression of unanimity (as in the final phases of a nominating convention.) Similar considerations may apply in times of war or crisis. Another reason why winning coalitions may not be minimal is that the solidarity of its members in subsequent actions is not always assured, as when coalition governments are formed by several political parties within which party discipline is not strict.

So far we have identified both the resources and the prizes of the political game with power, and indeed the behavior of some professional politicians may give the impression that political groupings have no other aim than to capture and retain power. The game-theoretic model of multi-lateral conflict presents the same picture. To be sure, the object of the game is to maximize payoff, but the nature of the payoff is not specified. In fact, one proposed "solution" of the N-person cooperative game, the so called Shapley Value, is an apportionment of the joint payoff attainable by the grand coalition of all players in proportion to the power of the individual players, the latter being calculated as the average increment a player brings to the value of a coalition he joins. This conception of solution rests on the assumption that all coalitions are a priori equally probable. In a political context, the assumption would imply that the politician has no preference except with regard to the amount of power (hence of payoff) that accrues to him in the coalition he joins. The model becomes the political counterpart of the classical *homo economicus* with power substituted for economic gain.

If one does not wish to accept this rather cynical view of politics, one is forced to take other constraints into consideration. Not all political coalitions are a priori equally likely. Political groupings are to *some* extent ideologically motivated. Political power is, at least in part, not just an end in itself or leverage for procuring personal benefits but also a means for effecting progress aimed at realizing ideological commitments. In other words, political coalitions are not formed in a vacuum. The political fluid has a viscosity, so that not all realignments are equally easy. There are some limitations on the old saw that politics makes strange bed fellows.

In the present monograph, the ideological factor is introduced into the political game in the form of a spectrum. The object of investigation is the multi-party political system of parliamentary democracies. Ordinarily a government requires the support of a majority of deputies in a legislative body. Typically, no single party commands an absolute majority. Therefore a coalition is necessary to form a government. So far the situation can be depicted by a cooperative N-person game with the "formation of the government" as the prize and with the distribution of the ministry portfolios among the coalition parties as the apportionment of the prize. It is assumed, however, that at least part of the payoff is embodied in the opportunity to effect certain programs. This can be done only if the positions of the members of the coalition are not too far apart on the political spectrum.

Political tradition in European parliamentary democracies makes a Left-Right political spectrum appear reasonable; so that every political party, except the extremes has a neighbor on the left and one on the right. Thus, the range of a coalition is roughly reflected by the portion of the spectrum spanned by it. The infusion of the ideological factor generates another criterion for singling out coalitions likely to form: those of minimum range.

The hypotheses mentioned so far derive from game theory only to the extent that they are suggested by the game-theoretic concepts: value of the game, winning coalition, etc., coupled in the last instance with the concept of the political spectrum. In this monograph, in addition, another type of theory is proposed that has a more direct bearing on the theory of the N-person cooperative game, the so called policy distance theory.

Here the point of departure is the individual actor's assumed preference order of the several coalitions of which he can be a member. This preference order is a reflection of the actor's preference order of the several policies. If both the policies and the actors can be assigned positions on the political spectrum, the preference order of policies can be naturally conceived as the inverse of the distances between the spectral position of the actor and those of the policies.

By the way the political spectrum is defined, the distance between an actor's position and the *expected* policy of the coalition of which he is a member is minimized if the actor occupies a "pivotal position" in the coalition, that is, commands what politicians call the "swing vote". The object of the game then becomes that of securing a pivotal position in a winning coalition. The concept of imputation now comes into its own, because payoffs can be defined in terms of distances between the actors' most preferred policies and the expected policies of the winning coalitions of which they are members. Further, in contrast to simple games with only one prize, the game is now non-constant-sum. As such it may have a "core", that is, a set of "undominated" imputations. (An undominated imputation is one to which no other is preferred by any subset of players who are able to enforce the latter by forming a coalition.) In one of its variants, the policy distance theory predicts the imputations of the core as the possible outcomes of this game.

In all, twelve different theories are presented and tested with reference to actual coalition governments formed at one time or another in eight European parliamentary democracies and Israel. Each theory singles out from all possible outcomes a particular subset. The success of a theory is assessed by matching the singled out sets of coalitions with those that have actually formed given a distribution of seats among the several parties. A completely successful theory would be one that singled out all those and only those coalitions that have actually occurred. However, correct prediction is not the only criterion by which the success of a theory is assessed. Another criterion, especially important in situations with indeterminacy, is the a priori improbability of the prediction. That is, a theory is the more credible the less likely it is that the predicted outcome could have occurred by chance. Comparison of rival theories is practically mandatory in the social sciences, where "definitive" theories, analogous to those of the physical sciences, derived from overwhelmingly corroborated "natural laws", are lacking. The comparative approach calls attention to the differential success of different theories in different situations and so provides opportunities for refining the theories.

By the criterion of statistical significance, the so called "closed minimum range theory" turned out to be the most successful. The minimum range refers to the portion of the political spectrum spanned by the winning coalition. The range is "closed" if the coalition contains every actor in its range, that is, contains no "gaps". It would seem that an experienced parliamentarian would predict the same result on common sense grounds: coalition partners are most likely to be "neighbors" on the spectrum, and homogeneity of ideology is desirable in a coalition. This concordance between theoretical and intuitive prediction would seem, at first sight, to minimize the importance of formal theory construction, all the more so because an experienced politician's prediction of the particular coalition expected in a particular political situation is likely to be more precise than the prediction of a theory that singles out a set of possible coalitions. However the formal theoretical analysis developed in this monograph does much more than single out the types of coalitions most likely to form. The main thrust of the analysis being comparative, it permits the political scientist to examine the extent to which the "components" (i.e., the constituent hypotheses) of each of the theories advanced contributes to the accuracy of the predictions. In particular, the analysis permits in principle a quantitative comparison of the relative importance of power politics and ideological considerations. The differential success of the several theories together with the differential contributions of the constituent hypotheses suggests further theoretical developments. In this way, the formalism of theory construction is firmly linked with the specifics of the subject matter, something not frequently achieved in social science, where the requirements of formal, rigorous theory are often at cross purposes with those of content relevance.

The theories presented here are all "static". That is, they single out final results and say nothing about the process that leads to them. In this respect the theories, especially those that predict on the basis of some "minimizing" principle, are analogous to the static theories of physical science that predict equilibrium or asymptotic states, for instance, the principle of minimal potential energy in mechanics or the principle of least action in optics or the principle of maximal entropy in the thermodynamics of isolated systems. These principles can also be derived from the dynamics of the systems involved. For instance, maximization of entropy can be shown to be a consequence of the laws of statistical mechanics, which, in turn, derive from mechanical laws governing the individual particles.

Of the theories presented here, the policy distance theory might eventually be extended to include the dynamics of the process. Resting, as it does, on hypotheses concerning the preferences for different coalitions of individual actors, the theory might suggest assumptions governing bids and counter-bids together with probabilities of these being accepted or rejected; assumptions concerning the viscous fluid process of wheeling and dealing that leads to the eventual stabilization of a winning coalition.

The policy distance theory was not the most successful by formal criteria. However it can perhaps be modified and brought into closer accord with observations. Of all the approaches mentioned here it has the closest affinity to the substantive (not merely terminological) aspects of N-person game theory. Extended to include the dynamics of coalition formation, this theory could be linked also with the theory of stochastic processes. In this way the deductive power of a mathematical apparatus could be brought to bear on the further development of the theory.

This suggestion is offered by way of illustrating the principal intellectual contribution of this monograph. It goes considerably beyond the empiricist goal — that of finding the most economical and accurate description of observed results; even beyond the "classical" goal of hard science — that of making accurate, a priori improbable predictions. Among the "dividends" gained from formal analysis of the sort undertaken here are insights that are frequently missed in routine statistical testing of more or less ad hoc hypotheses.

Anatol Rapoport
Toronto, May 21, 1973.

Contents

Author's Foreword xi

Preface, by Anatol Rapoport xiii

Part I: Constructing Theory

Chapter 1. Introduction 1
   Plan of the book 8

Chapter 2. The rational decision model 12
   1 Decision-making approaches 12
   2 The rational decision model 18
   3 Rationality and utility 18
   4 Knowledge 22

Chapter 3. n-Person game theory 26

Chapter 4. Theories of political coalitions 47
   1 Minimal winning coalitions: Von Neumann and
      Morgenstern 49
   2 Coalitions of minimum size: Riker and Gamson 52
   3 The bargaining proposition: Leiserson 65
   4 Policy positions and the range of coalitions 68
   5 Minimal range theory: Leiserson and Axelrod 71

Chapter 5. Policy distance theory 80
   1 Explaining non-minimal coalitions 81
   2 Policy distance theory 88

Chapter 6. Problems of testing coalition theories 120

Part II: Confronting History

Chapter 7. Empirical referents to the theories 125
  1 The nature of payoffs 127
  2 The majority requirement 129
  3 Actors and their weight 131
  4 The policy scale 132
  5 Membership of the coalition 143
  6 The parliamentary system and its environment 144

Chapter 8. A first evaluation: statistical 147

Chapter 9. Confronting history: Weimar, the Fourth Republic,
  Italy 160
  1 The Weimar Republic 161
  2 France 174
  3 Italy 192

Chapter 10. Confronting history: The Netherlands, Israel,
  Finland 205
  1 The Netherlands 205
  2 Israel 226
  3 Finland 237

Chapter 11. The Scandinavian monarchies 254
  1 Sweden 254
  2 Denmark 265
  3 Norway 276

Chapter 12. Conclusion 284
  1 Parliamentary coalition formation 284
  2 Coalition government and democratic theory 289
  3 Formal empiricist method and the study of politics . . 297

Appendix I. Computer programs 302

Appendix II. A simple model for testing coalition theories,
  by Robert J. Mokken 304
  1 The statistical test criteria 305

Notes 308

References 322

Index of names 335

Index of subjects 338

PART I: Constructing Theory

CHAPTER 1

Introduction

The purpose of this book is to test the claim that formal theories can explain important processes of political life. The theories investigated in this study deal with the interaction of rational actors as they join in coalitions with or against one another. Such coalition theories should be relevant for the study of collaboration and opposition in European legislatures when no single party controls a majority and some parliamentary groups must cooperate with one another in order to appoint and support a government and pass its legislation through the voting body. The formation of this governing coalition is crucial in these political systems since the elections as such do not indicate unambiguously which parties will be in power and what policy shall be carried out. That decision is the outcome of interaction among the leadership of the parliamentary groups once the elections have entrusted them with the command over a share in the votes of the legislature.

Those who are familiar with two-party systems, where the elections designate the winner, may be puzzled at the idea that a theory would be needed at all to determine what the composition of the government will be after the electorate has spoken already. Those who are familiar with multi-party systems ought to be puzzled too. The absence of an obvious relationship between the outcome of the elections and the selection of parties for the government confronts the theory of multi-party democracy with a gnawing paradox. If different governments, varying in party membership and policy, may result from a given election outcome, either there is no "verdict of the electorate" or, if such a concept is meaningful, the verdict is not necessarily, or even usually, realized

1

in multi-party systems. The coalition theory that could shed light on these questions would have great importance for democratic theory.

The coalition theories presented in this book are formal theories. They may be cast in the language of formal logic and they may be derived through formal operations from a universal axiomatic model of human behavior, *the rational decision model.* Moreover, the concepts of these theories may be made to correspond with some precision to things and events political: parties, votes, policies....... The theories are formal empirical theories of political coalitions*. The explanatory performance of these theories may increase understanding of political behavior, *i.e.* of collaboration and opposition in legislatures, but it will also reflect on the potential of the formal empirical method for the explanation of political life in general. The findings of this study present a case in point that bears directly on the current debate about the question of method in political explanation: what a theory of politics ought to be like, or whether a science of politics is possible and desirable.

Behind the immediate interest in the crucial decision of coalition formation in multi-party systems, and in the validity of formal empirical theories of political coalitions, stands a wider concern for the implications of this study for the theory of democracy and the method of political explanation.

In the past twenty years, the interest in formal theory construction has surged among social scientists, economists and psychologists especially. But the subject of politics has proven resistant to systematic generalization. Throughout the centuries, political thinkers have speculated upon the true laws of political life. Of late, this interest has led to the construction of models, couched in the language of logic and mathematics, that were meant to represent the laws underlying the political process. Examples which are already classical are the Hotelling—Downs model of party competition in one-dimensional preference space (Downs, 1957) and the system of differential equations representing an arms race by

---

*That is "hierarchical theories" after the usage of Kaplan: "A *hierarchical* theory is one whose component laws are presented as deductions from a small set of basic principles. A law is explained by the demonstration that it is a logical consequence of these principles, and a fact is explained when it is shown to follow from these together with certain initial conditions." Kaplan (1964) p. 298; *cf.* also Meehan (1965) p. 134 *et seq.* on "deductive theories" (on p. 136: "All deductive theories have the same fundamental structure or hierarchical arrangement.").

Richardson (1960). In accordance with the mood of this empiricist age, the authors of such proposals claim that their models may, in principle, be developed into empirical theories, amenable to confirmation or refutation through a confrontation of their inferences with political facts[1].

In practice, however, if empirical theories have been derived from the models at all, these were tested only rarely and almost never in a systematic manner[2].

On the other hand, at the same time and inspired by a similar quantitative empirical mood, great amounts of data were collected in research that was prompted mostly by specific questions and hypotheses of an *ad hoc* character. These data were usually organized according to statistical concepts — correlation coefficients, or, more sophisticated, multivariate analysis or scaling theory — rather than along the lines of a *political* theory. This has resulted in a vast mass of data on voting behavior on the one hand, while on the other hand there exists a small number of formal theories of voting (*e.g.*, Downs, 1957; Buchanan and Tullock, 1962; Davis and Hinich, 1966, 1967). The connection between the two is tenuous. The formal voting theories have been operationalized only rarely and their empirical implications have gone largely untested, while electoral studies have not often been subsumed into general statements fit for incorporation into a broad theory.

In the field of coalition studies the situation is different mainly because of the lack of systematic empirical research into coalition behavior outside the laboratory. Cabinet formations and the formation of legislative support coalitions are traditionally the subject of parliamentary historians. They provided the sources from which most of the data for this study were taken. Studies of a more systematic nature appeared only in recent years; the resurgence of European political science also revived professional interest in European political institutions, multi-party legislatures among them (*e.g.*, Dahl, 1966; various articles in *Scandinavian Studies*; Lipset and Rokkan, 1967; Lijphart, 1969).

The theoretical study of coalitions is more advanced. It originated with the publication of the work of Von Neumann and Morgenstern (1943), especially its less accessible part on n-person game theory. It took another twenty years before this conceptual apparatus was applied directly to the phenomenon of political coalitions[3]; Gamson (1961, 1962) studied American presidential conventions on the basis of his concept of the "cheapest winning coalition"; Riker (1962) attempted the derivation of the related

3

notion of the "minimum size principle" and used it to comment on a wide range of events in American history. Sawyer and MacRae (1962) investigated cumulative voting on the basis of game theory. The impact of these publications prompted studies by Leiserson (1966), Axelrod (1970) and De Swaan (1970) in which not only the resources, but also policy preferences of the actors were taken into account as major independent variables.

As a result, there are at present some six theories of coalition behavior, all specifically relevant to political coalitions and all originating in the theory of games, even though they may also be formulated independently of that theory. These are the theories that are tested in this study against the data on legislative coalition formation in support of the cabinet in nine European multi-party systems since 1918. A total of twelve "theories" have been submitted to a test by means of a Fortran computer program, "COAL", designed for this purpose by the author: four "theories" are minor modifications of the six main theories and have been included to check the effect of specific assumptions. Two other "theories" were incorporated in the program after the first results on the performance of the main theories were known: they appeared especially promising explanatory propositions.

The theories of political coalitions presented in this study have their common basis in the rational decision model and may be formulated in the conceptual system of the theory of games: game theory may be considered as the mathematical elaboration of the rational decision model for situations in which the outcome depends on the combined decisions of rational actors. This shared origin and common language allows to incorporate the theories of political coalitions into a general theoretical framework. Moreover, it greatly facilitates a comparative evaluation of the explanatory capacity of these theories, since differences in performance may be traced back with some precision to specific variations in a common theoretical structure. The performance of the theories, to some degree, also allows the validity of the assumptions in the rational decision model and game theory from which the theories have been derived to be judged.

The present theories of political coalitions may have their origin in universal and abstract maxims on the nature of rational decision, but even at this analytical level, the choice of assumptions has definite but hard to gauge implications for the view of the political world that inheres such theories. Political events are explained as the outcome of decisions based on individual prefer-

4

ences and not, for example, on supra-individual laws of history or of the social system. Rationality implies a knowledge of alternative actions and their consequences; it implies that one outcome is liked better than another and that all outcomes under consideration may be so ranked. In such a model, interests and values tend to be conceived as belonging to individuals, rather than as inherent in a collectivity, and they are generally treated as given, independent variables, rather than as outcomes themselves, or as products of the social environment. The egotistic, self-centered individual fits the model with more natural grace than would an altruist oriented towards some collective optimum. The minimaximizers of game theory are not at all adventurous[4] but strive for the greatest gain they can realize with certainty, and they will not settle for less.

These implications and tendencies contain in themselves, and before the theory is in its operational stage, a far-reaching view of politics, grim maybe, but unsentimental and hardnosed. Actors are interchangeable and all outcomes maybe reduced to the common denominator of the utility that attaches to them. In these theories not tragedy is the paradigm of politics but rather the market. And in normal times that may well be as it should: formal theory is geared to normalcy, "everything else remaining the same".

When it comes to operationalization of the theoretical concepts, the necessary definitions further delineate a conception of political reality. The "actor" of the theory is made to correspond to the "parliamentary group" in parliament, which therefore must be considered as a unitary entity for the purposes of the theory: all internal strife is mere "noise" until it reaches a level where the theoretician decides that there will be two or three actors instead of one, but all equally monolithic. Similarly, an actor with all his resources is either in or out of the coalition; there is nothing in between. The brinkmanship of the unwilling partner who is holding out for more, or the saving support of an opponent who does not want to be publicly identified with a government and yet does not want its downfall either, all these stratagems are ignored or eliminated as anomalies in this approach.

When policy preferences are introduced as variables they are reduced to choices on a few dimensions, most often a single dimension only. Moreover, all actors conceive of politics as dominated by this dimension. Political preference is assumed to be gradual in character: it is rarely a matter of all or nothing, or of a grand dichotomy. A small improvement on the existing state of

5

affairs will not be rejected in favor of the possibility of a great change at some future date, or because the matter is one of principle. Yet, all these distortions could be remedied by other assumptions that might, however, be more difficult to render in formal or operational terms.

The parliamentary system is treated in isolation from political and other social institutions and processes in the surrounding society: the influence of a king or a president, of pressure groups, finance, business, or of foreign powers is ignored. Either the forces in society are perfectly reflected in the composition of parliament, or they do not affect its decisions. Legislative coalitions are explained in terms of the legislative context itself.

Sometimes outside conditions do interfere with the process of coalition formation. In times of war the theories are suspended, only to resume for the subsequent period in the same manner, after adjustment of parameter values. The theories are entirely a-historical, the actors have no memory of success or failure, there is no hedging for future success or cashing in at the cost of future loss.

The application of the theories to different countries with only minor adjustments carries with it the implication that these political systems are comparable, at least with respect to those aspects that are taken into consideration by the theories. The statistical evaluation of the theories implies, moreover, that each correctly indicated historical government coalition is comparable to any other, from country to country, and throughout the period under study. Each "hit" earns the theory, after probabilities have been calculated, an equal score.

One reason for the choice of parliamentary coalition formation as the subject for testing the theories is precisely that there is a considerable number (about 100) of historical cases in which the actors may be identified with their resources and policies, and where the composition of the majority coalition can be ascertained more or less clearly.

All these considerations add up to the conclusion that it is not merely a specific, well-defined proposition that is tested with each theory, but that a far-reaching conception of political life, the implicit context of that proposition, is also involved.

The thrust of the preceding argument is not against the use of an approach that carries with it an underlying, encompassing view of politics. On the contrary, the same argument might be made about any other approach to political reality. What matters is that

6

the precise nature and implications of assumptions in formal theory are hard to decipher for those who are not conversant with its conceptual system. And those who are, have sometimes been somewhat lax in spelling them out. Maybe this has to do with the aversion of political *a priorisms* and *Weltanschauung* that often goes with the formal empiricist mood which inspired these theories. As a consequence, this approach has sometimes come to be identified with scientific method and with either the "objectivity" or the "amorality" that are ascribed to that method on the same inadequate grounds.

This is the reason why, in this study, special stress is laid on the character of the assumptions underlying the theories, their implications for political reality and the considerations that have led to their adoption. Each of these assumptions originated in a dilemma and a subsequent choice on the part of the theorist. This type of theory is not necessarily more aloof from social influences and shielded from personal belief than other forms of political theory. The theoretical framework of the theories carries with it a very "special" view of politics. Such a view has its political consequences, be it not in an immediately partisan sense. That view may as yet be shown to be adequate for an understanding of certain political processes, in certain periods, in certain contexts. It is put to the test along with the theories, although its validity is even harder to judge from the test results than the validity of specific theories.

There has been much confusion about scientific method on the one hand and the requirements that a theory of politics ought to satisfy on the other. At the same time that this study was written, these questions were the subject of an intense debate throughout the profession, a conflict that did not always remain an exchange of opinions and arguments at the universities of Berkeley, Cal. and Amsterdam, where this book was written. Questions were raised in the course of this conflict, that perhaps cannot be answered, but that cannot be ignored either.

This book is intended as a contribution to that debate, a demonstration of what the formal empirical method can achieve and what, at present, it cannot achieve for a theory of politics. In the course of this inquiry, most of the original theories are refuted and the rational decision model that has served as a point of departure is shown to be an inadequate approach to the study of coalition formation. But, from the analysis, a new explanatory proposition emerges that agrees with a different approach to political decision making.

7

Plan of the book

This study consists of two parts, the first discussing theory, the second confronting history. The structure of formal empirical theories of political coalitions is analyzed in the course of Chapters 2—4. Chapter 2 deals with the rational decision model, placing it in the decisionist traditions and sketching its relation to decision making and other approaches in contemporary social science. The formal structure of coalition theory is the subject of Chapter 3 which deals with game theory. The presentation concentrates on those concepts that are necessary for an understanding of the theories of political coalitions. It will present few mathematical difficulties to the uninitiated reader, but the number and the novelty of the technical terms may at times prove confusing or tiring. All arguments and conclusions are also rendered in plain language and an understanding of game theoretical notation is not absolutely indispensable.

Chapter 4 contains a review of the main theories of political coalitions that have been advanced in the literature. Some theories are reconstructed on the basis of the original hypotheses to fit them into the general theoretical framework of this study, or to resolve some ambiguities. The first sections deal with theories that take only the resources (size, or weight, or votes) of the actors into account. The "minimal winning set" defined by Von Neumann and Morgenstern (1943) contains all those coalitions that exclude an actor whose weight is not necessary for the coalition to be winning. The "minimum size principle" is a reconstruction based on the work of Gamson (1961) and Riker (1962). It entails a further restriction on the minimal winning set: it singles out the coalitions of smallest weight that are still winning. A different limitation is imposed by the "bargaining proposition" (Leiserson, 1968): the winning coalitions with the smallest number of actors are predicted. The second half of Chapter 4 is devoted to theories that also take into account the policy preferences of actors. Some definitions are proposed in relation to an ordinal policy scale and this allows the "range" of a coalition to be defined. "Minimal range theory", based on the doctoral dissertation by Leiserson (1966) excludes all those coalitions from the predicted set that contain actors that are not necessary for a coalition to be winning but which increase its range. Such a coalition would minimize "ideological diversity". According to Axelrod, actors strive to form a coalition that would minimize "conflict of interest". In the terms of this study, that would be a "closed coalition of minimal range": a minimal range coalition that contains all actors whose policy positions are within that minimal range.

The theoretical consequences of the factual assumptions are discussed in the opening sections of Chapter 5. The preceding theories all yield a prediction of coalitions that are minimal in some sense, with respect to their membership, weight, number of members, or their range on the policy scale. A number of alternative assumptions are reviewed in this chapter. This leads to the presentation of a different theory of political coalitions: policy distance theory. Its central behavioral assumption is that actors will strive to be included in a coalition with an expected policy that is as close as possible to their own policy position. This may well induce them to include actors that would render the coalition non-minimal in the sense of any of the preceding theories, if they expect those actors to influence the coalition's policy in the desired direction. On the other hand, the actors in the theory are maximizers (minimizers of policy distance) and the theory can easily be incorporated in the general theoretical framework of theories of political coalitions.

Coalition theories predict a number of coalitions for any given situation: the coalitions that are in mutual equilibrium. In contrast to most theoretical predictions, no probability distribution is postulated for the coalitions in the predicted set. This raises problems of statistical testing which are discussed in Chapter 6. A model for the statistical evaluation of coalition theories on the basis of a hypergeometric distribution of predictive results, developed by Robert J. Mokken of the University of Amsterdam, is presented by its author in Appendix II. After the discussion of theoretical problems, the theories that have been constructed are confronted with the data from parliamentary history in the second part of the book.

The adaptation of the theoretical assumptions to the conditions prevailing in European multi-party systems since 1918 is the subject of Chapter 7. The context of the coalitional game is defined as the parliamentary system of assembly and cabinet (and sometimes the senate too). Social economic progressivism versus conservatism is taken as the underlying dimension of the policy scale and it is described more precisely as referring to the share of the national income that should be assigned to the government budget, except defense expenditures, in the opinion of the party's activists.

Chapter 8 contains a discussion of the results of the statistical tests. The pattern of results indicates that coalitions tend to form from actors that are adjacent on the policy scale: the closed coalition proposition. And, especially in times of normalcy, coalitions will exclude those actors that are unnecessary for the coalition to achieve a majority, while increasing the coalition's ideological range: minimal range theory. The conjunction of these theories, closed minimal range theory, produces the best test results; it is, however, quite independent of the rational decision model. Another "theory", constructed after the results for the main theories were obtained, is used as a guideline in the discussion of historical coalitions in later chapters: it singles out the "basic alternatives" in a coalition situation, *i.e.* those coalitions that are both minimal winning and closed.

The remaining chapters of the book are devoted to a review of the actual conditions in each country in so far as they are relevant to the theories and to a case-by-case discussion of historical cabinets in those countries. Each country is treated in a separate section and particular attention is reserved for the determination of the position of the parties on the policy scale. The "polarized pluralist" (Sartori, 1966) systems of the German Weimar Republic, the French Fourth Republic and the Italian Republic since 1945 form the subject of Chapter 9. In Chapter 10 the pluralist systems of the Netherlands, Israel and Finland are discussed. Chapter 11 is devoted to the Scandinavian Monarchies, Sweden, Denmark and Norway with their particular feature of a Social Democratic party that gradually approaches majority during a period of minority cabinets.

The conclusion in Chapter 12 sums up the findings of this study as they relate to the subjects of parliamentary coalition formation in support of the cabinet and spells out the implications for the theory of political coalitions and for the theory of multi-party democracy. The bearings of this study on the question of method in political explanation are the subject of a final section. Appendix I contains a description of the computer program COAL for calculating the equilibrium sets of theories of political coalitions that fit the general theoretical framework. In Appendix II, a simple model for testing coalition theories is presented by Professor Robert J. Mokken.

The reader who is primarily interested in empirical results concerning coalition formation may begin with Chapter 8, which contains the outcomes of the statistical tests, and proceed from there to the sections in Chapters 9--11 dealing with the countries of special interest to him. The glossary of technical terms will aid his understanding of the discussions of historical situations. The final chapter may be read for the overall conclusions. In order to evaluate these empirical findings, however, it is necessary to read the operational definitions and decision rules that bridge formal theory and empirical analysis and that are presented in Chapter 7. In case these readings have whetted the theoretical appetite, the reader may go back to Chapters 2 and 3, Chapter 4 (omitting all of Section 2 except the first and last paragraphs) and Chapter 5 (omitting Section 2b and gleaning the main points from Sections 2c, d, and e). The social scientist without mathematical training will encounter few difficulties on this path. On the other hand, anyone who wishes to work with coalition theories or who is interested in formal political theory in its own right is well advised to read Part I of the book in its entirety, continuing with the chapters on operationalization and statistical evaluation (7 and 8) and from there on selecting whatever is of interest to him from the country by country analysis.

CHAPTER 2

The Rational Decision Model

The process of coalition formation is studied in this book from the viewpoint of decision-making analysis and, in particular, from that of the rational decision model as it has been elaborated in game theory. This is by no means the only possible approach. The same subject matter might be studied from another angle, such as institutional analysis, for example, in which institutions, norms and roles are the key concepts. Another starting point could be supplied by functional analysis, in which the requirements for the maintenance of equilibrium in the encompassing political system provide the point of departure. And again, the subject might be described and explained along the lines of historical monography.

1. Decision-making approaches

Before embarking upon a discussion of the rational decision model, it might be useful to place it in the context of the decision-making approach in its widest sense, then survey the other methods of decision-making analysis that are in use in contemporary social science and, finally, relate the decision-making approach to the major methodological alternative, functional analysis.

A decision-making approach of social reality attempts to arrive at an explanation of social phenomena as the outcome of decisions made by persons acting within a given social and physical context. The heroic tradition in historiography represents a classical form of the decision-making approach. Thomas Carlyle wrote[1] "all things that we see standing accomplished in the world are properly the outer material result, the practical realisation and embodiment, of Thoughts that dwelt in the Great Men sent into the world: the soul of the whole world's history, it may justly be considered, were the history of these."

It is in the keeping with this romantic view of history that the social context of the decision is neglected and that the person of the "Great Man" is stressed in the explanation.

A contemporary school of philosophy, existentialism, also focuses on the decision, the consequential choice among alternatives, in its description of human reality: Man chooses his way of being and in so choosing, he chooses for all mankind. In a phrase of J.-P. Sartre:

"en realité, les choses seront telles que l'homme aura décidé qu'elles soient." [2]

The common denominator between historic romanticism, existentialism and the decision-making approach in the social sciences may be small but it does exist: social phenomena are explained as the outcomes of individual choices.

The decision-making approach in contemporary social science explains social phenomena in terms of decisions made by human beings, in groups or on their own, under conditions of certainty, uncertainty, or risk, within a given social framework and constrained by the necessities and impossibilities that cannot be affected by the decision makers. One variety of this decision-making approach, and analytically the most elaborate one, is based on the rational decision model. This construct consists of a number of formal propositions; each one may be read as referring to a relevant aspect of the decision-making process in real life. The behavior of the actors is inferred from these propositions in combination with the central assumption of rationality, that an actor will choose from among all alternative courses of action that are open to him at any given moment the alternative that leads to the outcome he prefers most.

Because of the place it has occupied in economic theory, and because of the impact of game theory and related mathematical approaches in postwar years, the rational decision model has become the most important analytical tool for the formal study of decision-making processes in the social sciences.

Yet, within the field of political science proper, there are at least four lines of thought that may also be subsumed under the heading of the decision-making approach and that, nevertheless, differ considerably from rational decision analysis. There is the major revision of the maximization concept as proposed by Simon[3]: the rational decision model may be asking too much from real life actors by assuming that they will, indeed, attempt to achieve an optimal solution. It may be more realistic to attribute to the actors some level of aspiration which they will attempt to achieve even if it is not the highest conceivable level. Thus, according to Simon, actors do not optimize, but "satisfice" on the basis of their "bounded" of "limited" rationality.

This revision of the rational decision model modifies the notion of "complete information". The costs of collecting and processing the amount of information that would even begin to approximate "completeness" would be prohibitive. In the face of the complexity of day-to-day decision making, actors do not even attempt to achieve a perfect picture of the situation. Rather, they survey the decisional context for a solution that might satisfy their aspirations.

Braybrooke and Lindblom[4] have pursued a similar line of argument. They reject the idea of what they call "synoptic" decision making and replace it with the "strategy of disjointed incrementalism". Decisions are made step by step, in incremental departures from the existing state of affairs and they are prompted by visible and pressing problems, supported only by a partial analysis of alternatives and consequences.

A third approach to decision making within the realm of political science may be found in the works of Snyder et al.[5], who have attempted to construct a frame of reference for decision analysis inspired by the findings of their prior monographic study of U.S. foreign policy making in the Korean war. Their scheme consists of a checklist of motivational and situational variables. The decision maker is seen as operating within an organizational context; he arrives at his decision on the basis of (1) his definition of the situation, (2) his particular conception of his own role and (3) under the influence of his own personality traits.

Finally, research on the roles of elites in decision making in American cities has caused a renewed interest in the methodology of empirical decision-making research. A discussion has developed around Robert Dahl's (1961) study of New Haven city politics[6]. The evidence in this book is against a view of American politics as controlled by a unified elite in which business interests dominate. The book projects a pluralist image of politics: a variety of groups compete in the political arena for fulfillment of their demands, a

14

process described by Lindblom as "partisan mutual adjustment"[7] : just as there exists no grand strategy, there is no single, unified elite either.

All these currents of thought are concerned with decision making at the higher levels of the organizational and political structure within a well-defined institutional setting. Decision making throughout the citizenry is a subject of studies in electoral and consumer behavior. With the introduction in these fields of a scheme of analysis in which voters' orientation towards candidates, parties and issues replace sociological variables, the theoretical correspondence between decision theory and voting studies has increased; psychological models have taken the place of ecological models. Thus, one may encounter in the works of Campbell *et al.* (1960)[8] an empirical scheme of the voting decision. Downs, on the other hand, has applied the rational decision model to the theoretical analysis of voting behavior[9].

The rational decision model contains the *a priori* assumption that whatever counts for the decision maker in arriving at his decision must somehow be amenable to translation into a universal measure of preference, so that all alternative outcomes may be uniquely ranked as to their preferability and so that each and every action may be judged with regard to its consequences as measured along that scale. It is questionable whether human beings ever decide on the basis of such an universal rank-order of preference; but even if they do, at present no procedure exists to order all outcomes on a single preference scale on the basis of experimental data[10].

The main purpose of the contributions by Simon and Lindblom is to avoid the assumption of complete information by limiting the considerations attributed to the decision makers to some well-defined and restricted class of alternatives and outcomes. Thus the task of finding a preference ordering over all these outcomes is also facilitated. If some clear and consistent decision rules could be found to which real life actors are likely to adhere, then a limited but empirical theory of decision making would become feasible.

Decision rules that might be built into an abstract decision model might also be suggested by the outcome of empirical research, such as the study of Davis *et al.* (1966), on budgeting in the U.S. Congress[11], or Barber's work on Educational Committees[12]. On the other hand, one may search for plausible decision rules by first constructing a (modified) rational decision model,

15

simplified to its barest form, and by then surveying reality for the most promising empirical referents. This is the heuristic strategy pursued in this book[13]. Clearly, the two methods are not mutually exclusive, but rather complementary: research may produce plausible generalizations that may next inspire propositions to be built into a deductive system: the propositions that are inferred from this system may then again be tested against empirical data, as they are in the second part of this book.

The place of the rational decision model among the other approaches to the study of decision making has been roughly charted; at this point, it might be useful to discuss briefly the relationship between rational decision analysis and structural functional theory, the other major theoretical current in contemporary social science[14].

The nexus between the study of decision making and structural functional theory lies in a common interest in the more or less permanent rules of behavior that have originated in the social environment and that govern the behavior of the decision makers.

The fundamental notion in the functionalist scheme is that of a system consisting of mutually interdependent subsystems: in the last analysis, a social system is a network of relationships between actors[15]. The system requires for its survival the fulfillment of certain functions. Subsystems are described and defined in terms of their contribution to these functions. Decision making as a process does not serve any single specific function but may be found throughout the system, contributing to a variety of system requirements. The particular subject matter of this book — decision making for parliamentary coalition formation — is, therefore, not a separate category in structural functional analysis or in systems analysis. In Easton's scheme[16], its study would come under the heading of "structural regulation of support": coalition formation would serve to reduce the cleavage stress produced in the interaction among single-interest parties which the author considers a frequent phenomenon in multi-party systems.

Almond[17], who is more interested in a taxonomy of existing political systems, remains closer to the immediate observation of reality. The topic under consideration would fall under the study of competitive multi-party systems, especially from the viewpoint of the function of interest aggregation.

In the rational decision model, actors choose among alternative actions on the basis of their evaluation of the consequences of each course of action. This preference order is an essential element

16

of the rational decision model. In structural functional analysis, such evaluations are considered as a product of the surrounding political culture, in so far as they are common to all actors, and as a result of the particular role conception of each actor, in so far as they are specific to him. In this respect, structural functional analysis has a greater sociological content than rational decision analysis, in which, as in economic theory, the subject's preferences are treated as given and independent variables.

In structural functional analysis, the central question is what the process under study contributes to the system in its entirety, what its functions within the encompassing system are. Rational decision analysis does not provide explanations in terms of requirements of the system, but strives at an understanding of the social process in terms of the interdependent actions of persons who each strive to bring about a situation that is optimal for them, given certain initial conditions. The concept of system enters rational decision analysis only in so far as factors that are external to the specific setting of the decision making process impose constraints on the choices of the actors, and, in so far as they determine the motivations and evaluations of the actors (through political culture and role conceptions).

A teleological element may seem to operate in the conception of rational decision analysis also: actors act *in order* to maximize their utility, just as subsystems are said to function *in order* to fulfill certain requirements of the system. Yet, the decision-making approach avoids the assumption of a "superhuman" purpose that transcends individual volitions. The explanation with the aid of the rational decision model proceeds in terms of the goal achievement of individual maximizers but this may easily be reduced to a causal argument. The Dutch economist Kleerekoper has written[18]

> "The recognition that the ultimate cause in economics is a goal-image (*doelvoorstelling*) in no way contradicts our preceding argument that economics is a causal science".

The goal-images of individual actors serve as "last cause" in the explanation of facts through the rational decision model. These goal-images may themselves receive causal explanation in another body of knowledge, *e.g.*, psychology, or sociology. This applies not only to the explanation with the aid of the *homo economicus* in economic theory, but equally well to the more general application of this paradigm of the maximizing actor in the rational decision model. Whether such a reduction from teleological language to causal explanation is equally feasible in structural functional analysis is not clear[19].

2. The rational decision model

A number of theories in the social sciences share as their central assumption: "the actors whose behavior the theory is to explain are rational". The outstanding example of such a rational actor is of course the *homo economicus*, the economic man of classical economic theory. Through game theory, this theoretical construct, extended from a money maximizing into an even more universal and abstract utility maximizing actor, has entered the other social sciences. At present it would be inappropriate to speak of a single, unified rational decision theory that might be applied to decision processes throughout the social system. On the one hand, there is the body of classic economic theory, postulating rational behavior on the assumption that actors will strive to maximize their money-income over time, while ignoring all other considerations; on the other hand, there are a great number of models limited to specific social science phenomena, mostly of undetermined empirical validity, each postulating its particular definition of rationality. Rarely has such a model been formulated in operational terms, almost never has one been tested against empirical data. (Hypotheses derived from utility theory and game theory, however, have been tested in numerous experiments in a laboratory setting.)

All these constructs share the common foundation of the rationality postulate and the auxiliary assumptions that this postulate calls for. This theoretical common denominator might be termed the rational decision model.

3. Rationality and utility

In the context of the rational decision model, the term "rationality" has a specific, technical meaning. It is not meant to refer to some ethical concept, close in meaning to "reasonable" or "lucid" as opposed to "arbitrary" or "emotional".

"Rational", in the sense of the rational decision model, is a property of the behavior of actors. An actor is said to behave in a

18

rational manner whenever he acts in such a manner as to obtain the greatest possible satisfaction of his needs.

There are a number of ambiguities in the preceding sentence. Most of these are eliminated through the introduction of the technical apparatus of the rational decision model, but some will remain and they will be the subject of analysis in the discussion of game theory and its solution concepts.

Concerning the "greatest possible satisfaction", the question arises whether this "possibility" refers to what an omnipotent and omniscient actor might obtain for himself, or if it is intended to refer to the potential of an actor with a limited choice of actions and a limited capacity to process information.

Clearly, if the model is to have any relevance at all, it must specify certain limitations or minimum conditions on the information the actor is supposed to take into account and it must also define a set of "moves" open to each actor at any point in the game. These are necessary conditions to judge *ex post* if an actor's behavior satisfies the rationality postulate, *i.e.* whether the actor did achieve the greatest possible satisfaction given the alternatives he could choose from and the knowledge he had of their consequences.

A second ambiguity in the provisional definition of rationality concerns "the satisfaction of needs", that is of different needs at the same time or, as the case might be, of one and the same need at different moments in time or of different needs at different times. For example, a person attempting to maximize his income and his health at the same time might find himself confronted with a situation in which one course of action would improve his health more than any other, while a second alternative would bring his income to the maximum attainable and a third path would yield a reasonable financial reward and protect his health. The time dimension might be introduced by imagining that the person in question would have to choose between some short run enterprise and some investment that would yield its fruits only after some time.

Thus, if the actor would ask for advice as to what would be a rational choice in his case or if a theorist would wish to judge whether the actor's behavior was rational, some standard of comparison between the satisfaction of different needs and at different moments in time would be necessary. What is needed at this point is some kind of universal measure of satisfaction. And this is precisely the function of the most far-reaching concept in the rational decision model: the concept of utility.

19

A rational actor is an actor who chooses from among the alternative courses of action open to him the one that leads to the most preferred outcome or the outcome with the greatest utility.

Utility, in this sense, is a property of goods and services, their capacity to satisfy an actor's needs. For the present purpose, utility will be defined as a property of a state of affairs in which such goods and services are available for the satisfaction of the actor: when an actor prefers one state of affairs over another, the former state will be said to possess greater utility than the latter. Consequently, if an actor has ranked all events under consideration according to the value he attributes to them, this ordering is called the "utility function" of that actor over those states of affairs. A rational actor is one that acts so as to maximize his utility function.

The utility concept that emerges here is intended to reflect the preference of some individual over all outcomes under consideration, regardless of what kind of need satisfaction and what time expectation those preferences are based upon. The individual is assumed to have somehow brought his evaluations of all those states of affairs under a single, common denominator. The subject may say "I like to be with Marie because of her beautiful brown eyes" and "I like to be with Yvonne because she is so witty and gay", but he cannot say "I prefer Yvonne most and I prefer Marie most": he must either prefer the one to the other, or the latter to the former, or be indifferent between the two. In some manner he must have combined his appreciation of beauty, wit and gaiety into a single preference measure, which, to make matters worse, is called utility. This requirement — that between any two states of affairs, there can be only one of three relations of preference — is called the "requirement of connectedness of the preference relation". (It is always true that an actor i prefers outcome x to outcome y, or y to x, or that he is indifferent between the two: for all x, y and i, either xP_iy, or yP_ix, or xI_iy) [20].

The ordering of preferences that forms the basis of the utility function must also be transitive: if Marie is preferred to Sonya and Sonya is preferred to Yvonne, then it must also be the case that Marie is preferred to Yvonne (if xP_iy and yP_iz, then xP_iz).

So far, only the *order* of preference among the alternative states of affairs, x, y and z, has been discussed. This allows for the construction of an "ordinal" utility function. The question may be raised, *how much* one state of affairs is preferred to another. If this relationship could be defined, a "cardinal" utility function would result. Von Neumann and Morgenstern[21] constructed a utility theory that produced such a cardinal utility function. Each preference is defined as one between two lottery tickets, *i.e.* two "probability mixes": one lottery ticket presents the subject with a great probability of alternative x, and a small probability of y; the other lottery ticket, on the other hand, yields a great probability for y and a small one for x. By varying the probabilities for x and y, there might occur a pair of lottery tickets — probability combinations between x and y — that would be exactly equal in the preference ordering of the individual; he would be indifferent between the two tickets. This would give an indication of how much the individual preferred x over y or y over x. With an appropriate choice of axioms, this procedure results in a cardinal utility function[22]. More mathematical operations may be performed on such a function than on an ordinal function.

The concept of utility presented here may be of a sweeping nature in theory, it is clearly unfit for immediate application. In order to determine the utility function of an actor, it would be necessary to present him with a list of all relevant situations (and the corresponding probabilities) and to invite him to order these. Apart from the theoretical problem of transitivity (should intransitive choices be considered as mistakes to be corrected by the actor, or as characteristic properties of his preference structure?), there is the practical impossibility of making an interviewee answer the many thousands of questions necessary to establish his preferences while maintaining his interest, concentration and imagination of all those events. In reality this impracticality constitutes an impossibility. An alternative way of establishing a utility function would be to find some *a priori* rule for comparing all events under consideration. For example, any event that yields a greater monetary reward than another is preferred to the latter and it is preferred to the degree that its monetary reward is greater; no other considerations enter the evaluation. This *a priori* is problematical in economic theory and it is far too limited to embrace all preferences that are relevant for the other social sciences. In these fields comparisons between heterogeneous quantities such as "money", "prestige", "affection", etc. would be necessary. Even if agreement existed on the measurement of each of these values separately, no consensus is in sight on their reduction to a single unit of utility.

As matters stand now, the use of the utility concept would be only metaphorical if it were not for the mathematical theory that has been developed around the concept in order to deal with some of the theoretical intricacies in the comparison of preferences. It is this precise deductive apparatus which justifies the separate existence of the term "utility" next to non-technical expressions, such as "need", "value" or "satisfaction". Yet these are the concepts that provide the intuitive content for the technical notion of utility.

> "It is clear that every measurement — or rather every claim of measurability — must ultimately be based on some immediate sensation, which possibly cannot and certainly need not be analysed any further. In the case of utility the immediate sensation of preference — of one object or aggregate of objects as against another — provides this basis." [23]

Within the rational decision model the term utility and the technical terms that go with it exist merely as definitions, as symbols in an analytical construct. But they were not intended to remain so forever.

> "That is while [these notions] are in their immediate form merely definitions, they become subject to empirical control through the theories which are built upon them — and in no other way. Thus the notion of utility is raised above the status of a tautology by such economic theories as make use of it and the results of which can be compared with experience or at least with common sense." [24]

4. Knowledge

The next step is to determine what class of states of affairs is evaluated in the utility function of an actor. In an abstract construct it may be assumed that the actor has full knowledge of all courses of action open to him and of all the states of affairs that might result from these actions, each with its own probability. In any actual situation, the possible consequences of a single action branch out at an exponential rate: in little time they are beyond comprehension by any mind.

There are two ways of dealing with the problem of complete information: one is to assume simply that the individual does have an infinite capacity for the collection, analysis and evaluation of information. This allows concentration on analytical problems of optimalization and equilibrium, but it will take away much of the empirical relevance of the theory, since actors in real life adapt their calculations to their limited capacities. The other solution is to assume that an actor will take into account only specific kinds of information and that he will ignore the rest: in the process of coalition formation, for example, an actor might only consider the majority criterion and the distribution of seats among the parties in parliament, disregarding all other features of the situation. He may evaluate all possible coalitions only with respect to the number of seats they control. Such assumptions allow some of the optimalization and equilibrium concepts of the general model (based on the assumption of complete knowledge) to be related to the specific actions and events that may occur in real life, given certain initial conditions. If such actions and events occur, in fact, when the specific theory has led one to expect them, this increases confidence in both the general model and the specific theory but, if these events or actions do not occur, this may be due either to the faulty assumptions in the specific theory (concerning the information the actor takes into account, or his evaluative standards, or to the assumptions concerning the initial conditions of the system) or it may be due to the assumptions of the general model, *e.g.* the rationality postulate. The simplifications in the specific theory may to some degree be justified by the fact that actors in real life also apply rules of thumb and simple decision criteria, but these may well be different from those which the theory postulates.

A theory in which the actors' perception of the situation serves as the definition of the situation for the theory itself may very well provide a causal explanation of their behavior. It can also be normative in a specific sense: given the perceptions and evaluations of the actors it may tell them what is a rational choice. But the theory can no longer yield conclusions as to what constitutes the rational decision in the "true" situation, *i.e.* the situation as seen by a fully informed outside observer.

The rational decision model contains the assumption that all actors know what "moves" are open to each actor at each moment, what possible outcomes may result from these moves, and with what probability, and how each actor evaluates these outcomes; the actors are capable of carrying out all necessary calculations. This is called the assumption of "complete information". It goes very far indeed and is presented rather reluctantly: "we cannot avoid the assumption that all subjects of the economy under consideration are completely informed"[25].

The revisions of decision-making theory suggested by Simon and by Lindblom both do away with the assumption of complete information, the first by assuming that actors will only consider additional data until they have found a course of action that may satisfy their aspiration level, the second by holding that actors only envisage states of affairs that differ incrementally from the *status quo* and, even then, only if pressed by some manifest short-coming in their present situation. These modifications do sacrifice the universality and exactitude of the theory for a gain in realism. Shubik (1952) has proposed to built some measure for the cost of information gathering and processing into the model: however, no empirical measure that could cover a wide range of cases is available. The problem lies in determining beforehand the profit of knowing something, even if the cost of learning it were known.

For the purpose of empirical theory formation, the best way out seems to limit drastically the range of actions and outcomes the actors are assumed to consider: Riker[26] has proposed to attribute to the actors a motivation in terms of "money, power and succes" only: this would greatly simplify the calculations they are assumed to make, but since the three "values" still cannot be reduced to a single measure of preference, this simplification remains insufficient to make the theory fully verifiable.

It may be seen that a theory which attributes only a single motivation to the actors at the same time restricts the range of information which the actors are assumed to consider. If outcomes are considered only with respect to a single evaluative aspect, this simplifies the construction of the utility function as it narrows down the amount of information considered complete. If actors strive only to bring about a coalition of minimal size, all other aspects of that coalition are ignored in their calculations. This is the strategy pursued in the construction of theories of parliamentary coalition formation in the present book.

To sum up, the rational decision model is an analytical construct consisting of propositions that may be stated as follows:

(*1*) A rational actor is an actor who, if completely informed, acts so as to maximize his utility function.

(*2*) A utility function is determined by a complete and transitive ordering of preferences among all states of affairs that may result from the actions open to the actor.

(*3*) A completely informed actor is an actor who knows all courses of action open to him or to any other actor at any point in time and all outcomes that may result from those actions, and the utility functions for all actors over all these outcomes, and this actor is capable of performing all necessary calculations at no cost or at a cost that is known to him.

For the purpose of constructing an empirical theory of rational decision, a simplified motivation may be attributed to the actors; this restricts the set of relevant choices at each point, limits the evaluation of outcomes and narrows down the amount of information that the actors are assumed to consider.

Though this scheme goes far in eliminating the ambiguities of the original rationality concept, further analysis demonstrates that it does not go far enough to define a unique rational decision for each situation. Game theory provides a most precise language to discuss these matters.

n-Person Game Theory

Game theory is a branch of mathematics which borrows its procedures mostly from mathematical logic, set theory and functional analysis. Yet, from the time of its first presentation, this result of the collaboration by a mathematician, John von Neumann, and an economist, Oskar Morgenstern, proved of extraordinary interest to social scientists[1]. In game theory, the propositions that form part of the rational decision model are translated into formal symbols. The focus of interest is on the search for "stable standards of behavior" that might govern the actions of a rational actor in a situation in which the outcome does not solely depend on his own choices, but also on those of other actors and on "chance" or "nature". Game theory might thus be called the mathematics of rational actors in interaction with each other and with nature.

The solutions that are suggested by game theoretical analysis are based on a concept of equilibrium. No actor can do better than to adhere to his "equilibrium strategy", since any deviation from it may result in a loss to him. It will appear from the discussion that such "stable standards of behavior" can not be inferred immediately from the axioms of the rational decision model or of game theory. The rationality postulate is compatible with a variety of precepts for behavior and the equilibrium concept does not determine a unique solution either. Most often a number or even an infinity of strategies constitute an equilibrium together. It will be seen that solution concepts are justified by testing them against intuitively persuasive formal requirements or by comparing the consequences of some solution concept in a specific situation with intuitive insights of "fairness" or "elegance". Thus, the case for a certain solution concept can be made extremely convincing, but never as compelling as are the results of immediate deduction from the axioms of the rational decision model.

The main elements in game theory are the number of actors, the set of alternative moves available to every actor at each point in the game, the characteristic function, representing the evaluation by the actors of all outcomes that may result from their combined actions, and the information that may be exchanged between the actors, if any. The assumption is made that each actor knows these "rules of the game" including the evaluation by other actors of the various outcomes. This is the assumption of "complete information" which may be modified by imposing specific limitations on the information available to the actors.

The major divisions of the subject matter of game theory are based on these elements. Thus the overriding dichotomy within game theory concerns the number of actors: 2-person versus n-person games. Independent of this, games are classified as to the nature of the outcomes: if these outcomes are such that the gains of the winners equal the losses of the losers for every outcome, the game is called "constant-sum" *. If, on the other hand, this is not the case for every outcome and the winners do not necessarily gain as much as the losers lose, the game is called "non-constant-sum". Finally, an important distinction is made between games in which players may exchange information and enter into agreements and those in which no communication is possible, *i.e.* between cooperative and non-cooperative games.

The category of two-person zero-sum games has proven to be the most amenable to analysis. The actual mechanics of 2-person game theory are of limited importance for the purposes of this book. But a discussion of the central solution concept, the "minimax" strategy, is necessary for an understanding of n-person theory also.

In two-person zero-sum games, the interests of the players are perfectly opposed: there is no point in any cooperation, whatever is better for one player is worse for the other. Yet, every outcome

---

* Constant-sum games are also called "zero-sum games". The sum of the gains and losses of the players is constant and the payoffs may always be redefined so that they sum to zero by carrying out the appropriate linear transformation on the unit and origin of the utility scale in which the payoffs are measured.

in a game is a result of the choices of the players. When one player makes his move this leaves open a series of possible outcomes, dependent upon the choice of his opponent. Since this opponent gains from his losses, the player must reckon that the worst outcome that may come from his move will actually result. Therefore, he should survey every one of his moves to ascertain what is the worst outcome that could result from each. The "good way", according to Von Neumann and Morgenstern, to play the game is to choose that move, the worst possible result of which is at least as good as the worst possible result that may come from any other move[2]. This is called the "maximin" or "minimax" strategy. In some games, "strictly determined games", the opponent will, by following the same line of reasoning, aim for the same outcome: this is the "saddle point" of the game and if both players are rational and act as if they believe their opponent to be rational, this will be the outcome. If one player choses a different strategy while the second sticks to his minimax strategy, the latter will find that it is not the worst outcome that might result from his move which comes about, but one that is better or at least as good. Since the game is zero-sum, this improvement for the second player is, by definition, a loss for the first player; his defection is "punished", the saddle point represents an equilibrium.

Games that do not possess a saddle point do not yield such an immediate equilibrium outcome. However, if they are conceived of as iterated games, players may determine a sequence of moves in fixed proportion but in random order (so as not to be found out by the opponent); such a "mixed strategy" that an equilibrium comes about always exists for both players in the game[3].

Various modifications of the minimax principle have been proposed[4].

If the game is non-constant-sum, it may have outcomes in which both players are better off than in another outcome. However, there may be several of such outcomes and it may also be that when each player is aiming at a different one, both may end up at a point that is worse for either one or both of them. When the game is non-cooperative; no communication to coordinate the players' strategies is possible. It may be that the game allows simplification. A player may find that one of his moves results in a series of possible outcomes that are worse than the outcomes associated with another of his moves for every move his opponent makes. In such case, he will remove the first choice from consideration. It may be the case that the other player finds that if the first player removes one of his moves as "dominated", a move of this second player will be dominated in turn. After such deletions, the game may still turn out to possess points that are mutually advantageous and that cannot be missed even without coordination[5].

Various authors have pointed out that, even without manifest communication, players may still signal to one another[6]. In a sequence of games, for example, one player may play a mutually damaging move until the opponent "gets the message" and gives up his egocentric ways for a mutually advantageous strategy. The problem of coordination may also be solved because players tacitly coordinate their strategies on the basis of "cues" or "focal points", *e.g.* playing the number "seven", or giving up competitive strategies when the experimenter leaves the room.

Finally, games may be non-constant-sum and cooperative. Bargaining is possible and agreements may be reached. Various arbitration schemes have been proposed[7]; Schelling has remarked that those are compelling "only when the players perceive each other to be mathematicians"[8]. When everything else fails in such non-constant-sum games, players may fall back on their minimax strategies, striving at the best of the worst.

The study of n-person games is a continuation of 2-person theory, but at the same time fundamentally different aspects enter into the analysis. When three or more actors participate in the game, the option arises for some to collaborate against others. The emergence of such coalitions is the focus of interest in n-person theory. Again, "the aim of present-day game theory is to construct a notion of equilibrium social behavior and to investigate the properties of such a concept"[9]. As in 2-person theory, limitations may be imposed on the extent of communication and collusion going on among the actors. Yet, in the relatively small body of literature in this branch of game theory, the greatest attention by far has been given to games in which no such restrictions exist. For games in which all communication and collusion is ruled out, the analogy with 2-person games holds in that equilibrium points of mixed strategies may again be shown to exist for finite games[10]. But the same problems arise in this case, and with more force: the point may not be unique and as the number of players increases it is less and less likely that a solution set of equilibrium points will be found. Finally, games in which no communication among actors occurs are not very relevant for social scientists who are interested precisely in communication patterns and structures of collaboration. Therefore, the subject matter will be restricted to cooperative n-person games.

A group of actors that have decided to coordinate their choices into a common strategy is called a coalition* (S). The total payoff that the members of the coalition may expect is written as $v(S)$: the value of the coalition S. The quantity $v(S)$ depends in part on the behavior of the actors that are excluded from the coalition S; they may join together to form the counter-coalition $-S$. In general, $v(S)$ is defined in a conservative manner: it is the maximum that S may expect to obtain from a minimax strategy against its complement $-S$, on the assumption that this counter-coalition $-S$ has formed and that it also plays its maximax strategy. This is "the worst" that could happen to S. In many cases, however, the manner in which $v(S)$ is realized by the members of S, is left indeterminate: the game is completely defined by a "characteristic function"[11]. This function assigns a value $v(S)$ to all coalitions S that may be formed from N. (N is the set of all players in the game.)

This characteristic function must satisfy certain formal characteristics. First, the condition is imposed that an empty coalition, $\emptyset$, i.e. a coalition without actors, receives a value equal to zero.

$$v(\emptyset) = 0 \qquad (1)$$

In almost all cases, another condition is imposed. The value of a coalition is at least as great as the sum of the values of its component coalitions. Or, the sum of the values of a coalition S and a coalition T, that have no actors in common, is not greater than the value of their union ($S \cup T$).

$$v(S \cup T) \geqslant v(S) + v(T) \text{ for } S \cap T = \emptyset \qquad (2)$$

This is called the property of superadditivity of the characteristic function†. "It says that the whole does not obtain less than the sum of its parts"[12]. It is justified by Rapoport with the argument that "players joining in a coalition, hence coordinating their strategies, can always do at least as well as if they had not joined in the

---

* For reasons of convenience, the term "coalition" is also used for an actor operating on his own (a one-man coalition); a "coalition" without any actors is called an "empty coalition". This usage is analogous to that of the term "set" in mathematics.

† The condition of superadditivity may easily be misread as implying that a coalition has a larger value, the more members it has. This is not the case. The coalition T may have a value $v(T) < 0$. The coalition that represents the union of S and T (S and T have no members in common), consequently may have a smaller value than $v(S)$ but, according to condition (2), still larger than the sum of the values of both S and T. $v(T) < 0$; $T \cap S = \emptyset$; $v(S) \geqslant v(S \cup T) \geqslant v(S) + v(T)$.

coalition"[13]. Once the condition is derived for the constant-sum game, it may be proven for the class of non-constant-sum games[14].

For constant-sum games, a third condition is added.

$$v(S) + v(-S) = v(N) \tag{3}$$

In constant-sum games, the value of a coalition and of its complement always sum to a constant, the value of the coalition of all players.

All constant-sum games can be transformed into zero-sum games, for which it is true that

$$v(N) = v(S) + v(-S) = 0 \tag{4}$$

Commonly, though, in n-person game theory the value of $v(N)$ is set equal to 1^{*}.

A function that satisfies the first two conditions defines a game and in the case where the third is also satisfied, the game is constant-sum.

In order to determine what coalitions will or should form, it is desirable to know what share of $v(S)$ each prospective member of S may expect: an actor will base his decision whether or not to join S on that expectation. On the other hand, the share of $v(S)$ that may accrue to an actor is very likely to depend on the other coalitions that are available to that actor and to the payoff he may expect in those: this will provide him with the bargaining leverage

---

* The utilities in which payoffs are measured are defined up to an order-preserving transformation in the case of ordinal utilities and, in the case of cardinal utilities, up to a linear transformation. This allows, in both cases, multiplication of all payoffs with some constant and addition of a constant to the payoffs of each player without changing the formal characteristics of the game. Thus, a constant may be added to $v(i)$, so that $v(i) + a_i = 0$. Also, $v(N)$ may be multiplied by some constant, so that $v(N).c = 1$. The latter transformation is called the "0,1 normalization" of the game and it does not affect the mathematical properties of the game. Psychologically, of course, it would make a difference whether a player was involved in a game with stakes of millions of dollars or only a few pennies, or, whether $v(i)$ would stand for a definite loss, for playing even, or for receiving a small or a sizeable amount. In the 0,1 normalization of the game it is true that $v(S \cup T) \geqslant v(T)$ and $v(S \cup T) \geqslant v(S)$; $S \cap T = \emptyset$. This is the case, since the condition of superadditivity requires $v(S \cup T) \geqslant v(S) + v(T)$. In the 0,1 normalization, moreover, $v(i) = 0$ for all i. A coalition can only guarantee its members what they obtain on their own, $v(i)$, and thus be "individually rational" (cf. condition (5)), if the value of such a coalition, $v(S)$ or $v(T)$, is greater than or equal to zero. From $v(S \cup T) \geqslant v(S) + v(T)$; $S \cap T = \emptyset$; $v(S), v(T) \geqslant 0$, it follows that $v(S \cup T) \geqslant v(S)$ and $v(S \cup T) \geqslant v(T)$. In the 0,1 normalized version of the game, it is true that a coalition has the same or greater value the more members it contains.

to make threats and demands to his prospective partners. Thus, in order to know what coalition will form, it is necessary to know how $v(S)$ will be distributed or, in other words, which payoff vector will emerge; but, in order to determine what payoff vector may be expected to result, it is necessary to know the payoff vectors that could be enforced if other coalitions would form.

One way to break up this vicious circle might be to focus on payoff vectors and to select a certain class of these as more likely to emerge than others: the coalitions that are compatible with such payoff vectors are the ones most likely to form. The other tack might be to start from a given coalition structure and to investigate under what conditions such a partition of all actors over these coalitions might be stable in some sense. The former line of analysis, the investigation of payoff vectors, will be explored first.

It would be unlikely that a payoff vector would emerge in which a player would be worse off than he would be on his own, as the one-man coalition $\{i\}$. In that case, he would always be better off by playing on his own and guaranteeing himself $v(\{i\})$. Therefore, in a payoff vector x, each element x_i, representing the payoff to some actor i, should be at least as much as what the actor can obtain on his own.

$$x_i \geq v(\{i\}) \text{ for all } i \in N \tag{5}$$

This is called the condition of individual rationality.

Another limitation on the payoff vector is related to the Pareto-optimality condition: a situation in which it is possible to effect a change from which some will gain and no one will lose, cannot be considered stable, since no one will oppose the change and some are motivated to bring it about. Because of condition (2), the value of the coalition of all actors, $v(N)$, is at least as great as the sum of the values of the coalitions over which the actors have distributed themselves. Clearly, if this condition of superadditivity holds, $v(N)$ represents the highest amount that the players together can realize by playing the game. On the other hand, a payoff vector in which the payoffs to the players sum to less than this $v(N)$ is unlikely to be stable since another distribution of payoffs could be realized by moving to N, i.e. by forming the coalition of all actors and by distributing the surplus thus gained. Therefore, the sum of the payoffs in the payoff vector can not exceed $v(N)$, nor can the payoff vector be stable if the payoffs sum to less than $v(N)$; as a consequence the sum must exactly equal $v(N)$.

32

From $\Sigma x_i \geqslant v(N)$ over all $i \in N$
and $\quad \Sigma x_i \leqslant v(N)$ over all $i \in N$ follows
$\quad\quad \Sigma x_i = v(N)$ over all $i \in N$ $\hspace{3cm}$ (6)

Those payoff vectors that satisfy conditions (5) and (6) are called imputations[15]. Condition (5) is called the condition of individual rationality and it seems very compelling indeed. From the notion of Pareto-optimality, condition (6) also appears very persuasive. Thus it seems advisable to remove from consideration all those payoff vectors that are not imputations.

The analysis proceeds with the search for those imputations that for some reason appear more likely or commendable to form than others. At this point the concept of domination may render its services. In plain language, a payoff vector x dominates another payoff vector y, when there exists a set of actors S who are all motivated and capable to bring about x rather than y. The actors in S will be motivated to bring about x, when each of them is better off under x than under y: for each i in S, $x_i > y_i$; the actors in S will be capable, when the value of their common coalition S is sufficient to reward its members each with at least their amount x_i, i.e. the coalition S is "effective" for the payoff vector x: $v(S) \geqslant \Sigma x_i$ for all $i \in S$.

Thus x dominates y if, and only if, it is the case that

$x_i > y_i$ for all $i \in S$ and $v(S) \geqslant \Sigma x_i$ for all $i \in S$ $\hspace{1.5cm}$ (7)

As the actors in S are motivated and capable of bringing about x rather than y, there seems to be good reason to eliminate all dominated imputations y and to limit the equilibrium set to those imputations x that are not dominated. This proposal does offer a very attractive solution concept (known as the "core"). But there are some complications: as will be shown later, the core is empty in non-trivial constant-sum games: in these games no imputation is undominated. Von Neumann and Morgenstern, who were primarily interested in constant-sum games, therefore defined a different solution, V[16].

(a) No imputation in V is dominated by another imputation in V.

(b) All imputations not in V are dominated by some imputation in V.

Clearly, if an imputation is undominated by any other, it will be in V. However, an imputation x in V may be dominated by some

Vectors	Actors		
	1	2	3
x	$(\frac{1}{2}, \frac{1}{2}, 0)$			x dominates y; 1 and 2 are better off
y	$(0, \frac{1}{4}, \frac{3}{4})$			y dominates z; 2 and 3 are better off
z'	$(\frac{5}{8}, 0, \frac{3}{8})$			z' dominates x; 1 and 3 are better off
z	$(\frac{7}{8}, \frac{1}{8}, 0)$			z does not dominate x but it is dominated by y in which 2 and 3 are better off

Fig. 3-1. Domination among imputations in the 3-person constant-sum game.

imputation y that is *not* in V, but if it is, then there must be some other imputation in V that dominates y, the one not in V, because of (*b*). Thus V consists of the imputations that do not dominate each other, *e.g.* x and z.

At this point it should be made clear that the relationship of domination is not transitive. An imputation x may dominate another, y, which in turn dominates a third, z, but it is not necessarily true that x also dominates z. It may even be the case that z dominates x, as may be illustrated with an example from the three-person constant-sum game[17]. Consider the imputations in Fig. 3-1, where any two-person coalition is effective. This example illustrates the fact that cycles of domination may occur, as among imputations x, y and z'. If actors have to choose between these three imputations, nothing can be said about their choice since any imputation they decide upon may be undone by the actor who is left out and who may propose a dominating imputation in which he is better off. But if instead of z', the third imputation that might be brought about were z, then it could quite confidently be predicted that x would be the outcome: if z would form, player 3 could offer $\frac{1}{4}$ to player 2 in y; but player 1 would propose x with $\frac{1}{2}$ for player 2 who would accept this better offer.

This may clarify the definition of the solution V. Even if an imputation in V is dominated by one not in V there is per definition always a third imputation in V that dominates the second; thus, against every proposal that is not in V there exists a better proposal in V. Then, why not eliminate all those dominated imputations in V right away? The answer is that there may be no imputation left: in essential constant-sum games every imputation is dominated by some other, as will be shown hereunder (p. 37).

34

The solution concept V, as it stands, leads to somewhat disappointing results. In their analysis of the three-person game, Von Neumann and Morgenstern find that every imputation of this game is included in at least one solution. First, there exists a set V (of imputations that do not dominate each other) in which one player is assigned a fixed amount, $c*$, he is being discriminated against by the other two players. The other two players divide the remainder, $(1-c)$, among them. As long as neither of the two receives less than he would obtain on his own, $v(\{i\}) = 0$, each division among the two represents an imputation that is undominated by any other imputation in which the third player receives his fixed amount, c. Thus, this set V contains an infinity of imputations. And as any of the three players may be the one that is being discriminated, there are three sets, V, for a given amount, c, that is assigned to the discriminated player. As the amount that is assigned to the discriminated player may vary, and as there are three sets V, for each amount, there is a infinity of triples of sets V, each containing an infinity of imputations.

> "The interpretation of this solution consists manifestly of this: one of the players is being discriminated against by the two others...... They assign to him the amount which he gets, c. This amount is the same for all imputations of the solution, *i.e.* of the accepted standard of behavior. The place in society of player 1 is prescribed by the two other players; he is excluded from all negotiations that may lead to coalitions. Such negotiations do go on, however, between the two other players: the distribution of their share, $1-c$, depends entirely on their bargaining abilities."[18]

Notwithstanding its ingenuity, V, the solution advanced by Von Neumann and Morgenstern, is not a very useful criterion in selecting a small set of imputations that are in some kind of equilibrium and that may therefore be expected to form[†]. As a consequence, other solution concepts have been advanced.

The first criterion that suggested itself was that of the "core", the set of all undominated imputations[19]. When the core is not empty, it may be shown to be a subset of V: all imputations that

---

* $0 \leqslant c < 1/2$.

† Von Neumann and Morgenstern have suggested solutions for specific classes of games, such as "simple games" of special importance in the analysis of political coalitions, see Chapter 4 in this book; and also, for "weighted majority games" and "quota games". (Von Neumann and Morgenstern (1967) Chapter 10; see also Luce and Raiffa (1957) pp. 212, 224; Rapoport (1970) Chapters 14 and 15.)

are not in V are certainly dominated by one in V, thus as an imputation in the core is not dominated at all, it must be in V. The main drawback of the core concept is that the core is empty for non-trivial constant-sum games. This was the class of games that received most attention from Von Neumann and Morgenstern: they attempted to construct the theory of n-person non-constant-sum games as an extension of constant-sum theory by including a dummy player. Thus, it is not surprising that they did not choose the core as their central solution concept.

The core does have some very attractive properties. When defining imputations, condition (6) was imposed that they be Pareto-optimal with respect to the coalition of all actors, N. But one might very well argue that this condition should be extended with respect to all effective sets S. In other words, any imputation should satisfy the condition of "group rationality". The condition of Pareto-optimality was arrived at by imagining that the actors would compare their payoffs x_i, under some proposed payoff vector x, with what they would receive under a payoff vector y, that would become feasible if they would all decide to form N, the coalition of all actors. If they would all be better off under some y, for which N would be the effective set, x would not be stable; and it would not be an imputation. The same considerations might, with good reason, be extended from N to any coalition S. If some actors could form a coalition S and the value of this coalition, $v(S)$, would be sufficient to enable them to realize an imputation y in which all members of S would be better off than they would be in the imputation x which was proposed (e.g. by the members of T which is effective for x) then they would reject x, dominated by y. Thus the Pareto-optimality condition may be applied to the comparison with all coalitions S, in stead of only with N. In this form it is called the "condition of group rationality" and it defines the core, by eliminating all dominated imputations.

$$\Sigma x_i \geqslant v(S) \text{ for all } i \in S \text{ and all } S \subset N \tag{7a}$$

Or, an imputation x should guarantee to the members of every possible coalition together at least the value of that possible coalition (otherwise they would form it). If cond. (7) holds, the imputation is undominated, i.e. group-rational: there exists no coalition S with a value $v(S)$ that allows its members to realize an imputation y, such that $y_i > x_i$, for all members i of S. The set of imputations satisfying cond. (7a) constitutes the core.

Now it may be seen why the core is empty for constant-sum games. In such games the values of a coalition S and of its complement $-S$ (consisting of all actors not in S) always sum to the same value $v(N)$; this follows from condition (3). Thus, the sum of the elements of any imputation in a constant-sum game is constant and equal to $v(N)$. If, for a given imputation x, condition (7a) applies, there can be no coalition S that would enable all its members to realize an imputation in which they would be better off than they are under x. Now, might there be coalitions S in which the members are collectively worse off than they are under x? This would imply that there must be a coalition $-S$, in which the members together are *better* off than they are under x, since in a constant-sum game, $v(S)$ and $v(-S)$ always sum to the same amount $v(N)$! However, in that case x does *not* satisfy condition (7a) with respect to the coalition $-S$, all members of which are better off than they are in x and x does not belong to the core. If condition (7a) is to apply to x, there can be no coalitions whose members are collectively better off, nor coalitions whose members together are worse off then they are under x (because, in that case the members of the complement of that coalition would be better off). Thus, the only remaining possibility is that the members of S (or $-S$) together receive under x exactly the same amount that they would receive in any other S (or $-S$). Since S may also represent a one-man coalition $\{i\}$, this implies that no actor may receive more under x than he would receive on his own, as the one-man coalition $\{i\}$. If some $\{i\}$ would receive more under x than $v(\{i\})$, this would mean that the coalition of all actors except i, the coalition $(N-i)$, would receive under x less than $v(N-i)$ and they would all be motivated to form $(N-i)$ in order to distribute among themselves $v(N-i)$; x would not satisfy condition (7a). Imputations are individually rational (condition (5)) and therefore actor i cannot receive more, nor less than $v(\{i\})$, he must receive exactly that amount. Thus, in every imputation that satisfies condition (7a), every actor would receive exactly what he would obtain on his own. There is no incentive to form coalitions; all coalitions are "flat" and the game is "inessential". The conclusion must be that for constant-sum games either the core is empty — no imputation satisfies condition (7a) — or the game is inessential. However, in many non-constant sum games, the core exists and time and again it will turn out to be an element of a solution concept[20].

Perhaps the most literal application of the equilibrium notion is the one suggested by Vickrey[21]. His idea of a "self-policing" equilibrium is grafted on to the Von Neumann—Morgenstern solution concept. A "strong" solution in Vickrey's terminology is precisely the Von Neumann—Morgenstern solution V with the added characteristic that at least one of the group of defectors — the "heretic set" — will be certain to be worse off after equilibrium has been re-established than he was before the "heresy".

According to the definition of V, for every y not in V, dominating some x in V, there is a z in V which in turn dominates that y. By definition, the x and z in V do not dominate each other. A "strong" solution, according to Vickrey, is a solution V such that, for any "heretic" imputation y (not in V) it is the case that under any z in V that dominates y, at least one member of the effective ("heretic") set for y will be worse off than he was under x (the imputation in V, that was dominated by y). Since there will always be a member of the "heretic set" that will be worse off for some z than he was at the outset in x, the "strong" solution possesses a special kind of equilibrium: in any Von Neumann—Morgenstern solution, defections may occur and they will certainly be given up again for some imputation that is in V. But in a "strong" solution, any such defection will not only be undone by a return to V, it will actually be "punished", because at least one of the heretics will be worse off than he was before his defection. Thus deviations will not only be automatically corrected, they might not even be attempted.

Vickrey's "strong" solution very nicely catches the "mood" of the game theoretic search for stability. In the normalized three-person constant-sum game discussed before, it singles out as the "strong" solution precisely the three permutations of the imputation $(\frac{1}{2}, \frac{1}{2}\ 0)$ and condemns the other solution sets as "weak"; a satisfying result, at least to the esthetical sense. However, as the Von Neumann—Morgenstern solutions have not even been completely enumerated for the four-person game, let alone for larger numbers of actors, Vickrey's procedure suffers some of the drawbacks of the Von Neumann—Morgenstern solution V: it can only be applied after all solutions V have been calculated by inspecting each one of them. Thus, when n is greater than three, Vickrey's approach is of little help.

In the solution V, in the core as well as in the strong solution, the actors are assumed to compare their payoff under an imputation x with what they could obtain in each and every coalition that is effective for some other imputation. Theoretically this generality may be a virtue, but in the case of the solution V, the result is unwieldy and undiscriminating; the core, on the other hand, may be of more practical use but it does not exist for constant-sum games. For these reasons, a different approach may be useful: to find a criterion that would limit the comparisons among coalitions that the actors are assumed to make. This notion underlies the idea of ψ-stability and other approaches. Luce and Raiffa, after noting that the rationality postulate supplies the game theoretic model with its "psychology", suggest that their ψ-function may provide its "sociology" because it describes some limitation on the interactions of the participants[22]. The ψ-function specifies what coalitions may form, given a certain coalition structure τ, with an imputation x. A coalition structure, τ is a given distribution ("partition") of all actors in N over various coalitions. Thus, only comparisons between a given coalition structure and those coalitions that may be formed under the "boundary conditions" of ψ, the coalitions that are in $\psi(\tau)$, are relevant. The authors postulate that the actors will investigate all coalitions in $\psi(\tau)$ to see if there is a coalition S whose members do better in S than they do at present in the coalition structure τ with the imputation x. In that case, the pair (x,τ) will be rejected as ψ-unstable. This is again the condition of group rationality: "The only difference is that here it is not imposed for all coalitions but only for those determined by the coalition structure τ and the given function ψ"[23]. This defines the ψ-stable set, characterized by the conditions

for every S in $\psi(\tau)$ $\Sigma x_i \geqslant v(S)$, for all $i \in S$ (8)

and

if $v(\{i\}) = x_i$, then $\{i\}$ is in τ (9)

The last condition means that a player must do *better* in a coalition than he can do on his own as $\{i\}$, unless in the coalition structure τ he is already "isolated" as $\{i\}$ and may be willing to accept a coalition in which he is not worse off. Clearly, the ψ-stable set coincides with the core over all imputations that are allowed, given the coalition structure τ: "the core is, in effect, a special case of the ψ-stability concept", namely for the case in which the ψ-function allows all possible coalitions to form from any coalition structure.

Little work has been done in experimenting with various ψ-functions[24] or in trying to establish particular boundary conditions empirically.

The same notion of a given coalition structure and payoff vector is the starting point in the construction of two other solution concepts, those of the bargaining set and of the kernel.

In a paper by Aumann and Maschler[25], the authors call a given coalition structure with its corresponding payoff vector a "payoff configuration" (p.c.). All one-man coalitions may occur in such a partition, *i.e.* they also are "permissible", and they have the value zero: $v(\{i\}) = 0$. The other permissible coalitions are those that they have a value greater or equal to zero: $v(T) \geqslant 0$; all coalitions are, therefore, by definition, individually rational

$$v(\{i\}) = 0; v(T) \geqslant 0 \qquad (10)$$

The authors define an outcome as "coalitionally rational" (c.r.) when, in a given payoff configuration, the actors within a coalition receive at least what they could obtain if they were to form another coalition *from among some, but not all, the members of the present coalition*. Again, the group rationality condition is imposed, but this time only those coalitions are considered that can be formed from members that are already united in a coalition that is part of the given payoff configuration*.

$$\sum x_i \geqslant v(S), \text{ for all } i \in S, \text{ and for all } S \subset T \ (T \text{ is a coalition} \qquad (11)$$
$$\text{in the p.c.)}$$

Note that $S \subset T$, in other words S must be a "proper subset" of the existing coalition T, some member(s) must be left behind in the defection towards S. "Thus, we assume that a coalition will not form if some of its members can obtain more by themselves forming a permissible coalition". The condition may be considered as a particular ψ-function and it again defines the core over the imputations that satisfy that function[26].

Aumann and Maschler wish to single out those payoff configurations that are coalitionally rational and which convey a particular sense of "safety" to the actors involved. This would be the case, they argue, if every proposal for change could be met by a counter-proposal; in this counter-proposal, all actors whose consent is necessary to realize it do at least as well as they do under the terms of the first proposal and in the counter-proposal, moreover, some of the initial propounders of change would be left out, so that a deterrent to change is built in. Aumann and Maschler

---

* Note that condition (11) is analogous to condition (7), but is restricted to those coalitions S that can be formed from among members of a coalition T_i that exists in the payoff configuration. In the same manner the analogous condition (8) — for the ψ-stability set, restricts the condition to those coalitions S that are in $\psi(\tau)$.

reason that a c.r. payoff configuration will be "*M*-stable" if it can be shown that every "objection" made by some faction K within the coalition T could be answered with a "counter-objection" by another faction L in the same coalition T (K and L have no members in common), by showing that there is a c.r.p.c. in which L and its "partners" will be at least as well off as they are at present, while those "partners" of L who also are "partners" of K in its objection will be better or equally well off under the counter-objection, and some members of K will be left out of it.

An "objection" is defined as a c.r.p.c. for which

$$y_i > x_i \text{ for all } i \in K \tag{12}$$

and

$$y_i \geqslant x_i \text{ for all } i \in P_k; L \cap P_k = \emptyset \tag{13}$$

where P_k is the set of actors who in the new c.r.p.c. will be members of coalitions in which there will be also members of the K-faction: they are called "partners of K" and P_k contains K*. Moreover, no member of L belongs to P_k. "Verbally, in their objection, players K claim that, without the aid of players L, they can get more in another c.r.p.c. and the new situation is reasonable because their new partners do not get less than what they got in the previous p.c."[27].

A counter-objection is defined as a c.r.p.c. for which it is true that

$$z_i \geqslant x_i \text{ for all } i \in P_l \tag{14}$$

and

$$z_i \geqslant y_i \text{ for all } i \in (P_l \cap P_k); \text{ not all members of } K \text{ are} \tag{15}$$
$$\text{partners of } L$$

In these expressions, P_l is the set of "partners of L" who in the new payoff configuration will be in some coalition in which there is also a member of L; P_l has been defined so that it does not contain *all* members of K: "Sometimes, the members of L have to use the tactics of 'divide and rule' by using the members of K as partners, but they may not use *all* members of K". Under conditions (14) and (15), L, who defends the *status quo*, **x**, does not

---

* $K \subset T$; but note that P_k may contain actors that were *not* members of the coalition T in the initial c.r.p.c. The same goes for L.

have to propose a c.r.p.c. in which everyone does better than in the objection y by K; he must demonstrate that all those actors he needs to bring about his new c.r.p.c. (P_l) will do at least as well in z as they do under the *status quo* terms of x (14), and that those actors who also have been approached by K and whom he needs too, $(P_k \cap P_l)$ will do better or equally well in z as they would do if K had his way, *i.e.* under y. But there is at least one member of K to whom no such guarantee is made.

The bargaining set, M, consists of all M-stable coalitionally rational payoff configurations, that is, of all those c.r.p.c.'s for which there is a counter-objection of L against K for every objection of K against L.

The bargaining set has been defined with the aid of conditions (10)—(15) that have a somewhat *ad hoc* character. Also, condition (11), "the coalitional rationality assumption is a very strong one, as it forces the game to be essentially superadditive within those coalitions which are actually formed"[28]. However, a modified bargaining set, $M_1^{(i)}$, has been defined without the aid of condition (11)[29]. On the other hand, the bargaining set possesses some very attractive features. Even when the core is empty, coalitionally rational payoff configurations and M and $M_1^{(i)}$, may still exist. Moreover, for specific games with a small number of players, the bargaining set may consist of very few uniquely determined imputations or imputations whose elements may vary over a limited range. Finally, the mechanism captured in the ideas of objection and counter-objection seems to agree with intuitive insights and is corroborated to a degree by gaming experiments[30].

In a later paper, Maschler in collaboration with Davis[31] proposed another definition of a stable set of payoff configurations: the kernel. This time, all individually rational payoff configurations are considered. Since the characteristic function is chosen in a manner that $v(\{i\}) = 0$ for all $\{i\}$ this amounts to

$$x_i \geqslant 0 \text{ for all } i \in N \tag{16}$$

Moreover

$$\Sigma x_i = v(T) \text{ for all } i \in T, \text{ where } T \text{ is a coalition in} \tag{17}$$
$$\text{a partition of } N$$

Condition (17) requires that the members of T divide among themselves no more than is feasible, *i.e.* the amount $v(T)$, and, because of Pareto-optimality within T, no less, but exactly· the value of T.

42

Next, the authors define the "excess" of some arbitrary coalition, S, as the amount that the prospective members of S would gain together if they were to give up their present x_i and would form S^*. In the present notation, this excess, $e(S)$, may be written as

$$e(S) = v(S) - \Sigma x_i \text{ for all } i \in S \tag{18}$$

An actor k in T may thus survey all coalitions S and determine their excess. In order to determine his attitude to some other player l in T, the first actor, k, might be especially interested in those coalitions which could form without the consent of l, i.e. without l being a member, but in which k himself would join. Of all the "excesses" of all coalitions S that do contain k, but that do not contain l, the largest excess is called "the maximum surplus of k over l", which "therefore represents the maximal amount player k can gain (or the minimal amount that he must lose), by withdrawing from T and joining a coalition S which does not require the consent of l (since $l \notin S$), with the understanding that the other members of S will be satisfied with getting the same amount they had in T"[32].

From this point on, the argument is rather straightforward: two players within a coalition T are said to be in balance when the maximum surplus of k over l equals the maximum surplus of l over k. If in a coalition all players are in balance with each other, the coalition is said to be balanced. Finally, when all coalitions in an individually rational payoff configuration are balanced, this i.r.p.c. belongs to the kernel of the game. It may be shown that the kernel of a game is contained in its bargaining set, $M_1^{(i)}$; that is, any i.r.p.c. that is in the kernel is also in the bargaining set $M_1^{(i)}$.

Maschler and Davis interpret the maximum surplus of k over l as the most a player k may expect to win, or as the least he may expect to lose, without the consent of l. Yet, one might attribute a somewhat different meaning to the concept. The maximum surplus of k over l might also be taken to indicate the largest fund k could spend in buying other players away from l. When both have equal funds at their disposal, they are "matched" in some sense and they might therefore consider the i.r.p.c. as reasonable or stable.

---

* The expression "excess of S", written as "e_S" is also used in Chapter V, but in an entirely different sense.

The kernel is defined by starting from much the same premises as were used in the construction of the bargaining set $M_1^{(i)}$: a payoff configuration that is made to satisfy individual rationality and a notion of two players k and l (or factions K and L) within the same coalition, threatening to bid against each other to persuade other actors to join them and excluding the opponent in a new coalition structure and a new payoff configuration. And in both theories an equilibrium is established when in each coalition in the p.c. every player can demonstrate that he is able to counter the proposals of all his opponents in the coalition. Throughout n-person theory, the search has been for imputations, or sets of imputations, such that if one party (actor, faction) were to opt for an imputation outside this solution set, another (actor, faction) may bring about an imputation that is again an element of the solution, preferably in a manner that leaves the instigator of defection worse off than he was at the outset, thus creating a built-in deterrent to deviance.

It is in this light that ψ-stability, the bargaining set and the kernel must be judged. Essentially, they constitute attempts to limit the range of comparisons made by individually rational actors in a manner that seems formally and intuitively (i.e. "pre-empirically") acceptable; from the set of imputations constructed in this manner, those imputations are selected that in their totality seem to represent an equilibrium: any deviation will be followed by a return to some element of the equilibrium set. The idea of "punishment" — the requirement that a non-conformist will be worse off than he was at the outset, once the balance has been redressed — adds an additional element of stability to such an equilibrium set. It is strongly present in the "automatical" loss effected by applying a minimax strategy against a defector in the two-person constant-sum game; in the two-person non-constant-sum game, the notion adheres to the solution in the strict sense of Luce and Raiffa. In the n-person game, it may be found back in Vickrey's strong solution, and also in the bargaining set M, when it is postulated that at least some member of K (the defecting faction) will be excluded from the partners of L who act as the guardians of the balance.

All the solution concepts presented until now are justified with the reference to the calculations of individual actors motivated in last analysis by the utility maximization of individual rationality. With the Shapley value, for the first time a standard of fairness is introduced that in a sense transcends the individualist motivations of the actors, essentially by "making them accept" an *a priori* rule of distribution. The Shapley value is obtained by a particularly elegant mathematical procedure; when the formal context of the game is dominant in the perception of the actors, this esthetic virtue alone may cause acceptance of the Shapley value as an arbitration scheme.

The Shapley value is based on the idea that an actor by joining a coalition adds to its value and that the weighted average of these value increments effected by an actor are an indication of his importance ("power") in the game which should be reflected in the Shapley value of the game for the actor.

The increment — the difference in value of the coalition with the actor, i, and of the coalition without him — may be written as $v(S)-v(S-i)$[33]. The weighted sum of all the increments which i could bring about by joining all possible coalitions that hitherto excluded him, is the Shapley value of the game for i. It is assumed that each coalition S with s members has an equal chance of occurring; coalitions emerge at random.

If there are n actors in the game, the number of different coalitions with $s-1$ members, that exclude i, equals[34]

$$\frac{(n-1)!}{((n-1)-(s-1))!\,(s-1)!} = \frac{(n-1)!}{(n-s)!\,(s-1)!}$$

Since s may take the value of any whole number from 1 up to and including n (i may enter coalitions of 0 up to and including $n-1$ members), there are n times this number of different coalitions of which i is not a member and to which he may add his increment with random odds.

$$\frac{n!}{(n-s)!\,/(s-1)!} \qquad\qquad (19)$$

The Shapley value for actor i, $\phi_i(v)$, is obtained by adding the increments effected by i, each time multiplied by their probability coefficient, their weight (19).

$$\phi_i(v) = \sum \frac{(n-s)!\,(s-1)!}{n!}\,(v(S)-v(S-1)) \text{ for } 0 \leqslant s \leqslant n-1, \qquad (20)$$
$$\text{and } S \subseteq N$$

The mathematical elegance of this definition resides in the paucity and the persuasiveness of the conditions employed in its derivation. In this case the requirement is set that $\phi_i(v)$ be independent of the labelling of the actors; that the sum of the value $\phi_i(v)$ over all actors i in N be equal to $v(N)$, *i.e.* the value of the coalition of all actors; and, finally, that if the game is composed of various sub-games, it should be played by the actors involved in those sub-games as if these sub-games really were independent of one another, so that the values of these sub-games may simply be added to obtain the value of the (entire) game. In this context, the second condition is the most important; but it seems convincing that actors would agree to $v(N)$ as the total amount to be divided once they have agreed to submit to arbitration at all, and thus, in a sense, have already formed the coalition N. For political science, the most important category of games is that of the so-called simple majority games in which a coalition either receives 0 or 1, depending on the number of players s in S and on some majority criterion. The Shapley value allows an assessment to be made of the "value of the legislative game" to the actors concerned. Quite a few such analyses have indeed been made[35]. Since legislation normally occurs in different phases and within different bodies, for the purposes of analysis the entire process (game) is separated into various sub-games for the different bodies that participate in the legislative process. This explains Shapley's third condition and the importance he attaches to the problem of the decomposition of games.

This is not the place to attempt an evaluation of game theory. A multiplicity of solution concepts have emerged from the discussion. However, all of these could be traced back to an underlying concept of equilibrium. In the next chapters, especially the notions of permissibility and the core will play a central role.

As a branch of mathematics, game theory has been one of the most important innovations since World War II. Its value to social science is much harder to assess. It is easy to recognize the importance of the theory for operations analysis, the theory of competitive and ologopolistic markets and for other branches of economic theory. But the relevance of game theory to the other social sciences can only be evaluated as its concepts are being incorporated in social science theories. The yield of the minimax theorem and of two-person theory in general for sociology and political science has been somewhat meager. A major purpose of this study is to assess the possibilities and the results of an application of the theory of n-person games to the subject of politics.

CHAPTER 4

Theories of Political Coalitions

The theories of political coalitions presented in this chapter share an underlying analytical structure provided by the rational decision model and its mathematical elaboration, game theory. The empirical referents to the theories remain undefined at this stage of the analysis, but all theories are intended to apply, among others, to voting bodies that take decisions by some kind of majority.

The theories discussed in this chapter have been advanced by different authors and therefore vary in terminology, notation and in the assumptions that were used in their derivation. Here they are revised to fit the notational and conceptual system of this book. All theories are incorporated into a general theoretical framework. This allows the similarities and differences in their analytical structure to be demonstrated and a procedure for the testing of the performance of all the theories to be designed.

It will appear that the crucial decision for each theorist concerns the choice of the motivational assumption and the definition of the context of the game. The specific motivational assumption determines what it is that actors are assumed to maximize; it plays the role of the "general theoretical assumption" about the causal laws that govern the behavior of the actors in the system. The other assumptions may be understood as factual assumption about the initial conditions and subsequent external influences affecting the system[1]. These assumptions should be necessary and sufficient in conjunction with the general theoretical assumption to generate a number of statements about reality (*e.g.* which coalitions will form in a given situation); those statements are then tested in order to assess the validity of the general theoretical assumption. The most important factual assumption concerns the definition of the context of the game, whether or not it is constant-sum and whether or not payoffs may be transferred and side payments are allowed. This determines which solution concepts are applicable.

Other factual assumptions pertain to questions such as whether a parliamentary group may be considered a unitary actor or whether the parliamentary system is, in fact, the locus of decision making and whether it may be studied in isolation from other societal influences. These questions will be discussed in detail in Chapter 5, with an eye to their theoretical implications, and again in Chapter 7, when the rules for operationalization of the theories are presented.

The theories of political coalitions studied here are concerned with the patterns of collaboration and opposition in voting bodies, i.e. with the composition of coalitions, rather than with the distribution of payoffs to winners and losers or with the stability of coalitions once they have formed.

Often a more or less permanent coalition emerges in such voting bodies which is in a position to determine decisions if it controls a majority of the votes.

Allowing for a variety of voting procedures, voting bodies adopt as their decision the proposal that has been supported by more members than some other proposal (e.g. the "status quo"). Sometimes not just simple majorities but absolute or two-thirds majorities are required. The majority criterion, m, will be defined as the smallest number of votes that is sufficient to secure adoption of a proposal. If voting occurs by simple majority among n voting members with one vote each, m is defined as

$$\frac{n+1}{2} \leqslant m \leqslant \frac{n}{2} + 1$$

If voting occurs by simple majority among members with unequally weighted votes, as for example, in a stockholders' meeting, the weight of the vote of an actor i is written as "w_i". The sum of the weights of all members in the voting body may be rendered as "Σw_i". The majority criterion, m, is defined as

$$m = \tfrac{1}{2}\Sigma w_i + d \qquad \text{for all } i \in N$$

Here, d stands for any quantity that is larger than zero and smaller than the smallest unit of weight, w.

The weight of a coalition S may be written as w_S, which indicates the number of members of the coalition in the case of equally weighted votes and, in the case of votes with unequal weights, it refers to the sum of the weights of the members: $w_S = \Sigma w_i$, for $i \in S$. A coalition is called "winning" when it controls sufficient votes or a weight large enough to command a majority: $w_S \geqslant m$. The set of winning coalitions is written as "$w(S)$". A coalition S belongs to the set of winning coalitions $w(S)$, when w_S equals or exceeds m:

$S \in w(S)$ if, and only if, $w_S \geqslant m$, for all $S \in N$

Whether the actors that are not members of the winning coalition, S, join together in a coalition, $-S$, of losers, or distribute themselves over various coalitions, all losing by definition, or whether they remain on their own, is left indeterminate in the theory: they will do whatever keeps their loss at a minimum. The important thing is that for the purposes of the theory a coalition structure is sufficiently characterized by its winning coalition. In most cases, the assumption is made that this winning coalition has succeeded in "completely defeating" its opponents, *i.e.* holding them down to the amount they would obtain if each remained on his own[2]. In that case, the game is completely characterized by an enumeration of all winning coalitions and their values.

In a game with n actors, there exist 2^n different combinations, or coalitions, of actors, including the empty coalition. Since the complement of any winning coalition is a losing coalition (and the complement of any blocking coalition is another blocking coalition), a losing coalition corresponds to each winning one. Ruling out blocking coalitions, there must be as many winning coalitions as there are losing coalitions: half of 2^n, *i.e.* 2^{n-1} coalitions, are winning.

The coalitions that may be expected to form will certainly be winning coalitions. The task at hand is to specify conditions and criteria that allow the number of winning coalitions that may be expected to form to be restricted.

1. Minimal winning coalitions: Von Neumann and Morgenstern

The authors of *The Theory of Games and Economic Behavior* payed much attention to a specific class of *n*-person constant-sum games, called "simple games", and characterized by the property that the value of winning coalitions does not increase when new members are added. Or, a winning coalition, T, will not have a larger value, $v(T)$, than its subset, S, if S is also winning.

$$v(S) + v(-S) = v(N) \qquad \text{(constant-sum condition)}$$

and

$$v(S) \geqslant v(T) \text{ if, and only if, } S \leqslant T;\ S,\ T \in w(S)$$

A coalition is considered "losing" when its members cannot improve their position, either by staying on their own or by forming coalitions of losers: they are completely defeated. The complement of such a losing coalition in the simple game is a winning coalition. Of course, any superset of a winning coalition is again winning, any subset of a losing coalition is a losing coalition.

These simple games have a number of attractive properties for formal as well as empirical analysis. Most important in the first respect is the existence of a class of coalitions, W^m, the set of "minimal winning coalitions". The solution of the simple games consists of those imputations for which the minimal winning coalitions are effective, the "main simple solution".

On the other hand, simple games bear a resemblance to some situations in real life that are very relevant to the present purpose: a majority coalition in a voting body may conquer some fixed "prize", *e.g.* the cabinet portfolios and this "prize" may be considered the same, independent of the composition of the winning coalition that acquires it: the value of the coalition does not increase with its membership. The correspondence between simple games and these actual situations is fortunate, but not coincidental.

"In this connection we emphasize again that any game is a model of a possible social or economic organization and any solution is a possible stable standard of behavior in it."[3]

It should be noted that simple games may be visualized in different ways, all formally equivalent but involving very different images of the corresponding real-life situation. Two versions are especially important in this context. Von Neumann and Morgenstern present their analysis of simple games in the "reduced form", or, in "—1,0 normalization". The value assigned* to every (losing) one-man coalition $\{i\}$ is —1. All losing coalitions are completely

---

*Since utilities are defined up to a linear transformation only, a constant may be added to the utility scale of each actor, and the values of all coalitions may be multiplied by another constant.

defeated and therefore "flat"; therefore, a losing coalition with p members has a value of $p \cdot (-1) = -p$. The value of the coalition of all actors N, (and of the coalition of no actors, $\emptyset$) is set equal to zero: $v(N) = v(\emptyset) = 0$. The game is zero-sum. In a game with n members, therefore, the value of a winning coalition S, with $(n-p)$ members, equals the amount that the p losers have to give up: p. Thus as the number of losers p decreases, the number of members $(n-p)$ in the winning coalition S increases and its value, $v(S)$ does not increase, but decreases. The condition of simple games is satisfied.

This version of the simple game may be compared to a situation in which all players put the same amount, 1, at stake and the winning coalition takes all.

However, the simple game may also be visualized as a game about the division of a given amount c ($c = 1$). The value of being in a one-man coalition may be set equal to zero, $v(\{i\}) = 0$, and, because of the condition of complete defeat, this is the value of all losing coalitions. The coalition of all actors will have a value equal to c, or 1. The game is constant-sum. The value of a winning coalition, S, and its complement, $-S$, must sum to the value of the coalition of all actors: $v(S) = v(N) - v(-S) = 1 - 0 = 1$. All winning coalitions have the value 1. This is the simple game in "0, 1 normalization". Again, as the membership of the winning coalition increases, its value does not increase, but it remains the same. The condition of simple games is again satisfied. In the 0,1 normalization, the simple game conveys a resemblance to the situation in a parliamentary voting body where the opposition has no control over the government departments and the majority coalition acquires all cabinet portfolios.

Clearly, even though the two games are formally identical — they are "strategically equivalent" — their psychological features are very different.

Once a coalition is winning, the addition of a new member will not increase its value but the other members will have to share the same or a smaller value with the newcomer. Clearly, actors will strive to form winning coalitions that do not contain more actors than those necessary to win. An actor i without whose votes or weight a coalition S would also be winning is called an "unnecessary actor": $w_S - w_i \geqslant m$ ($i \in S$). A coalition without unnecessary actors is called a "minimal winning coalition": a winning coalition, such that the substraction of any single actor would render it losing. A minimal winning coalition S belongs to the "minimal winning set" W^m, and the coalitions in this set are expected to form*

$$S \in W^m \text{ if and only if } w_S \geqslant m > w_S - w_i \text{ for all } i \in S \qquad (1)$$

This solution applies under the restrictions of the constant-sum condition and the defining condition of simple games that the value of winning coalitions will not increase with their membership. It is not unrealistic to apply these conditions in the analysis of certain parliamentary situations. This "minimal winning theory" will be tested against historical data of European parliamentary coalitions in Part II of this book.

2. Coalitions of minimum size: Riker and Gamson

In situations that resemble simple games, minimal winning coalitions are predicted to form. But some persuasive rule that could restrict this predicted set further would, of course, be very attractive. Such a criterion has been suggested by Gamson (1962) and also by Riker (1962). It will be defined as follows: from among all winning coalitions, those are expected to form that have the smallest weight. Or, a coalition is of minimum size if, and only if*

$$S \in w(S) \quad and \quad w_S \leqslant w_T \quad \text{ for all } T \in w(S) \qquad (2)$$

Of course, a coalition S that is of minimum size must also be minimal winning. If the minimum size coalition S were *not* minimal winning, then it would contain an unnecessary actor i, so that the coalition without i, the coalition $\{S-i\}$ would also be winning. But the coalition $\{S-i\}$ would have a smaller weight than the coalition S: the coalition S would not be of minimum size, unless it contained no unnecessary actor i, *i.e.* unless it was, in fact, minimal winning. But, conversely, a coalition can be minimal winning without being of minimal size.

It may be noted that in games where all actors have an equal vote†, the minimal winning coalitions contain exactly m actors and all coalitions with m actors are minimal winning coalitions: every additional vote is unnecessary, one vote less would make the coalition losing. Thus, in games among actors of equal weight, the minimal winning coalitions are also the coalitions with the smallest weight or number of votes, w_S.

---

*For an example, see the Glossary of Technical Terms.
†Such simple games are called "symmetric simple games".

When actors have unequal weights*, this is not necessarily the case; coalitions may not have the smallest weight among winning coalitions and yet such coalitions may be minimal winning. Consider, for example, the three-person game with actors i, j, k, and with weights $w_i = 25$, $w_j = 35$ and $w_k = 40$ and, as a consequence, with the majority requirement, $m = 51$. All two-person coalitions are minimal winning; without either member they would be losing. Only the coalition of all three actors is not minimal winning, since it can do without any one of its members. Among the three minimal winning coalitions, the coalition $i\&j$ has the smallest weight; it is the minimum size coalition.

In the literature, these minimum size coalitions have not always been properly distinguished from the minimal winning coalitions[4]. There has been some confusion about the meaning and derivation of the minimum size principle which has most often been attributed to Riker. However, the minimum size principle may have been applied with great insight to political life by Riker but he has never adequately derived it. For games of actors with equal weight, e.g. individual players with one vote each, the set of minimum size coalitions is identical to that of minimal winning coalitions. The problem is to show that for games of actors of unequal weight the coalition of smallest weight, that is, the minimum size coalition, is most likely to form among all minimal winning coalitions.

In *The Theory of Political Coalitions*, Riker (1962) begins with a defense of the application of the zero-sum condition to the study of political life. Especially in societies that have a high degree of organization, the business of politics is carried on by fiduciaries who consider it their moral duty to defend the interest of their clientele to the exclusion of all other interests; they are true "maximizers". They will attempt to realize the outcome that is maximal in terms of "money or power or success". This definition does lift the utility concept out of its purely tautological state but it is not yet an operational definition: how to compare outcomes, when one of them yields more "money" and the other more "power", or how to measure "power" at all?

The term "success" risks throwing the definition back into tautology since it may mean "favorable or satisfactory outcome or result"[5] but it also has the more restricted meaning of "wealth. fame, rank etc."

---

*Such simple games are called "weighted majority games".

The "size principle" is introduced for the first time in the following wording [6].

> "In *n*-person zero-sum games, where sidepayments are allowed, where players are rational, and where they have perfect information, only minimum winning coalitions occur."

This statement is translated into a descriptive statement about the "natural world" [7].

> "In social situations similar to *n*-person, zero-sum games with sidepayments, participants create coalitions just as large as they believe will ensure winning and no larger".

The definition of the game at this point is not restricted to simple games. A "minimum winning coalition" is defined as "one which is rendered blocking or losing by the subtraction of any member" [8], *i.e.* the same definition as "minimal winning coalition" in this book except that here blocking coalitions have been ruled out.

It may be remembered that a game is considered a simple game only if a coalition T, which contains a coalition S as a subset ($S \in T$), does not have a larger value than this coalition S: $v(T) \leqslant v(S)$. Or, in simple games, the value of a coalition does not increase as its weight or membership increases. In a game where all actors have an equal vote, the weight, w_S, of a coalition is entirely determined by the number of its members. (If no players are considered "special" for some reason, the game is called "symmetric".) Thus, the various coalitions S, with increasing number of members, might be plotted on the abscissa and the values of the corresponding coalitions on the vertical axis: the characteristic function of a simple game would be graphically represented by a curve that would have no upward slope to the left (no increase in $v(S)$ as membership in S increases) at any point over its entire length. Thus, as new actors are added, the value of the coalitions that have been extended in that manner does not increase. On the other hand, when the curve does show an upward left slope over part of its length, the game is not simple.

Riker argues at this point that "natural situations" which exhibit such non-simple features, *i.e.* in which a coalition has a larger value than its subset which is also winning, "in concrete reality are probably nonexistent". In such games actors would continue to add new members to the coalition over and above those needed for a majority (because the larger coalition could secure larger gains). "The condition is extraordinarily restrictive." [9] But that is not quite the point. What matters is whether a definition that *excludes* such non-minimal winning coalitions with larger values, as does the definition of the simple game, is unduly restrictive. It appears that the restriction in the definition of simple games is reasonably plausible. But there exist "natural social situations" that contradict it. For example, the parliamentary game may be conceived as a game about the distribution of cabinet portfolios, thus satisfying the constant-sum condition. It may be redefined as a game, equally constant-sum, about the distribution of cabinet portfolios *and* seats in parliamentary committees. A simple majority is sufficient to capture the cabinet portfolios, but a larger majority, say two-thirds of the membership of parliament, may be in a position to oust the remaining opposition from the parliamentary committees*.

A second example may be taken from gang or tribal warfare over the control of a given territory, its installations and population. A minimal winning coalition could take the territory and its inhabitants with their possessions only after heavy warfare and costly destruction. A large coalition could, by a mere threat, take the territory without any damage to installations or loss of life among its population. The spoils of the large coalition would be greater.

> "My informants in Buganda told me that men relished war in the old days, and this seems to me very likely. Under such conditions, a party is likely to be coerced by the threat of battle only when defeat seems almost certain. Probably, then, something approaching a two-thirds majority would be required to win by threat of battle."[10]

These examples should be distinguished from situations in which a two-thirds coalition can change the rules of the game, *e.g.* by constitutional amendments, or where it can realize gains that do not correspond to a loss for the loser, *e.g.* because to each party the cost of warfare is spared[†].

---

*Something like this seems to have happened when Communists were excluded from major parliamentary committee-work in the French Fourth Republic, 1951. See Williams (1966) p. 258.

†Riker (1962) remarks: "There may exist in nature some situations that display these features, but if they do exist, they are so rare and obscure that one who has searched diligently to find them has been unable to do so." (*op. cit.*, p. 45) A situation in which a coalition gains more than its subset which is also winning, may not be so obscure or rare but often it may be more profitably studied as a non-constant-sum game.

In the appendix ("Derivation of the Size Principle") to his book, Riker demonstrates how some common rules for the division of payoffs among the members of the winning coalition lead to paradoxical results for those coalitions that contradict the condition of the simple game and this serves as an added argument to exclude such situations from consideration.

In Chapter 5 of *The Theory of Political Coalitions*, Riker makes the explicit assumption that

> "all characteristic functions slope downward and to the right (that is, assuming none are parallel to the abscissa except at zero)."[11]

This amounts to the condition for simple games in $-1,0$ normalization. In the same chapter, Riker introduces actors of *unequal* weight, "proto-coalitions", made up of the individual players in the voting body.

> "It is to be understood that these proto-coalitions are, for the purposes of the present analysis, indivisible units even though they may be composed of many individual players."[12]

At this stage of the analysis, therefore, the subject matter has been restricted to simple games and, moreover, the argument deals with games among actors of unequal weight, the "proto-coalitions". For actors with unequal weight it has been shown that not all minimal winning coalitions are also of minimum size. An additional argument is therefore necessary to derive the prediction of these minimum size coalitions.

In Chapter 5 of his book, Riker singles out the "uniquely preferable winning coalition" as especially likely to form. Such a coalition (*1*) "has a greater value than any other one possible....."; (*2*) "it is one in which all the participating proto-coalitions can satisfy their initial expectations." The initial expectation of an actor is the highest amount he can obtain in the best "nonminimal" coalition of which he could be a member[13].

In the argument that follows, a three-person game is presented with three "proto-coalitions", P^3, Q^3 and R^3, with weights $w_p > w_q > w_r$, such that no actor is winning on his own but any two of them are*.

---

*"P^3, Q^3, and R^3" indicate that P, Q, and R are proto-coalitions in a partition of the set of all players in three subsets.

"By reason of the size principle, the values of these coalitions are related thus:

$$\text{If}\begin{cases}v(Q^3 \cup R^3) = a = -v(P^3) \\ v(P^3 \cup R^3) = b = -v(Q^3) \\ v(P^3 \cup Q^3) = c = -v(R^3)\end{cases} \qquad \text{then } a > b > c."\ [14]$$

Note that the weights of coalitions $Q\&R$, $P\&R$ and $P\&Q$ decrease in that order.

First, whatever the "size principle" may imply at this point, it does *not* imply that the values of the coalitions decrease with their weight.

If, however, the postulated relationship between values and weights is accepted, for the time being, then the coalition of Q and R satisfies the first property of a uniquely preferable winning coalition: it has the largest value. Can it also satisfy the initial expectations of its members, Q and R? The initial expectation of Q appears to be the most Q can obtain in the "nonminimal"* coalition of Q and P, *i.e.* the entire value of that coalition, the amount c. Similarly, the most R can obtain in a "nonminimal" coalition is the entire value of the coalition of P and R, the amount b. Now, the coalition with largest value, the coalition of Q and R, should be in a position to guarantee b to R and c to Q. It has at its disposal the amount a. It can satisfy the initial expectations of its members if $a \geqslant (b + c)$. But this relationship "is, of course, determined by the shape of the curve of the characteristic function"[14].

The requirement that $a \geqslant (b + c)$ is a very restrictive condition: the "uniquely preferable winning coalition" exists only in special cases; the minimum size coalition is uniquely preferable only under these conditions.

However, the preliminary statement, that according to the size principle the value of coalitions decreases with their weight, can not be accepted, unless an additional premise is explicitly adopted: it must be assumed then that the value of a coalition is a function of its weight. (Note that the condition of simple games states only that the value of a coalition does not increase with its membership.)

It might be argued that the weight of a coalition is determined

---

*The expression is Riker's. If proto-coalitions are indissoluble, only an entire proto-coalition can be excluded from the coalition and without any such a proto-coalition the coalitions under consideration would be losing. In that sense they are minimal and not "nonminimal".

by the weight of its component proto-coalitions, which in turn is determined by the number of individual players — with one vote each — that are contained in each proto-coalition. When individual players, instead of proto-coalitions, are considered the actors of the game, the argument would continue along familiar lines: since each losing individual player has to give up an equal amount, the coalition that excludes the greatest number of individual players, that is, the coalition of minimum size, collects the greatest amount, or, has the greatest value. But in this manner the game has been reduced to one among equally weighted individual players instead of among unequally weighted proto-coalitions. In that case, all coalitions would continue to exclude individual players until their weight had been cut down to the minimum, $i.e.$ to exactly the size m. Only if by coincidence the weights of some proto-coalitions happened to sum to exactly this amount m, would they be maintained in their entirety in the minimum size coalition. In all other cases, the proto-coalitions would play no role. If, on the other hand, proto-coalitions are accepted as the (indissoluble) actors of the game, it does not follow from the condition of simple games that their value decreases with their weight once they are winning.

Moreover, for a voting body with n equally weighted players ($e.g.$ one man, one vote) and a majority criterion m, there exists $n!/(n-m)!m!$ coalitions that are minimal winning and of minimum size. In a voting body of 11 members, where six would control a majority, there would be 462 different six-man coalitions, all minimal winning, all of minimum size! For an assembly with some hundreds of members this would yield a rather unwieldy predicted set. The introduction of parliamentary groups in an assembly, and of proto-coalitions in the theory, serves the same purpose, to make the outcomes more predictable. That is the reason why unequally weighted actors (that may be thought of as sets of unequal numbers of individual players who have an equal vote each) are introduced as the proto-coalitions in Riker's theory.

In this stage of Riker's analysis, however, the actors in the game are apparently the indissoluble proto-coalitions made up of firmly committed individual players. These proto-coalitions may form coalitions in which individual players may be "unnecessary" in the sense that without them the coalition would still be winning. But as long as the proto-coalitions remain indissoluble, these redundant individual players will not be excluded. In the next stage of his argument, Riker discards the assumption of indissolubility of proto-coalitions because "in a dynamic world, this is, of course, absurd"[15].

Riker argues then that proto-coalitions which together form some minimal winning coalition from which no proto-coalition can be missed, will now exclude those individual players which are no longer necessary: as the condition of indissolubility of proto-coalitions is lifted, the "actor" in the analysis is no longer the proto-coalition, but again the individual player, and the game is no more among unequally weighted proto-coalitions but among equally weighted individual players. However, since in this "dynamic" model the "history" of coalition-building is taken into account, the argument produces more specific results. Not just any coalition of m individual players is expected to form, but some coalition of the minimum size m that originated as a coalition of proto-coalitions which was "uniquely preferable" (if there was one); this uniquely preferable coalition of proto-coalitions thereupon proceeds to exclude the individual players that can be missed.

The objection is that once individual players know that coalitions of proto-coalitions can always be cut down again to minimum size, the proto-coalitions will never be regarded as indissoluble. It does not matter how much bigger than minimum size a coalition of proto-coalitions is, corrections can and will always be made: the theorist must again face the situation of n individual players with all their coalitional combinations.

If, on the other hand, proto-coalitions must be considered as definitely indissoluble (which is not so absurd in a world with party discipline), then these proto-coalitions must be considered as the true actors in the game. In that case $v(\{i\})$ is not the value of what a losing individual player i has to give up, but of what a losing proto-coalition $\{i\}$ must give up and $v(\{i\})$ is the same amount for each proto-coalition $\{i\}$. In this view, $Q\&R$, $Q\&P$, $P\&R$ are all minimal winning and an additional assumption is necessary to single out any one of them as especially likely to form. This is the task of Riker's assumption that actors (proto-coalitions) will want to satisfy their "initial expectations", an assumption introduced at a stage of the analysis when proto-coalitions were still regarded as indissoluble. Under those assumptions* the "uniquely preferable winning coalition" is expected to form.

---

*That is, if it is accepted that the value of a coalition is a function of the number of individual players in a game with indissoluble proto-coalitions.

In the appendix ("Derivation of the Size Principle") to Riker's book, it is again demonstrated that, when the curve of the characteristic function at no point shows an upward-left slope (*i.e.* under the conditions of the simple game), and when players are of equal weight, the coalitions with the smallest number of players will form, *i.e.* the coalitions of smallest weight or: the predicted set is the set of coalitions of minimum size, which, in the case of equally weighted players is identical to the set W^m of minimal winning coalitions. In so far as the "derivation" applies to players of *unequal* weight, it demonstrates that unnecessary actors will be excluded from the coalition, *i.e.* only minimal winning coalitions will form; but it does not follow that only minimal winning coalitions of minimum size (smallest weight) will emerge when players are weighted unequally.

All this follows directly from the definition of the set W^m for simple games as advanced by Von Neumann and Morgenstern; no separate minimum size principle, that would allow a further restriction of this set W^m, has been derived.

In a later article, Riker (1966) makes the assumption that all players are "equally weighted persons". As has been shown for the simple game, in that case the set of minimum size coalitions is identical to the set of minimal winning coalitions W^m. The purpose of Riker's argument in this article is to show that even if the constant-sum game is *not* simple, *i.e.* when the characteristic function shows an upward slope over at least part of its length, only minimal winning coalitions are to be expected. In such case, there may exist two winning coalitions S and T, such that $v(S) < v(T)$ and $S \subset T$. There also exist some player(s), h, that are part of T and not of S, such that $T = (S + h)$. When these players h receive more in T than $v(T)-v(S)$, there is no incentive for the members of S to join the players h in T. But if the players h receive less in T than this difference $v(T)-v(S)$, then the members of S share in the increment and have a reason to bring about T together with the players h.

At this point[16], Riker argues that the members of $-T$ will not let this pass. If S forms, its members would demand the amount $v(S)$ from the losers, *i.e.* from the players in $-S$, who include the players h. When T is about to form, with the cooperation of players h, the remaining outsiders, $-T$, stand to lose a larger amount, $v(-T)$, to be paid by a smaller number of losers. They will therefore be ready to bid up to the amount of their additional loss, $v(-S)-v(-T)$, to keep the players h from joining with those in S to form T. This amount, by the zero-sum condition, equals $v(T)-v(S)$. Since the players h would receive less than $v(T)-v(S)$ if they would join T, they will accept the bid by the members of $-T$ and stay out of the coalition T. If the players h would receive exactly the amount $v(T)-v(S)$ as members of T, T would still not be "realizable" (or, expected to form); Riker defines a "realizable" coalition as one in which all members do *better* than in a smaller coalition and *at least as well* as in a larger one[17]. In this case, when the players h take the entire value increment, $v(T)-v(S)$, the members of S are not *better* off in the larger coalition T than in the coalition S. Riker's conclusion is that, regardless of the shape of the characteristic function, minimal winning coalitions will form when the constant-sum condition is satisfied.

There are several objections to this argument. First, the players h receive part of the value of coalition T, whether that part is visualized as a bid from the outsiders in $-T$ or as an offer from the members of S. It depends very much on the definition of "coalition" whether or not h should be considered a member of T or not when the value of T is, in fact, realized and acquired by S and h, and $(S + h) = T$. Secondly, the asymmetry in the definition of a "realizable" coalition that must guarantee its members *more* than a smaller coalition and *at least as much* as a larger one, appears somewhat arbitrary. If the members of S are equally well off in T, they might stay in T, once it formed, even though T is not minimal winning. Thirdly, there is some danger in an argument that singles out the "last added" actors h as especially likely to receive the increment $v(T)-v(S)$*. It gives rise to a similar debate as has occurred in economics around the attribution of a marginal increase in profit to the last added unit of a production factor or, a calculation of the cost of an added unit of product on the basis of the marginal cost for producing it[18]. As a matter of fact, in the present case, the argument can be turned against itself to prove that no minimal winning coalition will ever come about.

If the coalition T is a minimal winning coalition, $w_T = m$, and the coalition S is a smaller coalition, which is therefore losing, and if the members of S can form T with the aid of some player(s) h,

---

*The Shapley value of a game to a single actor, h, is also computed on the basis of this value increment $v(T)-v(S)$, for $T = S + h$. But, in this case the assumption is that the sequence in which h enters T is entirely random and the increments brought about by h are weighted for the probabilities that h is the 1st, 2nd,...., or nth actor to join in. The condition of independence of labelling is explicitly imposed; *cf.* Luce and Raiffa (1957) p. 247.

then it is rational for the members of S to offer the players h any amount up to $v(T){-}v(S)$, the difference in value between the two coalitions. The members of S cannot offer the players h the entire amount $v(T){-}v(S)$, since the members of S must be better off in the larger coalition T, for it to be realizable. The members of $-T$ will, according to the argument, offer the players h anything up to and including $v(T){-}v(S)$ and as a result h will not join in T. No minimal winning coalitions will form but the players h will receive the entire amount $v(T){-}v(S)$. Congratulations h! Riker's argument is self-defeating.

Riker has offered some very persuasive arguments for restricting investigations to those constant-sum games that are simple*. When, in simple games, all players are of equal weight, the predicted set consists of all coalitions that have just enough members to be winning and no more, *i.e.* the coalitions of minimum size, which are at the same time the minimal winning coalitions. When actors are of unequal weight, Riker has suggested that the uniquely preferable winning coalition is especially likely to form when (*1*) values of coalitions decrease with their weight, (*2*) actors strive to satisfy their initial expectation and (*3*) there exists a coalition of minimum size that has a value great enough to satisfy those initial expectations. If the game may be considered, in last analysis, as one among individual players of equal weight, coalitions made up of proto-coalitions that are of unequal weight may be expected to oust individual players until they have reached minimum size in terms of individual players.

Riker's arguments do not add up to the derivation of some "minimum size principle" that is distinct from the concept of minimal winning coalitions and that is defined for a specifies class of games†. The definition of the minimum size principle given at

---

*The author apparently identifies only $-1, 0$ simple games as simple, ignoring the fact that all linear transformations of such games are "strategically equivalent", among them those in $0,1$ normalization. This misinterpretation may be the cause of much of the confusion. In his most recent publication (with Ordeshook (1973)), *An Introduction to Positive Political Theory*, Riker makes a more modest claim for the validity of the size principle in non-simple constant-sum games: "We also offer some arguments to show that it holds — but, since in this category we are forced to rely in part on an argument from organizational costs, we regard this demonstration as less powerful" (*op. cit.* p.182). For the simple games, the analysis proceeds again in terms of individual actors with a single vote each. *Cf.* also Butterworth (1971), Riker (1971).
†The first to make the point in print, and very succinctly, was Michael Leiserson: "Riker says 'weights', but in his own applications uses member-

the beginning of this section will be maintained and investigated further: only coalitions of minimum size will form, that is coalition S, such that $S \in w(S)$ and $w_S \leqslant w_T$, for all $T \in w(S)$.

That these coalitions of minimum size are predicted in the case of simple games with equally weighted actors, followed immediately from the definition of minimal winning coalitions, which is in that case identical with that of coalitions of minimum size. For simple games with actors of unequal weight, an additional assumption is necessary. For the empirical study of coalitions, the assumption was advanced for the first time by Gamson:

> "Any participant will expect others to demand from a coalition a share of the payoff proportional to the amount of resources which they contribute to a coalition."[19]

Hence, players will attempt to maximize their "pro rata" gain, *i.e.* the proportion of the value of a coalition to its weight ($v(S)/w_S$).

> "Thus, where the payoff is held constant, he will favor the *cheapest winning coalition*." [19]

Or, in other words, in simple games in 0,1 normalization, where all coalitions have a constant value, $v(S) = 1$, the winning coalitions with the fewest resources, *i.e.* the smallest weight, w_S, are the coalitions expected to form, *i.e.* the coalitions of minimum size.

This holds true for all simple games. For example, when the game is in $-1,0$ normalization, the amount that a losing player is forced to give up is $v(i) = -1$. Accordingly, in a winning coalition of $n-p$ members, p players are excluded and they must give up the amount p, which is the value of the winning coalition: $v(S) = p$. The members of S, if they had not been in the winning coalition, would have had to give up an amount 1 each, or together, $(n-p)$. Thus together they stand to gain the amount $p-(-(n-p)) = n$. Now, when actors are unequally weighted, it may be that some minimal winning coalition has more (small) members than another minimal winning coalition and, yet, none of them is unnecessary. If the gains are divided proportionally to the weights of the members, it does not matter how many members are in the winning coalition as long as they are all necessary. What matters is that the weight of the minimal winning coalition is minimal, so that the pro rata gain is the highest possible; *i.e.* n/w_S is maximal when w_S is minimal.

---

ships. (If Riker's weights are the same as $N-M$'s weights, then his theory is no different from their's.)" Leiserson (1968) p. 784.

Thus the minimum size principle states that, in simple games, those coalitions will be stable that yield their members the highest payoff in proportion to their weight, w_i.

In simple games these are the coalitions S of minimum size, such that:

$$S \in w(S) \text{ and } w_S \leqslant w_T, \text{ for all } T \in w(S) \tag{3}$$

Moreover: $v(S) + v(-S) = v(N)$ (constant-sum condition)

and: $v(S) \geqslant v(T)$ if and only if $S \in T; S, T \in w(S)$

                                              (simple games)

This "minimum size principle", that only coalitions of minimal weight (size) will form in simple games, will be tested against the data.

When actors are of unequal weight, there may be only very few coalitions that are of minimum size. The principle generates a very precise prediction that is very sensitive to slight variations in the membership (weight) of parliamentary groups. Moreover, as Riker has argued, actors may not know exactly which other actors have committed themselves to the coalition and how many votes each actor may be trusted to deliver. Information will not always be "perfect and complete". In order to make sure, coalition leaders may add members over and above the minimum size. This is called the "information effect".

> "The greater the degree of imperfection or incompleteness of information, the larger will be the coalitions that coalition-makers seek to form and the more frequently will winning coalitions actually formed be greater than minimum size."[20]

The information effect cannot easily be estimated in real life situations; "this one change renders verification extraordinarily difficult". Coalitions of larger than minimum size may either be interpreted as a result of the information effect coupled to the operation of the minimum size principle, or, as evidence against that minimum size principle.

A very rough control for this information effect has been incorporated in another proposition tested in this study, "the two-thirds criterion": winning coalitions that are "large" will not form in simple games. A "large coalition" is one that controls more than two thirds of all the votes in a voting body that votes by absolute majority *i.e.* $(n + 1)/2 \leqslant m \leqslant (n/2) + 1$.

The implicit assumption is that, if both the minimum size principle and the information effect operate, the latter will cause coali-

64

tions to be larger than minimum size but not "very much larger", that is, not "large", as defined here.

The choice of the specific criterion is necessarily somewhat arbitrary: $w_S < 4m/3$. Or, a coalition with $w_S \geqslant 4m/3$ is large. In order to get a rough idea of the working of the information effect upon the minimum size principle, this "two-thirds criterion" will be tested against the data: in simple games only those coalitions S will form for which it is true that

$$m \leqslant w_S < \tfrac{4}{3}m \tag{4}$$

3. The Bargaining Proposition: Leiserson

It has been noted that in simple games with actors of unequal weight, minimal winning coalitions may differ in the number of members as long as all its members are necessary for a coalition to be winning. In a study on coalition formation and maintenance in Japan, Leiserson has advanced a "bargaining proposition" for simple games.

"The proposition regarding bargaining is that as the number of actors increases there is a tendency for each actor to prefer to form a minimal winning coalition with as few members as possible."[21]

Thus, again, a subset of the set W^m of minimal winning coalitions in simple games has been singled out as especially likely to form: the set of (minimal) winning coalitions with the smallest number of members*.

Clearly, when actors are weighted equally, all minimal winning coalitions are not only of minimum size, but they also have the smallest number of members, m, among all winning coalitions. When, however, actors' weights are not equal, one minimal winning coalition may have more members than another. And, whether actors' weights are equal or not, when a winning coalition has the smallest number of members among all winning coalitions, it certainly is a minimal winning coalition.

Von Neumann and Morgenstern found[22] that the coalitional possibilities of many simple games could be expressed by assigning a single set of weights to the actors. For example, in the simple

*For an example, see the Glossary of Technical Terms.

majority game of three persons, in which no actor holds a majority on his own, any two-person coalition is minimal winning. This may be represented by assigning to all three actors a weight $w_i = 1$. Every two-person coalition is minimal winning and has a weight $w_S = 2$. Since it is true for all three-person simple games that any two-person coalition is minimal winning, all these games may be described by assigning the set of weights 1,1,1 to the actors.

If blocking coalitions are ruled out or, in other words, if only "strong" simple games are considered, the weights may be chosen in such a fashion that all minimal winning coalitions end up with the same weight, w_S. Weights that satisfy this requirement are called "homogeneous". The strong simple four-person game may be described in all its coalitional possibilities by the set of homogeneous weights 1,1,1,2. In such games there will be a coalition of three small actors (with $w_S = 3$) or three coalitions of a large actor with any one of the small players (with $w_S = 3$); these are the minimal winning coalitions. Since there can be no blocking coalitions, not all actors can have the same weight; if the largest actor is assigned the weight 2, equal weights may be assigned to the three smaller ones and yet all coalitional possibilities are reflected by this set of weights.

The five-person simple game may be described in its coalitional possibilities by four sets of homogeneous weights. Already in the six-person simple game, however, some coalitional combinations can only be expressed by weights that are not homogeneous: some minimal winning coalitions end up with a larger weight than others.

In his study of Japanese diet politics, Leiserson has made use of this property of simple games, that a few sets of homogeneous weights may describe all or most coalitional combinations. The strength of factions in the diet cannot always be established with certainty and precision. Moreover, "intangible" factors, such as financial backing, play a role in the formation process. However, a rough and impressionistic idea of the "weights" of these factions may be obtained. This permits the selection of the set of homogeneous weights that best approximates these relations of strength and the assignment of these weights to the actors in the game[23].

The bargaining proposition as advanced by Leiserson asserts that, especially as the number of actors increases, coalitions will form that are minimal and winning and that consist of the smallest possible number of members (such as the factions in the Japanese diet). For example, in the four-person game, the coalition of the actor with $w_i = 2$ together with $w_j = 1$ is more likely to form than the coalition, equally minimal winning, of the three actors each with $w_j = 1$: the former unites only two actors, the latter embraces three.

Leiserson does not attempt to derive his proposition in systematic fashion. "In time it may be possible to integrate these propositions into the.....theory, but at present they are merely qualifications of the basic theory."[24] Instead, an argument is offered that should justify the bargaining proposition on intuitive grounds.

"The members of the smaller coalition will prefer to form it, since negotiations and bargaining are easier to complete and a coalition is easier to hold together, other things being equal, with fewer parties."[25]

The version of the bargaining proposition that is tested in this study makes no use of homogeneous weights but adopts, instead, the number of parliamentary seats controlled by an actor as an indicator of the weight of that actor. This should not cause divergences in the predictions of the bargaining proposition since no coalitional combinations are lost in the transition to homogeneous weights. However, blocking coalitions do sometimes occur and this may make for very slight distortions.

The number of actors in a coalition S may be written as "m_S". The bargaining proposition, tested in the second part of this book, asserts that in simple games those (minimal) winning coalitions will form, for which it is true that

$$S \in w(S) \text{ and } m_S \leqslant m_T \text{ for all } T \in w(S) \tag{5}$$

When evaluating the results of the empirical tests of this proposition, it must be taken into account that the described tendency is assumed to operate more clearly when the number of actors is large.

In simple constant-sum games, minimal winning coalitions will form. Among those, according to the minimum size principle, the coalitions with the smallest weight, w_S, and according to the bargaining proposition, the coalitions with the smallest number of members, m_S, are expected to form. The two-thirds criterion exclude large coalitions. The theories of political coalitions that remain to be discussed contain an additional element: the policy preferences of actors. Such preferences will be characterized by a quantity p_i, that will be discussed next.

4. Policy positions and the range of coalitions

With the introduction of some notion of policy preference, actors are no longer characterized by their weights, w_i, alone but also by some expression that indicates their location in a space of policy preferences. To simplify matters radically, it will be assumed that this space is one-dimensional and that the location of an actor may be described by a single number p, the most preferred policy, or the policy position, of an actor i.

The assumption that all relevant policy preferences may be subsumed in a single continuum is a very strong one. Its consequences for the empirical version of the theories will be discussed in Chapter 7. Once this assumption has been adopted, it is possible to make a weak assumption as to the nature of this single scale. The policy positions of the actors will be characterized by their sequence only: p_i is an ordinal number.

For each actor i, $i \in N$, there is one and only one number p_i, indicating its most preferred policy or its policy position.

For any two actors i and j, $i,j \in N$, either $p_i \geqslant p_j$ or $p_i \leqslant p_j$. The order is defined between all pairs of actors: it is a complete order*.

For any three actors, i, j, k; $i,j,k \in N$, if $p_i \geqslant p_j$ and $p_j \geqslant p_k$, then $p_i \geqslant p_k$. The order is transitive.

In order to derive the propositions necessary for the theories that are to be discussed, some concept of "distance" is needed†. Even when p is an ordinal variable, the distance between the policy positions of pairs of actors may be compared in certain cases.

---

*In the computer program for calculating the predictions of the various theories, provision has been made for one pair of actors that "ties" on the policy scale, or more precisely, whose ranking towards all other actors is identical but whose ranking *vis a vis* one another is indeterminate. Thus, two actors k and l are said to "tie", when it is the case that for all actors i and j, $i,j \neq k,l$, $p_i < p_k < p_j$, if and only if $p_i < p_l < p_j$. For the pair k and l: $p_k \overset{?}{\gtrless} p_l$. With respect to k and l, the order is therefore not complete.

†The word "distance", used here in quotation marks, does not refer to the concept of a relation that exists between all objects under consideration and that may be expressed in a common unit of measurement. Rather, it refers to the notion that "a is more similar to b than to c in some respect", and therefore "a is further away from c than from b", or, "more distant". It may be seen from the rest of the argument that the notion of "distance" can be dispensed with entirely; its use may help understanding, however. See footnote on p. 69.

The "distance" between the policy positions of actors i and j is written as "$d(p_i, p_j)$".

$$\text{If } p_i \leqslant p_j \leqslant p_k, \text{ and only then } d(p_i, p_j) \leqslant d(p_i, p_k) \qquad (5)$$
$$\text{and } d(p_i, p_k) \geqslant d(p_j, p_k)$$
$$\text{and } d(p_i, p_j) \overset{?}{\gtrless} d(p_j, p_k)$$

Or, the "distance" between an actor's policy position and the policy positions of actors on one side of him may be compared on the basis of the numbers p_i as defined. But, the "distance" between an actor's policy position and those of actors on either side of him cannot be compared on the basis of p_i as defined. The latter comparison will be called a "left—right comparison"; it is not defined when p_i is defined as an ordinal number but only when it is defined as an "ordered-metric"[26].

The theories that are discussed in the next section make use of the concept of a coalition's "range", that is the "distance" between the two members of the coalition that are extreme, or furthest apart, on the policy scale.

An extreme actor in a coalition S is an actor l_S who has a policy position p_l that is more to the left than the policy position of any other actor in the coalition S or, an actor r_S, whose policy position is rightmost among the policy positions of the members of S. The policy positions of l_S and r_S are written as p_l^S and p_r^S respectively.

Thus for the extreme actors l_S and r_S in the coalition S, it is true that

$$p_l^S \leqslant p_i \text{ for all } i \in S, \text{ and } p_r^S \geqslant p_i \text{ for all } i \in S.$$

The "range of a coalition" may be written as "D_S", and it may now be defined as*

---

*It may now be seen that the "range of a coalition" may also be defined as "the pair of extreme members of a coalition". When the policy positions of the extreme pair (p_l^S, p_r^S) of coalition S encompass the policy positions of the extreme pair of coalition T (coinciding or not at one or both extremes), then the policy positions of all members of T are encompassed by those of the extreme members of S. In that case, T is expected to form and S is not (cf. Section 5). These notions are captured efficiently by expressions such as "distance" or "range". Yet, such words carry with them the danger that it is not fully realized that only relations of order are defined. The situation may be compared to that of a set of traincars on a single track: they may be standing still or moving, some towards, some away from another, or maybe all in the same direction, some may be far apart, some close, but one thing cannot change on this single track: their order. And this knowledge makes the kind of statements that are being made in this section possible.

$$D_S = d(p_l^S, p_r^S) .$$

The distances between the pairs of extreme members of coalitions S and T, or the range of coalitions S and T, may be compared under the following conditions.

$$D_S \geqslant D_T \text{ if and only if } p_l^S \leqslant p_l^T \leqslant p_r^T \leqslant p_r^S \qquad (7)$$

or, conversely

$$D_S \leqslant D_T \text{ if and only if } p_l^T \leqslant p_l^S \leqslant p_r^S \leqslant p_r^T$$

Or, when the range of one coalition is contained (coinciding or not at one or both extremes) within the range of the other coalition, these ranges may be compared.

When the ranges overlap, or when they have no point in common, the ranges cannot be compared.

$$D_S \overset{?}{\lessgtr} D_T \text{ if } p_l^S < p_l^T \leqslant p_r^S < p_r^T \text{ or if } p_l^S < p_r^S \leqslant p_l^T < p_r^T$$

All this follows immediately from the definition of p and $d(p_i, p_j)$.

Finally, a "closed coalition" will be defined as a coalition made up of actors that are adjacent on the policy scale. Thus, for any two actors i and k that are members of S, an actor j whose policy position is between those of i and k must also be a member of the closed coalition S.

S is closed if, and only if, for any i, j, k, such that $p_i < p_j < p_k$ and $i,k \in S$, also $j \in S$. If this is not the case, the coalition is not closed but "open": there exists an actor j, such that $p_i < p_j < p_k$, and $i, k \in S$, but $j \notin S^*$.

These definitions make it possible to discuss theories of political coalitions that take into account the policy positions of actors.

---

*When one of a pair of tying actors, i and j, is an extreme member of the coalition S, e.g. $p_i = p_l^S$, it cannot be determined whether the policy position of the other tying actor, j, lies within or without the coalition's range, since the order of the policy positions of tying actors with respect to one another is indeterminate: $p_j \overset{?}{\geqslant} p_i = p_l^S$. When this actor j is *not* a member of the coalition S, $j \notin S$, this in itself is not sufficient to consider the coalition S an open coalition, since it may be that $p_j < p_i$. If all actors whose policy positions are certainly within the range of the coalition are members, the coalition is counted as closed, whether j is a member or not. The class of open coalitions is eliminated from the predicted set in some theories. In cases of indeterminacy such as the present one, the class that is eliminated as "non-permissible" or "unstable" contains those coalitions that can be assigned to it with certainty; the indeterminate cases are assigned to the classes from which the predicted set is still to be selected as "permissible" or "stable" coalitions, that is "not certainly non-permissible or unstable". Likewise "closed" is defined as "not certainly open".

5. Minimal range theory: Leiserson and Axelrod

The preceding theories took into account the numbers and weights of actors but ignored their mutual compatability*. In his unpublished doctoral dissertation, *Coalitions in Politics*, Leiserson presented a theory that incorporated a notion of "ideological diversity" among the actors: players search for those coalitions which they expect to secure them at least some minimal satisfactory payoff *and* which unite actors of minimal ideological diversity.

For the purposes of testing his theory, Leiserson assumes that players will expect a good enough payoff only from winning coalitions, S, $S \in w(S)$. Coalitions that are not winning are excluded from consideration. An actor i will survey all winning coalitions T of which he is a member in order to eliminate those that have a range that is larger than that of some winning coalition of which he is also a member. (It may not always be possible to compare a coalition S and a coalition T, because of the definition of "range"; in that case judgment must be reserved and actor i will maintain both coalitions until a third coalition U is found to have a range smaller than either S or T.)

Once actor i has selected the winning coalitions S of which he is a member and that have a range not larger than all other winning coalitions of which he is a member, he will propose forming any one of these coalitions S to those actors that are members of each. It may be that an actor j, who is a member of one such S, is also a member of a coalition U which he has found to have a smaller range than this S (and apparently i is not a member of this coalition U, otherwise he would have proposed it himself instead of this S). Since all members must agree to form a coalition, the refusal by j means that this S is removed from consideration. This may leave actor i without other coalitions S to propose or he may have another coalition S that is winning and that has a range not larger than other coalitions of which i is a member and i will try again.

When all members of some coalition S that is winning agree that it has a range not larger than that of any other winning coalition of which they are members, this coalition S is expected to form along with other coalitions for which the same holds.

---

*Gamson allows such "non-utilitarian strategy preferences" to decide, in case an actor is indifferent between outcomes whose payoffs are within the same range: *op. cit.* p. 375.

It may be noted at this point that every two winning coalitions have at least one actor in common. Since the weight of a winning coalition is more than half the weight of all actors together, all coalitions that have no members in common with this winning coalition must necessarily be losing. All coalitions that are not losing must therefore have a member in common with the winning coalition and these non-losing coalitions are the winning coalitions (blocking coalitions having been ruled out)*. This means that when a coalition S is accepted by all its members as a winning coalition with a range not larger than any other winning coalition of which they are members, this coalition S has a range that is not larger than any winning coalition in $w(S)$: because all winning coalitions have at least one member in common with the winning coalition S, this coalition S has been compared with every other winning coalition by at least one of the members of S. This comparison of the ranges of coalitions is based upon the order of the actors on the policy scale, an order upon which all actors are agreed, i.e. an "objective order". Therefore, the set of minimal range coalitions that is finally "found" by the actors is the set of coalitions that are "objectively" of minimal range, independent of the sequence in which the coalitions have been compared or of the actors that have made the comparisons.

To recapitulate the argument in formal notation: an actor i surveys all those winning coalitions T of which he is a member, $i \in T$, $T \in w(S)$, and selects from among these coalitions T the coalition S that has a range, D_S, not larger than that of any other winning coalition T of which i is a member.

(a) For any i, the coalition S, such that $i \in S$, $S \in w(S)$ and $D_S \not> D_T$, for all $T \in w(S)$, $i \in T$

These coalitions S, satisfying (a) are then proposed to the actors j, k, l... who are members of each of these coalitions S. A coalition S is then expected to form if each of the other members of S also

---

* Proof: if $S \in w(S)$ and $T \in w(S)$, then $S \cap T \neq \emptyset$.
(1) $S \cap T = \emptyset$ if and only if $T \subseteq -S$.
(2) $S \in w(S)$ if and only if $w_S \geqslant m > \frac{1}{2}\Sigma w_i$, for all $i \in N$
(3) $S \cup -S = N$
(4) $w_S + w_{-S} = w_N = \Sigma w_i$, for all $i \in N$
From (2) and (4):(5), if $S \in w(S)$, then $w_{-S} < m$; $-S \notin w(S)$.
From (1) $w_T \leqslant w_{-S}$; if $S \in w(S)$, then $T \notin w(S)$.
Therefore, if $S \in w(S)$ and $S \cap T = \emptyset$, then $T \notin w(S)$.
Given $T \in w(S)$ and $S \in w(S)$, it must be the case that $S \cap T \neq \emptyset$.

finds that the range of S is not larger than that of any other winning coalition of which he is a member, *i.e.* a coalition T, $j \in T$, $T \in w(S)$.

(b) The coalitions S, such that (a) holds *and* for every $j \in S$, $D_S \nsucc D_T$, for all T, such that $j \in T$, $T \in w(S)$.

The coalitions S that satisfy (b) — and therefore also (a) — are the winning coalitions with a range that is not larger than that of any other winning coalition of which a member of S is also a member. Since all winning coalitions have at least one member in common with S, S satisfies (b) only if it has a range not larger than that of *any* other winning coalition.

$$S \in w(S) \ and \ D_S \nsucc D_T \ for \ any \ T \in w(S) \tag{8}$$

This describes the set of minimal range coalitions*.

When the theory is adapted to the requirements of empirical testing, the payoffs are defined in terms of cabinet portfolios (in the case of France and Italy) and this may be interpreted as implying a constant-sum assumption. The game now exhibits all the features of a simple game†: all winning coalitions have the same value of control over all cabinet portfolios.

Under these conditions, only minimal winning coalitions are expected to form. In the context of minimal range theory this is especially important, since there may be actors who are unnecessary for the coalition to be winning and yet their inclusion does not add to the coalition's range: their policy position is in between that of two actors who are also members of that coalition.

An example may clarify the issue. In a voting body with actors h, i, j, k, l, ... with policy positions in that order, the majority criterion, m is $m = 51$. The weights of the first three actors are $w_h = 25$, $w_i = 19$ and $w_j = 27$. The actors h and j can form a minimal winning coalition, $h \& j$. The actor i is unnecessary in the coalition $h \& i \& j$, but i does not add to the range of that coalition, since his policy position is in between the positions of h and j. It may also be noted that extreme actors in a minimal range coalition are always necessary to win, otherwise they could be excluded and a winning coalition of smaller range would result.

A minimal range theory that would start from the definition of

---

*For an example, see the Glossary of Technical Terms.

†This conclusion has also been drawn by Leiseron on other occasions; Leiserson (1968) pp. 773—774; Leiserson (1970) p. 86, n. 11.

simple games would predict all minimal winning coalitions, under the added restriction that these minimal winning coalitions should be of minimal range: $h\&j$ would be predicted but not $h\&i\&j$ because the latter, though also of minimal range, is not minimal winning. Such a theory would be very similar in structure to the size principle which predicts among all minimal winning coalitions those with the smallest weight, or the bargaining proposition which singles out those minimal winning coalitions with the smallest number of members.

But a different coalition theory could start from the assumption that actors strive to join coalitions of minimal ideological diversity, rather than to maximize payoffs in terms of cabinet portfolios. Ideological diversity has been defined as the range of the coalition. This range remains the same, whether or not i joins $h\&j$ so as to form $h\&i\&j$. In a game where payoffs are measured in cabinet portfolios, h and j would have to give up some cabinet posts in order for i to gain some: the game is constant-sum. But when i joins $h\&j$, the coalition's range remains the same, no actor has to give up "something more" under $h\&j$ than under $h\&i\&j$ and yet i has gained "something", since he prefers to be a member of a minimal range coalition to being excluded from it: the situation is not constant-sum*.

Thus, a theory that incorporates the minimal range assumption as its general theoretical assumption must drop the constant-sum condition. Such a theory may predict both coalitions of the type $h\&j$ and of the type $h\&i\&j$, since their range is the same. Finally, a theory might predict only $h\&i\&j$ because it stresses the "homogeneity" of a coalition which will be defined as the property of a "closed" coalition†.

Leiserson's exposition of his theory is ambiguous on this point. His definition of the payoffs would rule out the prediction of coalition with unnecessary actors. Yet the tables for the various countries show that coalitions with unnecessary actors are predicted when those actors do not add to the range[27].

The theory will be redefined in this study to predict winning coalitions of minimal range whether or not they contain unnecessary actors and whether they are closed or open. The situation is

---

*The situation may not even correspond to a game: without further definitions it cannot be decided whether the characteristic function which describes such outcomes satisfies the condition of superadditivity. *Cf*, Chapter 3, condition (2) and Chapter 5, Section 2.

†See the discussion of Axelrod's conflict of interest and closed minimal range theory, below.

not constant-sum. Players wish to be members of winning coalitions with a minimal ideological diversity. Such coalitions may have unnecessary members and yet be in the predicted set, since without the unnecessary actor, if the coalition's range remains the same, the remaining actors are not better off in terms of the dimension of payoff: ideological diversity. This interpretation of the theory seems to be closest to the version that was used in Leiserson's discussion of the historical coalitions in Sweden, France and Italy. For the example of p. 73 the theory now predicts both $(h\&j)$ and $(h\&i\&j)$.

In summary, the theory that those winning coalitions will form that have the smallest range is called "minimal range theory" and it will be tested against the data*. The coalition S has a minimal range if, and only if:

$$S \in w(S) \text{ and } D_S \succ D_T \text{ for all } T \in w(S) \tag{8}$$

The range of S must be "not greater" than that of any winning coalition T because, in some cases, the ranges of S and T cannot be compared and in that case both T and S are predicted, unless there exists a coalition U with a range that can be compared with either D_S or D_T, and that is smaller than one or both of them.

A closely related theory has been proposed by Axelrod in his book *Conflict of Interest*[28]. The theory predicts "minimal connected winning coalitions". The term "connected" means that coalitions consist of actors that are adjacent on the policy scale. In the present terminology, such coalitions are called "closed coalitions". Moreover, these connected or closed coalitions must be winning and "minimal" in the sense that they contain no more members than is necessary for a closed coalition to be winning. Thus, the coalition may contain unnecessary members, but without these members the coalition would be open, *i.e.* the policy positions of such unnecessary actors must lie in between those of two actors that are members of the coalition. The extreme actors in the coalition must, therefore, always be necessary. In other words, a minimal connected winning coalition is, in the present

---

*So as to gain a first insight in the consequences for the test results of an ordinal definition of the policy scale, with the attendant indeterminacy in the comparison of the ranges of some coalitions, another theory is tested against the data. It is identical to minimal range theory except that instead of an ordinal policy scale, the policy scale is defined as an ordered-metric scale; p_i is a cardinal number, actors are equidistant: $p_1 = 1$, $p_2 = 2$, . . :, $p_n = n$. This theory is called "minimal range theory, interval version, when confusion might arise, the original theory is called "minimal range theory, ordinal version".

terminology, a closed minimal range coalition. The predicted set in the theory of Axelrod is a subset of the predicted set of Leiserson's theory, as revised, containing all those minimal range coalitions that are closed. For the example on p. 73, this theory predicts only $h\&i\&j$ and not $h\&j$.

The rationale for this coalition theory is to be found in Axelrod's theory on "conflict of interest". A measure for the conflict of interest was developed for the two-person bargaining game as the unique function satisfying certain "reasonable properties". For example, the measure must be "symmetric" (independent of the labelling of players) and "independent" (invariant as to the origin and unit of the utility scale, thus making interpersonal comparison of utilities unnecessary)[29]. The measure was generalized to the n-person game of a "whole society" in which actors may be distributed according to their policy position on some dimension.

> "Conflict of interest in society on a given policy dimension is the average conflict of interest between a pair of people, as each one of the pair takes on all the positions in the policy dimension in proportion to the position's frequency in society."[30]

The measure is identical to the variance of the distribution of policy positions along some dimension*.

> "Intuitively, this means that the more spread out or dispersed is the distribution of people along the policy scale......the higher is the average conflict of interest for the whole society."[30]

When it comes to operationalization of the concept of conflict of interest for a theory of political coalitions, the policy dimension is defined as an ordinal policy scale. The "spread" or "dispersion" of actors in a coalition is indicated by the range of the coalition. The smaller the coalition's range, the lower the conflict of interest among its members†. This correspondence between

---

*(Conflict of interest). $= k \cdot \Sigma_i\Sigma_j(x_i-x_j)^2/N^2$; the variable x_i is equivalent to p_i in the present notation except that x is defined up to a linear transformation and the ordinal quantity p_i up to any order preserving transformation. For this reason, Axelrod's conflict of interest theory does not allow the formal derivation of his coalition theory which is based upon an ordinal policy scale.

†A similar suggestion has been made in an unpublished paper by W.G.A. Hazewindus and R.J. Mokken, "A Distance Analysis of Party Preferences", University of Amsterdam, 1972. A city-block-type of metric indicates the distances between the preferences of individual representatives and the cohesion between groups of such representatives, i.e. parliamentary groups or coalitions.

the conflict of interest in a coalition and the range of that coalition is not derived formally but it is nevertheless very persuasive on intuitive grounds.

It remains unclear why a closed coalition should have a lower conflict of interest than an open coalition with the same range. A member somewhere "in the middle" of the coalition would probably add just about the average score to the total conflict of interest in the coalition; a coalition including this actor could still have a minimal conflict of interest. An "all-but-extreme" actor, however, would add a more than average score to the conflict of interest in the coalition, and therefore should be excluded, if he is unnecessary for the coalition to be winning and if members wish to minimize a coalition's conflict of interest.

A related objection[31] is that a coalition might have minimal conflict of interest without being a minimal connected winning coalition. An example may clarify this. There might be an actor i who could form a winning coalition with the large adjacent actor j or with the smaller (and not adjacent) actor k. Of course, everything depends on the manner in which a measure of "conflict of interest" is defined. But if such a measure would be at all analogous to that of variance, it would be easy to imagine that the coalition of i and k could end up with a lower "conflict of interest" than the coalition of i and j. If the ordinal definition of actors' policy is maintained, some rule would be necessary to decide on the comparison between $i \& j$ and $i \& k$ with respect to their "conflict of interest"*. But, as matters stand, there is no good reason to assume that a closed ("connected") coalition would have a lower degree of "conflict of interest" than some open coalitions of the type $i \& k$ (especially since k is smaller than j). It is hard to imagine a derivation of a measure of "conflict of interest" that would meet these objections, and maintain the definition of the predicted set as the set of minimal connected winning coalitions, that is the set of closed minimal range coalitions.

The theory to be tested against the data is the "closed minimal range theory", which states that only closed winning coalitions S of minimal range will form[†]. S is a closed minimal range coalition if, and only if

---

*The same problem is posed in the derivation of policy distance theory, (*cf.* Chapter 5, Section 2b).

†For an example, see the Glossary of Technical Terms.

$S \in w(S)$ and $D_S \gg D_T$ for any $T \in w(S)$, and for any $i, j, k,$ (9)
such that $i, k \in S$, if $p_i < p_j < p_k$ then $j \in S$

Theoretically, a third minimal range theory is possible. Coalitions will be of minimal range and minimal winning, that is unnecessary members are excluded; open coalitions may occur. The predicted set is a subset of W^m (in the context of the simple game). The coalition S is a "minimal winning, minimal range coalition" if, and only if

$$S \in w(S) \text{ and } D_S \gg D_T \text{ for any } T \in w(S) \qquad (10)$$
$$\text{and } w_S - w_i < m \text{ for all } i \in S$$

For the example on p. 73 this theory predicts only ($h \& j$).

The tests of minimal winning theory, of minimal range theory, and of closed minimal range theory will provide sufficient insight into the working of the various assumptions to make a test of this last theory superfluous: its potential performance may be inferred from the results of the other, related, theories*.

Theories of political coalitions have until now been built upon some minimization condition that tended to restrict the membership of the predicted coalitions. Minimal winning theory excluded all coalitions with unnecessary actors for the simple game. The minimum size principle and the bargaining proposition impose further restrictions upon this set W^m, singling out the minimal winning coalitions with smallest weight, w_S, or with smallest mem-

---

*Another related theory is tested against the data; "basic alternative theory": only closed, minimal winning coalitions are expected to form. (For an example, see the Glossary of Technical Terms.) It may be seen that a closed minimal winning coalition is also of minimal range. A closed coalition contains all actors with policy positions "between" the positions of its extreme members as members. A minimal winning coalition does not contain actors that are not necessary to win. A minimal range coalition is a winning coalition that cannot be shown to have a larger range than any other winning coalition. A winning coalition T could be shown to have a smaller range than some closed minimal winning coalition S only if the policy positions of the extreme members of T would lie "in between" the policy positions of the extreme members of S (cf. Section 4, proposition (7), p. 70). But if this is the case, all members of T must also be members of S since S is a closed coalition. And, since S is also a minimal winning coalition, the exclusion of any one of its members will render it losing. Therefore, all members of S, including the extreme members of S, must also be members of T. T cannot have a smaller range than S and S, as is every closed minimal winning coalition, is of minimal range. This argument does not apply when there is a pair of actors that tie on the scale. This "basic alternative" theory has been formulated only after the results of other, related theories became known. Its test against the present data is therefore not definitive.

78

bership, m_S. The introduction of an elementary notion of policy distance along an ordinal policy scale, led to the prediction of coalitions of minimal range, or to a subset of those, the closed coalitions of minimal range. All these theories impose restrictions on the size of the membership of the predicted coalition. This may not always be adequate to explain coalition formation in real life. In the next chapter, some alternative hypotheses will be discussed and a new theory of political coalitions, policy distance theory, is presented.

CHAPTER 5

Policy Distance Theory

The theories presented in Chapter 4 are all based on some assumption that leads to the prediction of coalitions that are minimal in some sense: the minimal winning set excludes all those coalitions that contain a member whose weight is unnecessary to satisfy the majority condition; coalitions of minimum size consist of those actors that combine the numerically smallest weight that still exceeds the majority requirement: the bargaining proposition singles out the winning coalitions uniting the smallest number of actors; minimal range theory excludes coalitions with actors that are unnecessary while adding to the coalitions' minimal range along the policy scale; the same goes for closed minimal range theory, with the added requirement that actors that are adjacent and within the coalition's range must be included.

Yet, non-minimal coalitions, *i.e.* coalitions with an unnecessary actor, or even with an unnecessary actor that adds to the coalition's range, are a very familiar feature of coalition politics. Not only in times of emergency, when grand or national coalition cabinets are formed, but also in periods of apparent normalcy do non-minimal coalitions occur. As a matter of fact, the data on the party composition of historical coalitions, collected in this study for the purpose of testing the theories, show that non-minimal coalitions are a quite frequent phenomenon in European parliamentary politics (*cf.* Chapter 8).

This is an intriguing phenomenon and a theory of political coalitions that could account for it would be at an advantage over theories that restrict their predictions to coalitions that are minimal in some sense. For this reason, it appears useful to investigate

80

a number of hypotheses that might explain the phenomenon of non-minimal coalitions and that may at the same time be incorporated in the general theoretical framework.

1. Explaining non-minimal coalitions

Various hypotheses suggest themselves.

(1) The political culture in which coalition formation and coalition management takes place attaches a high value to consensus: payoff maximization occurs in terms of "concord".

(2a) Constitutional requirements alter the definition of a "winning coalition" by prescribing qualified majorities or by bestowing veto power on at least one actor in the voting body that must be included in any coalition for it to be winning.

(2b) Political requirements alter the definition of a "winning coalition" because decisions adopted by a simple majority or without the concurrence of certain groups or individuals in the voting body will remain ineffective.

(3a) At least one group represented in the coalition is considered firmly committed to it, but with only part of its votes: the definition of "actor" (*i.e.*, parliamentary group) as a unitary entity is altered.

(3b) Uncertainty on the part of the actors as to the future parliamentary support of at least one group represented in the coalition alters the definition of "membership".

(4) The cabinet coalition is a supercoalition from which *ad hoc* coalitions for each bill or each category of issues are formed. (Corollary: minority governments are key proto-coalitions serving as the constant component in changing *ad hoc* coalitions.)

(5) The parliamentary system of cabinet and parliament is not isolated from outside factors to a degree that warrants its investigation from a closed-system viewpoint.

(5a) Constitutional requirements alter the definition of a "winning coalition" by bestowing veto power on at least one actor who is not represented in the voting body. (Corollary to (2a).)

(5b) Political requirements alter the definition of a "winning coalition" because decisions adopted by a simple majority or without the concurrence of certain groups or individuals not represented in the voting body will remain ineffective. (Corollary to (2b).)

(5c) When (5b) applies, but concurrence of such groups cannot be obtained, a threat of civil war or of war may prevail or materialize and the parliamentary system itself may come to be at stake.

(6) *Policy distance minimization*: coalitions emerge from the interaction among actors, each of which strives to bring about and join a coalition that he expects to adopt a policy which is as close as possible to his own most preferred policy.

All these hypotheses may contribute to the explanation of the occurrence of coalitions that are non-minimal in some sense. Some of them may be incorporated in the general theoretical framework as modifying conditions: (2a), (2b), (3a), (3b), (4), (5a) and (5b). Others may be included as limiting conditions, if they fit the facts, the theories do not apply: (1) and (5c). Other hypotheses, again, could serve as independent motivational assumptions for the new theories of political coalitions that fit within the general theoretical framework: (1) and (6).

The hypotheses will be discussed here in the context of analytic theory construction. In Chapter 7 the same and related issues are taken up again but, there, the purpose is to formulate factual assumptions that will allow operationalization of the theories in order to test them against the data that have been collected for that purpose.

Each time a country is introduced in Chapters 9—11, the validity of these assumptions for the system under study is investigated briefly.

There is, on the face of it, little doubt that assumption 1 points to a value that is, in fact, appreciated by many political actors: a decision in which all, most, or many concurred will meet with less (or no) opposition and is felt to be more legitimate than a decision adopted by a bare majority. There are examples of political systems where unanimity is indeed the norm, for example, the League of Nations Assembly or the *musjawara* of Javanese village meetings. And throughout its existence, the institution of representative democracy has been much criticized for its adherence to the "blind majority principle" or to the "one half plus one" rule, often in the name of more consensual methods of decision making. But in the systems under study, bills do pass into laws, proposals are accepted according to the criterion of simple majority, except in those cases where the constitution expressly prescribes a qualified majority. Consensus as a political value may be operative in the psychology of the individual representative, it may be embodied in the norms of political culture and it may even manifest itself in the election of a chairman to the Assembly, in the appointments to committees, in the adoption of solemn or festive resolutions, but it is not incorporated in the rules of parliamentary decision making when it comes to coalition formation or legislation*. Moreover, a "consensual" theory would explain the inclusion of the actors in the winning coalition, but it would leave the exclusion of the others unexplained. For the time being, it would appear that the parliamentary historian who can rely on a sensitive and expert impressionistic judgment, or a student of political culture who may use methods of attitudinal research, are in a better position to study the function of consensus as a political value than is the formal theorist who is at a loss for an unambiguous rule that could grasp the relevant phenomena. This, clearly, is a limitation of his method.

The status of hypotheses (2a), (2b), (3a), (3b), (4), (5a) and (5b) is different; they refer to such concepts as "actor", "membership in the coalition", or "winning coalition", "majority coalition", all of these being concepts that are already part of the general theoretical framework. Specific propositions referring to the actual conditions that apply in some or all systems under study could be incorporated into this framework. Thus, in the case of hypothesis (2a), it might be the case that a certain class of decisions (*e.g.* constitutional amendments) must be made by a two-thirds majority according to the constitution that governs the voting body. If the coalition is formed with the purpose of bringing about such decisions, that in itself would be sufficient explanation of "large" or other non-minimal coalitions. It may also be the case that the constitution prescribes that certain actors in the voting body must concur in the decision for it to be accepted, *e.g.*

---

*Leiserson's minimization of ideological diversity or Axelrod's minimization of conflict of interest are different motivations of actors' behavior than consensus in the above sense. In the former theories, actors strive for some kind of homogeneity *within* the winning coalition so as to make it a more efficient instrument to realize their objectives regardless of, and even against the wishes of, those excluded from their coalition. Thus, between the winning coalition and its opponents, diversity and conflict remain. The same goes for the minimization of policy distance in the theory to be discussed in the next section. When consensus, on the other hand, becomes an independent source of motivation, the actors strive to take the objectives of all, or almost all, actors into consideration when the composition and policy of the winning coalition is determined; this may be an all-party coalition or a coalition that is considered representative in some sense of the entire voting body.

the veto right of the "big powers" in the United Nations Security Council. Or, the voting body may really be divided in two bodies, both of which must support the decision: the bicameral parliament of many European countries. Such constitutional arrangements may quite simply be incorporated into the theoretical framework.

Students of parliamentary history have sometimes observed that for certain decisions the support of special categories of representatives is a political necessity. For example, in matters of legislation that touch upon religious practice, the consent of a religious party, or of the religious representatives throughout the voting body, may be a necessary condition for the law to be observed by the citizens[1]. Often such support is part of a logrolling arrangement with other parties and including other issues. Thus, hypothesis (2b) could contribute to an understanding of non-minimal coalitions (though, in itself, a veto position does not provide sufficient explanation for such coalitions: the coalition could include the veto group and still be minimal winning, or of minimal range, be it closed or open).

An actor in the sense of the general framework of the theories is a unitary entity and he is either a member of the coalition, or he is not. In fact, however, parliamentary groups may be divided, sometimes into more or less permanent and discernible factions, sometimes in groupings that change with the issues at hand[2]. If such is the case, the apparent inclusion of some parliamentary group in the coalition may, in reality, only commit a faction or a part of that group to the decisions of the coalition (hypothesis (3a)). If these subgroups can be identified, the definition of the actor should be changed so as to refer to those, rather than to the parliamentary group as a whole. A coalition which, on the face of it, appears non-minimal, may turn out to be minimal once the real member-actors have been identified in this manner.

A related, but different matter is the uncertainty on the part of the coalition leadership concerning the permanence of the actors' membership (hypothesis (3b)). Some actors may defect the coalition at crucial moments and therefore it may be necessary to form a "reserve" in terms of weight, i.e. votes. Riker's "information effect" is meant to take into account the uncertainty on the part of the coalition leadership at the time of formation, when it does not know whether it has already rallied sufficient support to clear the majority mark.

84

"The significance of incomplete and imperfect information in natural decision-making bodies is that coalition-makers tend to aim at forming coalitions larger than the minimum winning size." [3]

The effect may be somewhat less in parliamentary assemblies
where the strength of groups is often known but, on the other
hand, it may be stronger when future decisions are taken into
account at the time of the formation of the coalition. Theoretically, the term "membership" could be redefined to incorporate
some uncertainty or probability measure for the reliability of each
member's support. In practice, it would be difficult to find an
indicator for the estimated fidelity of prospective coalition partners.

Hypothesis (4) raises the question of what is the "real" winning
coalition in the parliamentary system. There may be different coalitions for each bill or for each category of issues. The notion of
parliamentary majority government carries with it the idea of a
more or less permanent coalition that ensures acceptance of all or
almost all government proposals. The parties that support the cabinet in parliament are represented in the cabinet by ministers holding portfolios. But sometimes there may be a minority cabinet
that is supported by a more or less permanent legislative coalition,
even though not all actors are represented in the cabinet*. In other
cases, such a minority cabinet is affiliated with one or more parliamentary groups that do not constitute a majority in parliament
but that form the nucleus for a multiplicity of coalitions, varying
from bill to bill†.

It may also be that the parties represented in the cabinet control a majority in the legislature, but that they do not constitute a
single winning coalition, but rather the union of a number of
winning coalitions, each of which may be minimal in some sense
and each coalition being effective for a specific set of issues‡.
Such a state of affairs would be hard to distinguish from one

---

*This was the case, for example, in Sweden, 1932—1936: the "Red—Green"
coalition of Social Democrats and Agrarians in parliament supported the
Hansson cabinet of Social Democrats only.

†For example the Ekman cabinets in Sweden, 1926—1932, consisted of
Liberals alone and remained in power through "jumping majorities" with
Social Democrats sometimes, Conservatives on other occasions.

‡Scheidemann's "Weimar coalition", for instance, could count on Socialists
and Democrats for the social economic policy of the early Weimar Republic,
whereas Social Democrats and Catholics passed the bills with regard to the
international situation.

which corresponds to the situation referred to by hypothesis (3b): coalitions are extended to hedge against possible defection by some of the members. In that case, parties vote against the coalition notwithstanding the agreement to support it. In case of a "supercoalition" which encompasses several winning coalitions for specific issues, a member of the supercoalition may be voting against the government because he is not a member of the particular coalition for the issue at hand and he was never expected to vote for the government in this matter. In general, it is not always clear whether coalitions are larger than necessary because some members may defect, or whether members defect unnecessarily large coalitions, because they can afford to without bringing the government down. In any case, supercoalitions that appear non-minimal in some sense may mask a variety of coalitions that are, in fact, minimal in the sense of some of the theories.

When the historical record shows that in the system under study no more or less permanent majority coalitions were formed for at least one major category of issues, then the theories do not apply in their present form and another framework, adapted to the study of parliamentary voting coalitions formed for specific bills, must be constructed.

Hypotheses (5a) and (5b) may be incorporated in the general framework of the theory as modifying factual assumptions in much the same manner as their corollaries, hypotheses (2a) and (2b). Thus, the existence of a presidential veto may contribute to the emergence of non-minimal coalitions because it could necessitate either the inclusion of the president's party in the coalition or the formation of a coalition large enough to override his veto, e.g. with a two-thirds majority (hypothesis (5a)).

Certain institutions and organizations in the surrounding society, e.g. business, finance, churches, trade unions, the army, universities, may entertain ties with only a relatively small number of representatives in parliament and yet such interests may occupy a position that makes it necessary to seek their consent, or to form large majorities in order to overcome their opposition, if the parliamentary decision is not to remain ineffective. Organs of state outside the parliamentary system, such as the king or the president, may be in a similar role quite independently of their constitutional position. The complete negation of hypothesis (5b) implies that the distribution of forces in parliament is a perfect reflection of the distribution of forces in society at large or that no outside force can influence the decisions of parliament.

Finally, hypothesis (5c) represents a limiting condition on the validity of the theories: the value of the payoffs in the parliamentary game rests upon the assumption that decisions accepted within the parliamentary system are, in fact, effective throughout the political system of which cabinet and parliament are a part, or what would remain of the value of controlling a department or of participating in the determination of government policy? When this assumption no longer fits the facts, the parliamentary system may break down or it must defend itself, for example, by forming a grand coalition against other forces in society or against the forces in some other society: war may be the continuation of politics with different means, but it certainly is an entirely different game.

Hypotheses (1)—(5) all refer to aspects of political life that may interfere with the predictions of the coalition theories presented in the preceding chapter; and the effects of these factors will be the emergence of coalitions that are larger than "minimal" in the various meanings this concept has in the different theories. However, the hypotheses do not so much appear to have the character of explanatory propositions on their own, but rather of factual assumptions to be incorporated, or expressly denied, in the various theories. Only the first and the sixth hypotheses attribute a motivation to the actors and may therefore serve as general theoretical assumptions for the explanation of coalition behavior. As regards the first hypothesis — actors strive to maximize concord — it appears to overestimate the importance of consensual strivings in parliamentary politics. The sixth hypothesis, on the other hand, looks promising: when each actor strives to join a coalition which he expects to adopt a policy as close as possible to his own most preferred policy, a pattern of preferences for coalitions among actors emerges that may result in the prediction of coalitions of varying size, from the all-party coalition to a coalition of minimum size. Though it is firmly rooted in the maximization model of the rational decision approach, policy distance theory might explain a wide variety of coalition types. In the next section a coalition theory based on the notion of policy distance minimization will be presented*.

Hypothesis (6) may function as the central behavioral assumption in a theory of political coalitions that has as yet remained unexplored.

---

*An early version of this theory was published by De Swaan (1970).

87

2. Policy distance theory

The basic notion of policy distance theory is that an actor strives to be included in a winning coalition that he expects to adopt a policy which is as close as possible to his own most preferred policy. This implies that considerations of policy are foremost in the minds of the actors and that the parliamentary game is, in fact, about the determination of major government policy. Coalitions are evaluated according to the proximity of their expected policy to the party's program. From the interaction of the actors on the basis of these preferences, certain coalitions are more likely to emerge than others, *i.e.* they are "undominated". Such coalitions are not necessarily minimal in the sense of any of the theories presented before: they may well include unnecessary members and those that add to the coalition's range. Even the coalition of all actors may sometimes be an outcome.

Although the theory does not necessarily predict minimal coalitions, the notion of policy distance minimization fits the concept of utility maximization of the rational decision model. Moreover, policy distance is defined in terms of weights and policy positions of the actors; the other concepts of the theory also have their place in the general framework which therefore serves as a cadre for policy distance theory too. The structure of the theory allows the application of game theoretic solution concepts. As such, the theory seems an attractive device to account for coalition formation in European multi-party systems.

2.a Verbal discussion

First, the assumptions of the theory are advanced in plain language, next they will be presented in formal notation and the implications and dilemma's of specific assumptions will be discussed. In the final part of this section some implications of policy distance theory are worked out, examples are given and two alternative versions of the theory are presented.

The central behavioral assumption of policy distance theory reads

(a) An actor strives to bring about a winning coalition in which he is included and which he expects to adopt a policy that is as close as possible, on a scale of policies, to his own most preferred policy.

This statement presupposes that an actor is able to place the expected policy of a coalition on the policy scale in such a manner that he can make the required comparisons with other coalitions, so as to decide his preferences among those coalitions. First of all, there must be a policy scale on which the actors' most preferred policies have a place, or at least a rank order.

(b) There exists a complete and connected order of the most preferred policies ("policy positions") of the actors, such that the most preferred policy of an actor is either "to the right", or "to the left", of the most preferred policy of another actor or the two most preferred policies tie with one another*.

This assumption is identical with that in the minimal range theories.

In order to define the place of the expected policy of a coalition in this ranking of parties' policies, some assumptions specifying what it is that determines that policy are necessary. At this point, two concepts are introduced that will receive exact definition when the theory is presented in formal notation. First, an actor will be said to be "pivotal" in a coalition when the absolute difference between the combined votes (weights) of members on his right and of members on his left is not greater than his own weight: the actor may "swing the vote", or he "holds the balance".

(c) An actor's most preferred policy is closer to the expected policy of a coalition in which he is pivotal than to the expected policy of a coalition in which he is not pivotal.

The next concept to be advanced is that of "the excess of a coalition": it represents the difference in the combined weights (votes) of the members on the left of the pivotal actor and of those on the right.

(d) Of two coalitions with the same pivotal actor, the coalition with the larger excess will have an expected policy that is placed more to the left on the policy scale than the expected policy of the other coalition.

Since the pivotal actor himself as a one-man coalition has an excess equal to zero, his expected policy as a one-man coalition coincides with his most preferred policy as an actor. Coalitions for which this actor is pivotal and with negative excess must have an expected policy that is to the right of the pivotal actor on the

---

*In the computer program for the testing of theories against historical data, provision is made for one pair of actors with most preferred policies that "tie" on the scale, (see footnote on p. 70).

policy scale. Or, the larger the excess, the more the left wing in the coalition outweighs the right wing. When the excess is negative, the right wing dominates and when the excess is zero both wings are evenly balanced, for example, because there are no wings, as in the one-man coalition.

The next assumption goes beyond the simple ordinal ranking of coalitions and actors that is obtained from the former three assumptions. It allows a specific actor to compare *all* coalitions for which he is pivotal, even if one is on his left and the other on his right side. In contrast to the assumptions (b)—(d) which establish a ranking that is one and the same for all actors, assumption (e) gives rise to a "subjective" ranking that is specific for each actor.

(e) The smaller the absolute excess of a coalition, the smaller the distance between the coalition's expected policy and the most preferred policy of the pivotal actor.

From assumption (a), it already follows that an actor prefers to be a member of any winning coalition to not being a member of any winning coalition. However, in the theories presented in Chapter 4, this followed immediately from the definition of the game as a simple constant-sum game. In policy distance theory, the game cannot be said to be constant-sum and this preference must explicitly be assumed.

These are the assumptions specific to policy distance theory. Assumption (a) defines the general theoretical assumption that characterizes policy distance theory. Assumption (b) is common to all theories that incorporate the policy scale. Together with assumptions (c) and (d), it serves to define the rank-order of expected policies of coalitions and of actors' policy positions. Assumption (e) together with the motivational assumption (a) defines the preferences of the actors for the coalitions on the basis of this rank-order. The theory, moreover, makes use of such concepts as belong to the theoretical framework of the preceding chapters: coalition, S; actor, i; weights and policies, w_i and p_i, the majority criterion m; the set of winning coalitions, $w(S)$; and "distance" and "range", $d(p_i, p_j)$, and D_S, as defined under the definition of an ordinal policy scale. A solution concept based on game theory, that of the core of group rational coalitions with undominated imputations, will be used to single out the set of predicted coalitions.

90

2.b Formal argument

After this first survey of the assumptions of policy distance theory, it is now time for a more precise formulation and a discussion of the issues raised by the choice of the respective assumptions*.

The expected policy of the coalition is assumed to be determined by its members. This may occur once and for all during the bargaining process at the formation stage, either in the form of some binding agreement among the coalition's partners or not; the coalition's policy may also emerge in the course of the existence of the coalition as decisions are being taken. Whatever the case may be, it is assumed that all actors have some kind of expectation about the future policy of the coalition and that they base that expectation on the policies and weights of the actors that are members of the coalition under consideration. This "expected policy of the coalition S", may be written as "p_S". The "distance between a coalition's expected policy and the most preferred policy of an actor i" may again be written as "$d(p_i, p_S)$".

Assumption (a) implies that among two winning coalitions S and T, when the actor i is a member of both ($i \in S,T$), the actor prefers† the one with the expected policy that is closest to his own most preferred policy‡.

For all i, such that $i \in S$ and $i \in T$; $S,T \in w(S)$: (1)
SP_iT if and only if $d(p_i, p_S) < d(p_i, p_T)$

Analogous to the definitional statements for the policy scale in Chapter 4 Section 4, assumption (b) may be written as

for all $i,j \in N$; either $p_i \leqslant p_j$, or $p_i \geqslant p_j$; and (2)
for all $i,j,k \in N$; if $p_i \leqslant p_j$, and $p_j \leqslant p_k$, then $p_i \leqslant p_k$

The expected policies, p_S, of the coalitions are to be related to this connected and transitive order of actors' policy positions.

Clearly, what needs definition at this point, is the expression

---

*While reading this section, the reader may find it helpful to look at the example with calculations of scale rankings, actors' preferences and the predicted set on pp. 104 *et seq.*
†The relation of preference is again written as "xP_iy". The expression "SP_iT" means: "actor i prefers coalition S to form, rather than coalition T".
‡ Verbal assumptions are referred to by letters between brackets, the parallel formal assumptions by bracketed numbers. For an explanation of "$d(p_i, p_j)$" see p. 69.

"p_S". Four criteria should be applied to such a definition. First, the expected policy of the coalition must be defined in terms of the weights, w_i, and the policies, p_i, of its members. In this way, policy distance theory is tied in with the general framework. Secondly, though it may not be necessary to define the comparison between *all* pairs of "distances", $d(p_i, p_S)$, $d(p_i, p_T)$, for each i and for all S and T, these "distances" must be defined in a manner that is sufficient to generate a preference matrix from which a manageable predicted set may be obtained, *i.e.* a predicted set that contains only a (small) part of all possible winning coalitions. Thirdly, the definition of "distance" must be such that a one-man coalition has an expected policy that coincides with the most preferred policy of the one actor who makes up that coalition on his own; if $(S = \{i\})$, then $(p_S = p_i)$.

And, finally, there is a fourth criterion based on the intuitively compelling notion that if an actor i joins a coalition S, $(i \notin S)$, so as to form a coalition T, $(T = S + i)$, the expected policy of that new coalition T will be no further away from p_i than p_S was from p_i and, conversely, that p_T will not be more distant from p_S than p_i was from p_S. Or the new expected policy, p_T, will lie somewhere in between the expected policy of the original coalition, S, and the most preferred policy of the actor to be added, i, or perhaps it will coincide with one of the two: $(p_i < p_S)$ if and only if $(p_i \leqslant p_T \leqslant p_S)$ for $i \notin S$; $T = S + i$. This criterion excludes the "boomerang effect" by which two parties in an agreement would find one another at a point further away from one of them than the original position of the other was. There would be no incentive for an actor to join a coalition that would not satisfy this fourth criterion. These four criteria do not define a "distance" function for all pairs of "distances" between an actor and a coalition, nor do they define an unique "distance" function. But they allow a function to be defined that is adequate for the present purpose of testing the central behavioral assumption of policy distance theory against the data collected to that end. The fourth criterion permits the ranking of the policies of all those coalitions T that may be obtained by adding an actor i to a coalition S $(i \notin S)$ when the position of the actor's policy with regard to that of the original coalition S is known (for example, because the original coalition S is a one-man coalition consisting of an actor j whose policy position on the policy scale is known). Thus, if the most preferred policies of a set of actors, a, b, c, d.... are ranked in that order, from this criterion the following order of actors' and coalitions' policy positions may be obtained.

92

a, $a\&b$, b, $b\&c$, $b\&c\&d$, d
or: a, $a\&b$, b, $b\&d$, d
   et cetera

The criterion is not sufficient, however, to relate two such orderings to one another, *i.e.* to decide on the relative position of $b\&c$, or $b\&d$, or on the rank-order among c and $b\&d$. For example, which actor by joining b in the coalitions $b\&c$ and $b\&d$, caused the greater "policy shift", c or d? Since the expected policies of coalitions are to be defined in terms of the weights and policies of the member actors, the question must be answered with reference to either the weights of c and d, or to their policy positions, or to both. Intuitively, it might be argued that d will cause a greater policy shift away from b than c would since d is further away from b. It could also be maintained that the actor with the greatest weight would cause the greatest policy shift. And maybe the problem could be solved by taking both into account, for example by choosing the product of weight and policy as an indicator of the policy shift away from b, very much as when mass and distance are multiplied in calculating the force of a lever. But, because the policy scale has been defined as ordinal, such a multiplication cannot be carried out in the present case. Nevertheless, there exists a way of taking both weights and policy positions into account.

If the actors in a coalition voted by weight between pairs of proposals, each supporting the proposal closest to his policy position, there would be one actor in the coalition whose policy proposals would never be outvoted when matched against the policy proposals of another actor. Such an actor might be called "pivotal": the difference between the combined weights of the members on one side of this actor and the weights of the members on his other side is less than the weight of this "pivotal" actor: he can throw his weight with either side and assure himself of a majority or prevent a hostile majority.

An actor, k, is pivotal if, and only if, it is the case that the difference between the combined weight (Σw_i) of the members of his left $(p_i < p_k)$ and the combined weight (Σw_j) of members on his right $(p_j > p_k)$ is less than or equal to his own weight, w_k.

Thus the definition of a pivotal actor k for coalition S may be written as*

k is pivotal for S if, and only if, for all i and j, such that $i,j,k \in S$, and $p_i < p_k < p_j$: $|\Sigma w_i - \Sigma w_j| \leqslant w_k$

The expression "$\Sigma w_i - \Sigma w_j$" is called the "excess, e_S, of coalition S"†.

This defines the pivotal actor k of the coalition S. The set of coalitions S that have the same pivotal actor k will be written as $k(S)$, "the set of coalitions for which k is pivotal".

Having defined the pivotal actor k, the set of coalitions $k(S)$ for which k is pivotal and the excess, e_S, of coalition S, it is now possible to present the assumptions pertaining to the ordering of p_S in formal notation.

Within each coalition S, an actor k has been singled out as "pivotal" because it is plausible that the coalition's expected policy will be especially close to k's policy position. This pivotal actor has been defined in terms of the combined *weights*, w_i, of the other members of S with *policy positions*, p_i, on either the one or the other side of the pivotal actor k. Assumption (3) is a formal equivalent of assumption (c) and postulates that this pivotal actor, k, will have a policy position, p_k, closer to the expected policy, p_S, of any coalition for which k is pivotal, $S \in k(S)$, than to the expected policy, P_T, of any coalition, T, for which k is *not* pivotal, $T \notin k(S)$.

For every actor k, $k \in N$, and for S, $T \subseteq N$;　　　　(3)
if $S \in k(S)$ and $T \notin k(S)$, then $d(p_k, p_S) < (p_k, p_T)$.

Not all actors are pivotal for some coalition; it may occur that

*If the difference between the combined weights exactly equals the weight of k, there must be another actor, l, who is also pivotal for S

$|\Sigma w_i - \Sigma w_j| = w_k$,　　or:　　$\Sigma w_i - \Sigma w_j = \pm w_k$

For $\Sigma w_i - \Sigma w_j = w_k$, $\Sigma w_i - (\Sigma w_j + w_k) = 0$. And for every l, $l \in S$, $p_l < p_k$: $\Sigma w_i - w_l - (\Sigma w_j + w_k) = -w_l$; or $|\Sigma w_i - w_l - (\Sigma w_j + w_k)| = w_l$
Among the actors i that make up the combined weight of Σw_i an actor l may be found, such that $p_l > p_i$ for all $i \notin l$. Since $p_k > p_i$ for all i including l, it is true that: $p_{i'} < p_l < p_k < p_j$, where i' indicates all those i that are not l. Thus, l satisfies all the properties of a pivotal actor, as does k. Also $p_l < p_k$ for $\Sigma w_i - \Sigma w_j = w_k$ and $p_l > p_k$ for $\Sigma w_i - \Sigma w_j = -w_k$.
†Apologies are due to Davis and Maschler who use the expression in an entirely different sense in their exposition of the theory of the kernel (see Davis and Maschler (1963) p. 62).

$i(S) = \emptyset$ for some $i \in N$, but all coalitions include an actor that is pivotal. Assumption (3) "groups" the expected policies of coalitions with the same pivotal actor, the sets $k(S)$, around the policy position of these pivotal actors and in this manner, among the sets of coalitions, $k(S)$, the same order prevails as among the actors, k, that are pivotal for the coalitions in those sets.

Thus, if there are three actors i, j, k, with policy positions ranked in that order on the policy scale and if there are among all coalitions, three coalitions, such that $S \in i(S)$, $T \in j(S)$, $U \in k(S)$, assumption (3) yields the following ranking for the expected policies of these coalitions:

According to assumption (3), actor i is closer to S than to both T and U; actor j is closer to T than to both S and U; actor k is closer to U than to both S and T. The statement concerning actor i is compatible with all six possible orderings of the three coalitions S,T and U; but, given the ranking of i, j, and k, the statement with regard to actor j contradicts three such rankings (T,S,U; T,U,S; and U,T,S); the statement about actor k eliminates two of the remaining sequences (U,S,T and S,U,T); only the ranking S,T,U is compatible with the repeated application of assumption (3) on the basis of the actors' ranking on the policy scale. Thus on the basis of assumption (3), sets of coalitions are ordered with respect to one another according to the order of the actors that are pivotal for each set.

The next step is to define an order within each set, $k(S)$, and relate the ranking of coalitions' expected policies with the policy positions of actors. Again, the excess, e_S, of the coalition S will provide an indicator that combines both the weights and the policies of the members of S. Parallel to assumption (d)

for every actor k, $k \in N$, for $S,T \subseteq N$, and if $S \in k(S)$ (4)
and $T \in k(S)$; $p_S < p_T$ if, and only if, $e_S > e_T$.

Assumption (4) orders the coalitions S and T within each set $k(S)$ in the order of decreasing excess from left to right along the policy scale. Since one of the coalitions in $k(S)$ is the one-man coalition k, with an excess $e_k = 0$, assumption (4) also relates the ranking of the coalitions' expected policies to the ranking of the policy positions of the (pivotal) actors: by substituting in assumption (4) "k" for either "S" or "T", the position of p_T or p_S relative to p_k is obtained.

From assumptions (2)—(4), an order of the expected policies of coalitions and of the policy positions of actors on a single policy scale is obtained, given the weights and policy positions of the actors. This order is the same for all actors, in that sense it may be called "objective", in contrast to the preference rankings of coalitions for each actor which vary with the actor concerned and might therefore be called "subjective". The rank-order of expected policies and policy positions is no longer purely ordinal at this point. Once it has been determined with the aid of assumption (4) that a coalition has an expected policy on one side of a pivotal actor, it follows from assumption (3) that this coalition is closer to that pivotal actor than any coalition for which that actor is not pivotal, including coalitions that are on the other side of that actor. A purely ordinal scale does not allow the derivation of such statements.

The next assumption is introduced to define left—right comparisons of this kind also for pairs of coalitions for both of which an actor k is pivotal. Only the pivotal actor would make such comparisons since he is the only actor who finds himself "in between" such coalitions that belong to the same set $k(S)$. For all actors to the left of k, all coalitions in $k(S)$ are to their right, for actors to the right of k, all coalitions in $k(S)$ are to their left on the policy scale. Moreover, assumption (5) does not define an order among coalitions and actors; this order has already been defined by assumptions (2)—(4) but it defines an order between the "distances" between pairs of coalitions in the same set $k(S)$. This order of "distances" is valid only for the pivotal actor who makes comparisons on the basis of assumption (5) so as to determine his preference ranking among the coalitions in $k(S)$.

If the absolute excess, $|e_S|$, of some coalition S, $S \in k(S)$, is smaller than the absolute excess, $|e_T|$, of some coalition T, $T \in k(S)$, then the "distance" of p_k to p_S must be smaller than the "distance" of p_k to p_T. Or, the "distance" of a coalition to the actor that is pivotal for it, increases with its absolute excess.

For an actor k, $k \in N$, and $S \in k$ (S) and $T \in k$ (S); (5)
$d(p_k, p_S) < d(p_k, p_T)$ if, and only if, $|e_S| < |e_T|$

If the excess of both S and T is larger than zero, it follows from assumption (4) that both coalitions must lie to the left of k, the one with largest excess most to the left and, conversely, to the right if both coalitions have a negative excess. Assumption (5) allows comparison of k's "distance" to a coalition within $k(S)$ with an expected policy to his left ($e_S > 0$) and one with an

96

expected policy to his right ($e_T < 0$). In terms of an ordinal policy scale, such comparisons would, of course, be undefined.

The expected policies of coalitions in $k(S)$ are distributed around p_k in such manner that those with positive excess are on a "subscale" to the left of p_k, with origin in p_k, and those with negative excess are on a "subscale" to the right of p_k, again with origin in p_k. Both these "subscales" are ordinal, be it with an origin. The coalition with the nth largest excess (whether negative or positive) certainly has an expected policy closer to p_k than the coalition with the $(n + 1)$th largest excess (whether larger or smaller than zero). One might imagine that for each coalition with a given negative excess, another coalition would be constructed with the same excess of positive sign. Each would be on another scale but both in the nth position, and therefore equally distant from the origin, p_k. Such a "double subscale" around p_k might be called a "symmetric-ordinal" scale, since each nth point on the one "subscale" corresponds to the nth point on the other "subscale" that has the same distance from the origin. From this origin, p_k, but only from there, left–right comparisons are possible and only within the range of the policy scale in which the expected policies in $k(S)$ are to be found. From assumption (3) it follows that this range for the p_S of coalition $k(S)$ does not overlap with the ranges of the coalitions for which actors adjacent to k are pivotal*.

Thus, an actor i may rank a pair of coalitions according to his preferences when he is pivotal for one and not for the other (assumption (3)), or when he is pivotal for both (assumptions (4) and (5)). When an actor i is pivotal for neither of the two coalitions, it follows from assumption (3) that the relations that obtain between the actor and the actors that are pivotal for these coalitions also prevail between the first actor and these coalitions. Therefore, when the pivotal actors of these two coalitions are both to one side of the first actor, the pair of coalitions can be compared. But, if the pivotal actors are placed on the policy scale on either side of the first actor, he cannot compare his "distances" to the expected policies of these coalitions, just as the "distances" to the pivotal

---

*Given that $S \in i(S)$, $T \in j(S)$, $p_i < p_j$. If the ranges of $i(S)$ and $j(S)$ overlap, an order such as $p_i < p_T < p_S < p_j$ could occur. With such an order it would be the case that $d(p_i,p_S) > d(p_i,p_T)$. But this would contradict assumption (3) which states that for $S \in i(S)$ and $T \notin i(S)$, $d(p_i,p_S) < d(p_i,p_T)$.

actors on either side of this actor can not be compared (assumption (2)). Or

$$\text{for } p_i < p_k < p_j; \text{ and } S \in i(S), T \in j(S), S,T \subseteq N;$$
$$d(p_k,p_S) \overset{?}{\lessgtr} d(p_k,p_T)$$

Under these conditions, the distance function is undefined and preferences will be left indeterminate. However, the distance function will turn out to be sufficient for its purposes.

After the preceding discussion of assumptions (b)—(e) and (2)—(5), on the coalition's expected policy and its "distance" to the actor's most preferred policy, it is now time to turn to the construction of the preference matrix on the basis of those "distances" and to the derivation of the predicted set from those preferences.

Assumption (a) states that an actor strives to bring about and be included in a winning coalition with an expected policy that is as close as possible to his own most preferred policy. Assumption (1) provides the formal notation for the preference of actor i among two coalitions, when he is a member of both. The theories in the preceding chapter that were based on a definition of the situation as a simple game, not only contained the constant-sum assumption but also — implicit in that definition — the assumption that the winning coalition will follow a strategy that results in the losing coalition being "completely defeated", that is, its members receive no more in that losing coalition than they would receive on their own or in any sub-coalitions they might form with one another[4]. As a consequence, in these theories actors prefer the membership in any winning coalition to being excluded from any winning coalition *and* they are indifferent as to which winning coalition it is they are excluded from.

In policy distance theory, it may occur that a winning coalition comes about that excludes some actor i, while this coalition's expected policy is very close to p_i, or even coincides with it. (Actors on either side of the excluded actor i and with the same combined weight on each side could have joined in a coalition.) It might be argued that actor i would prefer to see this coalition come about since it would carry out policies very close to his own most preferred policies, be it without i having a part in it. It might also be maintained that precisely this would be the worst fate that could befall actor i, since it would show that his participation in the government was unnecessary for the execution of his program; an embarassing situation with regard to the electorate.

98

It is not necessary to assume that the actor i is indifferent among all situations in which he is excluded from the winning coalition. He may well prefer to see one coalition without him come about, rather than another. The necessary assumption is that actor i prefers being a member of any winning coalition to not being a member of whatever winning coalition; i's preferences among losing coalitions may be left *indeterminate*. In the other theories the actors also prefer to be a member of any winning coalition over not being a member of any, but they are *indifferent* among all losing coalitions since these are "flat". Assumption (6) assures for policy distance theory that all preference vectors that go with winning coalitions are individually rational, *i.e.* that a member of a winning coalition will receive at least as much as he would receive by remaining on his own. And, finally, as a factual assumption on the preferences of actors in political life, it appears to be the most plausible single generalization, even if counter-examples may be advanced on intuitive or historical grounds.

$$\text{For all } i, \text{ such that } i \in S, i \in T, S \in w(S), T \notin w(S); SP_iT \qquad (6)$$

Or, actor i prefers to be a member of any winning coalition S to being a member of any non-winning, *i.e.* losing, coalition T. Because of the definition of $w(S)$ as the set of coalitions with $w_S \geqslant m > \frac{1}{2} \Sigma w_i$ for all $i \in N$, the complement $-S$ of every winning coalition S is losing: $w_{-S} < m$; $-S \notin w(S)$. Therefore, in assumption (6), "being a member of a losing coalition T" is equivalent to "not being a member of a winning coalition $-T$". Thus, assumption (6) may also be written as "an actor i prefers to be a member of any winning coalition S to not being a member of a winning coalition $-T$". Writing T in stead of $-T$

$$\text{for all } i, \text{ such that } i \in S, i \notin T, S \in w(S), T \in w(S); SP_iT \qquad (6')$$

When actor i is a member of neither winning coalition, his preferences are left undefined. This is sufficient to determine which coalitions are "effective" for an undominated preference vector, since the preferences of the actors that are excluded from both coalitions that are being compared are immaterial when establishing domination between the corresponding preference vectors: only the preferences of the members of either effective set (winning coalition) count.

It may be well to recapitulate at this point the function of the various assumptions concerning the ordering of coalitions on the policy scale with respect to their expected policies p_S. Assumption

(2) establishes a rank-order for the policy positions p_i of all actors on that scale. Assumptions (3) and (4) place the expected policies of the coalitions on that scale: assumption (3) ranks groups of coalitions with the same pivotal actor, the sets $k(S)$, in the same order as these pivotal actors k. Assumption (4) defines an order within each of these sets $k(S)$. This order of actors' policy positions and coalitions' expected policies, obtained from assumptions (2)—(4), does not depend on the viewpoint of one particular actor but it is "objective" in the sense that all actors agree upon this ranking.

When it comes to establishing a *preference* order for each individual actor over all — or, almost all — coalitions, matters are different. First, the particular preference ranking of each actor depends on his specific position on the policy scale. Secondly, an actor will rank some coalitions, irrespective of their expected policy, lower than others because they are losing coalitions of which he is a member or winning coalitions from which he finds himself excluded, *cf.* assumption (6). Finally, the ranking of actors and coalitions on the policy scale precludes certain comparisons. An actor cannot compare his "distance" to a coalition, or actor, on his right, to one on his left; whether an actor is "in between" the two, depends, of course, on his particular position on the policy scale. Assumption (5) allows for such "left—right" comparisons by an actor between coalitions only if he is pivotal for both.

An actor can compare "distances" to his left and to his right on the basis of the absolute excess of the respective coalitions: the one with smallest excess is closest to his own position. In this manner assumptions (2)—(4) establish a complete and transitive order of all coalitions, including losing coalitions, and of all actors upon a single policy scale. Moreover, on the basis of this order, assumptions (1), (5) and (6) define a preference order for each individual actor among all coalitions except between winning coalitions that are located on either side of this actor's position when he is pivotal for neither and except between two losing coalitions. The latter limitation is immaterial for the present purpose but the former rules out certain comparisons and therefore increases the indeterminacy of the theory and slightly augments the number of predicted coalitions.

The preferences of actors among coalitions of which they are a member are determined by the distances of their most preferred policies to the expected policies of the coalitions. Since these expected policies are determined by the weights and policy positions of the actors that make up these coalitions, there is for each member actor only one "payoff" that corresponds to this coalition: the one that is indicated by the particular preference rank which the coalition occupies in the preference order of this actor among all coalitions. Moreover, since these preferences are determined once and for all with the composition of the coalition, the question never arises whether the value of the coalition, "$v(S)$", is sufficient to guarantee its members their payoffs under some payoff vector x, or, whether S is "effective" for this payoff vector x. There is no quantity x to distribute; the payoff to an actor i consists in i being a member of or being excluded from S. In this sense there is only one payoff vector that goes with each coalition S and this vector contains the rank-numbers that the coalition S occupies in the preference orders of each actor i (S ranking lower in the orders of those actors i that are excluded from S than any coalition T from which these i are not excluded). In this sense the coalition S is always effective for the single corresponding payoff vector; it guarantees to its members the corresponding "payoffs" by the very fact that it emerges.

As every winning coalition S is effective in this sense, it may be said that the corresponding payoff vector dominates a payoff vector that goes with a coalition T when it can be shown that all members of S prefer S to form rather than T. In that case, for brevity, S is said to dominate T.

The preferences of one actor can in no way be transformed into the preferences of another. As the preferences are based on the "distances" $d(p_i, p_S)$ which are determined with the composition of the coalition from the given p_i and w_i of its members, there can be no additional inducements, bribes, or other "side-payments".

The preference matrix describes the situation entirely. It is analogous to the "characteristic function" (cf. p. 30). The first property of such a function, that the empty coalition receive a value equal to zero, can be satisfied by the matrix. The second property, that of superadditivity, is undefined in this case since the values of disjoint sub-sets of a coalition cannot be added: the value of a coalition can only be written as a vector of preference rank-numbers for the member-actors.

The context of the situation in policy distance theory is not constant sum: there is no reason to assume that a policy shift away from some actors and towards some others will increase the payoffs to the former with a total amount that equals the total amount with which the payoffs to the latter decrease. As a matter of fact, the preferences in the matrix cannot be summed at all and had they been defined in a manner that would allow for their summation, it would be easy to imagine that such sums would vary for different coalitions.

Every winning coalition S is effective for a preference vector that satisfies the condition of individual rationality (see p. 32), in so far as the elements of the preference vector are defined and when no actor on his own can form a winning one-man coalition.

The condition of individual rationality requires that no actor i be worse off under an individually rational payoff vector x than he would be on his own as the one-man coalition $\{i\}$. Or, $x_i \geq v(\{i\})$, for all $i \in N$. In the present context, this may be rendered as $SR_i\{i\}$, for all $i \in N^*$: an actor i prefers the winning coalition S to come about rather than to remain on his own as $\{i\}$, or he is indifferent between the two alternatives. When i is a member of S, this follows immediately from condition (6); i prefers to be a member of a winning coalition, rather than to be excluded from it in the (losing) one-man coalition $\{i\}$. When i is not a member of the winning coalition S, his preferences between being a member of some losing subset of $-S$ and being on his own as the losing one-man coalition $\{i\}$ have been left undefined.

In order to establish domination among pairs of preference vectors, it is sufficient to demonstrate that all *members* of a coalition S are better off under the corresponding preference vector than they are under the vector that goes with a coalition T. Such preferences are defined, with some exceptions (see p. 97—98), the preferences of actors excluded from both S and T need not be determined.

Though it cannot be shown that the preference vectors are Pareto-optimal in the sence of Chapter 3, the preference vectors that are considered stable satisfy a stricter condition of Pareto-optimality. Condition (6) of Chapter 3 required the payoffs to all actors to sum to $v(N)$, the value of the coalition of all actors. Since neither this sum, nor the expression "$v(N)$" are defined in the present context, this condition cannot be satisfied. But a coalition that is expected to form and be stable in policy distance theory corresponds to an undominated preference vector, *i.e.* a vector

---

*"xR_iy" is equivalent to "$xP_iy \cup xI_iy$": or, "i prefers x to y or is indifferent between the two".

that is also undominated by the vector that corresponds to the coalition of all actors, N. Thus, if a coalition is predicted, this implies that not all actors prefer the coalition of all actors to come about and such a predicted coalition is Pareto-optimal in the "strict" sence: there is no outcome that is preferred by every actor to an outcome that is in the predicted set*.

Under the assumptions of policy distance theory, a solution concept from n-person game theory is applicable: the set of undominated preference vectors, known as the "core", is expected to be stable. Coalitions that are effective for such preference vectors are called "group rational"[5]. When a coalition S is group rational, there exists no coalition in which all members are better off than they are when S forms. Or, in other words, in every coalition T there is at least one member who does not prefer T to form rather than the group rational coalition S.

For the coalitions S that are group rational it is true that

S, $S \subseteq N$, such that, for every T, $T \subseteq N$, there exists some actor i, $i \in T$, such that SR_iT

Clearly, no losing coalition can be group rational since there always exists a coalition T in which all members are better off: its winning complement.

On the other hand, a coalition S is dominated by a coalition T, if every member of T stands to gain from the transition: those actors that are members of S, but not of T, are not needed to form T and cannot prevent its formation; those actors that are members of T, but not of S, will prefer to bring about the winning coalition T rather than find themselves excluded from the winning coalition S when it forms. Finally, the computing program uses the concept of "weak domination". A coalition S is said to be "weakly dominated" by a coalition T when some members of T prefer T to S and at least one member of T is indifferent between S and T. Under such conditions at least one member of T (who must be a member of S also, otherwise he would prefer to see T come about,

---

*The requirement that the payoffs to the actors in N *sum* to $v(N)$ presupposes that side payments can be made, utilities are transferable between actors. Not every individual actor does have to gain from the transition towards N, the collective gain should be sufficient to make all actors gain *after* redistribution; this corresponds to Arrow's "compensation principle", Arrow (1963) pp. 34 *et seq.*; Sen (1970) pp. 28 *et seq.*. Without transferable utilities, such compensation is meaningless and every actor *on his own* should stand to gain from the transition.

rather than to find himself excluded from S) is not motivated to realize T. On the other hand, no member of T prefers S to T and therefore no member of T is motivated to prevent the emergence of T.

The assumption that coalitions belonging to the core will emerge and be stable is not specific to policy distance theory but belongs to the domain of game theory and, as such, is part of the general framework of coalition theories in this book.

2.c Computing example

In order to clarify the working of the theory and the function of the various assumptions, an example of the computation of the predicted set from the fictitious data given in Table 5-1 is presented. An example of the computer output for the calculations based on data from a historical situation follows this section. First, the summed weight, w_S, of all actors in the coalition is computed: $w_S = \Sigma w_i$, $i \in S$. Next, the pivotal actor of this coalition is determined, by summing the weights of member actors beginning with the leftmost actor and adding the weight of the next member until the weights summed in this manner just exceed half of the coalition's weight. The last added member must be the pivotal actor since his weight swings the balance to the other side. Calling all actors on this pivotal actor's left "i", and those on his right "j", the pivotal actor himself "k", the excess, "e_S", may be written as

$$e_S = \Sigma w_i - \Sigma w_j \; ; \quad |e_S| \leqslant w_k$$

TABLE 5-1

Actors:	a	b	c	d	(ranked in this order on the policy scale)
weights:	32	23	30	15	(majority criterion, $m > 50$)

winning coalitions:	total weight:	pivotal actor:	excess:
$S \in w(S)$	$\Sigma w_i, i \in S$	$k, p_i < p_k < p_j$	$\Sigma w_i - \Sigma w_j = e_S$
$a\&b$	55	a	$0-23 = -23$
$a\&c$	62	a	$0-30 = -30$
$b\&c$	53	c	$23- 0 = 23$
$a\&b\&c$	85	b	$32-30 = 2$
$a\&b\&d$	70	b	$32-15 = 17$
$a\&c\&d$	77	c	$32-15 = 17$
$b\&c\&d$	68	c	$23-15 = 8$
$a\&b\&c\&d$	100	b	$32-45 = -13$

On the basis of assumption (3), the coalitions with the same pivotal actor may be "grouped" along the policy scale with regard to their expected policy in the same sequence as the policy positions of these pivotal actors (an actor is pivotal to his own one-man coalition). The coalitions $a/a\&b/a\&c$, for which a is pivotal come first, next the coalitions for which b is pivotal (an oblique line does not indicate order, a comma does): $(a/a\&b/a\&c)$, $(b/a\&b\&c/a\&b\&d/a\&b\&c\&d)$, $(c/a\&c\&d/b\&c/b\&c\&d)$, (d). Within each group (between brackets), there is, as yet, no order. From assumption (4) an order is obtained within each group of coalitions that share a pivotal actor on the basis of their excess with respect to that pivotal actor. The larger the excess, the more to the left should the coalition be placed with respect to its expected policy. Thus, $a\&c$ with an excess -30 should be placed rightmost in the group of coalitions with pivotal actor a since it has the smallest excess. Next, coalition $a\&b$ with $e_S = -23$ is placed in the middle and the one-man coalition $\{a\}$, which is not winning, is leftmost among these three: a, $a\&b$, $a\&c$. Immediately to the right of these coalitions come those of pivotal actor b, in the order of decreasing excess: $a\&b\&d$, $a\&b\&c$, b, $a\&b\&c\&d$. The coalitions with pivotal actor c are $b\&c$, $a\&c\&d$, $b\&c\&d$, c. The rightmost coalition is the one-man coalition $\{d\}$ who is not pivotal for any winning coalition. Thus, the order of expected policies and policy positions obtained on the basis of assumptions (3) and (4) for the above example is a, $a\&b$, $a\&c$, $a\&b\&d$, $a\&b\&c$, b, $a\&b\&c\&d$, $b\&c$, $a\&c\&d$, $b\&c\&d$, c, d. The losing coalitions might be placed in this sequence according to the same assumptions and computational rules.

Assumptions (1), (5) and (6) serve to determine the preferences of each actor for all these coalitions. On the basis of assumption (6), an actor will prefer to be a member of a winning coalition to being excluded from a winning coalition. Thus, the coalition a and other losing coalitions may be left out of consideration. From assumption (1), it follows that an actor will prefer the winning coalition with the expected policy that is closest to his own policy position. This is sufficient to order all the preferences of a: the objective order on the policy scale, listed above, is also the order of decreasing preference from left to right for actor a. The same obtains for d, but in reverse order. Matters are more complicated for b and c: they are located in such a manner that they must make comparisons between coalitions with expected policies to their right and to their left. From assumption (3), it follows that coalitions for which an actor is pivotal are closer to him than those for which the actor is not pivotal. Therefore, actor b will start with the coalitions for which he is pivotal. In ranking his preferences, b places $a\&b\&c/a\&b\&d/a\&b\&c\&d$ highest. However, the first two are placed to his left, the third to his right on the policy scale. Using assumption (5), which allows comparison of coalitions with the same pivotal actor on the basis of their excess, b will rank the coalition with smallest absolute excess highest, since its policy is expected to come closest to his own: $a\&b\&c$, with excess of 2 coming first, followed by $a\&b\&c\&d$ and, next, $a\&b\&d$. Having ordered the coalitions for which he is pivotal, b next considers the remaining winning coalitions. They all rank lower on his preference list than those for which he is pivotal (assumption (3)). Coalition $b\&c$ is further away than $b\&c\&d$ and therefore b will place $b\&c$ higher on his preference order than coalition $b\&c\&d$. The coalition $a\&c$ is placed on the other side of b on the policy scale and can therefore not be compared with either $b\&c$ or $b\&c\&d$, though it is ranked lower in b's preferences than the coalitions for which he is pivotal. This results in the following order of preference for b:

$$a\&b\&c,\ a\&b\&c\&d,\ a\&b\&d,\ \begin{cases} b\&c,\ b\&c\&d \\ a\&b \end{cases}$$

The order is forked, when b begins to compare coalitions on either side of his own position and for which he is not pivotal.

In the same manner, the preference-order for c is calculated.

The resulting preference orders for this example are given below. (Figures between brackets indicate preferences, the higher the number the higher the preference.)

$$\text{For } a: \quad \overset{(6)}{a\&b},\ \overset{(5)}{a\&c},\ \overset{(4)}{a\&b\&d},\ \overset{(3)}{a\&b\&c},\ \overset{(2)}{a\&b\&c\&d},\ \overset{(1)}{a\&c\&d}$$

$$\text{For } b: \quad \overset{(6)}{a\&b\&c},\ \overset{(5)}{a\&b\&c\&d},\ \overset{(4)}{a\&b\&d},\ \begin{cases} \overset{(2 \text{ or } 3)}{b\&c},\ \overset{(1 \text{ or } 2)}{b\&c\&d} \\ \overset{(1, 2, \text{ or } 3)}{a\&b} \end{cases}$$

$$\text{For } c: \quad \overset{(6)}{b\&c\&d},\ \overset{(5)}{a\&c\&d},\ \overset{(4)}{b\&c},\ \overset{(3)}{a\&b\&c\&d},\ \overset{(2)}{a\&b\&c},\ \overset{(1)}{a\&c}$$

$$\text{For } d: \quad \overset{(4)}{b\&c\&d},\ \overset{(3)}{a\&c\&d},\ \overset{(2)}{a\&b\&c\&d},\ \overset{(1)}{a\&b\&d}$$

The losing coalitions are not included in these rankings: they come after the winning coalitions in each preference-ordering (*cf.* assumption (6)). Whatever the preference-number for these losing coalitions, it should be lower than the lowest preference for a winning coalition, although an actor does not necessarily have an equally low preference for all losing coalitions of which he is a member. In the matrix, the preference of actor i for being excluded from the winning coalition is indicated as "0", meaning "any number lower than 1". The above preferences give rise to the preference matrix shown in Table 5-2. In order to determine what coalitions are undominated, it is simplest to eliminate those that are dominated. A coalition — or, more precisely, the preference vector that goes with it — is dominated when there exists some other coalition all the members of which are better off than they would be if the former were to form. For example, the coalition $a\&c$: actor a prefers $a\&b$ above $a\&c$. Actor b is a member of $a\&b$ and is excluded from $a\&c$, a position valued as "0", or "less than 1". Membership of $a\&b$ is valued by b at "1—3": whatever the

TABLE 5-2

Preference matrix:

Actors:	a	b	c	d (ranked in this order on the policy scale)		
Weights	32	23	30	15	pivotal	
Coalitions:					actor	
$a\&b$	6	1, 2 or 3	0	0	a	b's preferences indeterminate*, dominated by $b\&c$, or $b\&c\&d$?
$a\&c$	5	0	1	0	a	dominated by $b\&c$, and by $b\&c\&d$
$b\&c$	0	2 or 3	4	0	c	dominated by $a\&b\&d$
$a\&b\&c$	3	6	2	0	b	undominated
$a\&b\&d$	4	4	0	1	b	dominated by $a\&c$
$a\&c\&d$	1	0	5	3	c	dominated by $a\&b$, and by $b\&c\&d$
$b\&c\&d$	0	1 or 2	6	4	c	b's preferences indeterminate*, dominated by $a\&b$?
$a\&b\&c\&d$	2	5	3	2	b	undominated

* Indeterminate, because b must compare $a\&b$, for which a on his left is pivotal, with $b\&c\&d$, for which c on his right is pivotal; see p. 97—98.

exact value, it is higher than "0". The only actor who stands to lose from the transition from $a\&c$ to $a\&b$ is c. However, c cannot prevent a and b from forming $a\&b$ since only their consent is needed to control a majority in the voting body. Therefore, there is a coalition in which all members are better off than in $a\&c$, this is the coalition $a\&b$, which dominates $a\&c$. If $a\&c$ might ever form, both a and b would be motivated to form $a\&b$ and since they are also capable of doing so, $a\&c$ cannot be considered stable. The matter is somewhat more complicated for coalition $a\&b$ itself: b's preferences are not defined up to a single rank-number but may range from 1 to 3. Together with c, b may form $b\&c$ and c is certainly motivated to join a winning coalition ($b\&c$) rather than be excluded from one ($a\&b$). Actor a cannot prevent b and c from joining together. Everything depends on b's preferences. But b must compare a coalition on his left ($a\&b$) with one on his right ($b\&c$) and b is pivotal for neither. His preferences in this comparison are indeterminate. It might even be a case of mutual "weak" domination. In that case, if b would be indifferent between $a\&b$ and $b\&c$, the two coalitions would weakly dominate one another since both a and c are better off when they are part of their winning coalition than when they are excluded from it. From inspection of Table 5-2, it may be concluded that two coalitions are certainly undominated: $a\&b\&c$ and $a\&b\&c\&d$ (the all-party coalition) and two other coalitions, $a\&b$ and $b\&c\&d$, cannot be shown to be dominated; either one may be undominated or both may weakly dominate one another. The predicted set contains these four coalitions, since they cannot be shown to be unstable*.

The central behavioral assumption of policy distance theory implies that actors first of all take into account the expected policy of the coalition, rather than its size, weight, range, "closedness" or the number of its members.

The minimization of policy distance in the sense of the theory may lead to behavior that goes against the maxims of other "minimizing" theories. Thus it may be desirable for a party, in order to bring about a coalition with an expected policy that agrees closely to the party's own most preferred policy, to add one or more parties over and above those that are necessary to win. In Table 5-2, for example, b could win with the support of either a or

---

*This indeterminacy of actors' preferences does not swell the predicted set as much as may appear from this example (33%). The increase over all historical data is an estimated 5%.

c alone. The highest preference for b, however, is $a\&b\&c$, followed by the all-party coalition $a\&b\&c\&d$, and both coalitions are "predicted" by the theory. In real life, b would probably be a "party of the centre", "ready and willing to cooperate with all responsible forces" and at times pleading for a "broadly based government", or even a "national coalition". In the historical chapters of this study, the reader will encounter quite a few of such parties, always in a strategic position that is similar to b's.

A similar phenomenon, equally inexplicable from minimizing theories, and yet quite common in political history*, is the preference of a "moderate" actor, (such as b or c) for a coalition that includes also the "extreme" actor on his side of the scale: thus, b prefers $a\&b\&c$ to $b\&c$ and c prefers $b\&c\&d$ to the same coalition $b\&c$. Of course, both b and c hope to strenghten their side in the coalition by adding a and d, respectively, and thus bring the expected policy of the coalition closer to their own position.

The type of actor that insists on minimal coalitions also in policy distance theory is the extreme actor on the scale who cannot use one actor's weight to balance it against that of another: a's highest preferences are $a\&b$ (smallest weight, smallest range for a) with $a\&c$ next. And d, who must accept two partners if he is to be a part of a winning coalition, prefers $b\&c\&d$ to the other two coalitions of which he is member: the adjacent actor c is pivotal in both and the former has the smaller weight.

An example of a computer analysis of the coalition situation in Norway may further illustrate the mechanism of policy distance theory.

2.d Historical example

Table 5-3 represents the situation of 1965 in Norway. There were five actors: the Social Democrats (SOCD), Liberals (LIB), Christian People's Party (CHPP), Center Party (CENT) and Conservatives (CONS), ranking in that order on the policy scale, except for the Liberals and Christians whose order *vis à vis* one another was indeterminate ("tying"). The row for resources indicates the number of seats each actor controlled in the *Storting*, the Norwe-

---

*On the other hand, the Social Democrats' apparent rejection of Communist support in many European countries for the greater part of the period under study provides a counter-example; it may be predicted by the theory in specific cases, however.

TABLE 5-3

COALITION FORMATION AS AN N-PERSON GAME OF POLICY DISTANCE MINIMIZATION — NORWAY 1965

```
NUMBER OF ACTORS            5
MAJORITY LARGER THAN    75.
TYING PARTIES       2 AND   3
```

```
CHECK =  28
NAME  =1656
```

ACTORS	SOCD	LIB	CHPP	CENT	CONS		COALITION STRUCTURE AND MEDIAN						REMARKS
RANK ON SCALE	1	2	3	4	5								NOTES AT END OF TABLE
RESOURCES	68.	18.	13.	18.	31.		SUM(K)	Q(K)	U(K)	V(K)	R(K)	MPARTY(K)	
K JJ(K)													
1 31	1	8	7	7	6	c c	148.0	68.0	19.4	80.6	62.0	49.0 2	UNDOMINATED (CORE) 16
2 30	0	5	5	8	7		80.0	31.0	9.0	9.0	31.0	31.0 4	UNDOMINATED (CORE)* 16
													ACTUAL COALITION
3 29	3	0	6	5	4	0 0	130.0	0.0	65.0	3.0	62.0	49.0 1	DOMINATED BY (AO) 15
4 27	2	7	0	6	5	0 0	135.0	0.0	67.5	.5	67.5	49.0 1	DOMINATED BY (AO) 15
5 25	4	0	0	4	3	0 0	117.0	0.0	58.5	9.5	49.0	49.0 1	DOMINATED BY (AO) 2
6 23	3	6	6	0	4	0 0	136.0	0.0	65.0	3.0	62.0	62.0 1	DOMINATED BY (AO) 13
7 21	5	4	3	0	2	0 0	112.0	0.0	56.0	12.0	44.0	44.0 1	DOMINATED BY (AO) 12
8 19	4	0	0	4	1	0 0	117.0	0.0	58.5	9.5	49.0	49.0 1	DOMINATED BY (AO) 11
9 17	7	4	4	4	1	0 0	99.0	0.0	49.5	18.5	58.5	31.0 1	DOMINATED BY (AO) 2
10 15	5	0	2	2	0	0 0	117.0	0.0	58.5	9.5	49.0	49.0 1	DOMINATED BY (AO) 9
11 13	7	3	2	3	0	0 0	99.0	0.0	49.5	18.5	31.0	31.0 1	DOMINATED BY (AO) 16
12 11	6	3	0	1	0	0 0	104.0	0.0	52.0	16.0	36.0	36.0 1	DOMINATED BY (AO) 9
13 9	8	0	0	0	0	0 0	86.0	0.0	43.0	25.0	18.0	18.0 1	DOMINATED BY (AO) 2
14 7	7	2	2	0	0	0 0	99.0	0.0	49.5	18.5	31.0	18.0 1	DOMINATED BY (AO) 13
15 5	9	0	1	0	0	0 0	81.0	0.0	40.5	27.5	13.0	13.0 1	UNDOMINATED (CORE)* 2
16 3	8	1	0	0	0	0 0	86.0	0.0	43.0	25.0	18.0	18.0 1	DOMINATED BY (AO) 15

EXPLANATIONS

ENTRIES IN TABLE INDICATE PREFERENCE OF ACTOR IN THAT COLUMN FOR COALITION IN THAT ROW. NUMBERS ARE
DEFINED SOLELY WITHIN EACH COLUMN AND IN AN ORDINAL SENSE ONLY - THE HIGHER THE NUMBER, THE HIGHER
THE PREFERENCE. A ZERO INDICATES THAT THE ACTOR IS NOT A MEMBER OF THE COALITION

JJ(K)   DECIMAL EQUIVALENT OF THE BINARY NUMBER THAT CHARACTERIZES THE COALITION - THE NTH DIGIT
         REPRESENTS MEMBERSHIP OF THE NTH ACTOR. 1 = IN, 0 = OUT

SUM(K)   TOTAL OF SEATS OF ALL PARTIES IN THE COALITION
Q(K)   TOTAL OF SEATS OF ALL PARTIES TO THE LEFT OF PIVOT PARTY
U(K)   TOTAL OF SEATS OF MPARTY TO THE LEFT OF COALITION MEDIAN
V(K)   TOTAL OF SEATS OF MPARTY TO THE RIGHT OF COALITION MEDIAN
R(K)   TOTAL OF SEATS OF ALL PARTIES TO THE RIGHT OF PIVOT PARTY
MPARTY(K) PIVOT PARTY, PARTY IN THE RANGE OF WHICH THE COALITION MEDIAN IS LOCATED

NOTE

IN THE CASE OF A TIE OF TWO PARTIES ON THE SCALE, AND WHEN THE COALITION MEDIAN LIES WITHIN THEIR COMBINED
RANGE,U(K) AND V(K) ARE EXPRESSED AS PERCENTAGES OF THE NUMBER OF SEATS (R(I)) OF THE TYING PARTY
THAT IS MPARTY. WHEN IN THAT CASE BOTH TYING PARTIES ARE IN THE COALITION, U(K) AND V(K) ARE PERCENTAGES
OF THEIR COMBINED NUMBER OF SEATS. ALL THIS FOR COMPARABILITY AMONG COALITIONS IN WHICH EITHER OR BOTH
TYING ACTORS ARE MPARTY. IN THE LAST CASE THE RANK NUMBER OF THE LEFTMOST TYING ACTOR APPEARS IN THE
```
```

gian parliament. The sixteen coalitions that controlled a majority are listed each with their preference vector. A "0" indicates that the actor in that column is not a member of the coalition in that row. The right hand columns present the key variables in the calculation of the excess, e_S, and the pivotal actor k. (The capital "K" in the table represents the number of the coalition; JJ(K) the decimal equivalent of the binary code for the coalition.) Thus, the column for "SUM(K)" lists the values for the various coalitions of the expression Σw_i for all $i \in S$. "Q(K)" and "R(K)" represent the values of Σw_i and Σw_j in the expression $\Sigma w_i - \Sigma w_j$, for all $i, i \in S$ and $p_i < p_k$, and for all $j, j \in S, p_j > p_k$, k being the pivotal actor. The columns for "U(K)" and "V(K)" indicate the values of $\frac{1}{2}(w_k - e_S)$ and $\frac{1}{2}(w_k + e_S)$, respectively. When a "tying" actor is the pivotal actor in the coalition, these values for U(K) and V(K) are calculated as percentages, so as to make them comparable when either the one, the other, or both tying actors are pivotal actors (when both tying actors are members and either one is pivotal, the two are treated as one actor). The column "MPARTY(K)" indicates the rank-number of the pivotal actor for coalition K, and of the leftmost actor in the case of two tying actors that are pivotal. The rightmost column, "REMARKS", lists whether a coalition is dominated and by which other coalition among others, which coalition is only weakly dominated and which one is undominated. A star indicates that this coalition could not be compared by at least one actor to at least one other coalition, one of which is mentioned.

In the much discussed situation that prevailed in Norway in 1965, the computer program calculates for policy distance theory a predicted set of three coalitions: the all-party coalition, which is the highest preference of the two parties of the centre who find themselves in a pivotal position, and the lowest preference among all winning coalitions for the Social Democrats who have to cope with all four neighbours on their right at once. The second un-dominated vector is that for the coalition of the four "bourgeois" parties. This was the coalition that succeeded in Norway at that time after twenty years of Social Democrat monopoly in government. Thus, the actual coalition was correctly predicted by policy distance theory. It may be seen from the table that the coalition was also minimal winning, all its members being necessary for the coalition to win, and of minimum size, its weight is the smallest among the winning coalitions. The all-bourgeois coalition is also closed, and such a closed minimal winning coalition, or "basic

111

alternative" coalition, is normally a (closed) minimal range coalition. In fact, the all-bourgeois coalition agrees with all but two of the theories: it contradicts the bargaining proposition since the Social Democrats can form winning coalitions of only two members with any one of the bourgeois actors; and, in minimal range theory interval version, where left—right comparisons are defined, the range of the Social Democrat and Liberal coalition would be smaller than that of the present all-bourgeois coalition.

The all-bourgeois coalition is starred in the table because the Christians and Liberals find themselves "in between" the pivotal actor for this coalition (the Center Party) and the pivotal actor of all but one of the other coalitions (the Social Democrats): they cannot compare the all-bourgeois coalition with all others, except for the all-party coalition in which the tying Liberals and Christians are pivotal, and which they prefer to all other coalitions. However, coalitions $K = 3$ to $K = 16$ are eliminated because they are dominated by coalitions that can be fully compared, except coalition $K = 15$ that is, again, not certainly dominated: The Christian People's Party cannot compare it to the all-bourgeois coalition, because if finds itself "in between" the pivotal actors. Coalitions $K = 2$, and $K = 15$ are not certainly dominated and therefore are classified as "undominated" and predicted. Moreover, the coalition of Social Democrats and Christian People, $K = 15$, because of the indeterminate rank of Christians and Liberals, is not certainly open and is classified as "closed".

2.e Some implications of the theory

Before embarking upon a discussion of the alternative versions of policy distance theory, it might be useful to comment briefly on the substantive implications of the assumptions (3)—(5) or (c)—(e) concerning the distance between an actor's most preferred policy and the expected policy of a coalition.

The underlying notion is that actors will attempt to influence the coalition's policy, be it at the time of its formation or in the course of its existence, in the direction of their own most preferred policy. Their success in influencing the policy of the coalition is proportional to their weight, or that is the rule of thumb the actors use in assessing the expected policy of the coalition (assumption (4)). The pivotal actor is in a position to throw in his weight with either side and thus win the vote, c.q. avoid losing it (assumption (3)). But each actor consists of individual represen-

112

tatives who make up its weight (voting strength). Some of those individual representatives may defect and, even when discipline is perfect, it has its costs to keep the individual representatives in line, as Riker has argued convincingly [6]. If a coalition is perfectly balanced, the pivotal actor could suffer the defection of all but a single individual representative and still win the vote. But as the excess grows, the pivotal actor will need more of his individual votes to swing the majority, or to avoid a hostile majority (assumption (5)). Thus the larger the excess of a coalition, the more likely it is for the expected policy of the coalition to diverge from the most preferred policy of the pivotal actor. At least, this is the rule of thumb which policy distance theory implicitly ascribes to the actors in their assessment of a coalition's expected policy.

This approach, in which the substantive assumptions remain implicit and rather rough, could be replaced by one in which the assumptions on the factual behavior of actors, and of the individual representatives that make up these actors, are made explicit and precise.

For example, it could be assumed (1) that the most preferred policies of the individual representatives that make up an actor all lie within a range that does not overlap with the range of another actor; and (2) that individual representatives vote individually according to preferences. In that case, there would be an individual representative (or pair of individual representatives) with an equal number of individual representatives on either side of the policy scale. Clearly, this individual representative (or pair) must belong to the pivotal actor. For that individual representative (or pair), the "excess" of the coalition would be zero (the weights of actors are equated here with the number of their individual representatives). Since the excess equals zero, the coalition is "perfectly balanced" and the coalition's expected policy, according to policy distance theory, coincides with the most preferred policy of this individual representative (or lies between the most preferred policies of the pair).

In his "theory of committees", Black[7] makes two assumptions: individual preference curves are single-peaked and individuals decide in a majority vote between any pair of policy proposals ("motions"). The committee will finally decide for the motion, or the coalition will adopt the policy, that coincides with the most preferred policy (preference-peak) of the median individual representatives; that is, of course, the individual representative who has an equal number of individual representatives on either side!

Policy distance theory, redefined* for individual representatives and their preferences, produces the same results as Black's theory of committees and elections.

When decisions are made by pairwise majority voting, as they are in Black's committees, it does not make any difference with what intensity or from what distance in policy position a voter rejects or supports a proposal; all that matters in his "yes" or "no". In policy distance theory, also, what matters in the assessment of a coalition's expected policy is what side of the pivotal actor a coalition member is on and what his weight is. Whether, on that side of the coalition, he occupies a moderate or an extreme position is immaterial to the theory. Yet, if the members of a coalition do'not make their decisions by majority voting alone but if there is an element of bargaining involved, which is quite plausible, these intensities of preference and these distances of policy positions would make a difference. For example, the coalition's majority may favor a proposal of a tax increase of 5%. If the decision is taken by simple majority voting, it makes no difference whether the minority proposes a 10, 20 or 90% increase, it is outvoted anyway. But in a bargaining process, a minority supporting a 90% increase — and defending its position with zest — might negotiate a larger rise in taxes than a minority with the same numbers that would propose an increase of only 20% and express its preference with resignation. It is an important drawback of policy distance theory that it does not take into account the intensity and the distance of an actor's most preferred policy unless the actor is pivotal; in that case, his position on the policy scale is a major determinant in defining the coalition's expected policy. If the actor is not pivotal, only his weight and what side of the pivotal actor he is on are taken into account; the intensity and the distance of his policy position do not enter the argument. Thus, according to the theory, a pivotal actor may prefer the addition of an extreme actor, whose weight happens to reduce the coalition's excess, over the inclusion of a moderate actor whose weight is such that a slightly larger excess results. However, such distance among actors cannot be taken into account without making much

---

*If policy distance theory were to be redefined in its entirety, an additional assumption would be necessary: the peaks of the preference curves of the individual representatives that make up an actor are distributed symmetrically around the preference peak of the individual representative that is in a median position among them.

stronger assumptions about the policy positions of actors than is justified, given the present state of empirical knowledge on the policy positions of historical actors. A parameter for the intensity of preferences would greatly increase these difficulties and also present baffling theoretical problems.

Policy distance theory as presented here may be modified by imposing certain permissibility conditions on the set of winning coalitions from which the core is computed. Non-permissible coalitions are ignored, whether they are undominated or not, or whether they dominate some permissible coalition or not.

In the course of the present study, two such permissibility conditions have been investigated in conjunction with policy distance theory. Both were inspired by the relative emphasis in the theory on the weight of an actor in determining the coalition's expected policy, rather than on the distance of his most preferred policy to that of other actors in the coalition. Thus, some extreme actor, whose weight will reduce the coalition's excess, may be preferred as a partner by the pivotal actor to a less distant actor whose weight may increase the excess. (This does not have to be the case; it is not in the example of Table 5-2 for pivotal actor c who prefers $b\&c\&d$ to $a\&c\&d$, nor for pivotal actor b who prefers $a\&b\&c$ to $a\&b\&d$.)

In order to eliminate the more implausible cases of this type of coalitions in which "the extremes touch", a permissibility condition was imposed in one version of the theory: the "$1,n$ permissibility condition" states that a coalition which contains either the extreme left (1st) or the extreme right (nth) actor, or both, is permissible if, and only if, these actors are better off in this coalition than they are in the coalition of all actors, the coalition N. This grand coalition N is therefore non-permissible by definition.

The leftmost actor on the policy scale is the actor l with a policy position p_l, such that $p_l \leqslant p_i$, for all i, i.e. a policy position to the left of that of all actors. The rightmost actor, or nth actor, r, is characterized by $p_r \geqslant p_i$, for all i. The set of permissible coalitions may be written as "$p(S)$", a subset of all winning coalitions: $p(S) \in w(S)$. The set of l,n permissible coalitions may be written as "$p_{1,n}(S)$".

The $1,n$ permissibility condition may be written as

S, $S \in w(S)$ is $1,n$ permissible, or $S \in p_{1,n}(S)$, if, and only if, for l, such that $p_l \leqslant p_i$ for all $i \in N$, and for r, such that $p_r \geqslant p_i$ for all $i \in N$: if $l \in S$, then $SP_l N$, and, if $r \in S$, then $SP_r N$.

The $1,n$ permissibility condition, and also other permissibility

115

conditions creating a permissible set $p(S) \in w(S)$, may be incorporated in a special version of policy distance through a specific assumption that is analogous to assumption (6) and, in the alternative versions, replaces it. For $1,n$ permissibility the conditions are written as

for all i, such that $i \in S$, $i \in T$, $S \in p_{1,n}(S)$, $T \notin p_{1,n}(S)$; SP_iT (6a)

or

for all i, such that $i \in S$, $i \notin T$, $S \in p_{1,n}(S)$, $T \in p_{1,n}(S)$; SP_iT (6a')

If "$p(S)$" is substituted for "$p_{1,n}(S)$", the general form of the permissibility condition is obtained. The set $w(S)$ forms a special case: all winning coalitions are permissible; by substituting "$w(S)$" for "$p_{1,n}S$" or for "$p(S)$", assumptions (6) and (6') are obtained, i.e. the "plain" or "pure core" version of policy distance theory.

The permissibility condition (6a) is an assumption of policy distance theory only in the $1,n$ permissibility version of the theory.

The particular condition has been chosen because the extreme actors in parliament tend to be less willing to participate in a coalition government and are more inclined to follow a strategy of maximizing future electoral support than are other actors. In judging coalitions, they would be likely to reject those coalitions that would not yield them an improvement over the coalition of all actors, i.e. the situation in which there is no majority coalition that was formed by some parties at the exclusion of others. When there exists a winning coalition that excludes some actors, it may impose its policy on the voting body because its members vote according to the coalition's strategy, which they have determined among themselves, rather than vote according to their own most preferred policies. When there is no such exclusive majority coalition, or when there is a coalition of all actors, all actors participate in determining the policy of the voting body or vote according to their most preferred policies.

The $1,n$ permissibility condition removes some odd coalitions from consideration; in the example of Table 5-2, $a\&c\&d$ (the 1st actor, a, is not better off than in $a\&b\&c\&d$) and $a\&b\&d$ (the nth actor, d, is not better off than in $a\&b\&c\&d$) and $a\&b\&c\&d$ (neither actor is better off than in $a\&b\&c\&d$).

As a consequence, in the example of Table 5-2, the core for policy distance theory, in the $1,n$ permissibility version, would contain $a\&b\&c$, $a\&b$ and $b\&c\&d$, as before and $b\&c$ (which was dominated by the now non-permissible $a\&b\&d$); depending on b's precise but unknown preferences, $a\&b$ may again be dominated by both $b\&c\&d$ and $b\&c$ or by $b\&c\&d$ only, or $a\&b$ may dominate the other two, but in the terms of the theory, all four coalitions may form. The all-party coalition, $a\&b\&c\&d$, is now excluded from the core as non-permissible by definition. Clearly, the $1,n$ permissibility condition is a first attempt to include some consideration of intensity of preference and to strengthen the role of the distance of actors' policy positions in policy distance theory, at least for the two extreme actors on the scale. It cannot replace an integrated, general theoretical treatment of actors' intensities and distance of preferences, but then the concepts of such a theory would be very far from being operational. In this study, the choice has been made for theories of a type that can be tested against available data. The $1,n$ permissibility condition may yet prove to have increased the realism of policy distance theory.

A second permissibility condition has been investigated in conjunction with policy distance theory. It will be discussed in a separate section since its inclusion in the theory appeared to affect the predictive performance so strongly that it was also adopted as a proposition on its own, independent of policy distance theory, and tested as such against the data in a later stage of the research.

2.f The closed coalition proposition

The closed coalition condition eliminates all open coalitions (*cf.* Chapter 4, Section 4) from consideration as "non-permissible" whether they are dominated themselves or not or whether they would have dominated other, permissible, coalitions, or not.

A permissible coalition, in this context, is a coalition for which it is the case that if i and j are members, and there exists an actor, k, whose most preferred policy is placed on the policy scale between those of i and j, $p_i < p_k < p_j$, then this actor, k, is also a member of the coalition. If there exists an actor, k, for which this is not the case, the coalition is open and, in this context, not permissible*.

---

*If there exists a pair of actors whose ranking on the scale is indeterminate, *i.e.* they are tying, $p_i \leq p_j$, the exclusion of either one of them is not sufficient to classify the coalition as "open", it is therefore counted as "closed", *i.e.* "not certainly open" (*cf.* p. 70).

The permissible set of closed winning coalitions is written as "$p_{cl}(S)$" and is defined by

S, $S \in w(S)$ is permissible, $S \in p_{cl}(S)$ if, and only if, for any two actors i, j, and for every actor k, such that $p_i < p_k < p_j$; if $i \in S$ and $j \in S$, then $k \in S$

The assumption that defines policy distance theory, closed coalition version, is obtained by substituting "$p_{cl}(S)$" for "$p(S)$" in assumption (6a) or (6a$'$) and comes instead of assumption (6) or (6a);

$$\text{for all } i, i \in S, i \in T, S \in p_{cl}(S), T \notin p_{cl}; SP_i T \qquad (6b)$$

Analogous to assumptions (6$'$) and (6a$'$), the assumption (6b$'$) may be obtained. As an assumption of policy distance theory, closed version, condition (6b) defines the class of permissible coalitions from which the core is computed. Condition (6b) does not contain a reference to the expected policy, p_S, of a coalition, S. It may be defined independently of assumptions (3)—(5) of policy distance theory. It does presuppose that actors may be ordered with regard to their most preferred policy, p_i, on a policy scale, an assumption also contained in the minimal range theories and policy distance theory.

Thus, condition (6b) may be incorporated in an independent "closed coalition proposition" which contains the assumptions that the actor's weights, w_i, are known, that the actors most preferred policies, p_i, are known and may be ranked on an ordinal policy scale and that some majority criterion, m, is given and must be exceeded by the total weight of the members of a coalition for that coalition to be winning.

Given these assumptions, the closed coalition proposition predicts that those winning coalitions will form that are closed as defined by (6b). As such, the proposition is independent of game theory, no solution concept is applied. The proposition is also independent of the rational decision model because it contains no concept of minimization or maximization, whether it be with regard to weight, size, membership, range or policy distance. In this form, therefore, the proposition should be understood as an independent generalization on the behavior of political actors. The emphasis on the policy positions of these actors increases the specific political character of the proposition. On the other hand, its reliance on these policy positions may increase the danger of circularity in the argument: if policy positions are not obtained independently from past coalition behavior, the proposition may explain one coalition from a series of preceding coalitions. Even this would be by no means trivial. The independence of the proposition from the underlying framework of the rational decision model of game theory reduces its explanatory capacity which should derive from a proposition's logical relationship to general axioms of behavior, that is, in the formal conception of theory construction that guides the present study. These considerations are quite separate from the predictive performance of the proposition.

CHAPTER 6

Problems of Testing Coalition Theories

The natural consequence of a formal approach to the study of cabinet formation is the statistical evaluation of the results achieved by these formal theories: from the theoretical point of view, the events under consideration are comparable and so are the theories themselves, constructed with common elements from a common underlying model.

But apart from the fundamental objection of historical unicity, which pertains to the present enterprise in its entirety, a statistical evaluation raises specific questions.

The comparison is between the results of six theories and their modified versions: minimal winning theory (Von Neumann and Morgenstern); the minimum size principle (Gamson—Riker), with a modification for evaluating the "information effect" roughly: the two-thirds criterion; the bargaining proposition (Leiserson, 1968); minimal range theory, (Leiserson, 1966), ordinal version and interval version; closed minimal range theory (Axelrod); policy distance theory (De Swaan, 1970), "pure core" version, and $1,n$ permissibility and closed coalition version. In the course of the investigations, two theories suggested themselves. They are tested along with the others and are closed, minimal winning (minimal range) or "basic alternative" theory and the closed coalition proposition. A dummy theory is included as a standard of comparison: "all majority coalitions may form", it is called "winning theory", not "the winning theory", for good reasons.

All in all, thirteen "theories" are to be tested against the data from 90 situations in nine different European multi-party democracies for the period after 1918.

A "situation" is characterized by a set of actors, a distribution of weights (votes) over these actors, an ordered scale of the policy positions of these actors and a majority criterion. Only situations in which no one party controls a majority of votes on its own and in which at least one majority coalition did come about are taken into consideration.

There are several ways to evaluate the performance of the theories relative to one another. The most common approach is to assess the probability that the results of a theory could have been achieved by chance, *e.g.* by someone making blind guesses from among all majority coalitions and as many guesses as there are elements in the predicted set of the theory under consideration. If the probability of equalling or surpassing the number of correct guesses is very low, then it is probable that something other than mere chance is at work: the mechanism postulated by the theory. This straightforward and time-honored approach is marred, however, by the presence of an "unknown" parameter: the number, p_j, of coalitions that *could have* emerged in each historical situation. This notion needs some discussion.

The coalition theories under study all predict *sets* of coalitions rather than unique outcomes. This is different from a theoretical prediction of the type: "the number of unkempt, barefooted, long-haired males passing by my window in the next 24 hours will be 17.5, and between 15.5. and 19.5 at a confidence level of 95%", as most theoretical predictions are formulated. Clearly, the observed number of said persons will be unique (and, hopefully, integer). The prediction consists, nonetheless, of an interval or of a set with an infinite number of elements. But this infinity of elements is distributed symmetrically with increasing probability around a single element: 17.5, and only one element occurs each time.

In contrast, coalition theories of the type presented here, generate a *finite* set of coalitions which *are not* arranged in some probability distribution: they are "in equilibrium". The underlying idea is that all predicted alternatives are equally likely to occur at any given moment, one is as good as the other, as far as the theory is concerned: which one or how many of them do in fact materialize during the period that the situation for which the prediction was made prevails is immaterial as long as each coalition that did emerge corresponds with an element of the predicted set.

"only V in its entirety is a solution and possesses any kind of stability — but none of its elements individually."[1]

And

"if one particular alliance is actually formed, the others are present in a 'virtual' existence. Although they have not materialized, they have contributed essentially to shaping and determining the actual reality."

"We emphasize that this stability — whatever it may turn out to be — will be a property of the system as a whole and not of the single imputations of which it is composed."[2]

Thus, if only one coalition from among those that were predicted for a situation j, and none of the others, materialized time and again, that would be equally strong evidence in favor of the theory, as would the emergence of different elements of the set one after the other. And, equally, if a coalition emerged that did not correspond to an element in the predicted set, that would constitute evidence against the set in its entirety and against the theory as a whole.

Now, the "true" number of coalitions that are in mutual equilibrium — and among which at any point in time one actually forms while the others remain in "virtual" existence — is unknown. Any theory that could determine it is itself to be tested at this point in the inquiry. This is different from a situation in which a person attempts to draw the aces from a deck of cards in which it is known that there are four aces. If the person announces that he will draw three or five times, it is not because he believes that there are that many aces in the deck but because these are the odds he wishes to take.

A coalition theory, on the other hand, predicts a set of coalitions with a certain number of elements because, according to the theory, that number of coalitions and those specific coalitions, are in equilibrium. However, the fact that a coalition does not materialize in actual fact though it is predicted by the theory, may be because the coalition was part of the equilibrium set but remained in virtual existence only, or it may not have materialized because the theory was wrong and the coalition "could" not have materialized since it was not in equilibrium at all. There is no way of telling from observation the difference between the two categories of coalitions that did not form. And, since the number of coalitions that are in equilibrium in a given historical situation is also unknown — some of them may remain in "virtual existence" — no direct statistical test of the theories is possible. Every theory that could determine the number of coalitions that are in equilibrium in a given historical situation is itself to be tested at this point.

The crucial point is that coalition theory implies a view of reality as partly, or mostly, invisible: any actual coalition is only the materialization of one among a swarm of virtual coalitions; "they have contributed essentially to shaping and determining the actual reality"[2]. Formal theory plus empiricist method here go beyond positivism: the real world cannot be inferred from the observable world.

Someone may object, at this point, that he is not interested in the world of virtual coalitions but that he wants to know what theory to put his money on in betting about what coalitions will and will not emerge. The answer must be that bettors will find more profit in the writings of pundits than of theorists.

There is no way out but there are some ways around. One of them is to take the position of positivist tradition: define the "real" equilibrium set as the set of coalitions that have been observed in the situation and ignore the coalitions that may have remained in virtual existence.

This changes the criterion to be applied to the theories. A theory should predict the coalitions that did, in fact, form in the given situation, preferably all of them, of course, *and* preferably no others: predicted coalitions that did not form will be equated with coalitions predicted wrongly.

The predicted set of a theory is determined, once the characteristics of a given situation j are known, *i.e.*, usually, after the elections. As long as these characteristics remain unchanged, no other information is taken into account by the theory, not even which coalitions have formed in fact in the course of time. The predicted set remains the same throughout and each different coalition that emerges constitutes an event that is predicted or not. It must be emphasized at this point that an "event" in the sense of the theory is the formation of a different (more or less permanent) majority coalition in parliament, including the first one that forms in the situation. When the same coalition forms several times, whether or not interrupted by the formation of others, this series of coalitions of identical composition constitutes a single event in the sense of the theory. Neither the number of times a coalition of given composition forms, nor the amount of time it lasts, is taken into consideration. This approach corresponds, of course, with the notion of a set of coalitions in equilibrium and with a stochastic model of testing but it is a profoundly unhistorical approach. This is compensated, to a degree, in the country by country discussion in Chapters 9—11 where the unit of analysis is the formation of a historical parliamentary majority coalition and where the formation of a coalition of a composition identical to the one that preceded it in the given situation does constitute a new event.

At this point, there is a situation j with certain characteristics; there are theories i which predict a set of coalitions that are in equilibrium and this set may number r_{ij} elements for theory i in situation j; in the given situation there are n_j majority (or, winning) coalitions from among which the theory must make its predictions. *Ex post* p_j coalitions are observed to be in equilibrium in the situation j. The problem at this point is to calculate the probability that in a situation j with n_j majority coalitions and p_j historical majority coalitions, q_{ij} of these p_j historical majority coalitions could have been elements of the "predicted" set of theory i, if it had been constituted at random. A statistical model developed to compute these probabilities is presented in Appendix II by Robert J. Mokken. The model is applied in Chapter 8.

PART II: Confronting History

CHAPTER 7

Empirical Referents to the Theories

The theories presented in the preceding chapters apply to the process of coalition formation in general. The formation of a parliamentary coalition in support of a cabinet is the subject to which these theories will be applied in the second part of this book. In this chapter, the technical terms of the theories are made to correspond to the phenomena of actual coalition politics in parliament. In this manner the theories are operationalized and thus they become theories specific to this particular field of political reality.

In Chapter 5, various hypotheses were suggested that might explain coalitions that were larger than minimal in the different senses of the theories advanced in Chapter 4. This theoretical discussion led to the presentation of policy distance theory, but in the course of the review of these hypotheses most of the problems were raised that an attempt at operationalization of the theories would have to deal with. In this chapter, these matters will be solved by the introduction of factual assumptions that establish a correspondence between the terms of the theories and the institutions and processes within the actual political systems under investigation in this study.

For this purpose it is necessary to determine (*1*) the nature of the payoff in the coalitional game, *i.e.* what is at stake in the process of coalition formation; (*2*) the actual majority requirement, m, that must be satisfied by a coalition in order to be considered winning; (*3*) the weights; and (*4*) the policy positions of the actors; furthermore, it is necessary to determine the composition of each historical coalition (*5*) and (*6*) the setting of the game; *i.e.* the parliamentary system must be described and separated from other components of the political and social system that surrounds it.

The definition of technical terms with reference to particular political phenomena implies the factual assumption that those phenomena do, in fact, satisfy the properties attributed to these technical terms in the context of the theories. For example, saying that a particular parliamentary party constitutes, at some point in time, an actor in the sense of the theories implies stating that it does, in fact, operate as an undivided entity; or, otherwise, that for the purpose of verifying the theories, such a group may indeed be regarded as an undivided entity, ignoring some contradictory evidence. In the face of such contrary evidence, the assumption may be revised so as to take it into account if the nature of the facts and the structure of the assumptions allow it. Thus, it is easy to revise the majority criterion, m, if the actual majority requirement is unambiguously stated in some constitutional rule. If, on the contrary, the majority requirement is informal, it may be hard to estimate as, for example, the "stampede point" in American presidential nominating conventions where most delegations switch their votes to a candidate once he has reached a certain plurality[1]. On the other hand, the facts may be unambiguous but the structure of the assumptions makes it difficult to incorporate them: for example, when an "opposition" party saves the government intentionally by abstaining from a critical vote. According to the definition to be advanced, such behavior will be insufficient to qualify the party as a member of the coalition.

When important contrary evidence cannot be incorporated and when, for the purpose of the theory, it cannot be ignored either, application of the theory is suspended, as it is, for example, in times of war and foreign occupation.

Thus, a number of factual assumptions are made in the course of this chapter, some quite plausible, others controversial but at least open to investigation and some that are very hard to decide upon through inquiry at all (*e.g.* the assumption that social economic policy, rather than any other cluster of issues, matters in parliamentary coalition formation). No special research underlies this chapter; the factual assumptions take into account knowledge considered expert and authoritative given the present state of the discipline.

126

1. The nature of payoffs

Cabinet governments in parliamentary systems need the tacit or explicit support of a majority in parliament. Constitutional law, written or unwritten, requires a cabinet to resign whenever a majority in parliament expresses its lack of confidence in the government or when it rejects a bill which the government has declared to be an essential part of its program. Usually, a more or less permanent parliamentary majority coalition supports the government: it ensures the formal investiture of the cabinet in some countries and in every country under study it effectuates the acceptance of major government bills and of the budget; it also prevents the opposition from passing a motion expressing lack of confidence. In other words, it provides the cabinet with a "working majority" in parliament and thus provides for its continued existence[2].

In most countries under study, parliament consists of two houses or chambers. Generally, one of these is selected directly by universal suffrage; it is the first to debate and vote upon bills and most often it has more constitutional privileges than the other which, normally, is elected indirectly by the representatives of local or regional bodies. In most cases, when there are two chambers, the parliamentary coalition that decides upon the fate of the cabinet is formed by the actors of the directly elected body, which, after French usage, will be called the "assembly", as distinguished from the other, the "senate".

Cabinets thus depend for their survival on a majority coalition in the assembly (though minority governments may rely on *ad hoc* coalitions for each legislative proposal). Governments can generally stay in power after the senate has rejected a major bill. The senate, moreover, most often refrains from expressing or denying its confidence in a cabinet.

For the purposes of the theories, in most countries the setting of the game may be defined to be the assembly. The senate, if it exists, will be ignored, except in Italy and Sweden (Joint Division).

As a rule, the parties in the legislative coalition are represented in the cabinet by individuals that are publicly identified with these parties: they hold a portfolio in the cabinet and this gives them the control over a government department and the right to vote in cabinet meetings. In this manner, and because in a parliamentary democracy the cabinet must resign in the face of a hostile majority in parliament, the legislative coalition exerts a measure of control over the cabinet.

Control over cabinet policy is also exerted because individuals affiliated with the parties in the coalition hold portfolios in the government. Recent research by Browne and Franklin (1970) has shown that actors, once they have joined in a winning coalition, tend to divide cabinet portfolios in proportion to the weight (number of parliamentary seats) of each actor. This evidence supports both the minimum size principle (Gamson used the proportionality rule in order to derive the principle) and policy distance theory (where proportionality agrees with the derivation of the coalition's expected policy as coinciding with the preference of the pivotal actor). It also highlights the problem in minimal range theory of the unnecessary actor who does not add to the coalition's range and who may well receive his full proportional share of portfolios.

Subsequent research[3] has shown that the relative weight of an actor in a coalition is an important factor in the assignment to that actor of the Prime Ministry, Economic Affairs, Finance and Defense. Although there exist qualitative differences in the valuation of portfolios, and parties differ among one another in their valuation on ideological grounds, the straightforward numeric relationship of proportional distribution is the most striking tendency. Apparently, the coalition partners bargain among one another over which portfolios each one should receive, not how many.

On the one hand, there are empirical findings on the valuation of cabinet portfolios, such as presented by Browne, and, on the other hand, the theories under investigation in this study allow certain factual statements with regard to the valuation of cabinet portfolios to be inferred.

It is interesting to note that when the payoffs are measured in terms of policy distance, the implication is that actors value a portfolio because it provides them with the right to participate in cabinet decisions, and thus to participate in the determination of major government policy, influencing the expected policy of the coalition. The other aspect of the portfolio's value — the control over a department — is ignored. Actors do not strive to maximize the number of portfolios under their control but they attempt to minimize policy distance, sometimes even at the expense of giving up some portfolio(s). These are factual statements immediately derived from the theory: thus the finding that actors do, in fact, stress the opportunity to participate in cabinet decision-making

128

conveyed by their portfolios and tend to make little of the control over a department would strengthen faith in policy distance theory. Also, the finding that an actor prefers a coalition in which he holds fewer portfolios but in which policy distance is smaller, to another, in which the opposite is the case, would again increase confidence in the theory. Finally, policy distance theory is more likely to hold true in systems where collective cabinet policy determines departmental policy than in countries where departments are administered with a great degree of autonomy.

This is also true for minimal range theory in so far as actors are *indifferent* to the addition of an unnecessary actor, unless, by his policy position, he adds to the coalition's range. As a consequence, the other actors are not unwilling to surrender some portfolio(s) to the newly added actor. In closed minimal range theory, the priority of collective cabinet policy over the control of individual departments is *a fortiori* a necessary condition for the theory to hold: coalitions that do not contain all actors within their range are not considered stable and actors will prefer to surrender portfolios to an unnecessary actor in order to bring about a coalition that is closed along the policy scale.

Minimal winning theory, the minimum size principle and the bargaining proposition, on the other hand, exclude the possibility that an actor would receive a portfolio if his membership was not necessary for the coalition to obtain a majority: these theories are also more likely to hold true when control over a government department is valued highly in itself.

2. The majority requirement

One of the purposes of this study is to explain the emergence of large coalitions. In this light the exact definition of the majority requirement is of great importance. If it were the case that, in actual assemblies, large majorities would be required by the rules of the game, this simple finding would close the discussion. However, in reality, almost all bills and motions are passed with a simple majority, the one significant exception being the final vote on constitutional amendments. Quite a few such constitutional revisions were completed in the period and in the countries under study. Yet, these revisions seem to have been a major matter of consideration in only very few cabinet formations*. It appears warranted to maintain the assumption that coalitions must control just over half the votes in the assembly to be considered winning, but not necessarily more. And whenever contrary evidence is strong enough, the majority requirement will be reconsidered.

Another matter worthy of consideration is whether, in fact, there exist actors that must be included in a coalition, not because they are necessary to achieve the required number of votes, but because they possess some kind of a formal or informal veto. Such is the position of the Great Powers in the United Nations Security Council or of the founder in the board meeting of a small corporation. Within the assemblies under study, no legal vetoes exist nor is there evidence that some actor would possess an informal veto in any of these countries. Some interest groups, whose representatives may be divided over several actors, have, however, at times achieved a near veto power in matters of concern to them; also, single-interest parties, especially religious ones, sometimes occupy such a position in matters that are their special province. Yet, the scope of such a near veto seems too narrowly defined in most cases to be of much concern to the actors while forming their coalition. Beyond the assembly, but still within the parliamentary system, are the veto positions of the king and the president, who never exercise this option in a parliamentary democracy, and of the senate, which is ignored for the purposes of this study except in Italy and Sweden (Joint Division)[+].

In the country there may exist political groups and institutions that ary in a position to exercise an informal veto: important tax legislation may remain ineffective without the concurrence of the organizations that unite entrepreneurs and *haute finance*; wage legislation may be undone if trade unions withhold their support.

---

*The constitutions of the Weimar Republic, the French Fourth Republic, of Italy and Israel were adopted by absolute majority. A constitutional amendment was of major concern during the formation of a large coalition in the Netherlands in 1948, but another non-controversial amendment was passed in 1922 under a coalition that controlled only 50 out of a 100 votes. In Finland, a $\frac{2}{3}$ majority ($\frac{5}{6}$ in constitutional matters) may prevent a suspensive veto by the remaining minority. Historical coalitions have ranged, however, from minority to large coalitions in this country.

[+]The Senate (in Italy) and the Joint Division (of both Lower and Upper House in Sweden) are incorporated into the theoretical framework by the assumption that a coalition is winning if, and only if, it controls a majority both in the assembly and in the former body.

Nevertheless, the assumption is made that such opposition in the country is expressed sufficiently in the assembly itself through the parliamentary representatives of such organizations and that as a system, the assembly is sufficiently isolated from its environment to ignore all outside factors for the purposes of the theory. In specific cases of strong evidence to the contrary, the assumption will be reconsidered.

When the concurrence of institutions outside the parliamentary system is required, for constitutional or political reasons, the parliamentary system cannot be treated as a (relatively) isolated entity, cf. Section 6.

3. Actors and their weight

The parliamentary groups are the actors, in the sense of the theories, whenever they control more than $2\frac{1}{2}\%$ of the vote in the assembly. Smaller groups are ignored though their votes are counted in calculating the majority over all votes in the assembly. Smaller parties were almost never included in a winning coalition*. Choosing a higher cut-off point would remove some parties from consideration that were considered by other actors for inclusion in the coalition and that were sometimes included.

In most countries, parliamentary parties enjoy some formal recognition under the rules of order for the assembly, with a view to the allotment of speaking time and the distribution of committee seats. These formally registered groups are normally accepted as the actors (when their vote exceeds $2\frac{1}{2}\%$) and their weight (w_i)

---

*Some parties, though very small, may have a strong "coalition-bargaining potential" because of their ideological position; Sartori has argued that they ought to be counted for this reason (Sartori, 1971, p. 325). For reasons of independence, parsimony and consistency of variables, the $2\frac{1}{2}\%$ criterion was maintained, however, even in the case of the Republican party in Italy after 1948 or the Democratic party in the Weimar Republic after 1930: government parties that became theoretically "invisible" because they were not counted as actors. The *Poalei Agudat Israel*, the labor wing of the orthodox religious party, supported Israeli governments in the sixties, even though on its own it was too small to count as an actor: it was lumped together with its sister party *Agudat Israel*. In the case of Denmark, the $3\frac{1}{2}\%$ mark was applied since it seemed to include those parties that played a role in the coalitional game, while excluding the others. For the Liberal Party in Italy, an exception was made in 1953: the party was counted as an actor even though it was two seats short of the $2\frac{1}{2}\%$ mark. This inconsistency yielded insight in the actual situation.

is set equal to their formally registered number of individual members. When there exists expert opinion reporting different voting strengths and alignments, this will be accepted especially in the later phases of an intra-election period*. Even though some parties may be divided sharply internally, they will be treated as unitary actors unless there is sufficient information as to the weight and policy position of the factions within the parliamentary group. The alternative would be to accept the individual parliamentary representative as the unit of analysis; this would lead to very unwieldy computations and predictions and it would ignore the evidence of cohesive parliamentary groups. At the risk of overlooking important factional differences, the parliamentary groups are accepted as the actors for lack of information on most of the internal factions.

4. The policy scale

In contrast to the other theories, minimal range theory, policy distance theory and the closed coalition proposition take into account the policy positions of the actors in explaining their coalition behavior. Adoption of this policy scale presupposes that such policy positions are, in fact, sufficiently independent of coalition behavior to serve as explanatory variables; on the other hand, it assumes that these policy positions may be ordered in a manner that does justice to the facts and yet is strong enough to generate a definite and limited set of predicted coalitions. These two matters are to be discussed in this section.

Popular opinion can be quite sarcastic when it comes to judging the intransigence of political actors and political theory has at times sided with this judgment. Also, in formal theory, there exists a line of thought that conceives of policy positions as the mere derivatives of strategic considerations in the struggle for votes or for office. This is clearly the view of Schumpeter: "a party cannot be defined in terms of its principles"[4].

---

*Thus, for the French Fourth Republic the distributions of seats are adopted as they are reported by MacRae for each investiture vote: as a control an analysis was made on the basis of Ph. Williams' data also; the latter indicate the distribution of seats after elections and for major parliamentary groupings only. In Italy, two splits in Socialist ranks that occurred between elections were taken into account.

"The social meaning or function of parliamentary activity is no doubt to turn out legislation and, in part, administrative measures. But in order to understand how democratic politics serve this social end, we must start from the competitive struggle for power and office and realize that the social function is fulfilled, as it were, incidentally — in the same sense as production is incidental to the making of profits."[5]

If "legislation" and "administrative measures" may be equated with policies, this means, in terms of the present subject, that a party adopts or supports policies as a result of its aspired or actual membership in a coalition, instead of assenting to form some coalition on the basis of the actor's policy position and that of his partners.

Downs, following Schumpeter's line of argument, states succinctly: "parties formulate policies in order to win elections, rather than win elections in order to formulate policies"[6].

Riker introduces this economic line of thought in the field of political coalition theory.

"If the market is thus controlled by those persons (possibly a minority) who behave in a maximizing way, then it can be said that the market institution selects and emphasizes rational behavior.

So, I believe, do other institutions, such as election systems, warfare, and other decision-making processes in which several persons must, for the sake of winning, come together for common action without much regard for considerations of ideology or previous friendship. Politics, in the old saw, makes strange bedfellows — and the very strangeness is the triumph of the maximizing motive in some (though far from all) participants."[7]

The position adopted in minimal range theory, policy distance theory and the closed coalition proposition differs sharply from this view and approaches more closely the classical theory of parties in a democracy. In the words of Edmund Burke

"Party is a body of men united for promoting by their joint endeavours the national interest, upon some particular principle in which they are all agreed"[8].

Or, policy positions precede and serve to explain membership in a coalition. The two divergent viewpoints are brought closer to one another in an argument advanced by Sjöblom and also by Downs. Sjöblom writes

"The voters have, in other words, expectations concerning the attitudes of the parties, expectations based on the concept of the relative sequence of the parties, who thus play certain 'roles' for the voters.

133

This is a circumstance that, to a considerable extent, should restrain the mobility of the parties at the choice between various standpoints."[9]

Thus, even a "maximizing" party might deem it necessary to hold on to its policies, quite independently of the coalitional situation, because credibility and cohesion of the party would be threatened by policy changes. Down likewise believes that parties must maintain a degree of "ideological immobility", "coherence" and "integrity" so as to remain reliable in the eyes of the voters. The original position, the "fundamental hypothesis of our model", as quoted before, is modified by Downs at a later stage, to read

"No matter which end — espousing ideologies or holding office — is viewed as the final one, the other will be a subsidiary end necessary to the attainment of the first." [10]

This leads Downs to assume for multi-party systems: "political parties cannot move ideologically past each other"[11]. Or, actors may be ranked on an ordinal scale, independently of their coalition behavior, an assumption that is identical to the one underlying the use of the policy scale for the respective theories in the present study.

In conclusion, it may be said that actors tend to maintain their policy position, quite independently of the coalition situation; this may be the case because of the ideological motivation of the party leadership and cadre or because of their desire to maximize their chance to office by persuading a sufficient number of voters to vote for a party of a given persuasion and apparent reliability: for the purposes of the present inquiry, the two theories amount to the same.

The second question raised by the introduction of a policy scale is whether the parties' policies may be subsumed into a pattern that allows definite predictions to be generated and yet reflects the variety of political preferences among the actors. The formal structure of this pattern will be a one-dimensional, ordinal scale.

The notion of a "left—right" or "left-center-right" ordering of parties is a familiar feature in the parliamentary history of the countries under study. However, even though historians often describe parties as "leftist", or "rightist", or "of the middle", or "in the center", the meaning of these terms varies with the context, with the country, the period and even the issues under discussion*.

In this study, the policy scale is made to correspond with the social economic dimension in politics. More specifically, the crucial criterion shall be based upon the degree of government intervention in the national economy that the party advocates: the percentage of the national income that the party wishes to see redistributed by means of the government budget, defense and police expenditures excepted, shall be an indicator of that party's social economic progressivism, or "leftness". The higher this percentage, the more progressive, or the more "leftist" the party will be.

The position adopted in this study is that, on the whole and in the long run, in the countries and for the period under study, the issues selected by this criterion were more important than any other set of issues. At the beginning of the period under review, the working classes were recently enfranchised and the parties that represented these new voters intended to increase material equality by conquering control over the government apparatus and utilizing the budget and legal powers to realize a more egalitarian income distribution. Expenditures on defense and police have been excepted because both in their political motivation and in their economic effect, they lack this egalitarian quality[12].

A political party is an organization that does not always speak with one voice, nor does it maintain the same position at all times. The party leadership, and equally the leadership in parliament, may speak with authority but its pronouncements are often prompted by the political exigencies of the day and may not be an adequate reflection of the party's position in the long run. Also, the statements of party leaders and the planks in the party program tend to stress goals to be achieved, dangers to be combated, with little mention of the costs of such objectives. For example, a party may advocate a policy of full employment and yet remain silent on the possible inflation that may result from such a policy. For these reasons, such statements of policy may not always be a reliable indicator of the preferences of the party.

---

*Cf. Lipschits (1969) who distinguishes as the most important meanings of the conceptual pair "left—right": progressivism vs. conservatism, secularism vs. clericalism, democracy vs. dictatorship and economic intervention vs. economic freedom. See also Sizoo on the meaning of "rightist"; Sizoo (1971) pp. 1—28, 40—41.

The perceptions of the electorate, on the other hand, are often too imprecise to yield an adequate ordering of the parties' policies and they may have been inspired by traditional loyalties, or past coalition behavior, rather than the party's real position on the issues.

It appears that the best overall indicator of a party's policy position in the long run would be the attitudes of its activists, *e.g.* those members that attend the party's yearly or biennial congress. They are sufficiently informed to be able to place parties with regard to one another on the issues involved. On the other hand, the pressures of day-to-day political life operate much less strongly on these members than on the leadership. Finally, this cadre is in a position to enforce its preferences with the party, at least by way of a veto in case the leadership sways too much from the line adopted by the activists. Thus, the cadre forms the anchoring ground that holds the party to its policy position while it manoevres on the high seas of politics. Therefore, in theory, some statistical aggregate of the policy preference of the party's activists might be taken as an indicator of its rank on the policy scale. As such data are rarely available for the period under study, the judgment of parliamentary historians on the long term policy position of the party will be accepted instead. Once a policy scale has been established in this manner, it will be maintained for a full period 1917—1940 and/or 1945 to the present.

In a widely quoted article, Stokes (1963) has criticized the use of one-dimensional spatial analogies for the description of the political positions of parties or voters. As this is the analogy adopted in the present study, his criticisms will be discussed briefly.

First, Stokes argues, both in a two-party system, as in the United States, and in such multi-party systems as are the subject of the present study, "the conception of a single dimension of political conflict can hardly be sustained"[13]. However, the conception need not be that there *is* only a single dimension of conflict but that, on the whole and in the long run, one such dimension is the most important in explaining coalition formation: the dimension of social economic conflict. Having adopted a formal empirical method of explanation, it is necessary to postulate unambiguous relationships between all explanatory variables. Including other dimensions of conflict would necessitate some rule to relate a certain position on, say, nationalism to another position of the same party in social economic matters. If it were the case that some theory of politics or some generalization from historical experience contained such a rule, *e.g.* "all nationalist parties are conservative in social economics", that rule would be incorporated in the present theoretical framework. But given the state of the discipline, there are no such general statements that may be adopted with sufficient confidence. Therefore, in the present approach, the social economic dimension is chosen as a starting point to see how much of coalition behavior can be explained on that basis alone. This procedure may produce generalizations that can serve in subsequent investigations taking into account additional dimensions of politics.

Stokes also argues convincingly that "the dimensions that are salient to the electorate may change widely over time"[13]. The same applies to the issues that count for the party leadership and cadre. Nevertheless, in this study, the policy scale is maintained without change for an entire inter-war or postwar period in order to satisfy such formal requirements as independence and parsimony of explanatory variables. Within the social economic dimension, changes may occur in the position of parties without affecting the validity of the policy scale as long as these changes do not reverse the sequence among parties. The latter type of change appears to be relatively rare; for a single pair of adjacent parties it can be dealt with by making them tie on the scale.

Stokes third and fourth objections against the one-dimensional policy scale are less relevant to the present enterprise. He raises the interesting point that not all political issues are of a kind that allows actors to be arranged in a sequence with regard to their position on such issues. For example, a party may come out strongly against crime but no party will present itself as "a little bit against crime" or "all for it". Such issues "involve the linking of the parties with some condition that is positively or negatively valued by the electorate"[14]. It may still be that such "valence" issues mask an underlying cleavage that allows sequential ordering: in the case of crime, for example, attitudes on civil liberties or on welfare, education and employment. Whatever the case may be, Stokes agrees that social economic issues such as the degree of government intervention in the economy give rise to preferences that can be subsumed in an ordered set which allows for the construction of a policy scale[15]. Stokes' fourth objection is that spatial models tend to assume that voters perceive the parties as they are in fact positioned[16]. This assumption has been avoided in this study by defining the party's position in terms of the preferences of its activists (or on the basis of its program), rather than in terms of the perceptions of the electorate as a whole.

Stokes' objections to a single, constant policy scale are most pertinent to the present enterprise. Clearly, the adoption of such a scale follows directly from the adoption of a formal empiricist method. Stokes concludes: "So few formalizations have added to our knowledge of politics that their potential value can be a matter for honest debate."[17] But there seems to be no other way of carrying on that debate than to put such formalizations to the test and assess what knowledge they can add. That is precisely the aim of the present enterprise.

In the country-by-country discussion of historical situations and the coalitions that emerged in them, the policy positions of actual parties will be discussed in terms that are common in political parlance and in the usage of parliamentary historians. Such labels are used in very different meanings. For that reason, the most common of these ideological labels will be roughly defined at this point. Apart from minor ideological movements and ethnic, denominational or single-issue and regional parties, European parties have been described most often with the following terms: Communist, Socialist, Social Democrat, Radical Democrat, Christian Democrat, Liberal, Conservative and Fascist (National Socialist)[18].

This enumeration follows a left—right order as defined above. In this sense, Communism clearly is the most leftist ideology: its adherents advocate an economic order in which the state is the sole producer and distributor of the important economic goods; the government budget almost coincides with the national income.

Socialism designates a variety of currents that have in common the advocacy of the nationalization of the major sectors of the economy (be it often under worker's control which differs, of course, from "government control"); only small parts of the economy, notably agriculture, retail trade, the crafts and professions, remain in private hands.

Social Democracy denotes the mainstream of the labor movement; it proposes a far-reaching equalization of wealth and income within the existent framework of representative democracy and within the existing order of private property and production for profit: a large government budget financed by progressive taxes and strong legislation along with a system of state-run agencies are expected to act as a counterweight against monopolistic economic power, to redistribute real income and to satisfy collective needs.

Radical Democracy stands for a variety of political programs

138

that all accept the capitalist economic system as legitimate and that staunchly defend parliamentary democracy. This school of thought may be classified as left of centre because of its acceptance of a strong administrative state apparatus in charge of carrying out the innovations and improvements necessary for continued economic growth: mass education, construction and transport, social security and public health.

Christian Democracy also refers to a multitude of programs, rather than to a unified doctrine: yet, there is a common core — the denial of the decisive and pervasive nature of the class struggle, and the affirmation, instead, of the concepts of evangelical solidarity and individual responsibility. In this conception, it belongs to the role of the state to safeguard the conditions for the fullest development of the individual and for the welfare of his community through legal measures that mitigate the adverse effects of a changing economy, and through an elaborate system of subsidies for social security, for education, or for imperiled farmers or small entrepreneurs. Since parties bearing the Christian Democratic label tend to unite a considerable working class following with bourgeois and agrarian supporters, the policy positions of such parties depend to a large extent on the outcome of intra-party struggles and vary from country to country. For that reason, Christian Democrats may be placed at times to the left of Radical Democrats, though always between Social Democrats and Liberals.

The irreconcilable contenders of the nineteenth century, Liberals and Conservatives, are lumped together for the purpose of the present study of twentieth century politics: though appreciable differences in style and opinion survive between the two traditions when religion, morality and individual rights are concerned, in matters of social economic policy the two currents have been united on a single platform. Such Liberal—Conservative parties strongly reject the entrepreneurial role of the state, combat all forms of nationalization and direct state intervention in economic affairs, accept state subsidies to individual entreprises only in specific cases and on an *ad hoc* basis and maintain that the economy will result in a socially optimal outcome as long as the state limits itself to the preservation of competition and, more recently, some anti-cyclical spending. In Scandinavian countries, however, Conservative and Liberal parties have maintained distinct characters.

The preceding ideological currents neatly fit the traditional left—right sequence, also when the share of the government budget is taken as the ordering criterion. Fascism*, however, presents a problematical case. Its adherents have advocated strong government and, as a consequence, a large government budget in relation to the national income. On the other hand, when fascist movements captured control of the state, they converted the economy into a war economy, which makes it difficult to separate defense and police expenditures from remaining budget posts. Where Fascist governments survived the war years, they reverted to a rather conservative economic policy of relatively small budgets and limited intervention in the economy, as in Portugal and Spain. Some peasant movements, such as surged in France, Holland and Finland and which were called Fascist by their opponents, can quite confidently be relegated to the right because of their vehemently anti-statist position. The same applies to the postwar Fascists in Italy. For the present purposes, only the National Socialists in the Weimar Republic pose a problem. Like the Italian Fascists of the interbellum, their propaganda contained proposals for far-reaching state control of the economy. At the same time, the leadership would meet many of the demands of business and finance. This ambiguity in the social economic propaganda and policy of the Italian Fascists and the German National Socialists has given rise to an unremitting debate on their classification as movements of the left or of the right. Scholars of each persuasion tend to push Fascism into the lap of the opponent. A contemporary American scholar, James A. Gregor, may provide the first example:

> "....both fascism and the variants of Marxism that today receive so much attention constitute species of a single genus: totalitarianism. Had Anglo-American political commentators not been under the pervasive influence of Marxist or quasi-Marxist analyses, this would have been evident long before the advent of World War II."[19]

The Dutch historian of Marxist background, Jan Romein, however, wrote on the eve of the war

> "Economically, there is nothing progressive in fascism. Its economic foundations are those of capitalism in its final agony."[20]

A German observer, Ernst Nolte, stated much more recently

---

*The term is understood here in a broad sense as to include National Socialism.

140

"The leftist elements in National Socialism are either historical anachronisms or sham acquisitions. It is quite otherwise with its rightist features.....National Socialism was a genuine party of the Right, clearly identifiable as such because its ideas and attitudes are in the tradition of the Right."[21]

Some authors deny the possibility to classify Fascism in terms of right and left.

"Fascism's ideology as well as its practices make it difficult to classify it as a movement of the traditional Right...."[22]

The author, Salvatore Saladino, concludes that Fascism "cannot be considered either essentially of the Right or of the Left*. The French political scientist Jean Meynaud considers the word at present hardly more than an ideological label with "emotional meaning" only[23].

However, this ambiguity in Fascist ideology is not pervasive; it pertains especially to social economic matters. Fascist thought is organized around the concepts of nation and leadership; social economic views are derived from this core which represents what Mannheim might have called the "basic intention" of Fascism[24]. Social economic positions are only derivatives of this core concept. Hans Rogger writes

"This entails that the economic and social conditions of the nation are not considered the prime movers of its history, but rather its sense of unity under one leader and with one binding faith, and its willingness to struggle and fight. Social and economic policies are only secundary and may be phrased for opportunistic reasons. A rank order that takes social economic policy positions as its decisive criterion will be ambiguous towards these movements."[25]

Fascist thought is quite determinate on the dimension of nationalism, the axis around which its philosophy is built. On a national-

---

*Seymour M. Lipset, in a comparative analysis of the electoral support of "extremist" movements, argues that such movements should be distinguished into those on the extreme left, such as Communism and Peronism, rightist extremists as for example the pre-1958 Gaullist movement and an extremism of the center: "classic fascism is a movement of the propertied middle classes, who for the most part normally support liberalism", though Nazism in Germany received some support from conservatives (*op. cit.* p. 174). The distinction is based on the social bases from which these movements receive support, rather than on their ideologies.

ism scale, a Fascist party would belong at the extreme right. On a social economic scale, its place cannot be determined with the present means of analysis. In this respect, the case of Communism is analogous though opposite. Socialist ideology is constructed on the axis of social economic issues, which in this philosophy determine the fate of society and the individual. It follows from this point of departure that the proletariat is without a fatherland; in their political practice, Socialist parties have adopted positions on issues of nationalism according to the exigencies of the concrete historical circumstances, or in an opportunistic fashion, as the opponents would call it. Thus, on a social economic scale, a Communist party should be placed at the extreme left and on a nationalism scale, its place cannot be determined once and for all.

This argument points to a solution of the left—right controversy. On a combined scale for nationalism and social economic issues, their social economic stand would anchor Communist parties at the extreme left and their nationalist position would place Fascist parties at the extreme right of the scale. *If* the ranking of all other parties on the one scale were to coincide with their order on the other, the other parties could be placed on the combined nationalism social economic scale in the same sequence. This would result in the construction of a formally correct scale that reflects the political reality of the countries under study.

The preceding discussion of the ideological mainstreams of political life on the European continent is intended as a brief guide to the use of the labels that are current in parliamentary history and not as an analysis of contemporary political philosophy. But it may be seen that the traditional left—right ranking of these ideological currents fits the left—right criterion advanced here quite well.

Parties will be ordered on a left—right scale according to the share of the national income they wish to see redistributed by means of the government budget, military and police expenditures excepted. When this does not affect the ranking of the other actors, the criterion of nationalism will be added to place the Fascist parties. The preference of the party's cadre will be taken as indicative of the party's stand and, in the absence of such information, the judgment of parliamentary historians and other expert observers will be accepted instead. The computer program used to analyse the data is capable of dealing with one pair of actors which tie in their ranking on the scale.

The present approach presupposes that policy positions are, to a large extent, independent of coalition behavior and that they may be subsumed in a single ordinal ranking for the purposes of the theory. Such a policy scale will be maintained without change for a full period 1918—1940 or 1945 to the present for reasons of independence and parsimony of the explanatory variables.

5. Membership of the coalition

The purpose of this study is to explain the composition of the parliamentary coalition that supports the cabinet. The membership of the actual coalition is inferred from the composition of the cabinet: generally the cabinet ministers are publicly identified with some parliamentary party which is then considered to be a member of the supporting coalition. When an actor is represented only by a minister without portfolio or with a very minor department, his membership will be considered doubtful.

On the other hand, when an actor is not represented in the cabinet but when he is nevertheless known to have supported the government consistently, and when there are grounds to believe that this support was based on some sort of an agreement with the leaders of the government parties, this actor will be counted as a member of the coalition. This has been the position, for example, of the Communists in Denmark in the late sixties and the Italian (Nenni and Sarragat) Socialists in the beginning of the "opening to the left".

When such support in parliament, without representation in the cabinet, consists mainly in a vote of abstention at critical times, as occurred for a time among the Socialists in Italy, for example, this will not be considered sufficient as a condition for membership of the coalition.

Thus, membership is assumed to imply that the member-actor is committed to support the cabinet with all the votes at his disposal whenever its continued existence is at stake. An actor is either in or out of the coalition, there is no "in between". When an actor who has been classified as a member of the coalition on the above grounds is found to vote against the government, it is assumed that the coalition leadership has decided to allow the actor to do so because, without his support, the coalition is still winning. This is an important assumptional choice: members vote at times against their own coalition, because these coalitions have sufficient weight to allow them to do so. The alternative assumption would be:

coalitions have more weight than is necessary to win because not all members can be trusted to vote with the coalition in all critical votes. The latter position is clearly the one Riker adopts in explaining why actual coalitions are often larger than minimum size: an "information effect" occurs; there exists uncertainty over the true strength and the reliability of the actors that are prospective partners[26].

The above matter cannot be settled by *a priori* argument but only by careful historical research into specific coalition formations. Here, the assumption is that membership of the coalition implies full support each time that the continued existence of the coalition is at stake. Coalitions are not larger than minimum size just to hedge against possible future defections but for other reasons, *e.g.* the desire to create coalitions of minimal range, closed or not along the policy scale, or of minimal policy distance for the actors concerned.

Minority governments present a special case for the theories since the membership of the supporting coalition — if it exists at all — cannot be inferred from the composition of the cabinet. Such minority governments may remain in existence by leaning on one majority at one time and on a different majority at some other time. However, when evidence is available as to the existence of a more or less permanent parliamentary majority coalition that supports this minority government, the analysis of such a coalition proceeds as in the normal case.

6. The parliamentary system and its environment

Once the election results are known, the cards are dealt in the game of coalition formation: the policy positions of the actors are given for an entire period, the setting of the parliamentary system and the majority criterion are also given, the elections decide what parties shall be parliamentary actors and with which weights. No other factors are taken into consideration by the theories in this study.

This does not necessarily mean that the assumption is that no other factors are at work. First, under certain conditions the validity of the theories is suspended, the assumptions do not apply. Secondly, outside factors may work without the assumptions of the theory being suspended or being invalidated, by determining *which* specific coalition may form from among the set of coalitions that is predicted by a particular theory for a given situation. This last possibility is quite characteristic of coalition theory since it predicts sets of coalitions in mutual equilibrium and "leaves it" to other factors to determine which of these "virtual" coalitions will materialize. Only when coalitions are observed that are *not* predicted by a theory does this constitute evidence against the assumptions of that theory.

Thus, outside factors operate on the parliamentary system first by determining its setting and rules (*e.g.* the majority requirement) and by shaping the identity and policy positions of the actors and, with each election, their weights. This is accounted for by the theoretical framework. Next, these outside factors may operate by determining which coalitions from among the coalitions that have been predicted by a particular theory for a given situation will, in fact, emerge. This does not contradict the assumptions of the theories. However, when outside factors operate in such a manner that a coalition emerges that is defined as unstable by some theory, this constitutes evidence against that theory. Lastly, certain outside factors are contrary to the assumption of the theory and when they apply, the validity of the theories is suspended.

The present approach implies the assumption that parliament is sovereign: its decisions can be enforced, regardless of opposition on the outside, be it from a constitutional body or from a political entity that has no such formal position and whether it be from domestic or foreign entities. During the period under study, decisions adopted in the parliamentary system did override those of all other constitutional bodies in each country. In the case of public policy, parliament could effectuate its decisions also against the resistance of political and social organizations in the country. Whether such forces were able to shape the decisions of parliament or to render them ineffective through the less visible techniques of political pressure is hard to determine. But in the case of an open, public contest, parliament would have its way.

Foreign influence on the parliamentary system is even harder to assess. It is uncommon for foreign powers to present their demands openly, except in times of grave international crisis. In normal times, especially in the politics of small countries, the influence of foreign powers is exercised with great discretion and it is largely anticipated in the sense that parliament will avoid certain decisions and even shun debate on the issues.

Thus, when in an open public conflict, parliament cannot enforce its will against some other constitutional body or against

145

some political or social organization in the country, or against the declared intentions of some foreign power, the validity of the theories is suspended: there exists clear evidence against the assumption that the parliamentary system operates as an isolated entity*. This is the case, for example, in the years during the second world war. The exclusion of the Communists from government in France and Italy, and their inclusion in Finland appear to have been greatly influenced by American and Soviet diplomacy respectively. In such cases, these influences will be discussed in the case-by-case review of the theories but in the statistical evaluation the theories will be applied without taking these factors into account.

From day to day, probably the most important outside influence on parliamentary coalition formation comes from social organizations such as trade unions, large corporations and financial institutions. The theories are not equipped to take such factors into consideration. In this respect the theories need amendment, or rather incorporation into a political theory of the parliamentary process. As they stand, the theories offer an explanation of parliamentary coalition formation exclusively within the context of the parliamentary system itself.

---

*When parliament cannot enforce its decision against the opposition of some other constitutional body in the political system, it is not the true locus for the determination of government policy. When parliament cannot enforce its decision against the opposition of social and political organizations in the country, a threat of civil war prevails; when it cannot enforce its decision against the opposition of a foreign power, a threat of war exists. Under these conditions the validity of the theories is suspended. Compare also hypotheses 5a, b, and c, Chapter 5, Section 1.

CHAPTER 8

A First Evaluation: Statistical

In this chapter, the theories that were advanced in Chapters 4 and 5 and operationalized in Chapter 7 will be submitted to the test proposed in Chapter 6.

Each theory produces a predicted set of coalitions that differ among one another in membership: therefore, the unit of analysis, or an "event", in this chapter is the occurrence of a different historical coalition, *i.e.* one that has not formed before in the same situation *j*. Repeated occurrence of the same coalition in the same situation *j* does not constitute a new event. However, in the historical discussion in Chapters 9—11, each formation of a more or less permanent majority coalition in parliament does represent a new event, even when a coalition of identical composition has occurred before in that situation.

The statistical test presents only a partial evaluation of the theories. Their analytical structure also plays a part in the judgment. Moreover, the historical discussion may reveal that a given theory is particularly well suited to explain developments in a specific period or in the coalitional politics of a single country.

In this chapter, the theories that fail badly in their empirical predictions according to the statistical criteria will be removed from further consideration. A few other theories will be "entertained"[1], that is the statistical evidence at this point is insufficient to accept them, but these theories have reached somewhat significant results and possess certain structural characteristics, especially in relation to other theories, that make them interesting enough for further consideration. One theory, finally, will be accepted as a

TABLE 8-1
Statistical analysis of results from COAL. A program for testing formal coalition theories

Nation	Winning (all majority coalitions)	Minimal winning	Minimum size principle	2/3 criterion	Bargaining proposition	Interv minim range
						Chi-square score
Denmark	0.000	32.445	53.006	32.841	30.588	64.09
Finland	0.000	7.556	5.416	15.242	4.734	4.73
France	0.000	2.938	0.000	10.903	0.000	0.00
Israel	0.000	3.393	0.000	7.353	4.445	6.80
Italy	0.000	10.558	13.588	17.443	5.416	25.39
The Netherlands	0.000	25.888	6.127	13.345	6.802	46.39
Norway	0.000	17.705	23.567	13.213	14.567	11.09
Sweden	0.000	19.245	13.467	16.601	20.842	26.28
Weimar	0.000	6.673	0.000	4.838	5.466	16.29
For all nations	0.000	126.401	115.171	131.779	92.861	201.09
						p-score
Denmark	1.000	0.445	0.011	0.426	0.538	0.00
Finland	1.000	1.000	1.000	0.976	1.000	1.00
France	1.000	1.000	1.000	0.996	1.000	1.00
Israel	1.000	0.998	1.000	0.920	0.992	0.94
Italy	1.000	0.836	0.629	0.357	0.993	0.06
The Netherlands	1.000	0.579	1.000	0.991	1.000	0.01
Norway	1.000	0.125	0.023	0.354	0.266	0.52
Sweden	1.000	0.256	0.638	0.412	0.185	0.05
Weimar	1.000	0.572	1.000	0.775	0.707	0.03
For all nations	1.000	0.999	1.000	0.997	1.000	0.13

theory of coalitional behavior for the countries and the periods under study.

In the 90 situations that were investigated in the nine countries under study, 108 more or less permanent parliamentary majority coalitions formed without an identical coalition having formed before in the same situation.

Not as an evaluation of the theories, but to convey a general idea of the characteristics of these historical coalitions, it may be noted that 85 of these 108 coalitions were closed, 78 were smaller than two-thirds of the assembly vote, *i.e.* 30 were large, 55 were of minimal range, all of them of closed minimal range, 51 coalitions were minimal winning and out of these 51 there were 33 that were

winning coalitions were found to be policy distance dominated among the closed coalitions and 19 historical coalitions were so dominated. Again, the closed condition is a much more discriminating eliminator than the domination criterion. Though these figures are only informal statistics, they do give a rough impression of the manner in which policy distance theory in its various versions attempts to cross off some 5000 coalitions until the 108 historical coalitions remain and how it fails in that task.

Having dealt with the inadequate theories, another glance at the last row of Table 8-1 or Table 8-2 reveals an equally striking conclusion, this time of a positive nature: closed minimal range theory produces a highly significant score. The odds for a random guesser to do better are one in five hundred! This result is sufficient to accept closed minimal range theory as an explanation of coalition formation in the parliamentary systems under study, at least for times of normalcy. The poor performance of the theory in the French Fourth Republic and Israel may well confirm the intuitive impression that these systems have not known normal times. The theory does best when the number of actors is five to six and this corresponds to its very good performance for the Netherlands and Denmark.

Minimal range theory, ordinal version, also produces very good predictions. The theory is not adopted as an independent explanation, however, because the conjunction of this minimal range theory and the closed coalition proposition, closed minimal range theory, performs even better: the theory is not rejected but superseded by a better one that contains its assumptions. As a component of another conjoint theory, basic alternative theory, it will be mentioned frequently in the country by country discussion.

Policy distance theory, closed coalition version, produces results that are significant at a level of 3.7%: not entirely sufficient to accept, yet too good to reject the theory. Obviously, the lion's share of its predictive success is due to its permissibility condition which leads an independent life as the closed coalition proposition. The closed coalition proposition on its own is not clearly insignificant: it scores at a level of 0.075. It is debatable if the improvement over this score obtained by the conjunction of this closed coalition proposition (as a permissibility condition) and policy distance theory is meaningful or an artefact of the data set. Moreover, it may be that the improvement is due to certain minimizing tendencies within policy distance theory that are expressed much more efficiently by minimal range theory: the conjunction

153

of minimal range theory and the closed coalition proposition — closed minimal range theory — is the most succesful. However, perhaps the improvement that results when the closed coalition proposition is combined with policy distance theory is due to a mechanism that is specific to policy distance theory after all: in policy distance theory, it often happens that a coalition of minimum size formed from actors on one side of the scale dominates most coalitions formed from actors on the other side of the scale. Thus, most predicted coalitions are on one side of the policy scale. For a given situation, policy distance theory tends to predict only left (—center) or only right (—center) coalitions, unlike other theories, It might be that this effect has caused the improvement of policy distance theory, closed coalition version, over the closed coalition proposition on its own. Further evidence is necessary to decide on the matter. Because of its (slightly) significant performance and because of the insight policy distance theory gives in the preferences of individual actors for the various coalitions, policy distance theory, closed coalition version, is entertained. It will not be mentioned frequently in the discussion because its predicted set coincides so closely with that of the closed coalition proposition which is always mentioned. Policy distance theory, pure core and $1,n$ permissibility version will, however, always be mentioned in the discussion of historical coalitions because, unlike other theories, they produce predictions that are difficult to compute by hand from the data.

After the discussion of the closed coalition proposition in conjunction with minimal range theory and with policy distance theory, it remains to discuss the proposition in conjunction with a third theory: minimal winning theory. This conjoint theory is called "basic alternative theory" and it produces a predicted set of closed minimal winning coalitions that are, almost always, also of minimal range. A predicted set that is the union of those of three other theories is interesting on purely theoretical grounds alone. But the theory performs very much better than one of its components, minimal winning theory, and somewhat better than the closed coalition proposition on its own. Apparently this interesting achievement, not clearly insignificant at the 0.067 level, is due to the fact that it predicts a subset of closed minimal range theory (those closed minimal range coalitions that are also minimal winning). Its statistical results are insufficient to accept it as an independent explanation of coalition behavior in the parliamentary system under study but its analytical characteristics make it a very efficient descriptive tool for the characterization of coalitional situations. For that reason, it is used to describe the situation that prevails after each election in the chapters dealing with historical coalitions. As an explanatory theory, it is rejected in favor of closed minimal range theory.

One theory remains, a theory that does not impose any minimizing criterion upon the predicted coalitions: the closed coalition proposition. As a component of conjoint theories (with minimal winning theory as basic alternative theory; in the closed coalition version of policy distance theory; in closed minimal range theory) it has resulted in improvements of performance compared with the results of the other component theory on its own, that were dramatic in at least two of the three instances. The proposition as a theory on its own was suggested because these improvements had been registered in the course of the present investigations. Therefore, it is not independent of the present data set. Moreover, though its results are not clearly insignificant, they are insufficient to accept the theory as an independent explanatory construct. However, it may be interesting to inspect the test results for a slightly different body of data. In Table 8-3, four additional cases have been included: the wartime situations in Finland, Denmark and Sweden (1940 and 1944). These situations gave rise to large

TABLE 8-3
Overall results for twelve theories for data set extended to include four wartime situations

Theories	Chi-square scores	p-scores
Minimal winning theory	125.984	1.000
Minimum size principle	117.677	1.000
Two-thirds criterion	132.285	0.999
Bargaining proposition	93.533	1.000
Interval minimal range theory	189.451	0.457
Ordinal minimal range theory	223.039	0.041
Closed minimal range theory	229.581	0.021
Basic alternative theory	210.313	0.127
Closed coalition proposition	223.481	0.039
Policy distance theory, pure core version	142.829	0.994
Policy distance theory, $1,n$ perm. version	181.512	0.619
Policy distance theory, closed coalition version	225.103	0.033
	94 cases	
	188 d.o.f.	

coalitions, sometimes even all-party coalitions. They have been excepted from consideration because the threat or the actuality of war prevailed. The parliamentary system could not be considered as a relatively isolated entity (*cf*. Chapter 7). However, outside factors may operate, not by causing coalitions to form that are unstable in the sense of the theories, but by causing particular stable coalitions to form from among the set of stable coalitions. Table 8-3 shows that for this slightly extended data set, closed minimal range theory is still the most significant. It also shows considerable improvement for the closed coalition proposition which is now significant at the 3.9% level. The closed coalition version of policy distance theory achieves a score that is only very slightly better.

The first conclusion should be that the test is very sensitive to slight changes in the data set: even the addition of four cases to the ninety situations of normalcy produce changes that alter the sequence of significance. But also, it allows a conclusion to be drawn which makes it possible to view the preceding statements about closed minimal range theory in a somewhat broader perspective: *historical coalitions tend to be closed coalitions and in times of normalcy these coalitions will be of minimal range also.* Or, in the conjunction of minimal range theory and the closed coalition proposition, closed minimal range theory is the explanation of coalition behavior in normal times; in times of crisis, this component, minimal range theory, loses its validity but the other component, the closed coalition proposition, remains valid on its own.

Students of coalition politics have sometimes checked the predictions of their theories against data on historical coalitions in parliament. Leiserson (1966)[3] and Leiserson (1968)[4] listed historical coalitions in Sweden, France and Italy in the first study, in Japan for the second study and calculated how many of these coalitions were predicted by the theory and for how much of the time. Axelrod did the same for Italy[5]. These tabulations were not meant as statistical tests but as a first attempt to assess the realism of the theories. Damgaard[6] investigated minimal winning theory, the minimum size principle and closed minimal range theory for the case of Denmark, again relying on tabulations rather than statistical measures. His results will be discussed in the section dealing with Denmark.

Independently of the present study, Browne studied the predictive performance of Riker—Gamson theory (the minimum size principle), Leiserson's bargaining proposition, and the Von Neu-

156

mann and Morgenstern set W^m (minimal winning theory) for thirteen countries* since 1945, restricting the definition of historical majority coalitions to coalitions of parties "that have agreed to accept responsibility for the government (or governing)"[7]. In the present study, parliamentary coalitions are determined on the basis of the parties that support the government, rather than on the basis of parties represented in the government. Even when this difference is taken into consideration, the data do not always match†. This pioneer attempt at a computer tabulated test of coalition theories is, however, marred by inadequate statistics. Browne adds all historical coalitions that formed in the countries and during the period under study: 125; next, he tabulates the number of coalitions that were winning in each situation: 19,205. The ratio of these two values ($\Sigma p_j / \Sigma n_j$ for all j, in the present notation) serves as a "random" criterion. For each theory, the ratio of the sum of all correct predictions and the sum of the number of predictions for each situation is computed: $\Sigma q_{ij} / \Sigma r_{ij}$ for all j, in the present notation. The values obtained are 0.007 for random, 0.043 for the minimal winning theory, 0.024 for the minimum size principle, and 0.120 for the bargaining proposition.

The measure is relatively meaningless since the procedure of summing over all situations masks the different values for n_j — dependent on the number of actors N in each situation — and r_{ij}.

In a footnote, a measure is proposed that is computed per formation instead of as an overall average. For each formation of a historical coalition a theory i obtains a score q_{ij}/r_{ij}; $q_{ij} = 0$ or 1. The overall score for a theory consists of the sum of these ratios: $\Sigma(q_{ij}/r_{ij})$ over all formations‡. Again, the same ratio for "winning theory" serves as a criterion: $\Sigma(p_j/n_j)$ over all formations; $p_j = 1$. The measure was not calculated by Browne. However, in the course of the present investigations, an almost identical measure

---

* Austria, Belgium, *Denmark, Finland,* Germany, Iceland, Ireland, *Israel, Italy,* Luxembourg, *the Netherlands, Norway,* and *Sweden.* (Countries in italics are also represented in the present study.)

† Browne finds 21 postwar majority governments in Finland, Törnudd only 15. In Denmark Browne counted the midterm successions of deceased prime ministers as new cabinets in contrast to Damgaard; for the postwar Netherlands, Browne observes 11 majority governments, the present data reveal only 9 for the period 1945—1969. See Browne (1970—1971) p. 399 and the sections and tables in this book dealing with the countries mentioned.

* Browne proposes division of this sum by Σp_j but this will not affect the ranking of the theories' results in the test as it is the same for all i.

TABLE 8-4

Overall results of thirteen theories for test $t_i = \Sigma(q_{ij}/r_{ij})$ for $j = 1, 2, ..., 90$

Theory	
"Winning theory" (all winning coalitions may form)	0.0499
Minimal winning theory	0.1181
Minimum size principle	0.2189
Two-thirds criterion	0.1170
Bargaining proposition	0.1327
Interval minimal range theory	0.2690
Ordinal minimal range theory	0.2347
Closed minimal range theory	0.2630
Basic alternative theory	0.2963
Closed coalition proposition	0.1129
Policy distance theory, pure core version	0.1414
Policy distance theory, 1,n perm. version	0.1660
Policy distance theory, closed coalition version	0.1616
	90 cases

was applied*: $\Sigma(q_{ij}/r_{ij})$ over all *situations* j; $q_{ij} = 0,1,2,3$ ... since more than one historical coalition may be observed in a situation j and predicted correctly. The ratio of "winning theory", $\Sigma(p_j/n_j)$ again served as a criterion. Results of this measure may be found in Table 8-4. Since the measure does not behave as a statistic with known distribution, no significance score can be computed.

The highest scores are obtained by basic alternative theory, interval minimal range theory, closed minimal range theory, ordinal minimal range theory and the minimum size principle. The theories that perform worst are the closed coalition proposition and the two-thirds criterion. Clearly, the test of Table 8—4 tends to favor unduly those theories that produce a small predicted set r_{ij} for each situation, thus keeping the value of $t_{ij} = q_{ij}/r_{ij}$ high. This explains the relatively high score of the very parsimonious size principle and the ranking of the minimal range theories: ordinal minimal range theory predicts a set that contains that of closed minimal range theory which, in turn, contains the predicted set of basic alternative theory; each subset achieves a higher score than its superset. The predicted set of interval minimal range theory is again a subset of that of ordinal minimal range theory.

Moreover, as the test does not take into account the number of

---

* Suggested by Dr. Helmut Selten of the University of Frankfurt in Berkeley, Cal. in May, 1968.

winning coalitions, n_j, from among which each prediction must be made and whereas r_{ij} tends to increase with n_j, but p_j and q_{ij} do not, the scores obtained in countries with a small number of actors, N, (and, as consequence, a small $n_j = 2^{N-1}$) load very heavily on the overall scores, whereas successes obtained in the more "difficult" situations with large numbers of actors hardly play a role. This discriminates very much against the closed coalition proposition and against policy distance theory.

Yet, the test of Table 8-4 corroborates the evidence from the main test with regard to the good performance of minimal range theory; again, theories that take only weights into account and not the actors' policy positions score very low with the exception of the minimum size principle. Policy distance theory is not rehabilitated in this test either. The theories that occupy the four highest places all take the policy scale into consideration. The first place of basic alternative theory (with a very small predicted set) and the bottom position of the closed coalition proposition (with a large predicted set), two theories that score almost equal in the main test, must be considered as an effect of the test's sensitivity to the average size of the theories' predicted sets, r_{ij}.

On the basis of the evidence in its entirety, the final conclusion to be drawn is that *parliamentary majority coalitions tend to be closed along the policy scale and, in times of normaly, of minimal range.*

Or, closed minimal range theory holds in normal times, the tendency to form coalition's of minimal range disappears in times of crisis but the propensity to form closed coalitions remains throughout. Of the four basic concepts in coalition theory, that of policy distance has no role in this general empirical conclusion but the other three remain central: historical coalitions are *closed* along the policy scale and contain no *unnecessary actors* that add to the coalition's *range*, except in times of crisis.

CHAPTER 9

Confronting History: Weimar, the Fourth Republic, Italy

In the next three chapters, the theories are applied to the process of cabinet formation as it occurred in nine European multiparty democracies. In a separate section for each country, the particular features of its parliamentary system are discussed in order to determine whether it fits the factual assumptions of the theories; especially, the policy positions of the actors are the subject of inquiry so that an adequate policy scale may be constructed. The predictions of the various theories are then compared with the outcomes of the parliamentary process in that country. This should provide further insight in the working of each theory and allow a further evaluation of its explanatory power beyond a performance score obtained by mere tabulation.

The arrangement of the countries in three chapters is mainly for convenience. But the combination of the German Weimar Republic, the French Fourth Republic and the Italian Republic in one chapter is also inspired by a classification suggested by Giovanni Sartori: he proposed the notion "extreme polarization" which is based on the distribution of the voting strength of parties arranged on a single left-right continuum; the notion applies to the three countries in this chapter which are explicitly discussed in the article[1].

. "The distinctive features of a polarized multipolar system are as follows: (1) the lack of centrality indicated by the physical existence of a center, and thereby the likely prevalence of centrifugal drives; (2) a high degree of ideological rigidity, or in any case a nonpragmatic approach to politics; (3)

160

marked cleavage at the elite level, which in turn deepens the fragmentation of basic consensus; (4) the absence of real alternative government; (5) the growth of irresponsible opposition* and thereby of the politics of out-bidding, of unfair competition."[2]

Sartori raises the question whether this framework might not also be applied to Finland and Israel and one is tempted to add the Netherlands — temptation that was succumbed to in Chapter 10. A more moderate pluralism is found in the Scandinavian monarchies, Sweden and Denmark, which have been grouped together in Chapter 11. If common conclusions were to emerge from each chapter, this would increase confidence in Sartori's typology and strengthen the unity of the theory of party systems.

1. The Weimar Republic

The Weimar Republic emerged after the defeat of the German Empire at the hands of the Allies. Its economy was heavily mort-gaged by the demands for reparation imposed by its neighbours, forestalling by its survival the resurrection of the old *Reich* on the one hand and the creation of a soviet republic on the other until it succumbed to the Nazi onslaught in 1933.

1.a The parliamentary system

The founders of the Weimar Republic opted for a moderately federal constitution with a strong presidency, elected by universal suffrage, and with a bicameral legislature consisting of the directly and universally elected Assembly (*Reichstag*) and a Senate (*Reichsrat*) that represented the *Länder*. However, the *Reichsrat* "was made distinctly subordinate to the Reichstag. Moreover, there was the all-important fact that the cabinet was to be respon-sible to the Reichstag alone"[3]. The *Reichsrat* will therefore be ignored when testing the theories.

Within the *Reichstag* no formal veto positions existed, nor is there evidence of any informal vetoes in this Assembly. Whether

---

* The term "irresponsible opposition" remains for Sartori's account if it implies that only a commitment to a national parliamentary democracy em-bodies "responsibility" and a commitment to the liberation of the working class does not.

major government policy was determined solely by the parliamentary coalition and by the cabinet government it supported is another question: formally the prime minister, or chancellor, was to determine the major course of policy; in fact, the other cabinet ministers did participate in the making of government policy[4]. Yet, the President could dissolve the *Reichstag*, subject laws to popular referendum or exercise broad emergency powers; all this with the counter-signature of the chancellor. Though the presidential powers were considerable, special assumptional provisions to the theories in order to account for them seem unwarranted for the period under study.

Two other major influences acted on the parliamentary system proper without being reflected in the operationalized theories; under the terms of the Versailles treaty, Germany was heavily indebted to the Allied powers and its defense was severely curtailed; in economic or military decisions the opposition of the Allies would weigh very heavily indeed. The other outside influence was domestic: "Control of the nation's economic life became the prerogative of a few men. The manner in which they used their power was to go a long way toward determining the ultimate fate of the German Republic[5]."

At the time of the founding of the Weimar Republic, the conditions of hypothesis (5c) (Chapter 5, Section 1) — threat of war and threat of civil war — were both realized; only gradually would the situation return to normalcy, to deteriorate again speedily after 1929.

All these considerations may serve to explain discrepancies between the predictions of the theories and the actual coalitions that governed Germany during the interbellum years; none of them is embodied in the operationalized versions by special assumptions.

Within the parliamentary systems of the *Reichstag*, decisions were made by simple majority, no vetoes are considered and no constitutional revisions seem to have required special majorities for the cabinet coalitions*.

Political life in the early Weimar Republic was dominated by the issues revolving around the constitution and the Versailles treaty on the one hand, and by the problems of an economy in upheaval on the other.

---

* The Constitution in art. 74 provided for its amendment by a $\frac{2}{3}$ majority, as occurred with the Railroad Reform Bill and the Dawes plan (Eyck (1962) Vol. I, p. 417).

The Weimar Republic was the creation of three parties: the *Sozialistische Partei Deutschland* (SPD) which controlled almost 40% of the votes in the constituent *Nationale Versammlung*, the *Deutsche Demokratische Partei* (DEMP) that counted many of the leading men in the Republic among its liberal democratic ranks and the Catholic *Zentrum* party. The latter split on the issue of federalism; the *Bayerische Volkspartei* (BAYR) opted for a separate existence and remained "sehr viel weiter rechts als das Zentrum" on both constitutional and economic issues.

The *Deutsche Volkspartei* (VOLK) voted against both the Weimar constitution and the Versailles treaty and only Stresemann's strenuous efforts could bring it into government coalitions[6]. The *Deutschnationale Volkspartei* (NATP) "was in its essence anti-republican and anti-democratic. It could work with the state only on behalf of a different constitutional system, an authoritarian philosophy, and the special economic interests of its members."[7] The party saw its *Reichstag* representation cut down to half its size by the advent of the German nazi party, the NSDAP, whose extreme views on Weimar and Versailles were not even muffled by a more moderate wing[8].

At the time of the founding of the Weimar Republic, the Independent Socialists voted against the constitution. This USPD faction was later to join with Majority Socialist dissidents in the Communist KPD. The Communists opposed the Republic but their alternative was also diametrically opposed to that of the *Deutschnationale*; they had supported the Berlin and Munich uprisings, so bitterly fought by the emperor's adherents.

With regard to the issues related to the Weimar constitution and the Versailles treaty, the "nationalism dimension", parties might be ranked in this order:

KPD (USPD) − SDAP (SPD) − DEMP + ZENT − BAYR + VOLK − NATP − NAZI.

(An oblique line indicates that the order between the adjoining parties is unknown; it may be a tie or even reversed.)

It will be shown that this order closely coincides with the social economic policy ranking and that both orders reflect general expert opinion on inter-party distance in the Weimar Republic.

In social economic matters, the Communists are placed leftmost almost by definition and the very doctrinaire German KPD should be no exception, given its insistence on a revolutionary takeover of political and economic life by a workers' state. The SPD opted for economic reform within the framework of the Republic. Its inter-

163

ventionist proposals were gradually replaced by a policy of crisis control in which the safeguarding of the purchasing power of the mass public came first[9]. The Democratic party may be placed immediately to the right of the SPD: "sympathetic to the idea of economic and social reform, indeed, it even went so far as to advocate the socialization of monopolistic industries."[10]

Policy positions are regarded in this study as the independent variables from which — in combination with other determinants — coalition behavior is to be explained. But the *Zentrum* party presents a case in which feedback from the coalition situation to its policy position is unmistakable: primarily organized as the political vehicle of German Catholics, it kept its options open to all sides, wishing to remain acceptable to all prospective partners and to alienate none of its socially heterogeneous factions. Its adherence to the papal encyclical *Rerum Novarum* implied an acceptance of the status quo, slightly modified by its strivings to improve the living conditions of the workers[11]. The Bavarian sister party was more conservative, at bottom "reactionary"[12]. The *Deutsche Volkspartei* represented the *"deutsche Bürgertum"* which strongly opposed any form of state socialism and stood for a "Marxistenreine Regierung"[13]. Its policy position is certainly to the right of the *Zentrum* party but its location relative to the Bavarian People's Party is hard to determine. Both, however, are surpassed in conservatism by the *Deutschnationale Volkspartei* which time and again gave in to the economic pressures from property holders, heavy industry and agricultural interests, finally closing ranks behind Hugenberg, "nur kapitalistischen Reaktionär"[14].

From the 1924 December elections on, a small party gained sufficient seats to be classified as an actor: the *Wirtschaftspartei* (WIRT), defending low taxes, a reduction of state intervention and government spending[15]. An offshoot from the NATP formed *Landvolk* (LAND), more moderate in its views than the NATP, mostly defending agrarian interest[16]. The latter two parties may have been less conservative than the NATP; they were probably to the right of the *Deutsche Volkspartei* in their single-minded opposition to taxation and government intervention. The positions of the *Deutsche Volkspartei* and the *Bayerische Volkspartei* in relation to each other are left indeterminate. For the *Reichstag* (1928), in which *Landvolk* and *Wirtschaftspartei* were both actors, results are not influenced by the ranking of these parties as long as they are placed to the right of the *Deutsche Volkspartei.*

164

It remains to place the National Socialists on this continuum and without doubt their case is the most problematic. Both the Communists and the National Socialists rejected the legitimacy of the Weimar Republic and vehemently protested the capitalist order of the economy. But where the Communists showed "theoretische Ambivalenz" towards the Weimar democracy[17] the National Socialists betrayed an "innere Zweispältigkeit" with regard to capitalism[18]. The Communists organized their doctrine around a historical critique of the capitalist economic order and proposed an unequivocal program of state intervention in order to equalize the distribution of income. The National Socialists based their teachings on the notions of the "Volk" and the "Rasse" and made their clearest statements on the issue of the rise of the German nation[19]. The ideologies moved, so to speak, along different dimensions; nationalism was a matter of pragmatic choices for Communist parties, social economic policy for the National Socialists was to be formulated according to the demands of the struggle for power.

The KPD should be placed on the extreme left of the social economic policy scale just as Communist parties in other systems. But it is hard to attribute a social economic policy stand to the National Socialists at all. If the NSDAP is to be anchored on the scale, a second criterion must be used*, that of nationalism. On this basis, the National Socialists are placed at the extreme right.

The resulting rank order reflecting social economic policy positions, and, in case of indeterminacy, nationalist attitudes (which for the other parties correspond with social economic positions) is KPD (USPD) — SDAP (SPD) — DEMP — ZENT — BAYR + VOLK — WIRT — LAND — NATP — NAZI.

This agrees with the ranking advanced "somewhat impressionistically" by Sartori[20].

1.b Historical coalitions

The first post-war elections in 1919 produced a *Reichstag* where two "basic alternatives" of government prevailed: a coalition of the Democratic Party with *Zentrum*, Bavarians, *Volkspartei*, and the Nationalists (NATP), or of the Democrats with the Socialists.

What emerged, in fact, was the "Weimar coalition" under Scheidemann (2/'19). In this coalition of Socialists (SDP), Demo-

---

* Cf. Chapter 7, Section 4.

```
WEIMAR 1919
MAJORITY LARGER THAN 211
ACTORS IN ASSEMBLY   USPD    SPD   DEMP   ZENT   BAYR   VOLK   NATP
POLICY SCALE ORDER      1      2      3      4    5,5    5,5      7
SEATS IN ASSEMBLY      22    165     75     73     18     19     44
SCHEIDEMANN (2/'19)           MEMBERMEMBERMEMBER
BAUER (6/'19)                 MEMBER        MEMBER
BAUER (7/'19)                 MEMBERMEMBERMEMBER
MÜLLER (6/'20)                MEMBERMEMBERMEMBER

RESULTS OF THEORIES   WIN   MWIN   MSIZ   BRGP   MRAN   CLMR   CLCP   PDST   PD1N    PD
                     2;61    1;8    0;1    1;2    0;2    0;2   1;13   0;10   0;10   1;13
```

crats (DEMP) and Catholics (*Zentrum*), either Democrats or Catholics were unnecessary and the Catholics added to the coalition's range. The Weimar coalition was large (controlling, in fact, a $\frac{3}{4}$ majority), closed, and p.d. dominated*, also under $1,n$ permissibility.

In the early days of the Weimar Republic, conditions prevailed that conflicted with the assumptions underlying all the theories: exclusion of the Socialists from government would have created "domestic dangers", participation of the Nationalists, on the other hand, would have been considered a "frivolous provocation" by the Allied Powers[21]. In terms of the underlying model, this may be translated as "threat of civil war" and "threat of war" or at least as major influence from factors outside the parliamentary system. Also, the assumption that membership of any permissible coalition is preferred by all actors to not being a member of any permissible coalition is of doubtful validity in this case: the first task of the parties in government was to conclude a humiliating peace treaty with the allied powers and that could only be achieved with a loss of electoral appeal. Moreover, in the light of the fundamental nature of the legislation on the agenda, the actors may have felt a strong need for a broad consensus, quite independent of formally required (simple) majorities. Finally, politics in the early Republic moved along the axis of nationalism (the Versailles treaty) and federalism (the constitution), as well as on the social economic dimension. All these considerations may explain the emergence of coalitions extending beyond a minimum.

---

* The expression "p.d. dominated" refers to "domination" under the terms of policy distance theory, pure core version; domination under the $1,n$ permissibility version is mentioned separately; domination under the closed coalition version is not mentioned in most cases.

Bauer (6/'19) governed with Socialists and Catholics in a minimal winning coalition, but not of minimal range, the Democrats having been skipped in this open coalition, p.d. dominated, also under 1,n permissibility.

Only after ratification of the Peace Treaty did the Democrats join the other parties in government in a renewal of the Weimar coalition which continued with Müller (3/'20). Interestingly enough, while Bauer attempted to lead the treaty through the *Reichstag*, the Allied powers submitted an ultimatum and the situation built up until an acute threat of war existed. Finally, a parliamentary coalition of all actors accepted the Allied terms, an occurrence nevertheless contained in the predicted set of policy distance theory[22].

In the elections of June 1920, the parties of the Weimar coalition lost their majority. The Socialists (from now on "Social Democrats", SDAP) had to surrender almost a third of their seats to the Independent or Left Socialists (USPD). This time the coalition of all bourgeois parties was of minimal range, while the Bavarians (BAYR) were unnecessary for the coalition to be winning. The Weimar coalition had to be extended with either the Left Socialists into a minimal winning, minimal range, closed coalition or, with the *Volkspartei*, the "Grand coalition", of minimal range and open but minimal winning without the unnecessary Democrats.

```
WEIMAR 1920
MAJORITY LARGER THAN 229
ACTORS IN ASSEMBLY  USPD  SDAP  DEMP  ZENT  BAYR  VOLK  NATP
POLICY SCALE ORDER    1     2     3     4   5,5   5,5    7
SEATS IN ASSEMBLY    84   102    39    64    21    65    71
Fehrenbach (6/'20)               MEMBERMEMBER     MEMBER
Wirth I (5/'21)            MEMBERMEMBERMEMBER
Wirth II (10/'21)         MEMBERMEMBERMEMBER
Cuno (11/'22)                    MEMBERMEMBERMEMBERMEMBER
STRESEMANN I (8/'23)      MEMBERMEMBERMEMBER     MEMBER
STRESEMANN II (10/'23)    MEMBERMEMBERMEMBER     MEMBER
Marx I (11/'23)                  MEMBERMEMBERMEMBERMEMBER

RESULTS OF THEORIES  WIN   MWIN  MSIZ  BRGP  MRAN  CLMR  CLCP  PDST  PDIN  PDCL
                    1;61  0;16   0;1   0;6   1;8   1;4   1;9   0;6  1;12   1;9
```

A series of minority cabinets followed, each supported by a more or less identifiable coalition in the *Reichstag*; yet, these alliances were not definite enough to count the partners as members of the coalition in the sense of the theories.

167

Fehrenbach (6/'20) consisted of Democrats, *Zentrum* and *Volkspartei* with "benevolent neutrality" from the Social Democrats in the *Reichstag*: a configuration that foreshadowed the emergence of the Grand coalition[23]. Wirth I (5/'21), another minority government, succeeded this time with the Social Democrats, Democrats and *Zentrum* (the old Weimar coalition) and with support from the Left Socialists, at least in its first days: a basic alternative of the situation had it become definite. Wirth II (10/'21) continued with the same parties in government. Cuno (11/'22) was composed of Democrats, *Zentrum*, *Volkspartei* and, for the first time, Bavarians, a minority government nevertheless. Finally, Stresemann I (8/'23) brought about the grand coalition of Social Democrats, Democrats, *Zentrum* and *Volkspartei*; the Democrats were unnecessary but they did not add to the coalition's minimal range; the coalition was p.d. dominated but undominated under 1,*n* permissibility; the coalition was not (certainly) open (*i.e.* "closed"), since the position of the excluded Bavarians *vis à vis* the *Volkspartei* is indeterminate.

After a crisis over the eight hour working day, Stresemann resigned but returned after a few days with a mended cabinet, Stresemann II (10/'23), of the same composition. The Social Democrats left the government within a month protesting the all too conciliatory attitude towards the breaches of the constitution by the Bavarian state government[24].

Until the elections, Marx I (11/'23) governed with the rump cabinet from Stresemann II, saved by the Social Democrats in the *Reichstag*[25].

```
WEIMAR 1924 MAY
MAJORITY LARGER THAN 236
ACTORS IN ASSEMBLY    KPD   SDAP  DEMP  ZENT  BAYR  VOLK  NATP  NAZI
POLICY SCALE ORDER      1     2     3     4   5,5   5,5     7     8
SEATS IN ASSEMBLY      62   100    28    65    16    45    95    32
Marx II (6/'24)                    MEMBERMEMBER       MEMBER

RESULTS OF THEORIES   WIN   MWIN  MSIZ  BRGP  MRAN  CLMR  CLCP  PDST  PDIN  PDCL
                    0;113  0;26   0;1   0;3   0;6   0;5  0;13  0;23  0;31  0;13
```

After the elections of May 1924, the new *Reichstag* allowed two basic alternatives. The old Weimar parties could have constituted a minimal winning, minimal range, closed coalition with the support of the Left Socialists, who now had constituted themselves as the German Communist Party (KPD), or the bourgeois parties could have combined in such a basic alternative coalition, excluding the Communists, Social Democrats and National Socialists (NAZI). In this situation, Marx II (6/'24) chose to form a minority cabinet of Democrats, *Zentrum* and *Volkspartei*, apparently keeping his options open towards either the grand coalition with the Social Democrats or the all-bourgeois coalition with the Nationalists. The Social Democrats proved to be the more dependable allies in the *Reichstag*, especially when it came to preventing disasters in foreign policy[26]. Nevertheless, the *Reichstag* was dissolved in the hope of a more amenable majority.

After the December 1924 elections, a new party, the *Wirtschaftspartei* (WIRT), or Economic party, achieved actor status. The National Socialists lost heavily. The parties of the old Weimar coalition, Social Democrats, Democrats and *Zentrum*, could form a minimal winning, closed coalition of minimal range together with the Communists or, on the other hand, with the Bavarians and/or the *Volkspartei*. *Zentrum*, Bavarians, *Volkspartei* and Nationalists could have formed a minimal winning, minimal range coalition, closed with the addition of the unnecessary *Wirtschaftspartei*.

```
WEIMAR 1924 DECEMBER
MAJORITY LARGER THAN 246
ACTORS IN ASSEMBLY    KPD  SDAP  DEMP  ZENT  BAYR  VOLK  WIRT  NATP  NAZI
POLICY SCALE ORDER     1    2     3     4    5,5   5,5    7     8     9
SEATS IN ASSEMBLY      45  131    32    69    19    51    17   111    14
LUTHER I  (1/'25)                       MEMBERMEMBERMEMBER       MEMBER
Luther II (1/'26)                 MEMBERMEMBERMEMBERMEMBER
Marx III  (5/'26)                 MEMBERMEMBERMEMBERMEMBER
MARX IV   (1/'27)                       MEMBERMEMBERMEMBER       MEMBER

RESULTS OF THEORIES   WIN  MWIN  MSIZ  BRGP  MRAN  CLMR  CLCP  PDST  PDIN  PDCL
                     1;250 1;36  0;2   0;8   1;9   0;5   0;17  0;33  0;32  0;17
```

Luther I (1/'25) opted for the coalition of Democrats, *Zentrum*, *Volkspartei*, Bavarians and Nationalists (NATP). The Democrats were unnecessary and added to the range but their single cabinet minister, Geszler, was considered an expert, whose presence did not commit his party[27]. The Bavarians, though unnecessary, had been included; they did not add to the range. The coalition was still open because the new *Wirtschaftpartei* had been excluded. Discounting the presence of the one Democrat expert, the coalition was of minimal range; it was p.d. dominated and also under 1,*n* permissibility.

Luther II (1/'26) succeeded after the Nationalists defected over foreign policy; the presence of the Democrats in the coalition was strengthened and this time they controlled three portfolios. But together with Catholics, Bavarians and the *Volkspartei* the coalition was still in a minority. In parliament, the Social Democrats came to its aid, especially on foreign policy; this made the *Volkspartei* unnecessary and it used its position to vote against the government on foreign policy issues[28]. This parliamentary coalition corresponds, of course, to a basic alternative in the situation. However, the coalition did not become a fully fledged support coalition and Marx III (5/'26) continued with the same parties in government as his predecessor.

The exclusion of the Social Democrats from the government, even though at decisive moments they had supported it in the *Reichstag*, should be explained, in part, with reference to an outside factor: the influence of President Hindenburg, elected in April 1925, and openly hostile to Social Democratic participation[29].

Marx IV (1,2/'27) extended the cabinet coalition to include the Nationalists again: the Democrats, who had become unnecessary and adding to the range, left the government. The coalition was of minimal range, but not minimal winning because of the unnecessary Bavarians, and open because the *Wirtschaftspartei* had been excluded; it was p.d. dominated and also under $1,n$ permissibility.

In the elections of 1928, the Nazi party lost its actor status. Social Democrats (SDAP), Democrats (DEMP) and *Zentrum* again could have formed a majority with either the Communists, in which the Democrats would have been unnecessary but not adding to the range, or with the Bavarians (BAYR), minimal winning, closed and of minimal range. The coalition of all bourgeois parties (excluding Social Democrats and Communists) was equally minimal winning, closed and of minimal range.

```
WEIMAR 1928
MAJORITY LARGER THAN 245
ACTORS IN ASSEMBLY    KPD   SDAP  DEMP  ZENT  BAYR  VOLK  WIRT  NATP
POLICY SCALE ORDER     1     2     3     4    5,5   5,5    7     8
SEATS IN ASSEMBLY     54    153    25    62    16    45    23    78
MÜLLER II (6/'28)            MEMBERMEMBERMEMBERMEMBERMEMBER
Brüning I (3/'30)            MEMBERMEMBERMEMBERMEMBERMEMBER

RESULTS OF THEORIES   WIN   MWIN  MSIZ  BRGP  MRAN  CLMR  CLCP  PDST  PDIN  PDCL
                     1;114  0;21  0;2   0;9   1;8   1;5   1;12  0;13  1;15  1;12
```

Müller II (6/'28) included Social Democrats, Democrats, Catholics and Bavarians with the *Volkspartei* that was unnecessary but did not add to the range of the closed coalition (tie!), p.d. dominated but not under 1,n permissibility. Significantly, the *Volkspartei*, although represented in the cabinet, declined formally to acknowledge its commitment to vote for it and thus may not have been a member of the coalition[30].

The (too) grand coalition continued for 21 months until the Social Democrats defected over a compromise on the funding of unemployment benefits. Brüning (3/'30) next formed a minority cabinet of Democrats, Catholics, Bavarians, *Volkspartei* and, for the first time, the *Wirtschaftspartei*. Two independent conservatives made the government more acceptable to Agrarians and Nationalists who saved it against Socialist opposition. However, the alliance failed to develop into a fully fledged bourgeois coalition[31].

In September 1930, new elections were held. The National Socialists (NAZI) in one stroke became the second largest party after the Social Democrats; the Democrats lost actor status and a conservative agrarian group, *Landvolk* (LAND), became an actor. Brüning's support coalition had lost its majority.

```
WEIMAR 1930
MAJORITY LARGER THAN 288
ACTORS IN ASSEMBLY   KPD  SDAP  ZENT  BAYR  VOLK  WIRT  LAND  NATP  NAZI
POLICY SCALE ORDER    1    2     3    4,5   4,5    6     7     8     9
SEATS IN ASSEMBLY    77   143   68    19    30    23    19    41   107
Brüning I  (9/'30)               MEMBER MEMBER MEMBER MEMBER      MEMBER
Brüning II (12/'30)              MEMBER MEMBER MEMBER              MEMBER

RESULTS OF THEORIES  WIN  MWIN  MSIZ  BRGP  MRAN  CLMR  CLCP  PDST  PDIN  PDCL
                    0;212 0;37  0;2   0;3   0;5   0;5  0;11  0;39  0;55  0;11
```

Under these circumstances, a coalition of Communists, Social Democrats and Catholics would have been one vote short of a majority but the few Democratic votes could have saved it. Social Democrats and Catholics would now need the support of the Bavarians, the *Volkspartei*, the *Wirtschaftspartei* and the new *Landvolk* to achieve a minimal winning, closed coalition of minimal range. Finally, all bourgeois parties were necessary in a coalition with the National Socialists against Social Democrats and Communists, again minimal winning, closed and of minimal range.

Until December 1930, Brüning remained in the saddle with the support of Nationalists and of the Social Democrats in the *Reichstag*[32], apparently collecting another half dozen needed votes from the Democrats. The *Wirtschaftspartei* left the government but Brüning succeeded once more, in October 1931, in obtaining a majority in parliament, when Social Democrats and backbenchers from the *Volkspartei*, against their leadership, voted down a motion of non-confidence from Nationalists and National Socialists together[33].

There existed a possibility of a majority without either Communists or National Socialists but a major outside factor worked against it: seven months later, Hindenburg dismissed the Brüning cabinet in an ultimatum demanding "from this moment on and *überhaupt* a government of the right"[34]. Under the circumstances, that could only mean a government with the National Socialists.

Von Papen (5/'32) formed a cabinet of mostly military men. In the following elections of July 1932, the bourgeois center parties virtually disappeared with the exception of the *Zentrum* and its Bavarian sister party; the Nationalists held their ground but the National Socialists more than doubled their seats. The elections of November 1932 did not change the situation much. The Weimar coalition, the grand coalition, any coalition excluding both the Communists and the National Socialists had become impossible. Neither Von Papen nor his successor Von Schleichen (12/'32) ever obtained a majority in the *Reichstag*; no supporting coalition can be discerned. Finally, Hitler (1/'33) formed a cabinet with National Socialists and rightist politicians which, within two months, did away with the parliamentary system in Germany.

```
WEIMAR 1932 JULY               (Not entered in statistical tabulations)
MAJORITY LARGER THAN 304
ACTORS IN ASSEMBLY    KPD  SDAP  ZENT  BAYR  NATP  NAZI
POLICY SCALE ORDER     1     2     3     4     5     6
SEATS IN ASSEMBLY     89   133    75    22    40   230

RESULTS OF THEORIES   WIN  MWIN  MSIZ  BRGP  MRAN  CLMR  CLCP  PDST  PDIN  PDCL
                     0;31  0;5   0;1   0;3   0;5   0;2   0;5   0;8  0;10   0;5



WEIMAR 1932 NOV                (Not entered in statistical tabulations)
MAJORITY LARGER THAN 291
ACTORS IN ASSEMBLY    KPD  SDAP  ZENT  BAYR  NATP  NAZI
POLICY SCALE ORDER     1     2     3     4     5     6
SEATS IN ASSEMBLY    100   121    70    20    51   196

RESULTS OF THEORIES   WIN  MWIN  MSIZ  BRGP  MRAN  CLMR  CLCP  PDST  PDIN  PDCL
                     0;30  0;6   0;1   0;2   0;3   0;2   0;5   0;8   0;9   0;5
```

172

Weimar is a difficult country for the theories. All of them score lower than they do on the average, no theory achieves a result that approaches statistical significance. Ordinal minimal range theory shows the best performance. Out of the twenty-two governments that ruled the Weimar Republic, three — Von Papen, Von Schleichen and Hitler — can hardly be accounted for in terms of the parliamentary system. Eleven others were minority governments. The remaining eight cabinets were based on a majority coalition. The three first cabinets leaned on the Weimar coalition; the two Stresemann cabinets were based on the Grand coalition ranging from Social Democrats to *Volkspartei*; Luther I and Marx IV embraced the span between Democrats and German Nationalists; Muller II reverted to the Grand coalition. Three coalitions (the Weimar coalitions) were large, six were closed, five were of minimal range, two were minimal winning, none was p.d. undominated, three were undominated under $1,n$ permissibility, one satisfies the bargaining proposition, part of the time (Bauer).

The two open coalitions that were winning both omitted the tiny new actor, *Wirtschaftspartei*. Bauer was closed after the Peace Treaty had been concluded. The three coalitions that embraced a larger than minimal range all occurred during the founding years of the republic.

Investigation of the actual parliamentary support coalitions might yield data that agree more closely with some of the theories. A cursory inspection of the parliamentary coalitions that supported the eight minority governments formed before Brüning I (3/'30) shows that the Social Democrats did, in fact, through support or abstention uphold the cabinets of Fehrenbach, Cuno (?), Marx I, Marx II, Luther II and Marx III; the Independent Socialists saved Wirth I and II. The addition of the excluded (Left) Socialist party would have left all but two of these coalitions closed, five out of eight would be of minimal range, only one would be minimal winning. Exchanging the *Volkspartei* for the Social Democrats in Luther II and Marx III would have made these coalitions also minimal winning and of minimal range. Outside factors appear to have worked strongly against the inclusion of leftist actors in the government. Only historical research as to the parliamentary coalitions that prevailed during the period can provide these speculations with a factual base.

2. France

The French Fourth Republic represents, as does the Weimar Republic, a closed historical period. Founded after the Liberation by the Resistance, victorious over the forces of Vichy, it crumbled in the face of the threat from military and colonialist groups and was succeeded by a regime under the man who had been its first leader, De Gaulle.

2.a The parliamentary system

The Fourth Republic was constituted as a parliamentary democracy with a bicameral legislature. The Assembly, "because it was the body to which cabinets were officially responsible" was far more important than the Senate[35]. Within the Assembly, bills were passed with a simple majority but for the present purposes the most important vote was the "investiture". At first, a cabinet was voted in office by a single absolute majority vote; in 1947, the custom of a double vote, one on the Prime Minister and one on his cabinet team, was revived presenting the Premier with a few dozens of extra votes in the first round from representatives still hoping to be included in the cabinet[36]. From 1954 on, the vote was by simple majority and on the cabinet as a whole only. Though, constitutionally, an absolute majority was required to vote down the Cabinet, most Premiers resigned in the face of an antagonistic simple majority[37]. For the reasons outlined in Chapter 7, it is assumed that a coalition had to comprise actors who nominally controlled an absolute majority of the votes in the Assembly; the Senate is ignored.

Within the Assembly, no veto positions, formal or informal, appear to have existed and in the constitutional system, Cabinet and Assembly were relatively supreme *vis à vis* the other organs of the state. No institutions, foreign or domestic, seem to have been so paramount that influence on the parliamentary system warrants the inclusion of special assumptions. Though the French army waged colonial wars throughout most of the life of the Fourth Republic, these wars did not unite the French nation as a whole against the colonial people; rather, colonial policy continued to be an issue within the French political system, reflected by the lines of cleavage in the Assembly. Thus, the "threat of war" condition did not apply, not even in 1954, and until the last years of the Republic the "threat of civil war" was not acute.

174

Having thus defined the French Assembly and the Cabinet supported by its majority coalition as the relatively "closed" setting, it is now necessary to determine the weights and policy positions of the actors.

Parliamentary politics in the Fourth Republic consisted in the interplay of six major political movements: the Communist (PCF), the Social Democrat (SFIO), the Christian Democrat (MRP), the Radicals (organized mainly in the UDSR and the RGR), the Conservatives (loosely assembled in various factional organizations), and the Gaullist (RPF). The Assembly has been called a "hexagonal" Chamber*[38].

Whether parliamentary politics in France should or can be described in terms of ideology, or even policy position, at all, is itself a subject of controversy. Leites, for one, writes

"Though there is little 'doctrine' in French politics, what does, of course, exist for each major political tendency, and what often gives the impression of 'doctrine', is a set of somewhat special and more or less emotion-laden phrases."[39]

On the other hand, French authors tend to make much of

"The intellectualism, the penchant for coherent systems of thought, and the value attached to symbols, which characterize French political life very often to the detriment of a sense of reality and a desire for concrete accomplishments."[40]

But this judgment, from 1951, may have become outdated:

"Car la pauvreté idéologique des années cinquante frappe surtout parce qu'elle contraste avec l'abondance d'écrits ou d'initiatives des années trente."[41]

Converse and Dupeux find in their study of the politicization of the electorate in France and the United States

"no striking reason to believe that the French citizen.....is predisposed to form political opinions which are more sharply crystallized or which embrace a more comprehensive range of political issues than do comparable Americans."[42]

Therefore "the ideological clarity or intransigence associated with

---

* It has also been characterized as "triangular": an egalitarian left, an authoritarian right, and a libertarian centre; Micaud (1956) p. 108.

French political elites" may not so much reflect properties of the mass public, but rather survives only because the multi-party system allows "the purest possible expression of the total configuration of positions adopted on crosscutting issue dimensions"[43].

In Leites' view, the game of French politics is one of dodging responsibilities and jockeying for cabinet positions, a conception that would agree with Riker's basic assumptions on the nature of politics. But MacRae, after extensive analysis of roll call votes in the French Assembly concludes

"We have examined the prevalent hypothesis that cabinets were overthrown by the ambitions of would-be ministers: yet statistical evidence for this has been hard to find."[44]

Discussing the divisions among coalition partners that brought about the downfall of the cabinet, MacRae states

"Among the many factors that contributed to these divisions ideology seems to have predominated."[45]

Granted that ideology did matter in French political life, the question arises as to what kind of policy space would reflect that political reality. Leites' incidental expression "hexagonal" seems to refer to the widespread notion that "les extrèmes se touchent" or that extreme parties were oppposed to each other in some respect, yet approached one another in others. Ideological space may not resemble a continuum, but a circle, or a horseshoe.

Another conception of the pattern of cleavage in French politics has had considerable influence: Duverger's overlapping of dualisms.

"It consists in the non-coincidence of a number of different dualisms of opinion with the result that their combinations produce a multi-partite division."[46]

Thus the Communists are "East, Planning, Anti-clerical"; the Right, in all respects their opposite, stands for "West, Freedom, Clerical". The other parties are also classified according to this binary system.

Very consistently, Duverger argues

"Such splits give rise to Centre parties. It has already been shown that there exists no Centre opinion, no Centre tendency, no Centre doctrine separate in kind from the doctrines of the Right or of the Left — but only a dilution of their doctrines, an attenuation, a moderate doctrine."[46]

Sartori presents an argument against this, concluding

"In any case, no matter how we wish to interpret a center opinion, the fact remains that Duverger's statement should be reversed. A center opinion, or a center tendency, always exists in politics; what may not exist is a center party."[47]

Whatever the true state of affairs, both arguments are more definitional than factual in character, the debate remaning mainly scholastic: no data on party policy positions have been tested on their scalability. Unfortunately the one major research study that could have provided an empirically founded spatial representation of French parties at the elite level stops short of drawing just the necessary inferences from the data: MacRae scales only individual deputies within a given party on scales obtained from clusters of roll call votes with a high index of similarity (Yule's Q) as computed over the votes of the deputies from that party only[48]. Scales differ with parties and therefore no overall continuum can be constructed.

From the literature on French parliamentary history, sufficient information may be gleaned to rank the parties with regard to their social economic policy positions.

The Communist party (PCF) is to be situated at the left extreme because of its adherence to Marxist doctrine. The Social Democrats, united in the SFIO, would fit the general pattern as adherents of a more moderate policy of equalizing income distribution through the means of the government budget and direct state intervention. In social economic matters, the MRP probably comes next:

"In Parliament, it came to be attacked by the Socialists, because of the latter's long standing anti-clerical animosities as well because of the fear that it might not want to be sufficiently progressive in social terms; it came to be attacked by the Radicals because it was felt to be too progressive."[49]

MacRae also places the MRP to the left of the Radicals on the issue of social legislation[50].

"the Peasants, the Independents, and the Radicals were in no way inclined to make concessions to socialism. Quite the contrary, they reasoned that it was necessary to decide squarely in favor of a liberal economic policy."[51]

The Radicals occupied "the centre of gravity" in the Assembly[52]. Their social and economic policy position was characterized by "their opposition to the political and social innovations of the Liberation and their fidelity to the traditional economic system of free enterprise and private initiative"[53].

The UDSR was founded as the party of the anti-Communist stream in the Resistance. At first, the association of many Radicals with the Vichy regime kept the UDSR away from them but, gradually, the parties grew closer, for some time after 1946 even uniting in a loose anti-Socialist, anti-clerical alliance, RGR, mostly for electoral purposes[54]. MacRae, who analyzes the votes of UDSR and Radicals together, does not seem to find cleavages that correspond with membership in the different factions. The parties must be considered tying and have not been lumped together as a single actor only because, at times, only one of them participated in the government while the other stayed out of it. That did not signify consistent support by the coalition partner and antagonism by the outside party: just as with the Independents and Peasants, one finds a "total lack of concern for discipline, except for occasional outbursts which soon fade"[55].

One is tempted to describe the Conservatives as similar to the Radicals, only more of the same: antagonism towards social reform, taxation and government intervention, support from peasants and shopkeepers, "but the Conservatives also receive considerable support from employers"[56]. The Conservatives (or, "Moderates" as they prefer to call themselves) were initially organized in two parliamentary groups, the PRL and the RI ("Independents"). Apparently, the Independents were more governmental than their PRL colleagues[57] but this is an aspect of coalition behavior rather than an independent indicator of policy position. MacRae, who scales RI and PRL members the same, does not mention cleavages that correspond with factional membership. On these grounds, RI and PRL, though both, without doubt, at the extreme right of the Assembly, can only be ranked *vis à vis* each other with a certain measure of doubt. The two factions joined ranks after 1951 in the CNIP and with some Peasant deputies and a number of former Gaullists, the CNIP group came to represent "the greatest unity the parliamentary Right had ever achieved"[58]. Yet, this unity was not always expressed in votes, discipline remained low and Independent support to the government involved an element of uncertainty.

After the split, the so called Antier-faction organized itself in the more "pro-Gaullist" PUS and it was placed immediately to the right of the Gaullist RPF. The *Action Paysanne* (AP) remained on the extreme, to the right of the Independents.

Two important but short-lived movements further complicate the pattern of cleavages on the right: Gaullism and Poujadism. Long before the RPF entered the Assembly under the banner of Gaullism, the movement counted representatives in the Chamber. Launching his *Rassemblement du Peuple Français*, general De Gaulle generously invited incumbent deputies of all parties to join, while remaining in their parties if they so wished. PCF, SFIO and MRP forbade their members to join; dissident MRP deputies formed the *Action Républicaine*[59], the first Gaullist group to achieve actor's status although it was for a short period only. In the meantime, the Gaullists swept the country in the municipal elections (1947) and a year later claimed a great victory in the Senate elections. But in that body occurred what was to repeat itself in the Second Legislature: candidates rode the general's coat-tails only to defect in great numbers once they had been securely appointed to their seat. Thus, even at a time when the Gaullists boasted large support in the First Legislature, they could only muster two dozen votes when they wished to impose party discipline and even that for a brief period only[60].

Gaullism has been called a resurgence of Bonapartism[61] and has been compared to Fascism, because of its authoritarian structure, nationalism and leadership cult; the "determination to come to power legally"[62] does not necessarily detract from the comparison but in combination with de Gaulle's personality, religious convictions and Resistance past, it checked the growth of Fascist tendencies within the movement. Twelve years of government experience with the moderate UNR may, in looking back, soften the contours of its predecessor RPF. Yet, in the context of the parliamentary system, what kept Gaullism from working as a Rightist surge was, except for De Gaulle himself, precisely what it had set out to combat: the egotistical politics of the deputies. Mostly Radical and Conservative representatives responded to the Gaullist call but, once elected, many of them quickly changed their tune and reverted to their old political positions and allegiances: RPF lost many deputies and split in two factions, URAS (later RS), following the Gaullist line, ARS gathering the veteran Conservatives[63].

The economic program of the Gaullists was based on the much celebrated phrase of "association of capital and labor". In fact, the parliamentary groups of the Gaullists took a moderately conservative stand in social and economic matters, not unwilling to support social legislation at times, and sometimes even attacking the great employers' organization *Patronat*[64]. Therefore, the Gaullist factions are placed between the Radicals and the Independents on the continuum, ignoring their positions concerning nationalism, the constitution and "the Republic", on which they might be situated more to the right, as they certainly were in the context of politics-in-the-country.

Poujade, more outspoken in his dislikes, more reticent in his sympathies than de Gaulle, headed the next surge movement that was to cause upheaval in the country and in the Assembly. His UDCA combined economic extremism with extreme nationalism, a profound disgust for the constitutional system, an authoritarian structure and a most personal leadership. Initial flirtations from the Communists passed quickly into bitter and mutual hostility[65]. As one proceeds to the right of the spectrum, attitudes among the other parties only very gradually become warmer[66]. Though favorably disposed toward an authoritarian state, it should have little or no power in economic matters in the Poujadist view: restoration of economic freedom, reduction of state intervention (*"desétatisation"*), return to private ownership of state enterprises: "les rémèdes proposés contre la condition actuelle du prolétariat sont singulièrement conservateurs."[67] On the social economic dimension, as on others, Poujadism may be situated at the extreme right, when its programmatic position is used as a criterion, as is the rule in this study. Its electoral support may have come from quite different directions.

In conclusion, the order proposed for the French actors, primarily based on social economic policy positions is

$$PCF-SFIO-MRP-RAD+UDSR-GAUL-\underset{(RI-PRL)}{\overset{CONS}{}}-PAYS\ (POUJ)$$

Only with regard to the position *vis à vis* each other of the Peasant (PAYS) groups and the Conservatives (and, among the latter, of RI and PRL) considerable doubt remains. The MRP should be placed to the right of the Radicals on the issue of clericalism: this apparently is how the voters perceive the situation, when asked to classify parties as right or left[68] or according to their patterns of change between consecutive elections[69]. With regard to nationalism and antisystem attitudes, the Gaullists belong further to the right. However, for reasons of theoretical necessity, the social economic ranking is maintained. Fox advances as his main hypothesis: "the basic division in French politics has been drawn along economic class lines"[70]. If the evidence supports the theories that have been operationalized with the continuum outlined above, it also supports Fox's hypothesis. The voting strenght, or weight, of the actors is based on data supplied by MacRae: they surpass sources for other countries in precision, especially with regard to the later years of each legislature, when defections and regroupings had changed the picture. As a result, some eight actors are part of each situation. For the constitutional Assemblies, data have been taken from Williams who mentions only the initial strength of the major political groupings, combining the Conservatives and Peasants under one heading.

2.b Historical coalitions

For the Constituent Assemblies of 1945 and 1946, only Williams' data are available. The Social Democrats (SFIO) held a key position in the 1945 Assembly: they could have formed a closed, minimal winning coalition of minimal range with either the Communists (PCF) or the Catholics (MRP). The other parties had no part in either basic alternative.

```
FRANCE 1945                     (Source of this Table: Ph. Williams)
MAJORITY LARGER THAN 293
ACTORS IN ASSEMBLY   PCF   SFIO   MRP    RAD   UDSR   CONS
POLICY SCALE ORDER    1     2      3     4,5   4,5     6
SEATS IN ASSEMBLY    161   150    150    28    29     64
DE GAULLE (11/'45)  MEMBERMEMBERMEMBERMEMBERMEMBERMEMBER
GOUIN (1/'46)        MEMBERMEMBERMEMBER

RESULTS OF THEORIES  WIN   MWIN  MSIZ  BRGP  MRAN  CLMR  CLCP  PDST  PD1N  PDCL
                     2;32  0;3   0;1   0;3   0;2   0;2   2;11  2;9   1;6   2;10
```

De Gaulle (11/'45) governed with a cabinet of all parties, all but the Social Democrats and either the Communists or the Catholics being unnecessary and adding to the range. The coalition was, however, closed and large and undominated in policy distance theory. It was, by definition, not 1,n permissible. Gouin (1/'46) succeeded with a cabinet of Communists, Social Democrats and Catholics, either the first or the last unnecessary and adding to the range of the coalition that was closed, large and undominated in policy distance theory.

181

After the elections of February 1946, only one basic alternative remained: the coalition of Social Democrats and Catholics, minimal winning and of minimal range. Bidault I (6/'46), however, continued the government of Communists, Social Democrats and Catholics, even though the Communists were unnecessary and added to the range of the large and closed coalition; it was still undominated in policy distance theory.

The constitutional legislation on the agenda may have inspired

FRANCE 1946
MAJORITY LARGER THAN 293

ACTORS IN ASSEMBLY	PCF	SFIO	MRP	RAD	UDSR	CONS				
POLICY SCALE ORDER	1	2	3	4,5	4,5	6				
SEATS IN ASSEMBLY	153	129	169	32	21	67				
BIDAULT I (6/'46)	MEMBER	MEMBER	MEMBER							
RESULTS OF THEORIES	WIN	MWIN	MSIZ	BRGP	MRAN	CLMR	CLCP	PDST	PDIN	PDCL
	1;31	0;5	0;1	0;2	0;1	0;1	1;10	1;17	1;11	1;10

the desire for a broad consensus and thus prompted the creation of large cabinet coalitions; the formal requirement for acceptance of the constitutional bills was only a simple majority in Parliament and subsequent ratification by referendum[71].

The elections of October 1946 robbed the Social Democrat SFIO of its key position: a coalition of Communists, Social Democrats and Catholics would have been closed and of minimal range but the Social Democrats were unnecessary. The second possibility was a coalition of Social Democrats, Catholics and Radicals minimal winning, closed and of minimal range. The other bourgeois parties were "hors concours" in any minimal range coalition.

FRANCE 1947   (Source of this and following Tables: MacRae)
MAJORITY LARGER THAN 309

ACTORS IN ASSEMBLY	PCF	SFIO	MRP	RAD	UDSR	RI	PRL			
POLICY SCALE ORDER	1	2	3	4,5	4,5	6	7			
SEATS IN ASSEMBLY	182	104	167	43	26	28	35			
RAMADIER I (1/'47)	MEMBER	MEMBER	MEMBER	MEMBER	MEMBER	MEMBER				
RAMADIER II (10/'47)		MEMBER	MEMBER	MEMBER	MEMBER	MEMBER	MEMBER			
RESULTS OF THEORIES	WIN	MWIN	MSIZ	BRGP	MRAN	CLMR	CLCP	PDST	PDIN	PDCL
	2;60	0;10	0;1	0;1	0;4	0;3	2;10	2;33	2;24	2;10

Ramadier I (1/'47) once more formed a government of all actors (except a small Conservative faction, PRL). The Communists left the government on the issues of the Cold War, the Indo-Chinese war and wage policy[72]. Ramadier II (10/'47) included all parties except the Communists and PRL. With or without the Communists, the Ramadier cabinets contained unnecessary members that added to the range of the coalition. And with or without Communist membership, these coalitions were undominated in policy distance theory; in both cases they were closed. With the Communists the coalition was large.

Though policy distance theory and the closed coalition proposition succesfully predict the foregoing governments, while minimal range theory and minimal winning theory exclude them, not much light is shed on the historical fact of the exclusion of the Communists. Policy distance and minimal range theory also include among their predictions coalitions in which right wing parties were ousted instead of the Communists. Therefore, factors outside the parliamentary system proper, such as the huge personal influence of General De Gaulle, the pressure against Communist participation exerted by the United States through financial aid and the hardening of Cold War attitudes, must explain the departure of the Communists.*

The succeeding governments show roughly the same pattern: a coalition of Social Democrats, Catholics, Radicals and UDSR with some right-wing faction(s) which were unnecessary and added to the range. Thus, Schuman (11/'47) governed with this combination, RI being the right-wing member. The coalition was open (omitting the Gaullist AR) until, in mid-term, the RI left the government and the new Schuman coalition was closed. (This coalition was entered in the tabulations.) With and without the RI the coalition is predicted by policy distance theory.

```
FRANCE 1947
MAJORITY LARGER THAN 309
ACTORS IN ASSEMBLY   PCF  SFIO   MRP   RAD  UDSR    AR    RI   PRL
POLICY SCALE ORDER     1     2     3   4,5   4,5     6     7     8
SEATS IN ASSEMBLY    184   103   155    43    27    18    25    34
SCHUMAN (11/'47)          MEMBERMEMBERMEMBERMEMBERMEMBERMEMBER

RESULTS OF THEORIES  WIN  MWIN  MSIZ  BRGP  MRAN  CLMR  CLCP  PDST  PDIN  PDCL
                   1;120  0;14   0;2   0;1   0;3   0;2  1;11  1;57  1;43  1;11
```

---

* Their departure came only briefly after a visit by Schuman to the United States. On that occasion Marshall aid was promised, but the U.S. government also expressed its displeasure in Communist participation in the French government. In May De Gaulle gave his Bayeux speech calling for unity against Communism; cf.Fauvet (1959) pp. 117—118.

FRANCE 1948
MAJORITY LARGER THAN 309

ACTORS IN ASSEMBLY	PCF	SFIO	MRP	RAD	UDSR	AR	RI	PRL
POLICY SCALE ORDER	1	2	3	4,5	4,5	6	7	8
SEATS IN ASSEMBLY	183	102	152	43	27	18	24	34
MARIE (7/'48)		MEMBER	MEMBER	MEMBER	MEMBER		MEMBER	MEMBER

RESULTS OF THEORIES	WIN	MWIN	MSIZ	BRGP	MRAN	CLMR	CLCP	PDST	PDIN	PDCL
	1;117	0;13	0;1	0;1	0;3	0;2	0;11	1;54	1;40	0;11

Marie (7/'48) continued the pattern, adding both RI and PRL as rightist members; the coalition is again open (still omitting the Gaullist AR) but predicted by policy distance theory. In the country, the Gaullists had rallied around the RPF and they had scored great victories in the municipal and cantonal elections. In the Assembly, representatives of Gaullist persuasion began to realign themselves and this led, among other things, to the disintegration of AR. Thus Queille (9/'48), of the same composition as Marie, was closed since AR had disappeared as the (omitted) actor. The UDSR also disintegrated through defections to a new Gaullist faction and thus the Social Democrat—Catholic—Radical—UDSR coalition lost its majority[73]. Both Marie and Queille had been p.d. undominated and under $1,n$ permissibility.

FRANCE 1948
MAJORITY LARGER THAN 309

ACTORS IN ASSEMBLY	PCF	SFIO	MRP	RAD	UDSR	RI	PRL
POLICY SCALE ORDER	1	2	3	4,5	4,5	6	7
SEATS IN ASSEMBLY	181	102	152	45	25	24	34
QUEILLE I (9/'48)		MEMBER	MEMBER	MEMBER	MEMBER	MEMBER	MEMBER

RESULTS OF THEORIES	WIN	MWIN	MSIZ	BRGP	MRAN	CLMR	CLCP	PDST	PDIN	PDCL
	1;55	0;9	0;1	0;1	0;3	0;2	1;9	1;29	1;20	1;9

Bidault II (10/'49) continued with the Social Democrats, Catholics and Radicals; RI was added and, unnecessarily and adding to the range, a Peasant group. With the Gaullists being omitted, the coaliton was open but it was predicted by policy distance theory. The Socialists "found themselves less and less at ease in govern-

FRANCE 1949
MAJORITY LARGER THAN 309

ACTORS IN ASSEMBLY	PCF	SFIO	MRP	RAD	GAUL	RI	PRL	PAYS
POLICY SCALE ORDER	1	2	3	4	5	6,5	6,5	8
SEATS IN ASSEMBLY	181	99	150	47	22	24	30	16
BIDAULT II (10/'49)		MEMBER	MEMBER	MEMBER		MEMBER		MEMBER

RESULTS OF THEORIES	WIN	MWIN	MSIZ	BRGP	MRAN	CLMR	CLCP	PDST	PDIN	PDCL
	1;113	0;15	0;1	0;1	0;3	0;2	0;12	1;57	1;39	0;12

ments where Moderates and Conservatives counted for more and more"[74] and as they had deserted Queille, they now abandoned Bidault. This time Pleven (7/'50) attempted a continuation: Social Democrats, Catholics and Radicals with RI and, unnecessary and adding to the range, PRL; the coalition was again open because of the exclusion of the Gaullists but predicted by policy distance theory. The same applies to Queille II (3/'51), who exchanged PRL for the Peasant group (PAYS).

```
FRANCE 1950
MAJORITY LARGER THAN 309
ACTORS IN ASSEMBLY   PCF   SFIO    MRP    RAD   GAUL    RI    PRL   PAYS
POLICY SCALE ORDER    1     2       3      4     5     6,5   6,5    8
SEATS IN ASSEMBLY    176    99     145     46    22     24    28    21
PLEVEN I (7/'50)           MEMBERMEMBERMEMBER        MEMBERMEMBER

RESULTS OF THEORIES  WIN   MWIN   MSIZ   BRGP   MRAN   CLMR   CLCP   PDST   PD1N   PDCL
                     1;112  0;17   0;2    0;1    0;3    0;2    0;12   1;55   1;38   0;12
```

```
FRANCE 1951
MAJORITY LARGER THAN 313
ACTORS IN ASSEMBLY   PCF   SFIO    MRP    RAD   GAUL    RI    PRL   PAYS
POLICY SCALE ORDER    1     2       3      4     5     6,5   6,5    8
SEATS IN ASSEMBLY    177    99     145     46    23     25    27    23
QUEILLE II (3/'51)         MEMBERMEMBERMEMBER        MEMBER        MEMBER

RESULTS OF THEORIES  WIN   MWIN   MSIZ   BRGP   MRAN   CLMR   CLCP   PDST   PD1N   PDCL
                     1;110  0;16   0;2    0;1    0;9    0;4    0;11   1;51   1;35   0;11
```

The first six years of the Fourth French Republic were marked by the persistence of coalitions with unnecessary members and exceeding the minimal range. Moreover, the presence of Gaullist factions, positioned on the social—economic policy scale between the UDSR and the Conservative factions and remaining in opposition throughout, made for a series of open coalitions. The extended membership of the coalitions cannot be explained well by reference to the uncertainty of coalition builders as to the reliability of the support by member parliamentary groups. In fact, the Communists (PCF), Social Democrats (SFIO) and Catholics (MRP) maintained a quite strict voting discipline; the Radicals suffered defections[75]. The unreliable partners were the Conservative groups, but then, why add them if they are not only unnecessary but also unpredictable?

Policy distance theory predicts all ten governments up to the 1951 elections. This remarkably good performance should be con-

185

sidered against the background of the large number of predictions made in every situation. But taking this into account, the success ratio still remains the highest of the theories. Apparently, at least in this period of French politics, actors did strive to bring about coalitions, the policy of which they expected to coincide most closely with their own most preferred policies; moreover, Catholics and Radicals succeeded in enforcing their preference for UDSR and Conservative support, even though unnecessary and adding to the range, against the objections of the Social Democrats.

In one stroke, the elections of 1951 made the Gaullist RPF movement the largest actor in the Assembly; the Conservative current was represented by two actors, the Independents and the Peasants[76]. UDSR made its comeback as a small actor.

Because of the Communist losses, an all-bourgeois coalition (without Communists and Social Democrats) had become a possibility for the first time: Catholics, Radicals, Gaullists and Independents could form a minimal winning coalition of minimal range but open without the unnecessary UDSR. Social Democrats, Catholics and Gaullists were one vote short of a majority and with either Radical or UDSR support the coalition would be minimal winning and of minimal range but open as long as not both were included. The coalition of Communists, Social Democrats, Catholics and Radicals was closed, minimal winning and of minimal range: a basic alternative in that situation.

Under the given circumstances, no minimal range coalition was possible without either the Gaullists or the Communists. Since the tripartite coalition of Social Democrats, Catholics and Radicals (plus UDSR), known as the "Third Force", had lost its majority through Gaullist defections long before the elections, the situation had come to resemble that in the Weimar Republic of 1920; there, the "Weimar coalition" of Social Democrats, Democrats and Catholics had lost its majority and the task was to bring these parties in one government with a bourgeois nationalist party, the *Volkspartei*; in France, the unwilling fourth partner was the Gaullist RPF.

The new Assembly first voted a minority government in power; Pleven II (8/'51) constisted of Catholics, Radicals, UDSR and Conservatives (Independents and Peasants). The Social Democrats supported the investiture[77]. The parliamentary coalition was minimal winning, but open because it did not include the Gaullists, and it exceeded the minimal range because it included the Conservatives instead. On the other hand, the very controversial compromise bill on education was passed with Gaullist support*, a parliamentary coalition that was closed (but not minimal winning or minimal range because of the presence of, amongst others, the Peasants).

FRANCE 1951
MAJORITY LARGER THAN 313

ACTORS IN ASSEMBLY	PCF	SFIO	MRP	RAD	UDSR	RPF	IND	PAYS
POLICY SCALE ORDER	1	2	3	4,5	4,5	6	7	8
SEATS IN ASSEMBLY	102	106	87	75	16	120	53	42
Pleven II (8/'51)			MEMBER	MEMBER	MEMBER		MEMBER	MEMBER

RESULTS OF THEORIES	WIN	MWIN	MSIZ	BRGP	MRAN	CLMR	CLCP	PDST	PD1N	PDCL
	0;117	0;29	0;3	0;1	0;8	0;4	0;10	0;10	0;21	0;10

The position of the Gaullists on the policy scale appears problematical. Leiserson places the RPF on the extreme right of his policy scale, until the URAS split off and joined the government[78].

In his case, Leiserson is justified in doing so, because his policy scale is based upon three factors: social conservatism, clericalism and system attitudes[†]. Once the URAS reconciled itself with the French system, its place on the scale changed accordingly. In the present study, the policy scale is based on social economic policy preferences alone and the attitudes towards the system (*i.e.*, towards the government in power) are to be explained, rather than to be assumed. It has been argued before that, on the score of social economic policy, the Gaullist factions are best positioned between UDSR and the Conservative groups.

Faure I (1/'52) continued the minority cabinet with Catholics, Radicals, UDSR and the two Conservative actors, IND and AP. In the Assembly, his government was also supported by the Social Democrats. The cabinet fell after Radicals and Independents deserted it over a wage and tax bill[79]. Pinay (3/'52) continued on the same basis but this time he received support from the "right-wing" faction of the Gaullists (ARS); MacRae for the first time

---

* See Fauvet (1959) pp. 186—187, for a discussion of different "majorities" on the dimensions of foreign policy, social policy, education and "support for the (Pleven) cabinet".
† The distance between any two parties is measured by attributing one unit to each (dichotomized) issue dimension on which the two parties take a different side.

187

places the Gaullist RPF between UDSR and Independents instead of at the extreme right[80]. In this study, the policy scale remains constant for an entire period 1918—1940 or after 1945.

Both coalitions — with Social Democrat or with Gaullist support — were p.d. dominated.

PUS was a Gaullist-oriented faction of peasants and conservatives, reuniting after a short time with the *Action Paysanne*.

```
FRANCE 1952
MAJORITY LARGER THAN 313
ACTORS IN ASSEMBLY   PCF   SFIO   MRP    RAD    UDSR   RPF   PUS   IND    AP
POLICY SCALE ORDER    1     2      3     4,5    4,5     6     7     8      9
SEATS IN ASSEMBLY    101   106    88     75      23    117    23    54     22
Faure I (1/'52)                   MEMBERMEMBERMEMBER          MEMBERMEMBER
Pinay (3/'52)                     MEMBERMEMBERMEMBER          MEMBERMEMBER

RESULTS OF THEORIES  WIN   MWIN   MSIZ   BRGP   MRAN   CLMR   CLCP   PDST   PD1N   PDCL
                    0;244  0;48   0;3    0;1    0;9    0;6    0;15   0;21   0;34   0;15
```

The split in the RPF became permanent when the pro-government deputies formed a separate faction, ARS, that voted for the cabinet of Mayer (1/'53). The government now received parliamentary support from the MRP, the Radicals and UDSR, and from ARS, Independents and Peasants, all necessary actors; this coalition was predicted by minimal winning theory but not by policy distance theory or minimal range theory, a coalition with RPF instead of the Peasant group having a smaller range. As an open coalition, it contradicted those theories that limit their predictions to closed coalitions.

```
FRANCE 1953
MAJORITY LARGER THAN 313
ACTORS IN ASSEMBLY   PCF   SFIO   MRP    RAD    UDSR   RPF   ARS   IND    PAYS
POLICY SCALE ORDER    1     2      3     4,5    4,5     6     7     8      9
SEATS IN ASSEMBLY    100   105    89     75      23    83    32    55     48
MAYER (1/'53)                     MEMBERMEMBERMEMBER         MEMBERMEMBERMEMBER

RESULTS OF THEORIES  WIN   MWIN   MSIZ   BRGP   MRAN   CLMR   CLCP   PDST   PD1N   PDCL
                    1;239  1;55   0;1    0;21   0;9    0;6    0;14   0;20   0;37   1;14
```

Because of an increase in organized membership on the right of the Assembly, a coalition without either Communists, Socialists or

---

* MacRae's order of parties is inspired by their attitudes towards the government in power, cf.MacRae (1967) p. 119.

Catholics had become a possibility. This coalition would have been of minimal range, minimal winning and of minimum size, closed and, of course, a basic alternative in the situation.

The presence of the RPF creates problems for minimal range theory, policy distance theory and the closed coalition proposition. The place of the Gaullists in the middle of the scale apparently does not correspond with its proclivity for oppositional tactics.

However, under Laniel (6/'53) the full incorporation of the Gaullists into the coalitional game was achieved; RPF enters the government under Laniel, a coalition of all parties except Socialists and Communists; every single actor except MRP can be missed and the Peasants add to the coalition's range but the coalition is closed and also predicted by policy distance theory, closed coalition version.

```
FRANCE 1953
MAJORITY LARGER THAN 313
ACTORS IN ASSEMBLY   PCF  SFIO   MRP   RAD  UDSR   RPF   ARS   IND  PAYS
POLICY SCALE ORDER     1    2     3    4,5   4,5    6     7     8     9
SEATS IN ASSEMBLY    100  105    88    75    23    78    33    54    48
LANIEL (6/'53)                  MEMBERMEMBERMEMBERMEMBERMEMBERMEMBERMEMBER

RESULTS OF THEORIES  WIN  MWIN  MSIZ  BRGP  MRAN  CLMR  CLCP  PDST  PD1N  PDCL
                   1;236  0;55  0;2  0;21  0;8   0;5  1;13  0;23  0;41  1;13
```

Laniel met his defeat over his Indo-China policy after the RPF (now calling itself URAS) and the Radicals defected. Under these conditions, Mendès-France (6/'54) formed a cabinet which, for the first time in the Fourth Republic, governed without the MRP. The government members, Radicals and UDSR, the Gaullist RS (formerly RPF and URAS) and ARS, and the Conservative RI and Peasants received Communist and Social Democrat support in the Assembly. Paradoxically, this cabinet without the Communists, Social Democrats and Catholics came before the Assembly at a moment that a majority without these three parties was no longer possible because the other actors had suffered some defections.

No theory predicts the coalition that *supported* Mendès-France in parliament: it was large, closed and contained, in addition to the cabinet coalition, the Communists and Peasants; either the Social Democrats or the Peasants were unnecessary members, all but the latter adding to its range. However, the position of the Communists is hard to classify. They voted for the government but Mendès-France declared before the vote that he would ignore their support[81]. Yet, even without the Communists, the parliamentary coalition contradicts every theory. Most likely it should be considered as a grand national coalition to carry the nation through the shock of the lost battle at Dien Bien Phu and the subsequent defeat in the Indo-China war. Even though France was involved in colonial warfare throughout the existence of the Fourth Republic, and though these expeditions were politically very controversial, they rarely created a situation in which a threat of war or civil war prevailed. In 1954, the crisis had become acute and the next time the colonial issues reached a crisis, the Fourth Republic collapsed.

Faure II (2/'55) formed an all-bourgeois government containing

```
FRANCE 1954
MAJORITY LARGER THAN 313
ACTORS IN ASSEMBLY    PCF  SFIO   MRP   RAD  UDSR    RS   ARS    RI   IND  PAYS
POLICY SCALE ORDER      1     2     3   4,5   4,5     6     7     8     9    10
SEATS IN ASSEMBLY      99   105    86    76    24    73    33    54    26    23
Mendès-France (6/'54)              MEMBERMEMBERMEMBERMEMBERMEMBER              MEMBER
FAURE II (2/'55)                   MEMBERMEMBERMEMBERMEMBERMEMBERMEMBERMEMBERMEMBER

RESULTS OF THEORIES   WIN  MWIN  MSIZ  BRGP  MRAN  CLMR  CLCP  PDST  PDIN  PDCL
                    1;460  0;90   0;6  0;14   0;7   0;5  1;16  0;43  0;65  1;16
```

the Catholics, the Radicals, UDSR, the Gaullist RS, the dissident ARS, RI, Independents and the Peasants. The Peasants unnecessarily added to the range of the closed coalition, which was p.d. dominated also under 1,n permissibility.

With the elections for the Third Assembly, the Communists once more became the largest party. The Gaullist movement virtually disappeared only surviving as an actor in RS (*Républicains Sociaux*). The followers of the new surge movement of Poujade formed an actor on the extreme right. RDA, a group of deputies mainly from overseas departments, closely affiliated to the UDSR, acquired actor status.

```
FRANCE 1956
MAJORITY LARGER THAN 298
ACTORS IN ASSEMBLY    PCF  SFIO   MRP   RAD   RDA    RS   IND  POUJ
POLICY SCALE ORDER      1     2     3   4,5   4,5     6     7     8
SEATS IN ASSEMBLY     150    98    74    58    32    22    85    40
Mollet (2/'56)              MEMBER      MEMBERMEMBERMEMBER

RESULTS OF THEORIES   WIN  MWIN  MSIZ  BRGP  MRAN  CLMR  CLCP  PDST  PDIN  PDCL
                    0;112  0;24   0;3   0;4   0;7   0;3  0;10  0;14  0;23  0;10
```

Two basic alternatives emerged, *i.e.* center—left (Communist, Social Democrats and Catholics) and center—right (Catholics, Radicals, RDA, Gaullists (RS), Independents and Poujadists). Both coalitions were minimal winning, closed and of minimal range. The centre coalition of Social Democrats, Catholics, Radicals and Independents was open without the unnecessary Gaullists and RDA.

```
FRANCE 1957
MAJORITY LARGER THAN 298
ACTORS IN ASSEMBLY    PCF   SFIO   MRP   RAD   RDA   RS   IND   POUJ
POLICY SCALE ORDER      1      2     3   4,5   4,5    6     7      8
SEATS IN ASSEMBLY     149    101    74    58    35   21    92     37
Bourgès Mannoury (6/'57) MEMBER      MEMBERMEMBER
GAILLARD (11/'57)         MEMBERMEMBERMEMBERMEMBERMEMBERMEMBER
RESULTS OF THEORIES   WIN   MWIN   MSIZ  BRGP  MRAN  CLMR  CLCP  PDST  PD1N  PDCL
                     1;117  0;23   0;2   0;5   0;9   0;3   1;10  0;13  1;23  1;10
```

Mollet appeared before the Assembly with a minority cabinet of Social Democrats, Radicals, RDA and Gaullists (RS). The majority in the Assembly came from Catholics and, unnecessarily and adding to the range, the Communists. This large and closed support coalition is predicted by policy distance theory and also under $1,n$ permissibility. The Mollet government survived for sixteen months, longer than any other cabinet in the Fourth Republic.

Bourgès-Mannoury (6/'57) formed a cabinet with, again, the Social Democrats, Radicals and RDA but without the RS. This minority received support from Independents and, through abstention, from the MRP. Since abstention is not counted as membership, no parliamentary winning coalition can be discerned.

The Catholics came back into the government under Gaillard (11/'57) in a coalition with Social Democrats, Radicals, Gaullists (RS), RDA and Independents. This was a winning coalition: closed, p.d. dominated, but not under either permissibility condition and, since any single actor except the Social Democrats was unnecessary, neither minimal winning nor of minimal range.

In the country and in the Assembly, the *Algérie Française* movement surged, causing the downfall of Gaillard when the Independents defected[82]. The investiture of Pflimlin (5/'58) on the fateful thirteenth of May was approved by the Assembly against the opposition of the Conservatives and the abstention of the Communists. By that time, however, forces outside the Assembly had taken over: the army and the *Algérie Française* movement

191

created a situation in which it appeared that only De Gaulle could prevent a further breakdown; he was voted into power under the acute threat of civil war. For some time to come the regime of parties was suspended.

2.c Discussion

Only the closed coalition proposition and policy distance theory, closed coalition version, achieve good scores for the Fourth Republic. Apparently, the politicians of the *quatrième* were no minimizers. Of 21 coalitions, 16 of which were majority coalitions, only one was minimal winning (Mayer), not even one was of minimal range, closed or open, none was of minimum size and none satisfied the bargaining proposition. Policy distance theory, however, predicts 11 coalitions correctly in the pure core and 11 in the $1,n$ permissibility version, 11 in the closed coalition version. The first two versions of policy distance theory, however, predict much larger sets and this results in relatively low statistical scores. The closed coalition proposition and p.d. theory, closed coalition version, predict the ten closed coalitions with much smaller predicted sets, though relatively large. As a result, the last two theories obtain significant results for the Fourth Republic.

A comparison of test scores for all theories for the data of Williams on the one hand and of MacRae on the other shows that all theories perform better for the more detailed figures of the latter, with the exception of the minimum size principle. This increases confidence in the general structure of the theories, as better data improve the performance of all theories but one.

3. Italy

Among Sartori's polarized pluralist systems, Italy is the only one that has survived to the present, notwithstanding the presence of a strong Communist party and the permanence of Fascist, Monarchist and Integralist Catholic groups, none of whom holds the Republic or the party system too dearly.

3.a The parliamentary system

The setting of parliamentary politics in Italy is a bicameral legislature consisting of an Assembly and a Senate, both elected direct-

192

ly and by universal suffrage. The two Houses have equal powers and the Government must have the confidence of both[83]. Accordingly, the distribution of seats in both Houses is taken into consideration.

Within the two Houses, no veto positions seem to exist, nor does the position of the President appear to be a major factor for consideration in the formation of coalitions. In the country, the Catholic church exerts strong influence over the voters and its intervention in coalition formations, at least in the early years, is a matter of record[84]. The U.S.A. also felt called upon to combine its financial aid with assistance in elections and formations[85]. The influence of the Church, however, is reflected by the strong numbers of the *Democrazia Cristiana* and does not warrant special assumptional provisions; American influence is impossible to assess and as far as elections were concerned, it may have been counteracted by the resentment it created[86].

Once the present constitution was drafted by the Constituent Assembly, no constitutional revisions requiring a qualified majority seem to have been a major matter of concern in the formation of coalitions and the majority assumption will be maintained unaltered.

Throughout the life of the Republic, three major actors dominated parliamentary politics: the Italian Communist Party (PCI), the Italian Socialist Party (PSI) and the largest, the *Democrazia Cristiana* (DC) which at times even achieved an absolute majority. The weight of these parliamentary actors is relatively easy to assess because voting discipline in the Italian parliament, including the DC, is tight[87].

A number of smaller parties had actor status for short periods, forfeiting it through loss of seats or through mergers with other parties: Monarchists, Fascists (MSI), Liberals (PLI), Republicans (PRI), Social Democrats (PSLI, PSDI, PSU) and Left Socialists (PSIU).

More than in most other countries, Italians parties seem to fall into a single policy scale.

"On the formal parliamentary level, Italian parties can be placed on a left to right continuum. While such a continuum is inadequate for the analysis of many political systems, it does not greatly distort the realities of Italian politics; furthermore, it is a useful way of viewing Italian parties."[88]

But in this case also, there is the usual *caveat*.

"The ideological divisions of Italian politics should be approached with considerable caution."[8] [9]

Barnes' continuum[90] boils down to
PCI—PSIU—PSDI—PRI—DC—(PLI, Monarchists, MSI).
The parties between brackets have been lumped together as composing "the right". Barnes does not make clear what the underlying dimension for his continuum is; he does, however, refer frequently to the parties' willingness to govern and for that reason the continuum seems to be insufficiently independent to qualify without further evidence as a basis for the policy scale.

Sartori proposes a similar continuum, this time placing the parties on the right in the order PLI—Monarchists—MSI. No justification is presented: "the polarity of the spectrum is self-evident."[91] Later in the same article, a threefold classification of parties is presented: Anti-system (PCI, MSI), "Half-way" (PSI, Monarchists) and Pro-system (PSDI, PRL, DC, PLI); Confessional (DC, MSI, Monarchists), and laical (PCI, PSI, PSDI, PRI, PLI); and, finally, left (PCI, PSI, PSDI, PRI, DC—centre-left) and right (MSI, Monarchists, PLI, DC—right). In Italy, also, being anti-system does not carry the same meaning for the Communists as it does for the Fascists, in fact they are diametrically opposed in the alternatives they propose and their antagonism against each other surpasses their hostility for the pro-system parties. Thus, "unfolding" the anti-system dichotomy into a more realistic trichotomy, one would obtain for the system dimension something like Communism—Democracy—Fascism. But then, the positions on Sartori's three "items" become almost scalable.

"Almost perfect", the PLI is really laical and should be placed to the left of DC on that basis. And, again, one might ask whether the Fascist system resembles the Monarchist ideal much more than that of the Communists. But from the patterns of persistent hostility, one is tempted to believe so: after all, the left has had its experience with Fascism and this antagonism has itself acquired an ideological character, long before the period under study.

The order obtained here agrees with the ranking by Sartori, with Barnes' continuum and also corresponds with the social economic policy positions of the parties. Communists, Socialists, Social Democrats, Republicans and Christian Democrats quite clearly, and according to the sources quoted, rank in this order on the social economic policy scale. For the remaining rightist parties, this ranking may be illustrated with some quotations.

194

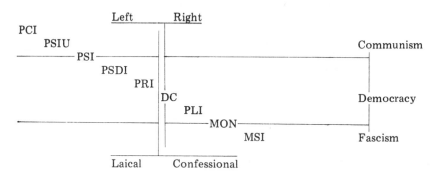

Figure 9-1.
The policy scale in Italy

The dichotomies for "left" *vs.* "right" and for "laical" *vs.* "confessional", and the trichotomy "Communism", "Democracy", "Fascism" together allow a single ranking of Italian parties, except for PLI, which is a laical party.

The Liberal party is conservative in economic matters and represents the large industrial interests, organized in *Confindustria*[92]. The Monarchist party, writing the restoration of the monarchy in its banner, "was not a revolutionary party, but rather a conservative or reactionary one. The party's conception of social consciousness was the distribution of a paternalistic largess to the unfortunate."[93]

In their history, the Italian Fascists display to the full the polyvalence of Fascist social economic thinking, oscillating between the early embrace of capitalism and the "social fascism" of the Republic of Salo[94]. The present-day MSI retains much of this indeterminacy but its positions are mostly far to the right: the MSI, silent or ambiguous on most points in its 1958 election program, does attack state intervention and restricts its demands on welfare legislation to "a more concrete and less illusory insurance system"[95]. In general its program is vague, but whenever it is specific, it is conservative.

In conclusion, it may be said, with some reserve concerning the mutual positioning of Monarchists and MSI, that social economic policy positions agree with the proposed ranking of actors for Italy.

3.b Historical coalitions

The elections of June 1946 for the Constituent Assembly pro-

195

duced a situation in which the Christian Democrats, without achieving a majority on their own, held a key position: they could have governed with the Socialist PSI, or with Republicans, Liberals and Monarchists, or with Liberals, Monarchists and Fascists (*Uomo Qualunque*): all three coalitions were closed, minimal winning and of minimal range and, as such, might be considered to be the basic alternatives of the situation*.

```
ITALY 1946
MAJORITY LARGER THAN 278
ACTORS IN ASSEMBLY    PCI    PSI    PRI    DCHR    PLI    MON    UOMO
POLICY SCALE ORDER      1      2    3,5    3,5      5      6      7
SEATS IN ASSEMBLY     104    115     23    207     41     16     30
DE GASPERI II
(6/'46)               MEMBER MEMBER MEMBER MEMBER MEMBER
DE GASPERI III
(2/'47)               MEMBER MEMBER        MEMBER
De Gasperi IV
(5/'47)                                    MEMBER MEMBER
DE GASPERI V
(12/'47)                     MEMBER        MEMBER MEMBER

RESULTS OF THEORIES  WIN  MWIN  MSIZ  BRGP  MRAN  CLMR  CLCP  PDST  PDIN  PDCL
                     3;59  0;8   0;1   0;2   0;3   0;3  2;13   0;6   0;8   0;4
```

The coalition that was, in fact, brought about by De Gasperi II (6/'46), consisted of the Communists, Socialists, Christian Democrats, Republicans and Liberals[96]. It was a closed coalition but large and neither minimal winning nor of minimal range since both Communists and Republicans were unnecessary, and the former also added to the coalition's range; it was p.d. dominated under either permissibility condition.

A high valuation of national consensus at the time of the foundation of the Republic and an attempt to diminish the threat of civil war by co-opting the left may explain the broad composition of De Gasperi II. A split within the Socialist party between the adherents of Nenni, who favored collaboration with the Communists, and, on the other hand, the followers of Sarragat who opposed that policy and who later formed the Social Democrat party, led to De Gasperi III (2/'47) in which Communists and Socialists participated but without support from the dissident Sarragat group:

---

* The coalition of Christian Democrats and PSI is closed, even though it does not contain PRI; PRI is tying, that is its position *vis à vis* the Christian Democrats is indeterminate and therefore the coalition cannot be said to be open: *i.e.*, it is closed (*cf.* p. 70).

the coalition must be considered open and, though the exact numbers of the Nenni and Sarragat factions are not known, the latter formed a minority[97]. The coalition must still have been large, the Communists being unnecessary and adding to the range. De Gasperi IV (5/'47) was a minority cabinet until December 1947; the Liberals and Social Democrats entered De Gasperi V, thus rendering it winning but neither minimal winning, nor of minimal range, ·again open since, this time, the Republicans were omitted[97]. Even though the exact strength of the Socialist factions is unknown, p.d. domination is certain for De Gasperi III and IV.

The elections of 1948 were fought on the theme of the Communist threat. The Christian Democrats, with the support of the Church, the United States and *Confindustria*, conquered a majority in the Assembly but not in the Senate, which was elected for the first time since the War.

```
ITALY 1948
MAJORITY LARGER THAN 287 (ASSEMBLY) 172 (SENATE)
ACTORS IN ASSEMBLY   PCI   PSLI   DCHR   PLI   MON
POLICY SCALE ORDER    1     2      3      4     5
SEATS IN ASSEMBLY    183    33    305    19    14
SEATS IN SENATE      119    24    148    27     8
DE GASPERI VI
(5/'48)                   MEMBERMEMBERMEMBER
De Gasperi VII
(1/'50)                   MEMBERMEMBER
De Gasperi VIII
(7/'51)                         MEMBER
De Gasperi IX
(7/'53)                         MEMBER

RESULTS OF THEORIES  WIN   MWIN   MSIZ   BRGP   MRAN   CLMR   CLCP   PDST   PD1N   PDCL
                    1;13   0;0    0;1    0;1    0;3    0;2    1;7    1;5    1;5    1;4
```

De Gasperi VI (5/'48) chose to form a coalition government with the Social Democrats (PSLI), the Liberals and the Republicans. The latter had become too small to be considered as an actor. The Liberals were necessary for a Senate majority but the Social Democrat PSLI could have been dispensed with. Since PSLI added to the coalition's range, De Gasperi VI was neither minimal winning nor of minimal range; it was p.d. undominated in all three versions of the theory. However, in the next cabinet, the Liberals, not the Social Democrats, were excluded. De Gasperi VII (1/'50) included Social Democrats, Christian Democrats and the theoretically "invisible" Republicans. The latter party, with its eight Senators, could have given the coalition its one missing vote for a

Senate majority. However, it does not "count" and the Gasperi VII is not entered as a winning coalition in the tabulations; it would have been closed, minimal winning and of minimal range. De Gasperi VIII (7/'51) was a coalition of Christian Democrats and Republicans, a minority in the Senate. The same is true of the short-lived government of De Gasperi IX (7/'53) which consisted of Christian Democrats only[97].

In the elections of 1953, the Christian Democrats lost their majority in the Assembly. Republicans and Liberals did not obtain sufficient votes to be considered actors but Monarchists and Fascists, who had fallen below actor status in the 1948 elections, again cleared the 2.5% mark. In this situation, a coalition of Christian Democrats and Monarchists would be open, minimal winning and of minimal range. The coalition of (Nenni) Socialists (PSI) and Christian Democrats would also be minimal winning and of minimal range, but open unless the unnecessary Social Democrats (PSDI) were added. Moreover, the Liberals (two seats short of actor's status but included) could have joined together with the Social Democrats in a majority coalition with the Christian Democrats that would have been closed, minimal winning and of minimal range (and p.d. undominated). The inclusion of the Liberals, who did not clear the $2\frac{1}{2}$% mark in the 1953 elections, is an exception. They were included because their presence proved decisive in the coalition situation. The very small Republican party was ignored, even though it did participate in the parliamentary support coalition.

```
ITALY 1953
MAJORITY LARGER THAN 294 (ASSEMBLY) 118 (SENATE)
ACTORS IN ASSEMBLY   PCI    PSI   PSDI   DCHR    PLI    MON    MSI
POLICY SCALE ORDER    1      2      3      4       5      6      7
SEATS IN ASSEMBLY    143     75     19    263      13     40     29
SEATS IN SENATE       55     31      4    114       3     15      9
Pella (8/'53)                            MEMBER
SCELBA (10/'54)              MEMBERMEMBERMEMBER
SEGNI I (7/'55)              MEMBERMEMBERMEMBER
Zoli (5/'57)                             MEMBER

RESULTS OF THEORIES  WIN   MWIN   MSIZ   BRGP   MRAN   CLMR   CLCP   PDST   PDIN   PDCL
                     1;60   1;6    1;1    0;3    1;5    1;3    1;13   1;6    1;6    1;7
```

Now that the Christian Democrats had lost their majority in the Assembly, they decided to govern alone: Pella (8/'53) "with technicians"[98] and the cabinet of Fanfani (10/'54) that was voted down immediately.

198

Scelba (10/'54) formed a government of Social Democrats, Christian Democrats and Liberals which obtained a majority in parliament. Segni (7/'55) continued on this basis[99]. This produced a closed, minimal winning coalition of minimal range and p.d. undominated.

When the Republicans withdrew their support, in February 1957, Segni continued for a few months with Monarchist support. This made the Social Democrats unnecessary and adding to the range of the coalition. Zoli (5/'57) formed a cabinet of Christian Democrats only but received support in Parliament from the Monarchists and also from the Fascists, "neither necessary nor desirable" in the words of the Prime Minister[100]. Apparently, because of Christian Democrat defections, the MSI votes could not have been missed[101].

The Liberals gained sufficient votes in the 1958 elections to be considered an actor again but the Republicans remained below that level. In the new situation, Social Democrats and Christian Democrats were three votes short of a majority in the Assembly and the Republicans could have given these votes. Under the definitions of the theories, the Christian and Social Democrats needed the support of the Liberals for a closed minimal winning, minimal range coalition. The other basic alternative was a coalition of Christian Democrats, Liberals and Monarchists. Fanfani II (7/'58) formed a cabinet of Christian and Social Democrats, with the

```
ITALY 1958
MAJORITY LARGER THAN 298 (ASSEMBLY) 123 (SENATE)
ACTORS IN ASSEMBLY   PCI   PSI  PSDI  DCHR   PLI   MON   MSI
POLICY SCALE ORDER     1     2     3     4     5     6     7
SEATS IN ASSEMBLY    140    84    23   273    16    23    25
SEATS IN SENATE       60    37     5   123     4     7     8
Fanfani II (7/'58)               MEMBERMEMBER
SEGNI II (2/'59)                          MEMBERMEMBERMEMBERMEMBER
Tambroni (3/'60)                          MEMBER
FANFANI III (7/'60)              MEMBERMEMBERMEMBER
Fanfani IV (2/'62)               MEMBERMEMBER

RESULTS OF THEORIES  WIN  MWIN  MSIZ  BRGP  MRAN  CLMR  CLCP  PDST  PD1N  PDCL
                    2;59   1;8   1;2   0;2   1;4   1;3  2;13   2;4   2;4   2;5
```

Republicans promising not to vote against the government and the Socialists (PSI) announcing that they would judge each bill on its

199

merits[102]. If the Republicans are ignored, Socialist support is necessary and the coalition including the latter is closed, minimal winning and of minimal range. But the Socialists commitment was as yet too vague to consider them a partner of a coalition, *i.e.* bound to support the government when its continued existence was at stake. A rapprochement of Nenni's PSI and PSDI seemed in the offing and some Sarragat Social Democrats defected the government to hasten its downfall and prepare the way for an "opening toward the left". Yet, the next government was a *"monocolore"* cabinet of Christian Democrats alone: Segni (2/'59), supported in Parliament by Liberals, Monarchists and Fascists[103]*. The Fascists were unnecessary and added to this coalition's range but the coalition was closed and p.d. undominated. Tambroni (3/'60) succeeded with another "monocolore" cabinet leaning on the Fascists in Parliament; the attitude of Liberals and Monarchists is not clear.

Until then, the right-wing factions within the Christian Democratic party had been succesful in preventing a left–center coalition but they had not been able to overcome opposition in the party against a coalition with the rightist groups. The Moro-faction had been trying for years to bring about the opening to the left. The vehement factional struggles within the Christian Democratic party certainly present a complicating factor in the analysis, obscured by the treatment of the party as a unitary actor, even if the representatives could almost always have been brought into line by the leadership when a crucial vote came up.

The Moro-faction scored a partial victory with the formation of Fanfani III (7/'60), a Christian Democrat *"monocolore"* cabinet with parliamentary support from Social Democrats, (Republicans) and Liberals[103]†. It was closed, minimal winning, of minimal range and p.d. undominated. The Socialists were to abstain. Fanfani IV (2/'62) moved a few steps closer to the left: Social Democrats (and Republicans) entered the cabinet, the Liberals were excluded. Since the Social Democrats had suffered a number of defections in the course of the parliamentary period, the three parties did not control an absolute majority[104]. The Socialists

*As the composition of this parliamentary support coalition seems reasonably certain, the parliamentary coalition is entered in the tabulations.
†The parliamentary support coalition can again be identified with reasonable certainty and is entered in the tabulations.

abstained at the investiture vote but were favorably disposed towards the government[105]. Nenni's party had become necessary and though it could not yet have been considered a member of the coalition, it presented a borderline case since it voted with the government on major occasions.

Monarchists and Republicans remained below the level of an actor in the 1963 elections. The Communists remained unnecessary to any minimal range coalition as they had been since 1946. The Fascists and the Liberals could have joined with the Christian Democrats in a minimal winning, minimal range, closed coalition and so could Social Democrats and Liberals. In the minimal range coalition of Socialists and Christian Democrats, the Social Democrats would have been an unnecessary member, but without them the coalition was open.

```
ITALY 1963
MAJORITY LARGER THAN 314 (ASSEMBLY) 157 (SENATE)
ACTORS IN ASSEMBLY   PCI   PSI  PSDI  DCHR  PLI   MSI
POLICY SCALE ORDER    1     2    3     4     5     6
SEATS IN ASSEMBLY    166    87   33   260    39    27
SEATS IN SENATE       85    44   14   133    19    15
Leone I (6/'63)                       MEMBER
MORO I (12/'63)            MEMBERMEMBERMEMBER
MORO II (7/'64)            MEMBERMEMBERMEMBER
MORO III (2/'66)          MEMBERMEMBERMEMBER

RESULTS OF THEORIES  WIN   MWIN  MSIZ  BRGP  MRAN  CLMR  CLCP  PDST  PD1N  PDCL
                     1;31  0;7   0;1   0;2   1;4   1;3   1;9   0;5   0;5   0;4
```

Leone I (6/'63) was a cabinet of Christian Democrats only, protected by the abstention of Socialists and Social Democrats. Half a year later, Moro I (12/'63) brought about his opening to the left by including Socialists, Social Democrats, (Republicans) and Christian Democrats in the cabinet — the first majority government in six years. It is interesting to note that the tendency towards a closed coalition prevailed over the tendency to a minimal winning coalition: the actual minimal range coalition did contain the Social Democrats (and Republicans), even though they were unnecessary, thus closing the coalition. The new union splintered at the flanks: PSIU, the "proletarian" Socialists, defected with some 17 representatives [106]*. After a crisis over the school issue,

---

* By the end of the legislative period, the "Proletarian" Socialists had 25 members in the Assembly and 12 in the Senate. (*Keesing's Historisch Archief*, January 17, 1964.)

201

Moro II (7/'64) returned with the same coalition, resigned again over the same issue and once more returned with a continuation of the coalition, Moro III (2/'66). The Moro cabinets were p.d. dominated, also under either permissibility condition. The defections did not change this.

```
ITALY 1966 INTERIM
MAJORITY LARGER THAN 314 (ASSEMBLY) 157 (SENATE)
ACTORS IN ASSEMBLY   PCI  PSIU  PSI   DCHR   PLI   MSI
POLICY SCALE ORDER    1    2    3     4      5     6
SEATS IN ASSEMBLY    166   24   95    260    38    26
SEATS IN SENATE       85   12   46    133    19    15
MORO IV (12/'66)                 MEMBERMEMBER

RESULTS OF THEORIES  WIN  MWIN  MSIZ  BRGP  MRAN  CLMR  CLCP  PDST  PD1N  PDCL
                    1;30  1;6   0;1   1;2   1;2   1;2   1;10  0;4   0;4   0;4
```

The Social Democrats and the Socialists of Nenni's persuasion merged into PSI. New factional alignments created a new situation. The PSIU came to control some 24 seats. Both Communists and Proletarian Socialists (PSIU) were unnecessary in any minimal range coalition. The Christian Democrats could have governed with either the Liberals and the Fascists, or with the newly merged Socialist party. Both coalitions were closed, minimal winning and of minimal range. Moro IV (12/'66) continued the opening to the left and his cabinet lasted until the elections of 1968; the coalition was p.d. dominated, also under either permissibility condition.

```
ITALY 1968
MAJORITY LARGER THAN 315 (ASSEMBLY) 157 (SENATE)
ACTORS IN ASSEMBLY   PCI  PSIU  PSI   DCHR   PLI   MSI
POLICY SCALE ORDER   1,5  1,5   3     4      5     6
SEATS IN ASSEMBLY    177   23   91    266    31    24
SEATS IN SENATE       87   14   46    135    16    11
Leone II (6/'68)                       MEMBER
RUMOR I (12/'68)                 MEMBERMEMBER

RESULTS OF THEORIES  WIN  MWIN  MSIZ  BRGP  MRAN  CLMR  CLCP  PDST  PD1N  PDCL
                    1;30  1;6   0;1   1;2   1;2   1;2   1;13  0;3   0;3   0;2
```

The elections of 1968 produced a situation with the same actors and the same basic alternatives. After a caretaker cabinet, Leone II (6/'68), Rumor I (12/'68) governed with the Nenni and Sarragat Socialists (PSI) until a new rift split the party's ranks. This time the "Unitarian" Socialists, opposed to any contemplated collaboration with the Communists, left the PSI and formed a new party, PSU, which was later renamed PSDI; about a third of the representatives of PSI left it for the new group[107].

This created a new coalitional situation. The new PSDI (PSU) can be placed between the PSI and the Christian Democrats on the scale, as heirs of the old PSDI of Sarragat. Under the new conditions, the Christian Democrats had three options: they could have formed a coalition with the Liberals and the Fascists, or they could have joined with the Liberals and the Social Democrats (PSDI). Both coalitions were basic alternatives. Thirdly, the Christian Democrats and the Nenni Socialists (PSI) could have formed a minimal winning, minimal range coalition which would have been open without the unnecessary Social Democrats.

```
ITALY 1969 INTERIM
MAJORITY LARGER THAN 315 (ASSEMBLY) 157 (SENATE)
ACTORS IN ASSEMBLY   PCI  PSIU   PSI  PSDI  DCHR   PLI   MSI
POLICY SCALE ORDER   1,5   1,5    3     4     5     6     7
SEATS IN ASSEMBLY    177    23   62    29   266    31    24
SEATS IN SENATE       87    14   34    12   135    16    11
RUMOR II  (8/'69)              MEMBERMEMBERMEMBER
RUMOR III (4/'70)              MEMBERMEMBERMEMBER
COLOMBO (8/'70)                MEMBERMEMBERMEMBER

RESULTS OF THEORIES  WIN   MWIN  MSIZ  BRGP  MRAN  CLMR  CLCP  PDST  PDIN  PDCL
                    1;62   0;10  0;1   0;2   1;4   1;3   1;15  0;5   0;5   0;4
```

Rumor II (8/'69) formed a minority cabinet of Christian Democrats only but with parliamentary support from both PSI and PSDI. These two parties entered the government with Rumor III (4/'70). Colombo (8/'70) succeeded with a government on the same basis. The three actual coalitions were closed and of minimal range: the actors apparently preferred a closed coalition (containing the Social Democrats) over one that would be minimal winning. The coalition is p.d. dominated in all three versions of the theory.

```
ITALY 1972
MAJORITY LARGER THAN 315 (ASSEMBLY) 157 (SENATE)
ACTORS IN ASSEMBLY   PCI   PSI  PSDI  DCHR   PLI   MSI
POLICY SCALE ORDER     1    2     3     4     5     6
SEATS IN ASSEMBLY    179   61    29   267    20    56
SEATS IN SENATE       94   33    11   135     8    26
ANDREOTTI (7/'72)              MEMBERMEMBERMEMBER
RESULTS OF THEORIES  WIN   MWIN  MSIZ  BRGP  MRAN  CLMR  CLCP  PDST  PDIN  PDCL
                    0;31   0;5   0;1   0;3   0;4   0;2   0;8   0;6   0;6   0;4
```

The elections of 1972 produced a situation that was quite similar to that of 1969. The Christian Democrats could have formed a

203

closed, minimal winning, minimal range coalition with the Liberals and Fascists (MSI) or a coalition that was also a basic alternative with Social Democrats and Liberals. Again, the coalition with the Socialists (PSI) would have been minimal winning and of minimal range but open without the unnecessary Social Democrats. The Proletarian Socialists disappeared as an actor; the Communists remained, as before, outside every minimal range coalition.

Andreotti (7/'72) formed a government of Christian Democrats, Liberals and Social Democrats: closed, minimal winning and of minimal range, p.d. undominated in all three versions of the theory, as far as the Assembly was concerned, but without a majority in the Senate.

3.c Discussion

From its foundation in 1946, the Second Italian Republic was ruled by 27 governments. Fifteen of these controlled a majority in both houses of parliament and four others (De Gasperi VII, VIII, IX and Andreotti) were supported by a majority in the Assembly alone. It may be that the importance of the Senate has been given too much weight by requiring that a coalition should also control a majority in this body in order to be considered winning.

All majority coalitions, except De Gasperi III, were closed. Once the period of large coalitions with the Communists was past, ten coalitions occurred that were of (closed) minimal range. Five others were minimal winning, three of these being also of minimum size and two satisfying the bargaining proposition. The three versions of policy distance theory predicted the center and center—right coalitions of 1948—1963. The failure of policy distance theory to account for the early governments with the Communists in a large coalition makes the success of this theory in predicting the similar French governments of the same period all the more puzzling.

Because of its economical predicted set, closed minimal range theory achieves a good result which is significant at the 4.4 level. The other minimal range theories and the closed coalition proposition are not clearly insignificant (under 10%). The remaining theories produce insignificant results.

CHAPTER 10

Confronting History: The Netherlands, Israel, Finland

In this chapter, three small European democracies have been grouped together, all characterized by a rather moderate form of pluralism: the bourgeois vote is divided over some four parties, some of traditional religious appeal as in the Netherlands and Israel, some recruiting their support among a particular linguistic community such as the Swedish Finns in Finland. A major part of the labor vote supports a large Social Democratic party, around which a number of smaller parties of various Socialist or Radicalist denominations may prosper and perish again; in Finland, however, the Communists have been a major actor since the second world war. The rural population has supported a party of its own and sometimes even several farmers' parties.

The "temperature" of politics, or the intensity of political conflict, appears to be somewhat less than in the countries of the preceding chapter and perhaps somewhat higher than in the Scandinavian monarchies.

1. The Netherlands

Contrasting sharply with the countries of the preceding chapter, the politics of the Netherlands are generally characterized as tranquil and stable, if not as dull and tedious[1] or rigid and traditionalist[2]. This is cause for wonder in a country that shared Europe's history of economic crisis, world war, decolonization and the cold war, while all the time internally divided into three distinctly organized denominational groupings: Catholics, Protestants and a secular sector which is sometimes divided into a Socialist and a "general" bourgeois section[3]. Yet, in the period under study, these "pillars", as they are called, came to support a unified national structure that withstood the upheavals of the century with remarkable imperturbility through gradual adaptation by accommodation among the elites.

1.a The parliamentary system

Dutch Parliament consists of two Chambers. An Assembly of 150 members — 100 until 1956 — and a Senate with half that number of seats. The King appoints the Cabinet but since 1868 unwritten constitutional law requires that the Government steps down when majority support in Parliament is lacking. On the other hand, cabinets can go a long way without, or even against, a majority in that body by adroitly avoiding tying their fate to an issue or by using a crisis as a threat that might bounce back on the opposition[4].

The Senate is indirectly elected, a fact that is assumed to diminish its political authority. Moreover, it lacks some of the legislative prerogatives of its opposite number, the Assembly, i.e. the right of amendment and of initiative. At the time of cabinet formation, only the chairmen of the factions in the Assembly are consulted by the Queen and, finally, the government program is debated in the Assembly alone. No cabinet was ever ousted by a Senate majority. The Senate is expected to exercise its legislative veto with considerable restraint[5].

For all these reasons, prevalent opinion has it that the cabinet ought to conform to the political relations within that branch of parliament that has been directly elected by the citizenry, the Assembly, or, as it is called in the Netherlands, the Second Chamber[6].

These considerations taken together justify the decision to ignore the Senate and to limit the definition of the parliamentary system in the sense of the theories to the Second Chamber and cabinet alone.

Within the Assembly, no formal or informal veto positions seem to exist even though, on specific matters such as agricultural policy, the united opposition of the members of the "Green front", represented in most parliamentary groups, may prove quite formidable.

206

One institution which is peculiar to the Netherlands deserves special mention *i.e.* the Social Economic Council, composed of representatives of employers, workers and crown appointees in equal parts. Its advice is obligatory but not binding, yet its unanimous opinion would be difficult to brush aside[7].

Its influence is therefore very great, but hard to assess. As no data exist that would enable this factor to be epitomized in an unambiguous operational statement, its presence must be borne in mind while explaining actual coalitions and evaluating the theories' performance for the Netherlands after 1950, when the Council came into existence.

Netherlands policy is not a law unto itself. In foreign policy, especially where it touches upon defense and the former colonies, the United States, as the leading NATO ally, at times exercises a strong influence.

In the sixties, economic policy came to be more integrated into the common policies of the EEC, the European Economic Community; these influences elude operational definition but should be considered in final explanations and evaluations.

Within the Assembly, laws and the budget are passed by a simple majority. Constitutional amendments require, for their final acceptance, a two-thirds majority in a newly elected parliament. Many such amendments passed into law during the period under study. However, only one was truly controversial at the time of its ratification. This amendment, on the status of Indonesia, was carried through by a very large coalition in 1948. But large coalitions remained a feature of Dutch politics in the succeeding years, whether or not constitutional revisions were on the agenda. In 1922 an amendment was ratified under a cabinet that controlled exactly half of the seats: not even a nominal majority. It appears that, only in 1948, was the qualified majority requirement a major consideration in the formation of the cabinet[8]. Thus, it appears warranted to set the majority requirement at just over one half of the total membership of the Second Chamber.

Five actors were represented throughout the past half century. Generally they are described in a trichotomy when social economic policy is concerned[9]. In the centre, the religious parties: the Catholic "KVP", and two major Protestants parties "ARP" and "CHU". On the right, a Liberal—Conservative party, at present the "VVD" (LIB), corresponding roughly to the "general" Bourgeois pillar; on the left, the Socialist parties, the major actor being the Social Democrat "SDAP", after the war "PVDA" (SOCD).

A radical-democrat (RAD) current achieved actor status in the years between the world war and since 1967. Another feature of Dutch politics is its Communist party (CPN), the oldest in Europe. Two fundamentalist Protestant parties, one of which achieved actor status at times, are also most characteristically Dutch. In the thirties, the NSB, a National Socialist movement, emerged and recently, a Poujadist-type Peasant Party (BP) achieved the 2.5% mark during one legislative period. Recently, DS'70, split off from the Social Democrat party and achieved actor status.

Most important for the present purposes is a study of party programs made by Lipschits: parties are ordered left to right on various scales, one of which is expressly social economic: "the antithesis between economic freedom and economic planning"[10]. The order on this scale is: Pacifist Socialists (PSP), Communists, Social Democrats, Catholics, Radical Democrats (D'66), Anti-Revolutionaries, Christian Historicals, Liberals, Political Reformed Party (SGP) and Peasants, *Boerenpartij* (BP). With two exceptions, this is the order that will be adopted in the present study. The Communists will be placed on the extreme left, the Pacifist Socialists to their immediate right. Lipschits found that the Pacifist Socialist program was stronger on nationalization than that of the Communists: "One would perhaps have expected a little more from a Communist party."[11] The other modification is the mutual rank of Catholics and D'66. Lipschits had some hesitation in this matter and ordered the parties provisionally until D'66, then in existence for only three years, declared itself more clearly[12]. In the present study, D'66 will be placed to the left of the Catholics.

Quite a few studies on the perceptions of the parties by the Dutch electorate, or parts of it, have been published in recent years. They show that informed and interested respondents, *e.g.* students affiliated with political organizations, tend to perceive similarities and differences among parties according to a "horse-shoe shaped curve ... This arrangement, in fact, corresponds very well with the order from left to right that could be defined on a priori grounds"[13]. The author, De Gruyter, clearly means an *a priori* left—right order along the social economic, rather than along the religious or the pro—anti-system dimenstion. Thus, De Gruyter finds the sequence: Communists, Pacifists, Social Democrats, Catholics, Anti-Revolutionaries, Christian Historicals, Liberals, Political Reformed Party, Peasants. This agrees with the ranking adopted in this study.

De Leeuw, in a replication study, found the same pattern and the same order except that Anti-Revolutionaries and Christian Historicals clustered together and so did the Political Reformed Party and the Liberals[14].

De Gruyter used multi-dimensional Kruskal scaling on data consisting of similarity judgments among triads of parties. De Leeuw used a non-metric multi-dimensional scaling technique on similarity orderings over all parties.

The order that these two authors found for their small student samples is corroborated by the findings of Koomen and Willems who asked a sample of voters from a representative Dutch village to order parties in the sequence of their preference: principal component analysis and varimax rotation yielded a two-dimensional space, in which the first component, accounting for 28% of the variance, again produced the same party sequence (except for Liberals and Peasants, who changed place this time)[15]. This component, moreover, correlated strongly (0.56) with the answers on questions regarding the equality of income and wealth and the desirability of worker's participation in company management: apparently a social economic dimension.

Jacobs and Jacobs-Wessels asked young, educated and informed voters to assign political parties their place on an ordinal scale (no ties allowed). In a frequency distribution of the responses of each party in each scale position, the greatest number of respondents placed the Communists on the extreme left, the mode for the Pacifists is immediately to the right and the modes for the other parties follow the sequence which is by now familiar[16].

Most of these studies were done with respondents whose interest and knowledge was above average. De Leeuw found quite different patterns for the preference orders of one hundred psychology students; the (then) government parties were placed on a different curved scale than were the (then) opposition parties; vote percentages (apparently treated as ranks on a preference scale) for eighty voting districts yielded patterns that could be interpreted in terms of the "well off" vs. the "discontented" neighbourhoods[17]. Stapel, who asked a representative national sample to judge the degree of "leftness" or "rightness" (from 1 to 7) for political parties found that Liberals and Peasants ended up much nearer the middle than would be expected. Apparently, the secular character of the first and the anti-system attitude of the second party induced many voters to consider these parties as leftist. Another poll made clear that 36% of the voters "cannot tell" what the terms left or right mean and 28% explains the term "right" in terms of "christian" or "religious"[18]. This is connected with traditional Dutch usage which describes the struggle between religious and secular parties as one between the right and the left.

Daalder and Rusk used data from a survey among Dutch parliamentary representatives in 1968. Respondents ordered all parties but their own according to how "close" they felt they were to each. A one-dimensional Kruskal solution separated the "left" from the "right" (religious, Liberal and Peasant parties) but with high stress and with some counter-intuitive sequences. Two-dimensional Coombsean party space reproduced the same curved dimension that has appeared in other studies, with the same sequences, except for a cluster of the big religious three and a most eccentric position for the Peasants[19]. The religious—secular dimension plays a part in the Kruskal configuration; the separation of parties eligible for coalition formation from the "outs" helped shape the Coombs pattern[20]. By scaling the preference of members within a given parliamentary group, an indicator of the coalitional preference of that group was obtained resulting in "a very realistic political picture"[21]. The Catholics would most prefer a coalition of the Social Democrats, the three religious parties and the Liberals. Liberals and Christian Historicals would prefer a coalition of the three religious parties and the Liberals without the Social Democrats. The Anti-Revolutionaries would prefer to govern with the three religious parties only and the Social Democrats would govern with Pacifist Socialists, D'66 and Anti-Revolutionaries. These preferences also score among the very highest in policy distance theory. Hazewindus and Mokken who converted the data of Daalder and Rusk into metric distance (on the basis of different rankings of the parties by the individual representatives), found the coalition of the three religious parties the most cohesive (smallest average distance between individual members) followed closely by the coalition of these three with either the Liberals or the Radical Democrats (D'66)[22]. The latter option is also very high on the list of Christian Historicals and Liberals in policy distance theory (and undominated in all three versions). It is not an outcome of the Daalder—Rusk analysis.

However, the Daalder—Rusk data, though of great value for an understanding of the coalitional mechanism, were acquired from parliamentary representatives and are not intended to furnish independent indicators of a party's policy position.

The evidence on the programmatic position of Dutch parties collected by Lipschits agrees, on the whole, with the data furnished by other authors on the voters' perceptions of the positions adopted by these political parties. On the basis of their programs, the five major parties, Social Democrats, Catholics, Anti—Revolutionaries, Christian Historicals and Liberals may be ranked in that order (the Catholics and the Anti-Revolutionaries tying in the postwar period).

General descriptions in the literature on the Dutch party system agree, in the main, with this ranking[23]. The order also seems to hold for the period between the two world wars, though in those years the three religious parties seem to have been closer to the position of the Liberal party in social economic matters, while a wider gap separated all these parties from the Social Democrats[24].

A brief review of the assessments made in the literature with respect to parties whose position has so far remained ambiguous may serve to complete the construction of the policy scale for the Netherlands.

The Left Socialists (PSP) will be placed to the immediate right of the Communists in contrast to the ranking proposed by Lipschits: though the wording of the Pacifist Socialist Party (PSP) program is stronger on the subject of socialization than the platform of the Communist Party, the information on the attitudes of the PSD cadre points to a less radical attitude in those circles. The emphasis among the Left Socialists may have been on community control of the means of production rather than on a redistribution by means of the government budget[25]. With regard to the pre-war Radical Democrats, though they split off from the Liberal movement, their place is on the side of "state socialism" instead of "freedom", as its more conservative opponents chose to characterize the cleavage[26]. Just as the later Democrats '66, they are placed immediately to the right of the Social Democrats. KVP and ARP are both parties that unite an agrarian, bourgeois and trade union following behind a religious banner. In the years between the wars, the ARP appears somewhat more conservative[27]. After the war the ARP gradually became more progressive and, at present, it may even be considered to the left of the Catholics. For the postwar period, its position with regard to the Catholics has been left indeterminate. The CHU, without organized workers' support, originally the organizational vehicle of the settled bourgeoisie and more liberal in its religious outlook, is somewhat more conservative in social economic matters than the more militant and religiously orthodox ARP, the party of "the little Man"[28]. As in the case of Israel, one is hard put to classify the fundamentalist parties; Lipschits' judgment, supported by the survey results quoted

211

above, has been followed. The case of the Peasants is comparatively unambiguous. They are vehemently opposed to state intervention on all counts. The paradox is on its peasant adherents which tend to favor government support more than their fellow agrarians voting for other parties[29]. The party must be considered extremely conservative in social economic matters[30]. This was also true for the National Socialist NSB. The party strongly opposed Communism and state intervention in the economy, considered itself the defender of the small entrepreneur and, generally, lacked the radicalism in social economic matters that was an element of corporatist Italian Fascism and of certain German National Socialist factions[31].

In conclusion, it seems warranted to rank the political parties in the Netherlands with respect to social economic matters as: Communists—Pacifist Socialists—Social Democrats—Radical Democrats (D'66)—Catholics($+$)Anti-Revolutionaries—Christian Historicals—Liberals—Peasants (or, National Socialists, or Political Reformed Party). Or, in the abbreviations as used in the tables CPN—PSP—SOCD—RAD (D'66)—CATH($+$)ARP—CHU—LIB—BP (NSB, SGP).

The sign "($+$)" indicates that Catholics and Anti-Revolutionaries were considered indeterminate in their position with respect to one another after the Second World War. The three parties that have been placed at the extreme right were actors in consecutive periods, they do not occupy the same place but the same rank with respect to the other parties.

By and large, individual representatives in the Dutch Assembly tend to vote with their parliamentary groups out of a sense of group cohesion[32]. The number of seats of an actor in parliament will be taken as a straight indication of his resources. And even though members of the coalition have considerable freedom of maneuver and do not always vote with their government, this is taken as an indication that the coalition management allows them to do so, rather than as a defection from the coalition on the actors' part. "No one party adopts the posture of all-out government — or all-out opposition — party...... If it is evident that an adverse vote would lead to an undesired ministerial crisis, these parties also tend to comply in Parliament, if often only under protest and not until after some give and take between ministers and parliamentary groups. In all other matters, the outcome remains an open question. Parties may more readily oppose, if they know for certain that other parties will see a particular bill through."[33] With its reservations and nuances this description still exactly fits the definition of membership in the present study: "support, whenever the coalition's continued existence is at stake".

1.b Historical coalitions

The elections of 1918 — the first in which all adult men had the right to vote — brought representatives of seventeen different parties into the Second Chamber. Eight of these parliamentary groups were large enough to be counted as actors. In this situation the Social Democrats and the Catholics together could have mustered a minimal winning coalition of minimal range but open without the unnecessary Radicals. The two Protestant parties (ARP, CHU) and the Catholics controlled exactly half the votes in the Assembly, strictly speaking a minority by one vote. If this coalition is considered winning ($m \geqslant 50$) — and in this fragmented Assembly a united opposition vote was very unlikely — the combination is minimal winning, minimal range, closed and, of course, of minimum size. Moreover, the three liberal and conservative actors on the right of the scale were excluded from any minimal range, minimal winning coalition.

Ruys de Beerenbrouck I (9/'18) formed the coalition of Catholics, Christian Historicals and Anti-Revolutionaries. The presence of a Free Liberal on Foreign Affairs indicated not so much the commitment of his party to the coalition, but rather the non-partisan character of neutralist Dutch foreign policy.

```
THE NETHERLANDS 1918
MAJORITY LARGER THAN   49
ACTORS IN ASSEMBLY    SOCD   RAD   CATH    ARP    CHU   ULIB   ECUN   FLIB
POLICY SCALE ORDER       1     2      3      4      5      6      7      8
SEATS IN ASSEMBLY       22     5     30     13      7      6      3      4
RUYS DE BEERENBROUCK
I (9/'18)                             MEMBERMEMBERMEMBER

RESULTS OF THEORIES    WIN  MWIN   MSIZ   BRGP   MRAN   CLMR   CLCP   PDST   PDlN   PDCL
                      1;107 1;17   1;5    0;1    1;3    1;2    1;14   0;46   0;22   1;10
```

With the majority condition revised downward by one vote, the Ruys cabinet was minimal winning, closed, of minimal range and minimum size. (It was, moreover, p.d. dominated, also under $1,n$ permissibility.) The cabinet suffered parliamentary defeat over a property tax bill but after tendering its resignation, it returned in essentially the same composition.

The elections of 1922 produced a configuration in the Assembly

213

that, with some variations, was to dominate Netherlands politics for the next half century: a large Catholic party in the center of the scale, flanking to its right the much smaller Protestant parties, Anti-Revolutionaries and Christian Historicals; at the extreme right, the Liberals. To the left the Social Democrat party, on average the second largest, and, during part of the period, the Radical Democrats, a small actor adjoining the Catholics.

```
THE NETHERLANDS 1922
MAJORITY LARGER THAN 50
ACTORS IN ASSEMBLY  SOCD   RAD   CATH   ARP   CHU   LIB
POLICY SCALE ORDER     1     2     3      4     5     6
SEATS IN ASSEMBLY     20     5    32     16    11    10
RUYS DE BEERENBROUCK
II (9/'22)                        MEMBERMEMBERMEMBER

RESULTS OF THEORIES  WIN   MWIN  MSIZ  BRGP  MRAN  CLMR  CLCP  PDST  PD1N  PDCL
                    1;29   1;8   0;1   0;1   1;4   1;3   1;9   0;14  0;6   0;6
```

In this situation, the Social Democrat—Catholic coalition was again of minimal range, minimal winning, but open without the unnecessary Radical Democrats. Radicals, Catholics and Anti-Revolutionaries could form a closed minimal winning coalition of minimal range and so could the three religious parties. The latter solution prevailed again under Ruys de Beerenbrouck II (9/'22), p.d. dominated in all three versions of the theory. The defection of Catholic representatives in a vote on naval appropriations caused an intermediary crisis that ended in the return of the cabinet.

The Second Chamber of 1925 showed the same basic alternatives and again the religious coalition provided the support for the cabinet. Colijn I (8/'25) was p.d. dominated but not under either permissibility condition. This time a vote on the continuation of a diplomatic ministry to the Vatican — an issue calculated to provoke the traditional animosity between Catholics and Protestants — toppled the Government. The Radicals made an attempt to

```
THE NETHERLANDS 1925
MAJORITY LARGER THAN 50
ACTORS IN ASSEMBLY  SOCD   RAD   CATH   ARP   CHU   LIB
POLICY SCALE ORDER     1     2     3      4     5     6
SEATS IN ASSEMBLY     24     7    31     13    11     9
COLIJN I (8/'25)                  MEMBERMEMBERMEMBER
DE GEER I (3/'26)                 MEMBERMEMBERMEMBER

RESULTS OF THEORIES  WIN   MWIN  MSIZ  BRGP  MRAN  CLMR  CLCP  PDST  PD1N  PDCL
                    1;30   1;9   0;3   0;1   1;4   1;3   1;9   0;8   1;7   1;8
```

214

form a government with Catholics on the one hand and Social Democrats on the other, an alternative that had been possible since 1918. They failed, however, and this seems strong evidence of the width of gap that separated the essentially clerical and conservative Catholics from the anti-religious Social Democrats, a rift widened and hardened in 1918 by an ill-timed and abortive revolutionary proclamation from the Social Democratic party leader Troelstra[34].

The crisis was resolved by De Geer (3/'26), an "Intermezzo cabinet of 'non-politicians' from all parties, except Socialists and Communists; both government and opposition uncertain"[35]. Except for the Free-Liberal who had held foreign affairs since 1918, the cabinet ministers were either connected with the religious parties or were without formal party-ties while sympathizing with the Liberal or Radical outlook. Thus, the government may have consisted of an "inner" coalition of the three religious parties — closed, minimal winning, of minimal range, a basic alternative — and an "outer" coalition, containing in addition to the former parties, the Radicals on the left and the Liberals on the right, both unnecessary and adding to the range; a closed but large coalition, p.d. dominated, also under $1,n$ permissibility. The former "inner" coalition is adopted in the tabulations since it is based on publicly identified parties.

```
THE NETHERLANDS 1929
MAJORITY LARGER THAN 50
ACTORS IN ASSEMBLY  SOCD   RAD  CATH   ARP   CHU   LIB   SGP
POLICY SCALE ORDER     1     2     3     4     5     6     7
SEATS IN ASSEMBLY     24     7    30    12    11     8     3
RUYS DE BEERENBROUCK
III (8/'29)                       MEMBERMEMBERMEMBER

RESULTS OF THEORIES  WIN  MWIN  MSIZ  BRGP  MRAN  CLMR  CLCP  PDST  PD1N  PDCL
                    1;57  1;12   0;2   0;1   1;3   1;2  1;11  0;17  0;10  1;10
```

The elections of 1929 produced a situation in which, again, the coalition of the three religious parties and the coalition of Catholics and Social Democrats were minimal winning and of minimal range, the former closed and the latter open, unless the unnecessary Radicals were included. Ruys de Beerenbrouck III (8/'29) continued the p.d. dominated coalition of the Catholic and Protestant (ARP, CHU) parties through the first years of the Great Depression. The Political Reformed Party (SGP), a fundamentalist Protestant group, had acquired actor status.

215

```
THE NETHERLANDS 1933
MAJORITY LARGER THAN 50
ACTORS IN ASSEMBLY   CPN  SOCD   RAD  CATH   ARP   CHU   LIB   SGP
POLICY SCALE ORDER    1    2     3     4     5     6     7     8
SEATS IN ASSEMBLY     4    24    7     28    14    10    7     3
COLIJN II  (5/'33)              MEMBERMEMBERMEMBERMEMBERMEMBER
COLIJN III (7/'35)              MEMBERMEMBERMEMBERMEMBERMEMBER

RESULTS OF THEORIES  WIN  MWIN  MSIZ  BRGP  MRAN  CLMR  CLCP  PDST  PDIN  PDCL
                    1;120 0;19  0;2   0;1   0;3   0;2   1;16  0;30  0;20  1;14
```

In the Second Chamber of 1933, the Communists (CPN) appeared as an actor; the basic coalitional features remained the same. Colijn II (5/'33) broadened the cabinet's base to include the parties that had been loosely represented in De Geer's "outer coalition": Radicals and Liberals governed along with the three religious parties. The two former were unnecessary and added to the coalition's range. The coalition was closed, but large, and p.d. dominated, also under 1,n permissibility. The defection of the Catholics caused an intermediate crisis, resolved by the return of the same cabinet, after a reshuffle, as Colijn III (7/'35). This government lasted until the elections of 1937.

```
THE NETHERLANDS 1937
MAJORITY LARGER THAN 50
ACTORS IN ASSEMBLY   CPN  SOCD   RAD  CATH   ARP   CHU   LIB   NSB
POLICY SCALE ORDER    1    2     3     4     5     6     7     8
SEATS IN ASSEMBLY     3    23    6     31    17    8     4     4
COLIJN IV  (6/'37)                           MEMBERMEMBERMEMBER
DE GEER II (8/'39)              MEMBERMEMBERMEMBER      MEMBER

RESULTS OF THEORIES  WIN  MWIN  MSIZ  BRGP  MRAN  CLMR  CLCP  PDST  PDIN  PDCL
                    2;119 1;17  0;3   0;1   1;4   1;3   1;17  0;34  0;21  1;14
```

This time the SGP lost actor status and a National Socialist Movement (NSB*) came to occupy the extreme right of the policy scale. In this situation, next to the two coalitional alternatives that remained unchanged, a third emerged: a coalition of Radicals, Catholics and Anti-Revolutionaries. But Colijn IV (6/'37) was forced to narrow the basis of his government so as to include only the three religious parties: minimal winning, closed and of minimal range, p.d. dominated, also under 1,n permissibility. This govern-

---

Nationaal-Socialistische Beweging: National Socialist Movement.

ment of "positive Christian inspiration" fell when the Catholic ministers resigned in protest against the cutting of unemployment benefits in a time of grave economic crisis [36].

Colijn V (7/'39) consisted of a minority coalition of Anti-Revolutionaries, Christian Historicals and Liberals, a rightist combination that was voted down immediately. Next, at a time of deepening international crisis, an attempt was made to bring about a grand coalition uniting all "democratic" actors; the Liberals bowed out and so did the Anti-Revolutionaries though one of their number, Gerbrandy, became an important cabinet member. Thus De Geer II (8/'39) came to consist of Social Democrats, Radicals, Catholics and Christian Historicals*. The Radicals and Christian Historicals were unnecessary, and the latter added to the coalition's range. Thus, the coalition was open (omitting the Anti-Revolutionaries)†, p.d. dominated, also under $1,n$ permissibility and it was large. It is interesting to note that when the Queen, after the breakdown of the religious coalition, proposed a coalition of Catholics and Social Democrats, the *formateur* in charge of forming the cabinet rejected this alternative, referring to objections made by the German ambassador [37]. Apparently, in this case, the menace of war and the influence of a foreign power play a part in explaining the broad base of this large coalition. However, the Social Democrats had been initiated and in a manner very much reminiscent of the way in which the Finns had gone about it in the Cajander III government two years before.

Shortly after the German invasion of the Netherlands in May 1940, the government fled the country. Gerbrandy succeeded De Geer as the leader of the government in exile which ruled without parliament and, therefore, remains outside the present analysis.

The parliamentary system came into operation again with the elections of 1946. The Radical *Vrijzinnige Democratische Bond* (RAD) had disappeared and its remnants, together with the Social Democratic Party, merged into a new Social Democratic Party of Labor. In the newly elected Second Chamber, the three religious parties (CATH, ARP, CHU) controlled a narrow majority and so did Catholics and Social Democrats; both combinations were p.d. dominated, minimal winning coalitions, closed and of minimal

---

* This is the cabinet composition according to De Jong (1969) Vol. I, p. 609.
† The Anti-Revolutionaries may well have been more conservative than the Liberals at the time. In that case the coalition was closed but the policy scale does not fit the facts (H. Daalder, private communication).

range. It may be noted that a coalition of Communists, Social Democrats and Anti-Revolutionaries — without the Catholics! — would have controlled a minimal winning majority, and (because of the tie between the ARP and Catholics) also closed (*i.e.*, not open) but not of minimal range.

```
THE NETHERLANDS 1946
MAJORITY LARGER THAN 50
ACTORS IN ASSEMBLY   COMM  SOCD   CATH    ARP    CHU   LIB
POLICY SCALE ORDER     1     2    3,5    3,5     5     6
SEATS IN ASSEMBLY     10    29     32     13      8     6
BEEL I (7/'46)             MEMBER MEMBER

RESULTS OF THEORIES   WIN   MWIN  MSIZ   BRGP  MRAN  CLMR  CLCP  PDST  PDIN  PDCL
                     1;30   1;8   0;1    1;1   1;3   1;3   1;11  0;3   0;2   0;2
```

This time a coalition of Catholics and Social Democrats was brought about: Beel I (7/'46). The question of the South East Asian colonies soon became of overriding importance: in July 1947 the first "policing action" against the Republic of Indonesia began. In Holland, a number of former Radical Liberals left the Labor Party and fused with the Liberal Freedom Party into a new Liberal People's Party for Freedom and Democracy.

```
THE NETHERLANDS 1948
MAJORITY LARGER THAN 50
ACTORS IN ASSEMBLY   COMM  SOCD   CATH    ARP    CHU   LIB
POLICY SCALE ORDER     1     2    3,5    3,5     5     6
SEATS IN ASSEMBLY      8    27     32     13      9     8
DREES I (8/'48)            MEMBER MEMBER         MEMBER MEMBER
DREES II (3/'51)           MEMBER MEMBER         MEMBER MEMBER

RESULTS OF THEORIES   WIN   MWIN  MSIZ   BRGP  MRAN  CLMR  CLCP  PDST  PDIN  PDCL
                     1;29   0;9   0;1    0;1   0;3   0;3   0;10  0;1   0;2   0;2
```

Elections in 1948 produced a majority for a coalition of either Social Democrats and Catholics or for a coalition of the latter with the two Protestant parties; both coalitions were minimal winning, closed and of minimal range. However, constitutional amendments to accomodate the new status of the former Asian empire required for their ratification a two-thirds majority in the newly elected Assembly*. This time the necessity for such an enlarged majority

---

* The "formateur" was commissioned "to form a cabinet that would enjoy the greatest possible confidence from the Chamber". "The words 'the greatest possible' referred to the requirement of a two-thirds majority for the second reading of the constitutional revision." Duynstee (1966) p. 16; *cf.* Lijphart (1966) p. 111.

seems to have been a major consideration in the formation of the cabinet. Yet not all actors seem to have been convinced of the necessity to have a permanent government coalition of that size: the Social Democrats opposed the broadening of the cabinet's base[38]. In fact, constitutional revisions have been prepared and ratified by governments with a small majority and large coalitions have governed without using their majority for an amendment of the constitution.

For a coalition with Social Democrats and Catholics to acquire a two-thirds majority, the inclusion of the Communists or of any one of the three rightist parties (the two Protestant parties and the Liberals) was necessary. Without Social Democrats *and* Communists such a majority could not have been achieved. On the basis of the (social economic) policy scale, the closest party on the right was the Anti-Revolutionary Party. But it had voted against the constitutional bill in its first reading. This left the Liberals and the Christian Historicals, who apparently not only insisted on cabinet membership in exchange for their support on the colonial issue, but, moreover, each demanded that the other be included also![39] This conflicts with every theory except policy distance theory. The final outcome, however, also conflicts with the latter. Drees I (8/'48) combined Social Democrats, Catholics, Christian Historicals and Liberals in a large and open coalition (the Anti-Revolutionaries were omitted); both Christian Historicals and Liberals were unnecessary for a simple majority, either one was unnecessary for a two-thirds majority and both added to the coalition's range. Drees I was p.d. dominated, also under $1,n$ permissibility. No explanation in terms of the present theories is available for this coalition but the idea of policy distance suggests that either one of the two small parties that were necessary for achieving the required majority in the vote on the constitutional bill, wished to trade its support for membership in the cabinet and hoped to shift expected cabinet policy further in its direction by making way for inclusion of the other also. The Catholics were agreeable to this, since it would have given them a well-balanced position in the cabinet. Social Democrat opposition was overruled.

Drees II (3/'51) was again an open coalition and also large: Social Democrats, Catholics, Christian Historicals and Liberals formed the cabinet, the latter two unnecessary and adding to the range. The coalition was p.d. dominated, also under $1,n$ permissibility.

The basic alternatives remained the same after the elections of

1952. The problems revolving around the liquidation of the South East Asian empire had been reduced to the determination of the status of New Guinea. Though the constitutional amendments on the agenda were uncontroversial this time, a large coalition emerged once more: Drees III (9/'52) united Social Democrats and Catholics with Anti-Revolutionaries and Christian Historicals; either the latter two or the Social Democrats were unnecessary and added to the range of the large, but closed, coalition that was p.d. dominated and under 1,n permissibility. The cabinet lasted the full parliamentary period even though, in 1955, it resigned and was subsequently reinstated in the course of a crisis over rent policy.

```
THE NETHERLANDS 1952
MAJORITY LARGER THAN 50
ACTORS IN ASSEMBLY  COMM  SOCD  CATH   ARP   CHU   LIB
POLICY SCALE ORDER    1     2   3,5   3,5    5     6
SEATS IN ASSEMBLY     6    30    30    12     9     9
DREES III (9/'52)            MEMBERMEMBERMEMBERMEMBER

RESULTS OF THEORIES  WIN  MWIN  MSIZ  BRGP  MRAN  CLMR  CLCP  PDST  PDIN  PDCL
                    1;30  0;7   0;4   0;1   0;3   0;3   1;10  0;5   0;3   0;2
```

The Second Chamber of 1956 once more showed the configuration that was familiar since 1946. Social Democrats and Catholics, or the latter with the two Protestant parties, could have formed a minimal winning, closed coalition of minimal range. Communists and Liberals were excluded from either basic alternative. It took four months to form the new government, Drees IV (10/'56), composed of the same parties as the preceding cabinet. The coalition was again large and closed but neither of minimal range or minimal winning and again p.d. dominated, also under 1,n permissibility.

```
THE NETHERLANDS 1956
MAJORITY LARGER THAN 75
ACTORS IN ASSEMBLY  COMM  SOCD  CATH   ARP   CHU   LIB
POLICY SCALE ORDER    1     2   3,5   3,5    5     6
SEATS IN ASSEMBLY     7    50    49    15    13    13
DREES IV (10/'56)           MEMBERMEMBERMEMBERMEMBER
BEEL II (12/'58)                  MEMBERMEMBERMEMBER

RESULT OF THEORIES   WIN  MWIN  MSIZ  BRGP  MRAN  CLMR  CLCP  PDST  PDIN  PDCL
                    2;31  1;7   0;1   0;1   1;3   1;3   2;10  0;5   1;3   1;2
```

The impression prevails that the Drees cabinets in fact consisted of a "super-coalition" of two coalitions: on the one hand, Social Democrats and Catholics, a basic alternative of the situation and on the other hand the Catholics with Christian Historicals and, in Drees III and IV, Anti-Revolutionaries, again a basic alternative of the situation. The Catholics occupied the key position of being a member in both minimal range, minimal winning coalitions. It appears that they were able to extend this privileged position into the cabinet coalition proper by including both alternatives in the "super-coalition", thus holding on to their options beyond the moment of formation*.

The six years of Drees' "super-coalition" ended with a crisis over tax legislation which prompted the Social Democrats to resign. Beel II (12/'58) governed with Catholics, Anti-Revolutionaries and Christian Historicals — the remaining basic alternative — minimal winning, of minimal range, closed and p.d. dominated but not under $1,n$ permissibility. The Catholic party was not too happy to govern with the rightist parties alone[40]. The Second Chamber was dissolved and in the elections the Communists lost actor status and the three religious parties gained exactly half of the seats, as in 1918. This time the alternative to a coalition of Catholics and Social Democrats (minimal winning, minimal range and closed) was a coalition of the three religious parties with the Liberals (also minimal winning, minimal range, closed and p.d. undominated). It was the latter basic alternative that was realized

```
THE NETHERLANDS 1959
MAJORITY LARGER THAN 74
ACTORS IN ASSEMBLY  SOCD  CATH   ARP    CHU    LIB
POLICY SCALE ORDER    1     2    3,5    3,5     5
SEATS IN ASSEMBLY    48    49    14     12     19
DE QUAY (5/'59)            MEMBERMEMBERMEMBERMEMBER

RESULTS OF THEORIES  WIN   MWIN  MSIZ  BRGP  MRAN  CLMR  CLCP  PDST  PDIN  PDCL
                     1;15  0;6   0;1   0;1   0;2   0;2   1;7   1;8   1;5   1;4
```

---

* The outspoken preference on the part of the Catholic People's Party for "broadly based" governments, even at the cost of losing some portfolios to the additional partners (*e.g.* Duynstee (1966) p. 293) is explained by its desire to maintain its options; this, in turn, springs from the urgent necessity to keep the internal factions of trade union, farming, and entrepreneurial interests at bay by avoiding a clear commitment to one political side or another (*cf.* Daalder (1955) p. 7).

by De Quay (5/'59). The government lasted the full parliamentary period, though an intermediary crisis occurred over government-subsidized housing. This time the Protestant factions demanded an increase in the volume of government funded construction and this led the government to resign; it returned when the dissenting parliamentary groups had renewed their guarantee for support[41].

The three religious parties gained the vote necessary for a majority in the elections of 1963; their coalition again emerged as the basic alternative next to the Social Democrat—Catholic coalition. Communists (CPN) and Pacifist Socialists (PSP) gained actor status in these elections but both were unnecessary to either minimal range coalition, as were the Liberals.

```
THE NETHERLANDS 1963
MAJORITY LARGER THAN 75
ACTORS IN ASSEMBLY    CPN   PSP   SOCD   CATH   ARP    CHU    LIB
POLICY SCALE ORDER     1     2     3     4,5    4,5     6      7
SEATS IN ASSEMBLY      4     4     43    50     13     13     16
MARIJNEN (7/'63)                         MEMBERMEMBERMEMBERMEMBER
CALS (4/'65)                       MEMBERMEMBERMEMBER
Zijlstra (11/'66)                        MEMBERMEMBER

RESULTS OF THEORIES   WIN   MWIN  MSIZ  BRGP   MRAN   CLMR   CLCP   PDST   PD1N   PDCL
                     2;59  0;10  0;5   0;1    1;3    1;3    2;15   1;9    1;5    1;3
```

Marijnen (7/'63) continued the existing coalition of the three religious parties and the Liberals, even though after the elections the latter had become unnecessary and added to the coalition's range. Except for uncertainty over the narrow majority the government would have possessed without the Liberals*, the motivations for the formation of this coalition are hard to find, especially so, since there was opposition in the Catholic parliamentary group against a center—right combination. The coalition is, however, p.d. undominated and may have been the result of policy distance calculations.

The rupture in the coalition came over the issue of radio and television broadcasting. The Liberals who had no close ties with

---

* "A majority of 76 or 77 votes (out of 150) was too small", according to the Catholics (Duynstee (1966), pp. 382—383). Constitutional amendments, on the agenda for a second reading with a two-thirds majority, do not seem to have been the reason for including the Liberals, with whom the cabinet still did not control two-thirds of the vote.

any of the existing broadcasting organizations favored an "open system" while the other actors, allied to like-minded broadcasting organizations, opposed the creation of new and competing bodies. Marijnen resigned and Cals (4/'65) formed a cabinet of Social Democrats, Catholics and Anti-Revolutionaries, the latter unnecessary but not adding to the range, since Anti-Revolutionaries and Catholics tie on the policy scale. The coalition was closed, but large, p.d. dominated under either permissibility condition.

The Catholic parliamentary leadership voted against the cabinet over social economic policy (the budget) and a minority cabinet, Zijlstra (11/'66), of Anti-Revolutionaries and Catholics prepared early elections.

The new Second Chamber counted nine actors, among which were D'66, a radical democratic party, and a right-wing Peasant party; both appeared as actors for the first time. As in the pre-war period, Social Democrats and Catholics could form a minimal winning, minimal range coalition, which was open without the unnecessary Democrats. The three religious parties had lost their majority but with either D'66 or the Liberals they could have formed a closed, minimal winning coalition of minimal range. Communists, Pacifist Socialists and Peasants were not members of any minimal range coalition.

```
THE NETHERLANDS 1967
MAJORITY LARGER THAN 75
ACTORS IN ASSEMBLY    CPN    PSP   SOCD   D'66   CATH   ARP    CHU    LIB    BP
POLICY SCALE ORDER      1      2      3      4    5,5    5,5      7      8     9
SEATS IN ASSEMBLY       5      4     37      7     42     15     12     17     7
DE JONG (4/'67)                                  MEMBERMEMBERMEMBERMEMBER

RESULTS OF THEORIES   WIN    MWIN   MSIZ   BRGP   MRAN   CLMR   CLCP   PDST   PD1N   PDCL
                     1;240   1;29    0;8    0;1    1;6    1;4    1;21   0;15   1;17   1;11
```

De Jong (4/'67) chose the basic alternative of a coalition with the three religious parties and the Liberals, p.d. dominated, but undominated under $1,n$ permissibility. This cabinet lasted the entire parliamentary period until the elections of 1971.

This time the Pacifist Socialists and the Peasants disappeared as actors but a group of dissident Social Democrats, DS '70, with a platform of government savings, achieved actor status on the right-hand side of the policy scale. Catholics and Social Democrats lost the combined majority they had possessed since 1918. D'66, which in the elections had collaborated with the Social Democrats,

223

now became necessary to this closed, minimal winning, minimal range coalition of left-center. The three religious parties needed the support of both DS'70 and the Liberals for a closed, minimal winning, minimal range coalition. A third basic alternative, the three religious parties with DS'70 and D'66, was practivally excluded and theoretically doubtful: Social Democrats and D'66 had entered the elections with a common program, excluding collaboration with the Catholics unless the latter would commit themselves to it before the elections. In the new Second Chamber, Social Democrats and D'66 operated as distinct factions but their freedom to enter coalitions on their own was certainly much less than that of normal actors.

```
THE NETHERLANDS 1971
MAJORITY LARGER THAN 75
ACTORS IN ASSEMBLY    CPN  SOCD  D'66  CATH  ARP   CHU  DS70   LIB
POLICY SCALE ORDER     1    2     3    4,5   4,5    6    7      8
SEATS IN ASSEMBLY      6    39    11    35    13   10    8     16
BIESHEUVEL (7/'71)                    MEMBERMEMBERMEMBERMEMBERMEMBERMEMBER

RESULTS OF THEORIES   WIN  MWIN  MSIZ  BRGP  MRAN  CLMR  CLCP  PDST  PD1N  PDCL
                     1;105 1;26  0;4   0;6   1;5   1;4   1;13  1;21  1;11  1;6
```

Biesheuvel (6/'71) opted for the right-center alternative of the three religious parties with the Liberals and DS'70, minimal winning, of minimal range, closed and p.d. undominated.

The defection from the coalition by DS'70 resulted in early elections in November 1972. The Pacifist Socialists lost actor status but the Political Radicals, PPR, became an actor and are, provisionally, placed to the left of the Social Democrats. The Biesheuvel coalition of the Christian parties with DS'70 and the Liberals remained a basic alternative of the situation but because of heavy losses among Catholics and Christian Historicals, it had become a minimum size coalition (p.d. undominated in all three versions). A second basic alternative was represented by the coalition of Social Democrats, D'66 and Catholics (still closed and of minimal range with the tying Anti-Revolutionaires). It was p.d. dominated in all three versions. However, the Political Radicals, the Social Democrats and D'66 had committed themselves as the "Progressive Three" to join the government together and to reject a coalition with the Catholics unless it had been agreed to before the elections (which it hadn't). Finally, a basic alternative coalition without the Catholics appeared; Communists, Progressive Three and Anti-Revolutionaries could form a closed and minimal winning coalition of minimal range, an unaccustomed combination, which had been a possibility only once before, in 1945. Moreover, this basic alternative coalition is not of minimal range; and exception due to the fact that the pivotal Catholics and Anti-Revolutionaries are also tying parties; Catholics and Progressive Three span a smaller range, even with the addition of the Anti-Revolutionaries.

The latter coalition emerged after the longest crisis in Dutch parliamentary history: Den Uyl (5/'73) was supported by the Progressive Three, Catholics and Anti-Revolutionaries: closed, but not minimal winning and not of minimal range, unless the Progressive Three are considered as one actor. In both cases the coalition is dominated in all three versions of policy distance theory.

```
THE NETHERLANDS 1972                (Not entered in statistical tabulations)
MAJORITY LARGER THAN 75
ACTORS IN ASSEMBLY  COMM   PPR  SOCD  D'66  CATH   ARP   CHU  DS70   LIB
POLICY SCALE ORDER    1     2    3     4    5,5   5,5    7    8      9
SEATS IN ASSEMBLY     7     7    43    6    27    14     7    6      22
DEN UYL  (5/'73)            MEMBERMEMBERMEMBERMEMBERMEMBERMEMBER
RESULTS OF THEORIES  WIN   MWIN MSIZ  BRGP MRAN  CLMR  CLCP PDST  PD1N  PDCL
                   1;230   0;40 0;14  0;8  0;4   0;3   0;18 0;28  0;18  0;5
```

1.c Discussion

Since 1918, the Netherlands have been governed by a succession of 21 majority cabinets, two "intermezzo" minority ministries and the war cabinet in exile.

Among these 21 majority governments, eighteen were closed along the social economic policy scale. In the Netherlands, a configuration of party cleavages along religious lines overlaps a pattern of social economic differences between parties. Religion, and after the Second World War, the liquidation of the South East Asian empire, have determined political life along with social economic issues. Yet, the policy distance scale remains a very powerful explanatory guideline: the closed coalition proposition is significant at the 2.9% level. Moreover, minimal range theory performs very well for the Netherlands, predicting twelve cabinets at a significance level of 0.3%. When coupled to the closed coalition proposition, it achieves even higher scores: closed minimal range theory is significant at a level of 0.1%!

Only three cabinets were based on a p.d. undominated coalition, seven for p.d. theory in the 1,n permissibility version. The closed coalition version of p.d. theory predicted twelve coalitions,

225

a significance score of 4.9%. The poor performance of policy distance theory is important evidence against the theory in its present operationalization. Though the actors manifested at many instances precisely those coalitional preferences that were ascribed to them in terms of policy distance theory, the final outcome of the predictions of this theory does not fit reality very well. It appears that in the calculation of domination, the basis of the actors' preferences does not correspond with actual mechanisms at work in coalition formation: the calculations may be far too complicated and much too dependent on rather subtle numerical variations.

There was a clear propensity among the Dutch coalition builders to extend the cabinet's support beyond the parties that were numerically necessary for a majority, even if this meant decreasing the number of portfolios available to each actor that was indeed necessary. The key position of the Catholic party as a member of all minimal range coalitions that were possible in a given situation, may have presented it with so much bargaining leverage, that it could force a "super-coalition" upon its partners thus extending its advantage right into the cabinet coalition.

These characteristics of the Dutch coalitional game are accounted for much better by minimal range theory, especially the closed minimal range theory, than by minimal winning theory, which predicts only five coalitions correctly, or the minimum size principle and the bargaining proposition, each predicting only one historical coalition.

On the whole, the theories that have shown good overall test results achieve very good results for the Netherlands.

2. Israel

Immediately after its National Council proclaimed statehood for Israel in 1948, war with the surrounding Arab nations broke out. The Israeli army won, but from then on a permanent threat of war prevailed and materialized twice more in actual warfare: in 1956 and in 1967. Notwithstanding the constant state of near-war, the Israeli game of politics continued. Conflict between parties remained lively but whenever a foreign threat required it, partisan differences were transcended by national unity toward the outside world. Thus, with some brief interruptions in time of war, domestics politics in Israel continue to be dominated by inter-party cleavages, relating to social economic issues and also to religion and foreign policy.

2.a The parliamentary system

The setting of the parliamentary game in Israel is the unicameral legislature, the *Knesset*, a parliament of 120 members elected by universal and direct suffrage. The *Knesset* approves of a new government by a simple majority vote of confidence[42]. The parliament has passed a number of bills of a consitutional nature but they were all accepted by simple majority[43]. Though some such laws contain provisions for qualified majorities necessary for their amendment, no such revision has as yet been undertaken[44].

All relevant votes appear to have been simple majority decisions, and it is assumed that a coalition had to command at least half plus one of the *Knesset*'s 120 votes.

No formal or informal veto positions have been found to exist in the *Knesset** but this does not mean that the legislature and the cabinet together hold the monopoly on social economic decisions. Another, most remarkable, institution plays a critical role in Israeli political and economic life: the *Histadrut*, a federation of trade unions that almost monopolizes social security and medical services, controls important sectors of the economy as an entrepreneur and as an employer and unites about 90% of the working population in its ranks[45].

Under such conditions, one could hardly imagine a cabinet decision on social economy policy to become effective if it were diametrically opposed to the wishes of the *Histadrut*. Yet, the parties that participate in the elections of the *Histadrut* governing body are also represented in the *Knesset*, which body as a consequence certainly reflects the influence of the *Histadrut* in its own composition. Arian finds that "leftist" parties, that is labor-supported parties, are "over-represented" in the *Knesset* in proportion to their support among the electorate[46].

Throughout Israeli history, these labor parties have controlled roughly half the votes in parliament, not counting the seats of Communist, Arab, or religious labor representatives. Thus, the possibility of a *Knesset* majority hostile to the *Histadrut* never arose. Therefore it does not seem necessary to add to the theories an

---

* But Ben Gurion's position at times came close, *cf*. Badi, pp. 174—178.

additional assumption that could have accounted for the influence of the *Histadrut.*

The acute threat of war that has haunted Israeli politics must also have influenced the parliamentary process profoundly. This is a condition that may explain the emergence of unnecessarily large coalitions. The particular international situation of the Israeli system will be taken into consideration in the discussion of the results of the theories.

Israeli politics are characterized by a proliferation of parties, mostly organized around a body of doctrine that goes back to the history of the Zionist organizations "in exile". At the same time, more research data on the ideological positions of parties are available in the case of Israel than for most other countries. A pioneer of scaling analysis, Louis Guttman, was also the first to suggest the application of his "scalogram method" to the Israeli party system. The problem of unidimensionality has been a special subject of scrutiny[47]. Guttman's scaling technique is characterized by the rule that "if the data do not meet the necessary conditions for an ordinal scale, one will not be obtained"[48].

Antonovsky found that the responses to four questions he submitted to a representative sample did fall into a scalable pattern. Arian, after having ranked political parties on Antonovsky's scale according to their "official position", found in a replication study that the respondents' answer to these scale items also corresponded with their reported party affiliations[49]. Next, Arian decided to confront the question of unidimensionality specifically, by adding to each of the original four scale items two new questions in order to check whether a scalable pattern could still be discerned. "This attempt failed decisively. Even after excluding two 'offending' items, an acceptable scale could not be constructed"[50].

Five items were then combined in an "economic" scale, connected with attitudes on socialism and the *Histadrut*; this scale possessed satisfactory characteristics, as did another made up of five remaining items all related to foreign policy[51].

These Guttman scale analyses were carried out for the secular parties only; the religious parties were ignored. On the basis of evidence from the studies quoted by Arian, the secular parties may be ranked with regard to social economic policy as Communists—MAPAM—Ahdut—MAPAI—Progressives—Zionist—Herut. The descriptions in the literature of the ideological character of these parties agree with this ranking[52].

The religious parties remain to be placed on this continuum; a task that is complicated by the fact that up to four distinct religious parties were sometimes seated in the *Knesset*, at least one of them profoundly unconcerned about such worldly matters as social economic policy. There are, however, indications with respect to the positions in social economic matters of the religious actors in Israel.

The *Mizrachi* party, in origin a religious Zionist organization, consists of members "who follow a conservative, right-of-center program and oppose the dominant position of the Histadrut in the affairs of the country"[53]. The party never occupied actor status on its own. In 1949, it participated in the elections together with the three other religious parties. In 1951, it was lumped together in the analysis with the *Mizrachi* labor party with which it combined, in fact, in 1955 under the shared label of National Religious Party, *Mafdal*. The *Mizrachi* labor wing operated within the *Histadrut* and "sought a formula for combining socialism and religious orthodoxy"[54]. As a combination of these two currents, the *Mafdal* may be considered to be analogous to the Christian Democratic parties of Western Europe with respect to social economic matters. Its place seems to be between the Mapai and the Progressives.

The *Agudat Israel* is "more conservative, militantly orthodox, and aggressive than Mizrachi in its opposition to secularism"[54]. Its labor wing, *Poalei Agudat Israel* has not joined the *Histadrut*. For 1951, the two factions were lumped together as one actor and in 1955, they united in fact as the Torah Religious Front. The attitudes of *Agudat* members on the issues of Zionism, the supreme rule of the Torah (next to which a constitution is unnecessary and offensive) and the maintenance of religious custom, are equally intense as they are vague in social economic matters: "Autrement dit, il n'existe pas en Israel, dans les milieux religieux, de judaisme social"[55]. The combined *Agudat* factions are placed to the right of the *Mafdal* and to the left of the General Zionists, tying therefore with the Progressives.

The preceding ranking, including the location of *Mafdal* and *Agudat* parties, agrees well with another indicator of inter-party distance, one that is, however, not entirely independent of coalition behavior. The factions in the *Knesset* may be ranked according to the percentage of their members that indicate which particular parties "they regard as closest to their views". The result is the familiar left—right continuum except for the preferences expressed by Progressives and *Herut* members for the socialist parties (42% and 30%, respectively); none of these representatives opts for the religious parties which have been ranked closer to them on the present continuum. The jump over the religious parties is reciprocated by 23% of Mapai members preferring secular rightist parties, while only 10% in the Mapai faction opt for the Mafdal, even though it adjoins them on the present continuum[56]. Clearly, the religious dimension of Israeli politics influences these preferences. Ignoring all other dimensions out of sheer theoretical necessity, Israeli parties have been ranked on the continuum of social economic policy in the order Communists—MAPAM—Ahdut—MAPAI—MAFDAL—Agudat—PROGR—Zionist—Herut.

Three actors appeared only once on the Israeli scene: the National Religious Front, combining all four religious parties: it was placed to the right of the Mapai and to the left of the Progressives, tying with another ephemeral grouping, the Sephardic Party, which sat astride the Labor—Conservative division[57]. In 1965, Rafi was placed to the immediate right of Mapai[58].

2.b Historical coalitions

The analysis of Israeli cabinet formations is complicated by the large number of actors represented at any time in the *Knesset.* Yet, and notwithstanding war and threat of war, the parliamentary system has functioned throughout the brief history of Israeli statehood and time and again parliamentary majority coalitions were found to support the government.

```
ISRAEL 1949
MAJORITY LARGER THAN 60
ACTORS IN ASSEMBLY    CPI  SOCL  SOCD  SEPH  NREL  PROG  ZION  HRUT
POLICY SCALE ORDER      1     2     3     4     5     6     7     8
SEATS IN ASSEMBLY       4    19    46     4    16     5     7    14
BEN GURION II  (3/'49)              MEMBERMEMBERMEMBERMEMBER
BEN GURION III (11/'50)             MEMBERMEMBERMEMBERMEMBER

RESULTS OF THEORIES   WIN   MWIN  MSIZ  BRGP  MRAN  CLMR  CLCP  PDST  PD1N  PDCL
                    1;121  0;12   0;2   0;2   0;3   0;2  1;16  0;22  0;23   0;9
```

In the first elected *Knesset*, eight actors participated and one of them, the National Religious Front (NREL), in fact represented a rather loose alliance of four religious parties. Yet, one party dominated the scene, the Social Democratic Mapai (SOCD)[59]. Together with the Socialist Mapam (SOCL), it could have controlled a majority in a closed, minimal winning coalition of minimal range.

230

The Mapai could also have governed with the National Religious Front, an open coalition of minimal range, that would have been closed with the addition of the small Sephardic party (SEPH) which was unnecessary but not adding to the range of the coalition. What emerged, however, was the Ben Gurion II government (3/'49) of Mapai, Sephardim, the Religious Front and the Progressive party; the latter, as the Sephardim, was unnecessary but, moreover, adding to the range of this closed, p.d. dominated coalition. The government resigned after "defeat on a minor issue"[60] and was succeeded by Ben Gurion III (11/'50). The cabinet was supported by the same coalition as the preceding one. It fell over a conflict concerning education which led to dissolution of the Knesset[61].

```
ISRAEL 1951
MAJORITY LARGER THAN 60
```

ACTORS IN ASSEMBLY	CPI	SOCL	SOCD	MAFD	PROG	AGDH	ZION	HRUT
POLICY SCALE ORDER	1	2	3	4	5	6	7	8
SEATS IN ASSEMBLY	5	15	45	10	4	5	20	8
Ben Gurion IV (10/'51)			MEMBER	MEMBER		MEMBER		
BEN GURION V (12/'52)			MEMBER	MEMBER	MEMBER		MEMBER	
SHARETT I (1/'54)			MEMBER	MEMBER	MEMBER		MEMBER	
Sharett II (6/'55)			MEMBER	MEMBER	MEMBER			

RESULTS OF THEORIES	WIN	MWIN	MSIZ	BRGP	MRAN	CLMR	CLCP	PDST	PDIN	PDCL
	1;115	0;16	0;4	0;1	0;3	0;3	0;14	0;20	0;13	0;8

After the 1951 elections, Mapai (SOCD) and Mapam (SOCL) together fell one vote short of a majority in the Knesset: they would either have needed Communist (CPI) support or have had to ally themselves with the combined Mizrachi and Mizrachi workers' parties (MAFD). Thirdly, Mapai could have governed with the Mizrachi, the Progressives and the (fundamentalist religious) Agudat Israel (AGDH), now operating as a separate actor. All three coalitions were closed, minimal winning and of minimal range. Ben Gurion IV (10/'51) consisted of Mapai, Mizrachi and Agudat Israel: the coalition controlled exactly 60 out of 120 votes and was, therefore, strictly speaking, a minority government*. Once Agudat Israel withdrew over the issue of military service for religious women, the Ben Gurion V government (12/'52) came to include, as well as Mapai and Mizrachi, the Progressives and General Zion-

---

* Czudnowski (1970) p. 222 (Table II) mentions the support of 7 votes from "others", non-actor representatives.

ists — an open coalition, with *Mizrachi* and Progressives unnecessary, and of larger than minimal range (p.d. dominated, also under $1,n$ permissibility). After Ben Gurion resigned "for personal reasons"[62], it took 53 days before Sharett I (1/'54) emerged with the same coalition partners. After some time, the General Zionists defected and the other parties, two votes short of a majority*, continued as Sharett II (6/'55) until the election of the third *Knesset.*

```
ISRAEL 1955
MAJORITY LARGER THAN 60
ACTORS IN ASSEMBLY   CPI   SOCL  AGAV  SOCD  MAFD  PROG  AGDH  ZION  HRUT
POLICY SCALE ORDER    1     2     3     4     5     6     7     8     9
SEATS IN ASSEMBLY     6     9    10    40    11     5     6    13    15
BEN GURION VI (11/'55)  MEMBERMEMBERMEMBERMEMBERMEMBER
BEN GURION VII (1/'58)  MEMBERMEMBERMEMBERMEMBERMEMBER

RESULTS OF THEORIES  WIN   MWIN  MSIZ  BRGP  MRAN  CLMR  CLCP  PDST  PD1N  PDCL
                    1;238  0;33  0;7   0;10  0;3   0;3   1;19  1;29  1;31  1;14
```

The elections of 1955 brought a new Socialist actor, the *Ahdut Ha'Avoda* (AGAV), to the *Knesset* which now counted nine parties of actor status. An all-Socialist government of the Communists, the Mapam, *Ahdut Ha'Avoda* and Mapai, or the latter two with Mafdal (the combined *Mizrachi* and *Mizrachi* workers parties), which would have been of minimum size, and, finally, Mapai, Mafdal with Progressives and *Agudat Israel* (AGDH) would all three have constituted basic alternatives in the situation: closed, minimal winning, p.d. undominated and of minimal range. Ben Gurion VI (11/'55) united Mapam, *Ahdat Ha'Avoda,* Mapai, Mafdal and Progressives. Mapam (SOCL) and Progressives were unnecessary and added to the undominated and closed coalition's range. This was the war-cabinet that presided over the Suez campaign in 1956 and that alone may explain the width of its range. Yet, it lasted with this broad support for more than two years and Ben Gurion VII (1/'58) continued the same coalition until the elections of 1959.

In the new *Knesset* the Communists had become too small for actor status. But Mapam (SOCL), *Ahdut Ha'Avoda* (AGAV) and Mapai (SOCD) controlled a majority; *Ahdut Ha'Avoda*, Mapai and

---

* 5 individual "others" supported the government (Czudnowski (1970) p. 222, Table II).

Mafdal, or the latter two with the Progressives, also formed majorities. All three coalitions were closed, minimal winning and of minimal range. Ben Gurion VIII (7/'59) governed with Mapam, Mapai, *Ahdut Ha'Avoda*, Mafdal and Progressives: the latter or the former two were unnecessary and all four added to the coalition's range. However, the coalition was closed and beautifully balanced around Mapai (yet, the coalition is p.d. dominated, also under $1,n$ permissibility).

```
ISRAEL 1959
MAJORITY LARGER THAN 60
ACTORS IN ASSEMBLY  SOCL  AGAV  SOCD  MAFD  PROG  AGHD  ZION  HRUT
POLICY SCALE ORDER    1     2     3     4     5     6     7     8
SEATS IN ASSEMBLY     9     7    47    12     6     6     8    17
BEN GURION VIII
(7/'59)            MEMBERMEMBERMEMBERMEMBERMEMBER

RESULTS OF THEORIES  WIN   MWIN  MSIZ  BRGP  MRAN  CLMR  CLCP  PDST  PD1N  PDCL
                   1;119  0;15  0;2   0;1   0;3   0;3  1;15  0;10  0;10  1;7
```

Ben Gurion VIII lasted the full parliamentary period. In the Fifth *Knesset* the Communists regained actor status. The Progressives and General Zionists had united into a new actor, the Liberal Party. The Mapai, as always in the key position, could have formed a coalition with the Communists and the other two Socialist parties, or it could have joined with *Ahdut Ha'Avoda* and Mafdal, or, finally, with Mafdal, *Agudat Israel* and (with one vote short of a majority) the new Liberal Party. Up to this point, the General Zionists had always been unnecessary and adding to the range of any minimal range, minimal winning coalition; the Nationalist *Herut* still was. This time, since they were part of the Liberal Party with the Progressives, the General Zionists were necessary for a single vote in one of the three minimal range, minimal winning and closed coalitions.

```
ISRAEL 1961
MAJORITY LARGER THAN 60
ACTORS IN ASSEMBLY   CPI  SOCL  AGAV  SOCD  MAFD  AGDH   LIB  HRUT
POLICY SCALE ORDER    1     2     3     4     5   6,5   6,5    8
SEATS IN ASSEMBLY     5     9     8    42    12     6    17    17
BEN GURION IX (11/'61)          MEMBERMEMBERMEMBER
ESHKOL I (6/'63)                MEMBERMEMBERMEMBER
ESHKOL II (12/'64)              MEMBERMEMBERMEMBER

RESULTS OF THEORIES  WIN   MWIN  MSIZ  BRGP  MRAN  CLMR  CLCP  PDST  PD1N  PDCL
                   1;120  1;22  0;2  1;13   1;5   1;4  1;19  0;12  0;16  1;12
```

233

Ben Gurion IX (11/'61) consisted of *Ahdut Ha'Avoda*, Mapai, Mafdal and, unnecessarily and adding to the range, the labor wing of *Agudat Israel: Poalei Agudat Israel*. The two factions of *Agudat* (AGDH) have been considered as a single actor in the computer analysis and the support of the labor faction in the *Agudat* was ignored, since it was too small to be counted as an actor on its own. The coalition of *Ahdut Ha'Avoda* (AGAV), Mapai (SOCD) and Mafdal was one of the basic alternatives of the situation (yet, p.d. dominated, also under 1,n permissibility). Eshkol I (6/'63) and Eshkol II (12/'64) continued on the same basis. Thus the coalition, with unclassifiable support from the *Poalei Agudat Israel*, lasted for the entire parliamentary period.

In the elections of 1965, the Communist Party again lost its actor status. The Socialist *Ahdut Ha'Avoda* (AGAV) merged with the Social Democrat Mapai and a new labor list, Rafi, acquired actor status. The Liberal Party united with the *Herut* into the Gachal. The Independent Liberals left the combination to form an actor on their own. Thus, Mapam (SOCL), the newly extended Mapai (SOCD) and the new actor Rafi or, Mapai, Rafi and Mafdal could have formed closed, minimal winning and minimal range coalitions.

```
ISRAEL 1965
MAJORITY LARGER THAN 60
ACTORS IN ASSEMBLY  SOCL  SOCD  RAFI  MAFD  AGDH  ILIB  GACH
POLICY SCALE ORDER    1     2     3     4    5,5   5,5    7
SEATS IN ASSEMBLY     8    45    10    11     6     5    26
ESHKOL III (1/'66) MEMBERMEMBER        MEMBER      MEMBER
ESHKOL IV (5/'67)  MEMBERMEMBERMEMBERMEMBER        MEMBERMEMBER

RESULTS OF THEORIES  WIN  WMIN  MSIZ  BRGP  MRAN  CLMR  CLCP  PDST  PD1N  PDCL
                    2;56   0;9   0;3   0;1   0;2   0;2  0;11  1;10  0;10  0;11
```

Under these conditions, Eshkol III (1/'66) opted for a coalition of Mapam, Mapai (as extended), Mafdal and the Independent Liberals: an open coalition, omitting Rafi and *Agudat Israel* (and again, with support of the *Poalei* wing of *Agudat Israel*, unnecessary but not adding to the range)[63]. The coalition was p.d. dominated, also under 1,n permissibility. There is little doubt that Rafi, though excluded from the coalition, did lie within its range. Rafi was less progressive in economic matters than Mapam, more so than the Independent Liberals, and probably no less than Mafdal. The *Agudat Israel* was also "omitted" but both the membership in

234

the coalition of its labor-wing and the indeterminacy of its policy position *vis à vis* the Independent Liberals, further complicate this case. The explanation for the exclusion of Rafi must apparently be sought in the vehement resentment on both sides that went with the defection of the Mapai leaders who left to found Rafi.

Another war was in the offing: just before the June war, Eshkol IV (5/'67) was formed and this time Rafi's strong man, Moshe Dayan, joined Mapam, Mapai and Mafdal; the Independent Liberals, and now also the Gachal, entered the government, *Agudat Israel* (AGDH) stayed out. This was a large and open coalition, apparently with the special mission of guiding the country through the war; it was neither minimal winning nor of minimal range but p.d. undominated, even though 1,n non-permissible! Eliminating the Independent Liberals and Gachal, obviously underrepresented in the cabinet, what remained was a coalition of Mapam, Mapai, Rafi and Mafdal — a closed coalition in which either Mapam or Mafdal was unnecessary and added to the range. This may well have been the coalition that supported the government in domestic matters, especially social economic policy. (It was p.d. dominated, also under 1,n permissibility.)

```
ISRAEL 1969
MAJORITY LARGER THAN 60
ACTORS IN ASSEMBLY   MAKI   ILAB   STP  MAFD  AGDH  ILIB  GACH
POLICY SCALE ORDER     1      2     3     4   5,5   5,5    7
SEATS IN ASSEMBLY      4     56     4    12     6     4    26
MEIR I  (3/'69)             MEMBER      MEMBER      MEMBERMEMBER
Meir II (8/'70)            MEMBER      MEMBER      MEMBER

RESULTS OF THEORIES   WIN   MWIN  MSIZ  BRGP  MRAN  CLMR  CLCP  PDST  PD1N  PDCL
                     2;60   0;6   0;1   0;3   0;3   0;2  0;11  0;5   0;5  0;11
```

In the election of 1969, Mapam, Mapai (already merged with *Ahdut Ha'Avoda*) and Rafi presented a single list and they entered the Seventh *Knesset* as a united actor, the Israel Labor Party (ILAB), only five votes short of a majority. Ben Gurion had stayed out of the merger with his State Party (STP), which acquired actor status, as did the Communists (MAKI). The Labor Party would need the support of both the Communists and the State Party to form a closed, minimal winning coalition of minimal range. Together with Mafdal, the Labor Party also controlled a majority, minimal winning and of minimal range but open without the unnecessary State Party.

Meir I (3/'69) continued the grand coalition of Eshkol IV, after the death of the prime minister and beyond the elections: Israel Labor (Mapam, *Ahdut Ha'Avoda*, Mapai, Rafi), Mafdal, Independent Liberals and Gachal (Liberals and *Herut*). Apparently, for domestic matters, the rump coalition of Israel Labor and Mafdal constituted the governing majority, since Independent Liberals and Gachal again received only a minor portfolio. The extended coalition was large and neither minimal winning nor of minimal range; it was open because both the State Party and *Agudat Israel* were omitted; moreover, it was $1,n$ non-permissible and p.d. dominated. The rump coalition without the unnecessary Independent Liberals and Gachal was of minimal range and minimal winning but (with the State party excluded) open and p.d. dominated, also under $1,n$ permissibility. Once Gachal defected, the coalition was no longer large but still open, p.d. dominated and not minimal winning with the unnecessary Independent Liberals: Meir II (8/'70)[64].

2.c Discussion

There is a marked tendency in Israeli politics to include some unnecessary actor(s) so as to broaden the base of government. Yet, there is a striking propensity in forming coalitions to move along the policy scale and build closed coalitions. This, notwithstanding a party system in which a multitude of parties compete for the vote, sometimes affiliated with each other in varying degrees, all differentiated along cross-cutting lines of cleavage with regard to religion, foreign policy and social economic matters.

Probably, the permanent threat of war should explain the fact that only three out of fourteen majority cabinets were minimal winning, (and also conform the bargaining proposition) whereas three others may be considered as minimal winning but extended to deal with war policy (Eshkol III and IV, Meir I). Eight of fourteen majority coalitions were closed (Ben Gurion V and Sharett omitted *Agudat*, Eshkol omitted *Agudat* and Rafi, Meir excluded *Agudat* and the State party). Only three coalitions were of minimal range but, again, Eshkol IV and Meir may have consisted of a rump coalition for domestic matters within the extended cabinet coalition and therefore may also be considered as being of minimal range. All but three of the historical coalitions were p.d. dominated, two under $1,n$ permissibility: negative evidence of special significance since the Israeli party system with its many parties, its one actor, Mapai, in a key position (a member of all minimal winning, minimal range coalitions) and its tendency towards broadly based governments, seems well-suited to the assumptions of policy distance theory.

Israel is a difficult country for the theories. Most of them score below their average over all countries. The closed coalition proposition performs best, the closed coalition version of policy distance theory comes second, but neither theory achieves a significant level (26% and 31.7% respectively).

3. Finland

For Finland, the October Revolution in adjoining Russia meant the end of over eight centuries of foreign domination. The "Whites" proclaimed independence and defeated the "Reds" and the Soviet troops. The Republic of 1919 steered between Russian and German influence and on the domestic scene between Communists and Finnish Patriots until it was attacked by the Soviets, while Germany imposed first an alliance and then its troops upon the Finnish nation. Since the Second World War, Finland has maintained a precarious and detached friendship with the Soviet Union, coming to terms with the sizable Communist party within its own borders.

3.a The parliamentary system

The constitution of 1919 presents a number of features that are peculiar to Finland. The universally elected parliament, *Eduskunta*, is unicameral and consists of 200 members. There is "a kind of bicameral element" in the form of a Grand Committee composed of 45 members elected annually by the entire membership of the *Eduskunta*[65].

The advice of this Grand Committee must be asked for each legislative project (except the budget), but it is not binding. The Committee is elected on the principle of proportionalism[66]. As an advisory and proportional body, it probably does not affect the composition of cabinet coalitions very much.

The Cabinet does not have to solicit a vote of confidence from Parliament but a vote of no-confidence may be taken upon interpellation and has always been sufficient to bring the government down[67].

A vote of over one-third of the members of the *Eduskunta* is enough to halt acceptance of a bill until after the next elections; a presidential veto has the same effect. Constitutional revisions become law only after acceptance by a two-thirds majority in the next elected *Eduskunta*. The procedure may be shortened to a single legislative period if a five-sixths majority so decides. This means that a minority that controls over one-third of the votes (or one-sixth in constitutional matters), has a suspensory veto of up to four years and so does the President [68].

"The President is a power factor of considerable importance"[69]. He appoints the Cabinet, heads it while in session as the "Presidential Council" and maintains close informal contact when it deals with business in its capacity of Council of Ministers. In the Presidential Council the ministers may advise but the President alone decides. The ministers, on their part, may refuse to carry out a decision and are, in fact, obliged to do so when they believe it to be unlawful. The President, universally elected, be it indirectly through an Electoral Council, wields considerable political authority. As a result, "the Cabinet is in a tricky position between the President and Parliament"[70]. However, in drawing up the balance, Kastari concludes "The characteristics of parliamentarism, after all, control the normal course of events completely, nor has their dominance of principle been upset even in exceptional situations"[71].

No operational rule to define the peculiarities of the President's impact on the Finnish system suggests itself; it seems best to keep this special factor in mind when discussing the historical course of events in the *Eduskunta*.

No doubt Finnish foreign and military policy has been greatly shaped by the presence of Germany and Russia, but even though this foreign influence may have been more marked than in other countries, it is no less elusive. It must be considered an imponderable outside factor.

The weight of parliamentary actors may quite confidently be inferred from their nominal strength in the *Eduskunta*: "the general impression gained from the (Stuart Rice party cohesion) index numbers is the relatively high degree of cohesion within all the parliamentary groups"[72].

A Finnish author has identified a "special Nordic party system" characterized by the fact that at least five parties are represented in parliament: (*1*) the extreme left; (*2*) moderate socialist workers' parties; (*3*) a party of farmers and country dwellers; (*4*) a liberal bourgeois center party; and (5) "the bourgeois right, the upholders of conservatism and national tradition"[73]. This five-fold division in itself suggests a basic policy scale. Observers agree in placing the Democratic League for the People of Finland (PDEM), a communist-dominated organization, on the "extreme left"[74]; it is the successor of the communist movements that were represented in the *Eduskunta* from 1919 until 1939 when they were outlawed[75].

"Immediately after independence the Social Democrats were on the whole a disappointed and radical party; only gradually they followed the common Nordic trend away from Marx towards a programme of social and economic reform"[76].

The Agrarian League (AGR), since 1965 Center party (CENT), has of old been the party of small holders and rural proletarians. The Finnish Conservative Party (CONS) is, indeed, "a conservative party, emphasizing private enterprise, and, in general, the interests of economic life"[77]. A peculiar feature of the Finnish party system is the Swedish People's Party (SWPP) safeguarding the interests of the Swedish speaking minority, the Swede-Finns; it "includes all shades from right-wing conservatism to left-wing liberal radicalism bordering on socialism"[78]. The liberal movement was represented in Finland by a succession of parties: from the National Progressive (PROG) to the Finnish People's Party (FFP) and, from 1965, the Liberal League (LIB).

Two parties achieved actor status for only a brief period. The Finnish Patriotic Movement (NPF) was an actor in the thirties and entered some wartime coalitions. All the difficulties of ranking that are customary for a party of its type apply to this case. As its first goal it proclaimed "the entire Finnish race must be united into one Greater Finland on the basis of national self-determination"[79]. Within the party, the leadership principle obtained; democracy was rejected for the country. Its program was inspired by the corporate thinking of the Italian Fascists. The party saw itself as transcending the bourgeois-marxist antithesis: "Down with parties, down with Socialists and Bourgeoisie! There is only one Finnish nation."[80] In social economic matters, one suspects in the Finnish Patriots a similar indeterminacy as in the Weimar Nazis.

More recently, in 1958 and 1966, a split-off from the Social Democrats, the Workers' and Smallholders' Social Democratic League (SDWS), gained sufficient seats to be considered an actor.

In the construction of a social economic policy scale for these actors, the results of recent research in Finland are of great help. Parties have been ranked on the "Basic Ideological Ordinal Scale" (BIOS) which "refers to an ordinal scale based from right to left, on the intensity [sic] to preserve, develop or change the social order and political system of the country..... This order is controlled by a study of voters' opinions on the average image of parties."[81] The readiness to change the social order is a different criterion from the one underlying the definition of the policy scale in the present study. Fortunately, in a later phase, the author has applied a more elaborate content analysis to the party programs, tabulating for each party the frequency with which words belonging to 24 different categories appear in the programs, each category referring to some general political, economic, social or cultural value. These frequencies for each category for all parties are then correlated to the original BIOS scale. Thus, the categories "Socialist economy", "Patriotism" and "Bourgeois society" have a rho-correlation of over ±0.90 with the BIOS rank-order; "Capitalist economy" scores 0.83*. This strongly suggests that the original BIOS order did, in fact, correspond closely with a Socialism—Capitalism dimension and with the concomitant issue of the share of the government budget in the national income, *i.e.* the left-right dimension of this study.

Clearly, the original BIOS scale is strongly, but not only, associated with social economic party positions and some such positions do not agree with the original scale. With these considerations in mind, the order proposed is that of BIOS, *i.e.*,COMM—SOCD—SDWS—AGR—PROG($\neq$)SWPP—CONS(—NPF).

The amendments to BIOS are given in parentheses. On the basis of Andrén's description, it appears warranted to assume a tie between the Swedish and the Liberal Progressive or Finnish People's Party. The Patriots have been placed at the extreme right. Roughly the same argument as applies to the case of the Nazi party in Weimar appears to be valid here: the Patriots are to be considered indeterminate in social economic matters, but they have a clear and extreme position on nationalism. The "patriotism" category correlates with BIOS at 0.95 and, surveying the Finnish parties, one is tempted to believe that, in the thirties also, the patriotism dimension yielded the same party ranking as did the social economic dimension. Thus, an indeterminacy in the one continuum is

---

* The related categories of "Expansion of social security" and "Social justice" correlate much less with BIOS (0.36 each).

again combined, in this case, with a determinate and extreme position in another continuum that leaves the parties' ranking unaffected. In the present case, however, doubt is generated by the very low correlations with BIOS that Borg finds for the related (?) categories "Nationalism" and "National Independence", (-0.31 and -0.10 respectively)[82]. The present ranking will nevertheless be maintained as the least implausible[83].

3.b Historical coalitions

The 1919 elections in Finland resulted in a victory for the parties of Republican persuasion: the Socialists, the Agrarians and the Progressives. The Socialists and Agrarians together controlled a majority, one that was minimal winning, closed and of minimal range. The Socialists, however, had been deeply involved in the preceding Civil War on the side of the "Reds". The alternative to a Republican government was an all-bourgeois coalition that would have united Agrarians and Progressives with the parties that opposed the Republic, the Swede-Finns (SWPP) and the Conservatives (National Union Party). This coalition would also have been closed, minimal winning and of minimal range, p.d. undominated.

```
FINLAND 1919              (Source for coalitions in this Table and the following:
MAJORITY LARGER THAN 100 Tornudd)
ACTORS IN ASSEMBLY   SOCD   AGR  PROG  SWPP  CONS
POLICY SCALE ORDER      1     2     3     4     5
SEATS IN ASSEMBLY      80    42    26    22    28
Castrén (4/'19)             MEMBERMEMBERMEMBER
Vennola I (8/'19)          MEMBERMEMBER
ERICH (3/'20)              MEMBERMEMBERMEMBERMEMBER
Vennola II (4/'21)         MEMBERMEMBER

RESULTS OF THEORIES  WIN  MWIN  MSIZ  BRGP  MRAN  CLMR  CLCP  PDST  PDIN  PDCL
                    1;16   1;5   0;1   0;4   1;2   1;2   1;5   1;2   1;2   1;5
```

After a ten month period of minority cabinets with Progressives and Agrarians, these two joined with the Swede-Finns (SWPP) and Conservatives to form the all-bourgeois coalition, Erich (3/'20)[84], the p.d. undominated basic alternative.

```
FINLAND 1922                        (Not entered in the tabulations)
MAJORITY LARGER THAN 100
ACTORS IN ASSEMBLY   SOCL  SOCD   AGR  PROG  SWPP  CONS
POLICY SCALE ORDER      1     2     3     4     5     6
SEATS IN ASSEMBLY      27    53    45    15    25    35
Kallio I (11/'22)                MEMBERMEMBER

RESULTS OF THEORIES  WIN  MWIN  MSIZ  BRGP  MRAN  CLMR  CLCP  PDST  PDIN  PDCL
                    0;32  0;12   0;1  0;10   0;4   0;3   0;8   0;3   0;6   0;8
```

241

The elections of 1922 brought a Communist actor in the *Eduskunta* (SOCL). Communists, Social Democrats and Agrarians could have formed a minimal winning, closed coalition of minimal range and the coalition of the Agrarians with other bourgeois parties was closed and of minimal range but not minimal winning if the unnecessary Progressives were a member. A new basic alternative had emerged: a coalition of Social Democrats, Agrarians and Progressives. Until the next elections, however, no majority coalition appeared, in fact. After the 1924 elections, Social Democrats and Agrarians together could have controlled a majority, and so could the four bourgeois parties together. The former coalition was a basic alternative but in the latter the Progressives were again unnecessary. Ingman II (5/'24) opted for the all-bourgeois coalition which, when the Agrarians defected after six months, gave way to a succession of minority cabinets. The only government of interest here is Tanner (12/'26), an all-Social Democrat minority cabinet that gave this party its first taste of government.

```
FINLAND 1924
MAJORITY LARGER THAN 100
ACTORS IN ASSEMBLY   SOCL   SOCD   AGR    PROG   SWPP   CONS
POLICY SCALE ORDER     1      2      3      4      5      6
SEATS IN ASSEMBLY     18     60     44     17     23     38
INGMAN II (5/'24)                   MEMBERMEMBERMEMBERMEMBER
Ingman II (11/'24)                         MEMBERMEMBERMEMBER
Tullenheimo (3/'25)                 MEMBERMEMBER        MEMBER
Kallio II (12/'25)                  MEMBER              MEMBER
Tanner (12/'26)              MEMBER

RESULTS OF THEORIES   WIN    MWIN   MSIZ   BRGP   MRAN   CLMR   CLCP   PDST   PD1N   PDCL
                      1;31   0;8    0;1    0;1    1;3    1;2    1;9    0;4    0;6    1;9
```

```
FINLAND 1927
MAJORITY LARGER THAN 100
ACTORS IN ASSEMBLY   SOCL   SOCD   AGR    PROG   SWPP   CONS
POLICY SCALE ORDER     1      2      3      4      5      6
SEATS IN ASSEMBLY     20     60     52     10     24     34
Sunila I (12/'27)            MEMBER
Mantere (12/'28)                    MEMBER        MEMBER
Kallio (8/'29)               MEMBERMEMBER
SVINHUFVUD II (7/'30)        MEMBERMEMBERMEMBERMEMBER

RESULTS OF THEORIES   WIN    MWIN   MSIZ   BRGP   MRAN   CLMR   CLCP   PDST   PD1N   PDCL
                      1;32   0;8    0;2    0;1    1;3    1;2    1;9    1;5    1;7    1;9
```

The Progressive party was again unnecessary (but not adding to the range) in the all-bourgeois coalition after the elections of 1927. No majority governments were formed until a few months before the new elections when Svinhufvud II (7/'30) formed the closed, minimal range all-bourgeois coalition that was p.d. undominated.

In the months preceding the 1930 elections, strong agitation by the Communist party was matched by heavy oppression from the government which finally excluded the party from participation in the elections[85].

```
FINLAND 1930
MAJORITY LARGER THAN 100
ACTORS IN ASSEMBLY  SOCD    AGR   PROG  SWPP   CONS
POLICY SCALE ORDER    1      2     3     4      5
SEATS IN ASSEMBLY    66     59    11    21     42
SVINHUFVUD II (10/'30)     MEMBERMEMBERMEMBERMEMBER
SUNILLA II (3/'31)         MEMBERMEMBERMEMBERMEMBER
KIVIMAEKI (12/'32)         MEMBERMEMBERMEMBERMEMBER

RESULTS OF THEORIES  WIN   MWIN  MSIZ  BRGP  MRAN  CLMR  CLCP  PDST  PD1N  PDCL
                    1;16   0;3   0;1   0;3   1;5   1;2   1;5   1;5   1;2   1;5
```

The outcome of the elections was a situation in which Social Democrats and Agrarians could have formed a closed, minimal winning, minimal range coalition, while Agrarians and Conservatives could have joined in an open minimal winning, minimal range coalition of minimum size, to which Progressives and Swede-Finns (SWPP) were unnecessary without adding to the coalition's range. Svinhufvud II kept his cabinet intact, even more clearly than before the elections, opting for a closed rather than a minimal winning coalition. The same applies to the succeeding cabinets of Sunila II (3/'31) and Kivimäki (12/'32). The coalition is p.d. undominated, also under either permissibility condition. Kivimäki

```
FINLAND 1933
MAJORITY LARGER THAN 100
ACTORS IN ASSEMBLY  SOCD    AGR   PROG  SWPP   CONS   NPF
POLICY SCALE ORDER    1      2     3     4      5      6
SEATS IN ASSEMBLY    78     53    11    21     18     14
KIVIMAEKI (6/'33)         MEMBERMEMBERMEMBERMEMBER

RESULTS OF THEORIES  WIN   MWIN  MSIZ  BRGP  MRAN  CLMR  CLCP  PDST  PD1N  PDCL
                    1;30   1;9   1;2   0;1   1;2   1;2   1;7   1;8   1;7   1;5
```

continued his coalition after the 1933 elections, in which the Conservatives lost heavily, and a party of near Fascist character, the Patriotic People's Movement (NPF), emerged as a new actor. Because of this, all four members of the coalition became necessary, the coalition was minimal winning and, moreover, of minimum size! It was also p.d. undominated.

```
FINLAND 1936
MAJORITY LARGER THAN 100
ACTORS IN ASSEMBLY  SOCD    AGR   PROG   SWPP   CONS   NPF
POLICY SCALE ORDER    1      2     3      4      5     6
SEATS IN ASSEMBLY    83     54     8     22     19    13
Kivimaeki (2/'36)           MEMBERMEMBER        MEMBER
Kallio IV (10/'36)          MEMBERMEMBER
CAJANDER III
(3/'37)              MEMBERMEMBERMEMBER

RESULTS OF THEORIES  WIN    MWIN   MSIZ   BRGP   MRAN   CLMR   CLCP   PDST   PD1N   PDCL
                     1;32   0;6    0;1    0;3    0;2    0;2    1;7    0;6    0;5    0;4
```

The elections of 1936 produced the same basic alternatives; the Kivimäki coalition barely maintained its majority (though, strictly speaking, it was no longer of minimum size). Yet, the Swede-Finns left the coalition and Kivimäki continued as a minority government, as did its successor Kallio IV (10/'36). Cajander III (3/'37) included the Social Democrats for the first time in a coalition government in which Agrarians and Progressives also participated, the latter unnecessary and adding to the range. The coalition was closed, large (controlling more than two-thirds of the Assembly vote) and p.d. dominated, also under either permissibility condition. The inclusion of the Progressives may well have been induced by the desire on the part of the Agrarians to counerbalance the much larger Social Democrats[86], a motivation akin to policy distance theory's behavioral assumption. Yet, in its present operationalization, policy distance theory does not account for Cajander III. As the international situation grew worse, and on the eve of the Soviet invasion, the Swede-Finns joined the cabinet. This contradicted minimal winning and minimal range theory once again and it enlarged the already large coalition, which remained closed and p.d. dominated. Under conditions of actual war, Ryti I (12/'39) continued the coalition of Cajander III in its final composition[87]. Both coalitions are ignored in the tabulations. The conditions underlying all the theories no longer apply to this period. The threat of war had materialized in the form of invasion and occupation of

244

```
MAJORITY LARGER THAN 100
ACTORS IN ASSEMBLY  SOCD   AGR  PROG  SWPP  CONS   NPF
POLICY SCALE ORDER    1     2    3     4     5     6
SEATS IN ASSEMBLY    85    56    6    18    25     8
RYTI  I  (12/'39)   MEMBERMEMBERMEMBERMEMBER
RYTI  II (3/'40)*   MEMBERMEMBERMEMBERMEMBERMEMBER
RANGELL (1/'41)     MEMBERMEMBERMEMBERMEMBERMEMBERMEMBER

RESULT OF THEORIES   WIN   MWIN  MSIZ  BRGP  MRAN  CLMR  CLCP  PDST  PD1N  PDCL
                    3;31   0;5   0;1   0;3   0;2   0;2   3;7   2;7   1;5   2;4
```

large parts of the Finnish territory; the Assembly was no longer the main centre for the determination of major government policy because of Soviet interference in Finnish politics[88]. A gradual rapprochement with Nazi Germany developed, however. In addition to the Parties of the preceding coalition, Ryti II (3/'40) contained also the Conservatives, a closed coalition and p.d. undominated this time. Next, Rangell (1/'41) added the Patriotic People's Movement (NPF) to the other parties, thus forming a grand national coalition of all six actors. The closed coalition was p.d. undominated, but, by definition, not 1,n permissible! At a time when the tide of war seemed to change and turn against Germany[86], Linkomies (3/'43) excluded the Patriotic People's Movement, going back to the coalition of Ryti II; the shortlived cabinet of Hackzell (8/'44) and that of Castrèn (9/'44) continued on the same basis as Linkomies.

As the balance of international power had shifted once more, Paasiviki II (10/'44) formed a government that included a party not even represented in the Assembly, since it had been illegal until then, i.e. the Finnish People's Democratic League (PDEM) (an organization with Left Socialists, but dominated by the Communists)[89]. Though Paasiviki was a Conservative, his own former party, the National Union Party, did not participate in the government[90]. The coalition of Communists, Social Democrats, Progressives and Agrarians anticipated the outcome of the 1945 elections in which Communists, Social Democrats and Agrarians each captured a quarter of the seats in the Assembly. Any two of these parties together would have been two or three votes short of a majority but the three of them could form a left-center coalition that was closed, and at once minimal winning, of minimal range

---

* Of the same composition as Ryti II: Linkomies (3/'43), Hackzell (8/'44) and Castrèn (9/'44).

and large! On the other side of the policy scale, the Patriotic People's Movement (NPF) had vanished as an actor; the all-bourgeois coalition of Agrarians, Progressives, Swede-Finns (SWPP) and Conservatives was one vote short of a majority. As a consequence, the only other basic alternative next to the center-left coalition was one of Social Democrats, Agrarians and Progressives, again minimal winning, closed and of minimal range.

```
FINLAND 1945
MAJORITY LARGER THAN 100
ACTORS IN ASSEMBLY   PDEM   SOCD   AGR   PROG   SWPP   CONS
POLICY SCALE ORDER     1      2      3     4      5      6
SEATS IN ASSEMBLY     49     50     49    ·9     14     28
PAASIVIKI III
(4/'45)              MEMBERMEMBERMEMBERMEMBER
PAASIVIKI III
(7/'45)              MEMBERMEMBERMEMBER        MEMBER
PEKKALA (3/'46)      MEMBERMEMBERMEMBER        MEMBER

RESULT OF THEORIES    WIN    MWIN   MSIZ   BRGP   MRAN   CLMR   CLCP   PDST   PD1N   PDCL
                     2;30   0;11   0;1    0;10   0;2    0;2    1;7    0;9    2;9    1;7
```

Passiviki III (4/'45) extended the already large center-left coalition to include the Progressives who were unnecessary and adding to the range of the closed coalition. Three months later, the Progressives left the government, and the Swede-Finns, who were equally unnecessary, joined, making the coalition an open one. Both Paasiviki III coalitions were p.d. dominated but not under $1,n$ permissibility. Pekkala (3/'46) continued the open Paasiviki III coalition.

The Communists in the Paasiviki and the Pekkala government were embedded in a large coalition, reminiscent of the cabinet of Cajander III which had initiated the Social Democrats into coalition politics, counterbalancing them with bourgeois partners. Again, policy distance theory, as presently operationalized, does not account for this coalition, even though it was brought about by actors who appear to have been motivated by a desire to minimize policy distance. The influence of the Soviet Union (and the related victory of the Democratic League) is a plausible explanatory factor in understanding the formation of these very large coalitions[91]. Electoral alliances of Communists and Social Democrats, moreover, had set the stage for their collaboration in government.

The elections of 1948 changed the situation since they provided the Social Democrats and Agrarians with a majority, one that was minimal winning, closed and of minimal range. The latter could now have governed with the Swede-Finns (SWPP) and the Conservatives in a minimal winning, minimal range coalition, open without the unnecessary Progressives[92], but closed if including them, and no longer minimal winning.

```
FINLAND 1948
MAJORITY LARGER THAN 100
ACTORS IN ASSEMBLY  PDEM  SOCD  AGR  PROG  SWPP  CONS
POLICY SCALE ORDER    1     2    3    4     5     6
SEATS IN ASSEMBLY    38    54   56    5    14    33
Fagerholm (7/'48)          MEMBER
Kekkonen I (3/'50)              MEMBERMEMBERMEMBER
KEKKONEN II (1/'51)        MEMBERMEMBER      MEMBER

RESULT OF THEORIES   WIN  MWIN  MSIZ  BRGP  MRAN  CLMR  CLCP  PDST  PD1N  PDCL
                    1;32  0;7   0;1   0;1   0;3   0;2   0;9   0;6   1;6   0;5
```

After the minority cabinets of Fagerholm (7/'48) (with only Social Democrats) and Kekkonen I, with Swede-Finns, Agrarians and Progressives, a new majority came about. Kekkonen II (1/'51) united Social Democrats, Agrarians and, unnecessarily, the Swede-Finns in an open coalition, neither minimal winning nor of minimal range and p.d. dominated, but not under 1,n permissibility.

```
FINLAND 1951
MAJORITY LARGER THAN 100
ACTORS IN ASSEMBLY  PDEM  SOCD  AGR  PROG  SWPP  CONS
POLICY SCALE ORDER    1     2    3    4     5     6
SEATS IN ASSEMBLY    43    53   51   10    15    28
KEKKONEN III (9/'51)      MEMBERMEMBER      MEMBER
Kekkonen IV (7/'53)             MEMBER      MEMBER
Tuomioja (11/'53)               MEMBERMEMBERMEMBER

RESULTS OF THEORIES  WIN  MWIN  MSIZ  BRGP  MRAN  CLMR  CLCP  PDST  PD1N  PDCL
                    1;32  0;9   0;3   0;1   0;2   0;2   0;9   0;4   0;7   0;9
```

In the new Assembly, Kekkonen III (9/'51) continued on the same basis, even though the Swede-Finns (SWPP) were still unnecessary. The basic alternatives in this situation were again the coalition of Agrarians and Social Democrats or the all-bourgeois coalition in which, this time, all four parties were necessary. Both coalitions were of minimum size. But Kekkonen III contradicted all theories for another twenty-two months and no plausible explanation suggests itself.

247

```
FINLAND 1954
MAJORITY LARGER THAN 100
ACTORS IN ASSEMBLY  PDEM  SOCD   AGR    FPP   SWPP   CONS
POLICY SCALE ORDER    1     2     3      4     5      6
SEATS IN ASSEMBLY    43    54    53     13    13     24
TOERNGREN (5/'54)          MEMBERMEMBER        MEMBER
KEKKONEN V (10/'54)        MEMBERMEMBER
FAGERHOLM II (3/'56)       MEMBERMEMBERMEMBERMEMBER
Sukselainen I (5/'57)      MEMBERMEMBER

RESULTS OF THEORIES  WIN   MWIN  MSIZ  BRGP  MRAN  CLMR  CLCP  PDST  PDIN  PDCL
                     3;32  1;9   0;1   1;1   1;2   1;2   2;9   0;4   1;3   1;5
```

After the minority governments of Kekkonen IV (7/'53) and Tuomioja (11/'53), new elections yielded the same basic alternatives that had prevailed before. Törngren (5/'54) once more resorted to the coalition of Kekkonen II and III; the Swede-Finns remained unnecessary, the p.d. dominated coalition was open and of larger than minimal range. Kekkonen V (10/'54) governed for sixteen months with a cabinet of Agrarians and Social Democrats, a basic alternative, p.d. dominated under either permissibility condition. Fagerholm II (3/'56) extended the government's base to include the Swede-Finns and the Finnish People (FPP, formerly Progressive party), both unnecessary and adding to the coalition's range; because of the presence of the Finnish People, however, the coalition was this time closed, p.d. dominated but not under either permissibility condition.

```
FINLAND 1958
MAJORITY LARGER THAN 100
ACTORS IN ASSEMBLY  PDEM  SOCD  SDWS   AGR   FPP   SWPP  CONS
POLICY SCALE ORDER    1     2     3     4     5     6     7
SEATS IN ASSEMBLY    50    38    13    48     8    14    29
FAGERHOLM III (8/'58)      MEMBER      MEMBERMEMBERMEMBERMEMBER
Sukselainen II (1/'59)                 MEMBER
Miettunen (7/'61)                      MEMBER

RESULTS OF THEORIES  WIN   MWIN  MSIZ  BRGP  MRAN  CLMR  CLCP  PDST  PDIN  PDCL
                     1;63  0;16  0;2   0;9   0;4   0;3   0;9   0;8   0;14  0;9
```

Sukselainen I (5/'57) was the first of a series of three minority cabinets that continued until the elections of 1958. A new actor emerged, The Social Democratic League of Workers and Small Farmers, (SDWS). It was founded by a group of Social Democrat dissidents, the "Independent Social Democrats", later "Social Democratic Opposition", which shortly after the elections defected from the Social Democratic Party and held 13 seats in the

Eduskunta, thus qualifying as an actor[93]. The SDWS is placed between Social Democrats and Agrarians on the BIOS scale[94]. Democrats and Agrarians lost their majority and the Social Democrats could not have governed with the Communists either. The all-bourgeois coalition also remained under the majority mark. Therefore, the basic alternatives were a coalition of Communists, Social Democrats and Smallholders (minimum size!); or of Social Democrats, Smallholders (SDWS) Agrarians and Finnish People (FFP). Fagerholm III (8/'58) added to Social Democrats, Agrarians and Conservatives the unnecessary Swede-Finns and Finnish People, thus increasing the range of the coalition beyond the minimum and its weight beyond two-thirds of the Assembly vote. The coalition was closed, however, but p.d. dominated under either permissibility condition. No theory accounts for it.

```
FINLAND 1962
MAJORITY LARGER THAN 100
ACTORS IN ASSEMBLY   PDEM  SOCD   AGR   FPP   SWPP  CONS
POLICY SCALE ORDER     1     2     3     4     5     6
SEATS IN ASSEMBLY     47    39    53    13    14    32
KARJALAINEN (4/'62)              MEMBERMEMBERMEMBERMEMBER
VIROLAINEN (9/'64)               MEMBERMEMBERMEMBERMEMBER

RESULTS OF THEORIES   WIN   MWIN  MSIZ  BRGP  MRAN  CLMR  CLCP  PDST  PD1N  PDCL
                     1;29  1;11  0;1   0;8   1;3   1;3   1;8   0;6   1;11  1;8
```

After some four months, the cabinet fell and until the 1962 elections a series of minority cabinets governed the country. In the new Assembly, the all-bourgeois coalition was closed, minimal winning and of minimal range and so were the coalitions of Social Democrats and Agrarians if either the Communists or the Finnish People were added. Karjalainen (4/'62) brought about the all-bourgeois coalition, a basic alternative this time, p.d. dominated but not under either permissibility condition. Internal dissension over agricultural price policy led to the downfall of the government. After nine months of caretaker government under Lehto (12/'63), Virolainen (9/'64) revived the all-bourgeois coalition which lasted another twenty months until the elections of 1966.

Before the elections, the Agrarians changed their name to Center Party and the Finnish People's Party, formerly the Progressives, now called itself the Liberal People's Party (LIB).

This time the Social Democrats had made sufficient gains to govern with either the Center Party alone or with Communists

(PDEM) and Smallholders (SDWS), the latter having regained actor status (but as a reconstituted party). The coalition of Communists, Social Democrats and Smallholders was closed, minimal winning and of minimal range: a basic alternative. The coalition of Center Party and Social Democrats was open without the unnecessary Smallholders but it embraced a minimal range. The all-bourgeois coalition remained in the minority.

```
FINLAND 1966
MAJORITY LARGER THAN 100
ACTORS IN ASSEMBLY  PDEM   SOCD   SDWS   CENT   LIB   SWPP   CONS
POLICY SCALE ORDER    1      2      3      4      5     6      7
SEATS IN ASSEMBLY    41     55      7     49      9    12     26
PAASIO I (5/'66)    MEMBERMEMBERMEMBERMEMBER
KOIVISTO (3/'68)    MEMBERMEMBERMEMBERMEMBER        MEMBER

RESULTS OF THEORIES  WIN   MWIN   MSIZ   BRGP   MRAN   CLMR   CLCP   PDST   PD1N   PDCL
                    2;63   0;10   0;2    0;1    0;4    0;3    1;10   0;10   2;11   1;10
```

Paasio (5/'66) formed a coalition of Communists, Social Democrats, Center Party and Smallholders: either the Communists (adding to the range) and the Smallholders, or the Center Party (also extending the coalition's range) were unnecessary. The coalition was large, closed and p.d. dominated but not under the two permissibility conditions. The next prime minister, Koivisto (3/'68), extended this large coalition to include the Swedish People's Party. The only theory to predict this alliance is policy distance theory in the $1,n$ permissibility version. Perhaps, the efforts to balance the presence of the Communists in the cabinet are reflected in the fact that the coalitions of 1945 and 1966 are p.d. undominated under $1,n$ permissibility. Koivisto lasted for more than two years, until the end of the parliamentary period.

With the elections of 1970, a new actor entered the Assembly, the "Vennamo" Peasant Party (PAES), situated at the extreme right of the policy scale*. Because of the new party and the gains of the Conservatives, the bourgeois parties could have formed a majority coalition in which the Liberals were unnecessary without adding to the range. The Smallholders had disappeared as an actor

---

* The Vennamo Peasant party, founded in 1959 as the Finnish Rural Party, has been characterized as "populist" and compared to the French Poujadist movement: a charismatic leader, strong opposition to big business and big government, to progressive taxation and the secularization of modern life, recruiting mostly from small rural farmers and businessmen. See Sänkiaho (1971) pp. 37, 41—43.

on the left. Social Democrats and Center Party had lost their majority and needed either the support of the Communists (PDEM) to form a closed, minimal winning coalition of minimal range, or the support of the Swede-Finns to bring about a minimal range coalition, minimal winning but open without the Liberals.

```
FINLAND 1970
MAJORITY LARGER THAN 100
ACTORS IN ASSEMBLY  PDEM  SOCD  CENT  LIB  SWPP  CONS  PAES
POLICY SCALE ORDER    1     2     3    4    5     6     7
SEATS IN ASSEMBLY    36    52    37    8   12    37    18
KARJALAINEN II
(7/'70)              MEMBERMEMBERMEMBERMEMBERMEMBER
KARJALAINEN III
(3/'71)                    MEMBERMEMBERMEMBERMEMBER

RESULTS OF THEORIES  WIN   MWIN  MSIZ  BRGP  MRAN  CLMR  CLCP  PDST  PD1N  PDCL
                     2;63  0;13  0;2   0;9   1;5   1;3   2;9   0;7   0;12  2;9
```

Karjalainen II (7/'70), after some months of negotiations and a caretaker cabinet, formed a government of Social Democrats, Communists, Center Party, Liberals and the Swede-Finns[95], a large, closed coalition in which the Communists were unnecessary and added to the range, or the Liberals and Swede-Finns were unnecessary and adding to the range. The coalition was p.d. dominated under $1,n$ permissibility but not in the closed coalition version of the theory. In March 1971, the Communists left the government[96]. Karjalainen III (3/'71) was no longer large but was still closed and this time of minimal range: the Liberals were still unnecessary but without them the coalition would have been exactly of minimum size, a somewhat uneasy majority. The coalition was p.d. dominated, also under the $1,n$ permissibility condition but not under the closed coalition condition.

```
FINLAND 1972
MAJORITY LARGER THAN 100
ACTORS IN ASSEMBLY  PDEM  SOCD  CENT  LIB  SWPP  CONS  PAES
POLICY SCALE ORDER    1     2     3    4    5     6     7
SEATS IN ASSEMBLY    37    55    36    7   10    34    18
PAASIO II (2/'72)          MEMBER

RESULTS OF THEORIES  WIN   MWIN  MSIZ  BRGP  MRAN  CLMR  CLCP  PDST  PD1N  PDCL
                     0;6'  0;13  0;2   0;9   0;4   0;3   0;9   0;8   0;9   0;9
```

The elections of 1972 did not produce dramatic changes. A caretaker cabinet led by Aura (1/'72) was succeeded by a Social Democrat minority government under Paasio II (2/'72)[97]. The coalitional options of the situation remained unchanged in comparison with 1970.

3.c Discussion

There has been a marked tendency in Finnish politics to govern either with minority cabinets or to bring about coalitions of larger than necessary membership. It is also remarkable that in Finland, as in the Netherlands and Israel, all major actors were accepted, in the long run, as partners in government.

Ignoring the war-time governments, Finland was ruled after 1919 by some 44 cabinets, 20 of them without a parliamentary majority coalition to support them. Of the remaining twenty-four governments, nineteen were closed along the policy scale. The five that were open either omitted the Progressives, while including the Swede-Finns (four times), or the coalition (Fagerholm III) excluded a new actor, the Smallholders. It may be, that additional information on the relative position of Progressives and Swede-Finns will show them to tie in their position on the scale, thus rendering most of these coalitions also closed.

Thirteen out of twenty-four majority coalitions were large (so were, as a matter of fact, all coalitions in the fateful period between 1937 and 1948). The coalitions containing the Communists were all among them.

As might be expected, minimal winning theory performs quite poorly in the case of Finland, only five coalitions satisfy its criterion (and only one the minimum size principle, one other coalition the bargaining proposition). Eleven out of the 24 majority governments were based on (closed) minimal range coalitions (among them all those that were also minimal winning and therefore basic alternatives).

Policy distance theory predicts six coalitions, all of them before the war. However, with the 1,n permissibility condition, there is a surprising improvement: fifteen coalitions are predicted. The closed coalition condition coupled to policy distance theory produces fourteen correctly predicted coalitions.

The statistics for Finland, however, are somewhat disappointing: no theory achieves a significant result, though closed minimal range theory comes close, at a 10.9 level. The closed coalition proposition and policy distance theory, 1,n permissibility version, are runners up with a meagre score of ±20%. The only theory that could have dealt with the extended Finnish coalitions, policy distance theory, does not reach significance, not even if the wartime coalitions are included (though this results in dramatic improvement of the performance of the closed coalition proposition and of p.d. theory, closed coalition version).

CHAPTER 11

The Scandinavian Monarchies

The Scandinavian monarchies display common features not only in the constitution of the three countries but also in their party system and in the process of coalition formation. Generally, four to five parties are actors in parliament. After the Second World War, the Social Democrat party has grown to be the largest actor, at times holding a majority on its own, confronting several bourgeois parties of social—liberal and liberal—conservative persuasion, sometimes devoted especially to the agrarian interest. Minority governments have been a common occurrence in Sweden, Denmark and Norway but, especially since the thirties, coalition government has occurred frequently in the Scandinavian monarchies.

1. Sweden

Of all countries under study, Sweden is the only one which, though threatened, was never involved in actual warfare. A policy of neutrality has shielded it from foreign influence more than other countries; this has added to the relatively closed nature of the Swedish political system. In domestic politics, the Swedes' homogeneity of language, religion and ethnic origin has resulted in a certain degree of consensus and has prevented such upheavals as might constitute a threat of civil war. Thus, the parliamentary system has continued to function as a more or less closed system within which the determination of major government policy has taken place.

254

1.a The parliamentary system

The Swedish parliament, *Riksdag*, was bicameral until 1971[1]. The constitutional equality of the Lower and Upper House[2] was not merely a formal matter[3]. Both Houses acted on the same questions simultaneously[4], and, most important in the present context

> *"Le cabinet était responsable aussi bien devant la seconde que devant la première Chambre* l'égalité entre les Chambres n'avait fait que se confirmer."[5]

The Lower House was elected directly for four years by universal suffrage; the members of the Upper House were appointed for eight years by local representative bodies whenever a seat came up for re-election.

Decisions in both Houses were made by simple majority[6]. This also applies to constitutional amendments (in the second and final readings passed by a re-elected Lower House)[7].

The King appoints the Cabinet but his decision depends exclusively on the confidence that the ministers enjoy in the *Riksdag*[8]. Even though some years after the establishment of this groundrule, in the beginning of the period under study, some conflict between King and ministers still occurred in the council, the King's veto exists only *pro forma*[9].

A consultative referendum has been held three times since it was instituted in 1922 but these rare popular pronouncements do not seem to have influenced coalition politics very much except, perhaps, for the boost that the last referendum gave to the pension scheme of the minority government in 1957[10].

The constitutional equality enjoyed by the Upper House opens, of course, the possibility of disagreement between Upper and Lower House.

> "The votes in both Houses are put together and the opinion which at this 'joint division' *(gemensam votering)* has attracted a majority of the aggregate number of the votes in both Houses constitutes the decision of the Riksdag."[11]

In this manner, a veto from either House can be overruled by the aggregate decision of the two Houses of Parliament. For this reason the "Joint Division" of the *Riksdag* has been chosen as the Senate in the technical sense of the theories. That is, a coalition is considered winning only if it has a majority in the Lower House *and* in the Joint Division.

Since 1971, however, the *Riksdag* is a unicameral body of 350 seats elected directly for three years with a mixed constituency—proportional system[12].

No other formal or informal veto positions seem to exist in Swedish politics; not of sufficient importance, that is, to warrant the amendment of the theories with some special provision to account for them.

Voting discipline among parliamentary groups in the *Riksdag* is tight.

"To most party members it must seem more important to preserve the unity and power of their own party than to act independently whenever they disagree with the official party line."[13]

For the last fifty years, four parties have divided amongst themselves more than ninety percent of the seats in the Lower House and almost all the seats in the Senate. The only other party that at times qualified as an actor by capturing more than 2.5% of the seats in the Lower House, was the Communist party.

Särlvik writes

"For a multi-party system, the Swedish political scene has a remarkably one-dimensional character. The major parties can be arranged along a right—left continuum which forms the ideological basis of the party system..... This characterization clearly is applicable to four of the five major parties: the *Conservative Party....*, the Liberal *People's Party*, the *Social Democratic Party* and the *Communist Party*..... A partial exception from the prevailing unidimensionality is the *Center Party....* The Center Party shares the position at the 'political centre' with the People's Party."[14]

Särlvik is of the opinion that social economic matters constitute the predominant dimension of Swedish political life and that this dimension corresponds with voters' attitudes on the welfare state[15].

Hence, the Communist party, with its close adherence to the international Communist movement[16], may be placed at the extreme left of the policy scale. The Social Democratic Party comes next.

"The Social Democratic Labour Party abandoned its purely Marxian principles at an early date and developed into a reformist, moderate socialist party, stressing instead of direct measures of socialism, social reform, the levelling of incomes, and various state controls."[17]

When it came to power in 1932, the party shifted from a program of nationalization to one of social welfare policy: "The Socialists wanted a higher level of state activity and an economy planned by the state." The underlying reason for this agrees well with the postulates of the policy scale: "Social welfare programs were seen as another means of leveling incomes."[18]

The bourgeois parties may be placed to the right of the Social Democrats.

"The Conservatives and the Liberals still acted as protectors of the structure of society and opposed state regulation. The Center Party however, was able to accept state regulation in agriculture."[18]

This places the Center Party (*Centerpartiet,* formerly *Bondeförbundet,* or Agrarian Party) immediately to the right of the Social Democrats.

The program of the Liberal (People's) Party has been described as "social liberalism, in which a considerable number of social welfare policies are combined with a program to promote individual initiative and freedom of enterprise"[19]. The party split in 1923, the larger Ekman-faction favoring prohibition. In 1934 the two factions reunited as the People's Party[20].

The Conservatives, of old opponents of welfare policy and disarmament, "have accepted the basic tenets of the welfare state," but hold "that social welfare measures may be carried too far"[21]. The Conservative Party is to be placed at the right end of the scale.

Stjernquist signalizes a development "from cleavage to consensus" in Swedish politics.

"The main aim of Swedish economic policy has been to secure social welfare and full employment and to raise the standard of living. Democracy has become equated with social services. To realize this aim it has been necessary to give priority to actions that can lead to an increase in production. On this point the government, the opposition, the organizations, and big business are united."[22]

The author goes on to remark that a Socialist government may be in a better position to put pressure on the unions.

"All these considerations taken together have many times made the nonsocialist parties and the Socialists accept the same policy. In the process ideological differences have been pushed aside."[22]

In the course of the years, the policy scale may have come to span a decreasing range but its order has remained the same.

"Cleavages sometimes occur *within* the parties. During the last few decades, however, the parties have been so well established and party identifications among the electorate so strong that new political issues have not produced changes in the party system."[23]

The preceding considerations are best summed up in the following policy scale.

Communists—Social Democrats—Center Party (+) Liberals—Conservatives

The position of Agrarians and Liberals *vis à vis* one another is classified as indeterminate until 1940, even though the Agrarians may have shifted to the left around 1932: however, this shift may still be explained from the theories if the policy scale is held constant for the entire period between the wars.

1.b Historical coalitions

In 1917, the principle of parliamentary government was affirmed when a government that had been appointed by the King against the wishes of a majority in the *Riksdag* was forced to resign[24].

```
SWEDEN 1917
MAJORITY LARGER THAN 115 (ASSEMBLY) 190 (SENATE)
ACTORS IN ASSEMBLY  COMM  SOCD   AGR   LIB  CONS
POLICY SCALE ORDER     1     2   3,5   3,5     5
SEATS IN ASSEMBLY     11    86    12    62    59
SEATS IN SENATE*      13   105    12   105   145
EDÈN (1917)                MEMBER       MEMBER
Branting I (1920)          MEMBER

RESULTS OF THEORIES  WIN  MWIN  MSIZ  BRGP  MRAN  CLMR  CLCP  PDST  PD1N  PDCL
                    1;16   1;3   0;1   1;3   1;4   1;4   1;8   0;8   0;4   0;4
```

The elections that followed produced a Lower House in which Liberals and Conservatives could have formed a closed, minimal winning coalition of minimal range. Social Democrats and Liberals could have formed a minimal winning, minimal range coalition, closed (that is "not certainly open") even without the unnecessary Agrarians, whose position *vis à vis* the Liberals is indeterminate. The Conservatives controlled an absolute majority in the Upper House but not in the Joint Division, so that this aggregate voting procedure was very important.

The electoral victory of the Social Democrats and the Liberals moved the King to consent to their joint government: Edén (1917) governed with the two parties in a minimal winning, minimal range and closed coalition that was p.d. dominated, also under 1,n permissibility. After the government carried out its program of reform, if fell over a bill on local taxation[25]. A Social Democrat minority cabinet, Branting I (1920), governed until the elections of 1921.

---

* The "Senate" in the case of Sweden is the Joint Division.

SWEDEN 1921
MAJORITY LARGER THAN 115 (ASSEMBLY) 190 (SENATE)

ACTORS IN ASSEMBLY	COMM	SOCD	AGR	LIB	CONS
POLICY SCALE ORDER	1	2	3,5	3,5	5
SEATS IN ASSEMBLY	8	93	21	41	62
SEATS IN SENATE	9	143	39	79	103
Various minority governments		MEMBER			
				MEMBER	

RESULTS OF THEORIES	WIN	MWIN	MSIZ	BRGP	MRAN	CLMR	CLCP	PDST	PD1N	PDCL
	0;15	0;4	0;1	0;2	0;3	0;3	0;8	0;4	0;2	0;3

The coalitional features of the new *Riksdag* were to remain mostly unchanged for the remainder of the years between the wars; there were two basic alternatives: the all-bourgeois coalition (p.d. undominated, moreover) and the coalition of Social Democrats and Liberals, closed even without the Agrarians, because of the indeterminate policy position of Liberals and Agrarians with respect to one another. Thus the Liberals were in the key position of being a member of both basic alternative coalitions throughout the period. From 1924 on, the Agrarians were in a similar position: they could have formed a basic alternative coalition with the Social Democrats (in 1928 the Left Socialists were also necessary). From this time on, the Social Democrats could also have chosen between two basic alternatives, one with the Agrarians, the other with the Liberals.

SWEDEN 1924
MAJORITY LARGER THAN 115 (ASSEMBLY) 190 (SENATE)

ACTORS IN ASSEMBLY	SOCD	AGR	LIB	CONS
POLICY SCALE ORDER	1	2,5	2,5	4
SEATS IN ASSEMBLY	105	23	33	65
SEATS IN SENATE	157	41	68	109
BRANTING III (1924)	MEMBER		MEMBER	
Ekman I (1926)			MEMBER	

RESULTS OF THEORIES	WIN	MWIN	MSIZ	BRGP	MRAN	CLMR	CLCP	PDST	PD1N	PDCL
	1;8	1;4	0;1	1;3	1;4	1;4	1;5	0;4	0;3	0;4

Various minority and caretaker cabinets governed until Branting III (1924) formed a Social Democrat minority cabinet supported by the Liberal parties in parliament[26], a basic alternative, although p.d. dominated in all three versions of the theory. Ekman I (1926) was a Liberal minority cabinet that relied "on support from the Social Democrats on the defence budget and from the Conservatives on unemployment"[26], a good way to keep the government budget low! A good way, moreover, to exploit membership in two basic alternative coalitions. However, the parliamentary base of the Ekman I government is too uncertain to qualify as a more or less permanent parliamentary majority coalition. Such a clear parliamentary majority emerged again in 1932.

```
SWEDEN 1932
MAJORITY LARGER THAN 115 (ASSEMBLY) 190 (SENATE)
ACTORS IN ASSEMBLY  COMM  SOCD  AGR   LIB   CONS
POLICY SCALE ORDER    1     2   3,5   3,5    5
SEATS IN ASSEMBLY     8    104   36    24    58
SEATS IN SENATE       9    162   54    47   108
HANSSON I (1932)            MEMBERMEMBER
Pehrsson-Bramstorp
(1936)                            MEMBER
```

RESULTS OF THEORIES	WIN	MWIN	MSIZ	BRGP	MRAN	CLMR	CLCP	PDST	PD1N	PDCL
	1;16	1;4	0;1	1;3	1;4	1;4	1;9	0;4	0;2	0;3

In the elections of 1932, Social Democrats and Agrarians together captured enough seats to control a majority in both Houses: a minimal winning, closed coalition of minimal range, although it was p.d. dominated. The all-bourgeois coalition also remained a basic alternative. Thus, the Agrarians, as members of both basic alternative coalitions, were in a key position. The Social Democrat minority government Hansson I (1932) succeeded after some months in concluding a support agreement with the Agrarians in parliament: a basic alternative parliamentary coalition, set up to deal with the great crisis.

With the 1936 elections, the bourgeois parties lost their majority in the Lower House. The coalitions of Social Democrats with either Agrarians or with Liberals were basic alternatives; the Agrarians were no longer in the key position. This was the moment that they entered the cabinet to bring about the first majority cabinet of the period: Hansson II (1936), a basic alternative (but still p.d. dominated).

```
SWEDEN 1936
MAJORITY LARGER THAN 115 (ASSEMBLY) 190 (SENATE)
ACTORS IN ASSEMBLY  COMM  SOCD  AGR   LIB   CONS
POLICY SCALE ORDER    1     2   3,5   3,5
SEATS IN ASSEMBLY     6    112   36    27    44
SEATS IN SENATE       7    178   58    43    89
HANSSON II (1936)          MEMBERMEMBER
HANSSON III (1939)         MEMBERMEMBERMEMBERMEMBER
```

RESULTS OF THEORIES	WIN	MWIN	MSIZ	BRGP	MRAN	CLMR	CLCP	PDST	PD1N	PDCL
	2;14	1;3	0;1	1;3	1;3	1;3	2;8	1;4	1;5	1;6

Not surprisingly from the standpoint of policy distance theory, the Agrarians pressed for a coalition of the "big four", excluding only the Communists. This was the Agrarians' first preference in p.d. theory and Pehrsson-Bramstorp had tried in vain to bring it about during his three months of government[27].

With the formation of Hansson III (1939), the four-party government became a fact. War had broken out on the continent. Liberals and Conservatives joined the cabinet, even though they were unnecessary and added to the range. But the coalition was large, closed and p.d. undominated, also under either permissibility condition.

The Social Democrats obtained a generous majority in the Lower House in 1940 and by that time they held an ample majority in the Joint Division also*. Throughout the war years — a period of neutrality, but also of great international insecurity for Sweden — the National Coalition Government of Hansson III maintained itself. No theory predicts the coalition since the Social Democrats had an absolute majority on their own. As a war coalition, it is not tabulated.

Shortly after the war, the coalition fell apart. The Liberals began to waver in their support and the Social Democrats intended to carry through their planned reforms[28].

The Social Democrats were one vote short of a majority in the Lower House after 1944 but secure in the Joint Division. The basic alternatives were coalitions of the Social Democrats with either the Communists or the Agrarians. Hansson IV (1945) consisted of the Social Democrats only. Erlander (1946) who succeeded after Hansson's death kept the Social Democrat government in power until 1951.

In 1948, the Social Democrats again lost a few seats in the Lower House but the bourgeois parties were still outnumbered. Only with Communist aid could they have toppled the Social Democrat cabinet. The Social Democrats retained their key position as members of both the basic alternative coalition with the Communists and with the Agrarians.

In 1951, Erlander II (1951) brought about the "red—green" coalition between Social Democrats and Agrarians: a basic alternative but p.d. dominated.

In the elections of the following year, the Communists lost their actor status and, as a consequence, the "red—green" coalition was the only remaining basic alternative. (The bourgeois parties were one vote short of a majority.) Erlander II continued his govern-

---

* For that reasons the tables for 1940 and 1944 have not been reproduced.

ment until 1957, after 1952 as a minimum size coalition, undominated in all three versions of policy distance theory.

```
SWEDEN 1948
MAJORITY LARGER THAN 115 (ASSEMBLY) 190 (SENATE)
ACTORS IN ASSEMBLY  COMM  SOCD    AGR   LIB   CONS
POLICY SCALE ORDER    1     2      3     4     5
SEATS IN ASSEMBLY     8    112     30    57    23
SEATS IN SENATE      11    196     51    75    47
Erlander I (Ctnd.)         MEMBER
ERLANDER II (1951)         MEMBERMEMBER
```

RESULTS OF THEORIES	WIN	MWIN	MSIZ	BRGP	MRAN	CLMR	CLCP	PDST	PD1N	PDCL
	1;15	1;4	0;1	1;4	1;2	1;2	1;7	0;1	0;1	0;1

```
SWEDEN 1952
MAJORITY LARGER THAN 115 (ASSEMBLY) 190 (SENATE)
ACTORS IN ASSEMBLY  SOCD   AGR   LIB   CONS
POLICY SCALE ORDER    1     2     3     4
SEATS IN ASSEMBLY    110    26    58    31
SEATS IN SENATE      189    51    80    51
ERLANDER II (Ctnd) MEMBERMEMBER
```

RESULTS OF THEORIES	WIN	MWIN	MSIZ	BRGP	MRAN	CLMR	CLCP	PDST	PD1N	PDCL
	1;7	1;3	1;1	1;3	1;1	1;1	1;3	1;3	1;2	1;3

```
SWEDEN 1956
MAJORITY LARGER THAN 115 (ASSEMBLY) 190 (SENATE)
ACTORS IN ASSEMBLY  COMM  SOCD   CENT   LIB   CONS
POLICY SCALE ORDER    1     2      3     4     5
SEATS IN ASSEMBLY     6    106     19    58    42
SEATS IN SENATE       9    185     44    88    55
ERLANDER II (Ctnd.)        MEMBERMEMBER
Erlander III (1957)        MEMBER
```

RESULTS OF THEORIES	WIN	MWIN	MSIZ	BRGP	MRAN	CLMR	CLCP	PDST	PD1N	PDCL
	1;15	1;3	1;2	1;3	1;1	1;1	1;6	1;5	1;5	1;6

The year before, in 1956, elections were held. The Communists regained their actor status but they were unable to muster enough votes to provide an all-Socialist coalition with a majority: the Social Democrats had lost votes, as had the Center Party, formerly the Agrarian Party, but the two retained a majority and could have constituted a basic alternative coalition, p.d. undominated, moreover. Under these circumstances, the "red—green" coalition came to an end and Erlander III continued as a Social Democrat minority government until the Lower House was dissolved following a popular referendum on the pension schemes of the various parties[29]. Early elections were held in 1958.

```
SWEDEN 1958
MAJORITY LARGER THAN 115 (ASSEMBLY) 191 (SENATE)
ACTORS IN ASSEMBLY  COMM  SOCD  CENT   LIB  CONS
POLICY SCALE ORDER     1     2     3     4     5
SEATS IN ASSEMBLY      5   111    32    38    45
SEATS IN SENATE        7   190    54    70    61
Erlander III (Cntd.)        MEMBER

RESULTS OF THEORIES  WIN  MWIN  MSIZ  BRGP  MRAN  CLMR  CLCP  PDST  PD1N  PDCL
                    0;16  0;5   0;1   0;4   0;2   0;2   0;7   0;1   0;1   0;1
```

The elections of 1958, 1960 and 1964 did not change the coalitional features of the situation. The bourgeois parties remained a few votes short of a majority and so did the Social Democrats; their key position between Communists and Center Party, with both of whom they could have formed basic alternative coalitions, remained unchanged. Erlander continued to govern with a minority cabinet of Social Democrats but he received "firm but independent support" from the Communists who "had pledged themselves not to endanger the position of a 'labour' government"[29]. On the other hand, in 1961, Social Democrats and Agrarians concluded a support agreement on important financial legislation[30].

To all appearances, the Social Democrats used their key position to the full by using either basic alternative coalition instead of basing themselves upon a more or less permanent parliamentary majority coalition. Their behavior is reminiscent of the tactics of the Agrarians used in the period 1932—1936 when they were in a key position between a bourgeois basic alternative coalition and one with the Social Democrats.

In the elections of 1968, the Social Democrats gained an absolute majority in both Houses and that suspended the coalitional game. After twenty-three years, Tage Erlander was succeeded by Palme (10/'69).

In 1970, the first elections were held for a unicameral *Riksdag*; the Senate was abolished and so, of course, was the Joint Division.

```
SWEDEN 1970
MAJORITY LARGER THAN 175
ACTORS IN ASSEMBLY  COMM  SOCD  CENT   LIB  CONS
POLICY SCALE ORDER     1     2     3     4     5
SEATS IN ASSEMBLY     17   163    71    58    41
PALME (10/'69)          MEMBERMEMBER

RESULTS OF THEORIES  WIN  MWIN  MSIZ  BRGP  MRAN  CLMR  CLCP  PDST  PD1N  PDCL
                    1;16  1;5   1;1   1;4   1;2   1;2   1;7   1;1   1;1   1;1
```

The Social Democrats lost their majority but continued their key position in the basic alternative coalitions with either the Center Party or the Communists. This time a support agreement was concluded with the Communist Party[31]. Palme continued his government with a coalition that was predicted by every theory in the book.

1.c Discussion

Looking over the evidence, it appears rather striking that the "red—green" coalition could only have come about in the thirties after the Agrarians had lost their key position in two basic alternative coalitions and that after a period of National Coalitions during the war years, the "red—green" coalition came to an end when the Social Democrats were in a similar key position between Communists and Agrarians (Center Party). This phenomenon may point towards an explanation of these minority governments in Sweden; actors in a key position may prefer a minority government which allows both basic alternatives to be exploited at once.

The Edén and Branting coalitions of Social Democrats and Liberals, the Hansson and Erlander coalitions of Social Democrats and Agrarians and the Palme coalition of Social Democrats and Communists were all basic alternatives: they were closed, of minimal range and minimal winning. The four-party coalition of Hansson III (1939) was large, closed and p.d. undominated in all three versions of the theory. Counting a cabinet continuation after the elections as a new cabinet, and ignoring the wartime governments of 1940—1945, there were nine majority governments, all but one of them (Hansson, 1939) minimal winning and of minimal range. In addition, all of them satisfied the bargaining proposition. Two coalitions were of minimum size (Erlander II, 1952 and 1956). All three versions of p.d. theory predict four coalitions correctly.

The statistical scores of most of the theories are insignificant; the indeterminacy of the Liberal and Agrarian policy positions increases the predicted set of the theories that use the policy scale. Minimal range theory scores at a level of significance of 5% for the Swedish case. Closed minimal range theory achieves the same result but basic alternative theory (closed, minimal winning, minimal range coalitions) is significant at the 2% level.

2. Denmark

The discussion of coalitions in Denmark will not proceed along the same lines as in preceding chapters. The Danish case is special, not because in Denmark conditions prevail that might require adaptation of the assumptions underlying the theories (in fact the postulates of the theories fit the parliamentary system in Denmark quite well) but because all theories produce such convincing results that it is hard to single out some as more adequate to explain coalition formation in Denmark than others. Moreover, an excellent analysis of Danish coalitions has been published by Erik Damgaard. It therefore seems appropriate to review the findings of that inquiry and compare them with those of the present study, rather than to discuss theoretical predictions and actual coalitions in chronological order. The Danish system first will be reviewed.

2.a The parliamentary system

The *Folketing* is the setting of parliamentary politics in Denmark. A senate, the *Landsting*, existed alongside the *Folketing* until 1953 when the former was abolished. Though the formal powers of the two Houses were equal, the role of the *Landsting* was secondary[32] and there is no evidence that the desire to achieve a "law-making majority" in the Senate was effective in coalition formation[33].

A cabinet minister cannot stay in power in the face of a hostile majority in the *Folketing*[34]. Constitutional amendments may be passed in several ways but none requires a special majority. Delegation of powers to international authority requires a five-sixths majority in parliament or simple majority and ratification by popular referendum[35]. According to the letter of the constitution, the King holds veto power but the Danish system is parliamentary and in his cabinet appointments the King follows the wishes of the parliamentary majority[36]. Decisions adopted by popular referendum may overrule a majority in the *Folketing*; this occurred, in fact, in 1963; In such a case, the government is under no obligation to resign: "The referendum has no direct effect on the life of the Government, although it certainly may increase its difficulties."[37]

There is no evidence of other institutions or groups, inside or outside the *Folketing*, that might wield a veto against decisions taken in that body.

Party discipline in the Danish parliament is very tight: "members take a stand contrary to their group only in rare instances"[38]. Thus, the weight of an actor in parliament may safely be set equal to the number of his individual representatives.

Throughout the period under study, four political parties have held actor status: the Conservatives, the Liberals (*Venstre*), the Radicals (*Radikale Venstre*) and the Social Democrats. After the Second World War, the Communist party achieved actor status; in 1960 a Left Socialist party, led by the former leader of the Communists, became an actor. Followers of Henry George, the "single taxers", formed the Justice party (JUST), which qualified as an actor in the years 1947 until 1960. The definition of "actor" has been altered for the Danish case so as to include the preceding parties and to exclude some short-lived parties such as the Trade party, the National Socialists and the Agrarians, none of whom seems to have played any role in the coalitional game and all of whom remained under the level of 3.5% of the *Folketing* seats. Therefore, 3.5% rather than the usual 2.5%, has been chosen as the cut-off point.

The policy positions of these actors may be best determined by taking the Social Democratic party (SOCD) as an anchoring point. It had been the largest party in parliament since 1924 and in its policy it "was clearly reformist, rather than revolutionary". And: "the emphasis from the beginning fell on change that would benefit the working class in the existing society."[39] The three bourgeois parties in Denmark clearly belong to the right of the Social Democrats on the policy scale, the Communists — who adhered to Marxist—Leninist doctrine concerning the state management of the economy — belong to the left. The Left Socialist party (LSOC) under Axel Larsen, which captured enough seats on the left to succeed the Communists as an actor in 1969, occupies the same rank on the scale: it stood for far-reaching nationalization in key sectors of the economy and for workers' control[40].

The bourgeois parties, all to the right of the Social Democrats, are harder to order with respect to one another. It is sometimes said that the equator of the *Folketing* runs right through the Radical group, not only in terms of numbers — it has often held the balance between a Socialist and a bourgeois majority — but also in terms of policy: the *Radikale Venstre* (RAD) advocates "the social—liberal society, where the state ensures freedom and order, so that the economically strong cannot misuse their power to exploit the economically weaker."[41]

266

The Liberal party, *Venstre* (LIB), defends a society where the individual can prosper through his own efforts, even though those for whom economic possibilities fail through misfortune or social conditions should benefit from the aid of the welfare state[42].

The Conservatives consider it the main role of the state to protect the conditions of a free economy: "Inequality is something essential for man's common life because inequality, joined with freedom, impels men towards constantly more excellent results .....there must also exist 'Equality at the start'."[43]

On the basis of the above, the Liberals may be placed between the Radicals on the one hand and the Conservatives on the other. Most difficult to classify in Danish politics is the Justice party. It is characterized by a "generally individualistic philosophy"[44]. The survival value of its narrowly conceived program has puzzled observers[45].

The party advocates a single tax: on land property. In the meantime, it adopts positions on nearly all other social economic issues that can only be termed conservative: it has been a "vigorous critic of 'welfare state' measures," it opposed a progressive income taxation and it favored "laissez-faire enterprise"[46]. In the given situation of Danish politics, it should be considered as a conservative actor on the social economic policy scale.

The above analysis results in a policy scale with the following order[47].

Communists—Social Democrats—Radicals—Liberals—Conservatives—Justice Party

The Left Socialists succeed the Communists on the left extreme of the policy scale.

Now, the results of the theories in the present study may be compared with the outcomes of Damgaard's analysis.

2.b Historical coalitions

Damgaard begins his study with an evaluation of Danish coalitions in the light of the minimum size principle. To that end the author first eliminates from consideration what he calls "overwhelming majorities", as occurred in the period 1901—1905 and during the German occupation and its aftermath[48].

The period 1901—1905 lies before the start of this analysis and the large coalitions that occurred during and just after the German occupation may be ignored because the German presence conflicted with the assumption that the parliamentary system may be studied in isolation from outside influences. Damgaard's data on the composition of historical parliamentary coalitions will be adopted in this study.

Damgaard's study takes into consideration only the four major parties with the Justice Party and the Left Socialists included only for the time that they were, in fact, part of the historical coalition. The Communists are ignored throughout. In terms of the present analysis, these parties are included as actors whenever they control more than 3.5% of the seats.

Having thus defined his empirical terms, Damgaard sets out to determine the meaning of Riker's minimum size principle. His hesitations are the same as those expressed in the discussion of the minimum size principle in this study. If a proto-coalition is understood as a dissoluble entity, the individual representatives are the real actors in the situation. A minimum size coalition is, in that case, one which controls exactly one half plus one of the Assembly votes. Damgaard[48] finds four such coalitions in Danish parliament since 1906. This is not enough. Nor is the "information effect" accepted as an attenuating circumstance: parties "are characterized by a very high degree of cohesion, particularly with respect to government formation. This implies that every participant has complete and perfect information about any other."[49]

However, such coalitions of one half plus one cannot emerge when the numbers of seats controlled by some of the parties do not happen to sum to that amount: the Danish parliamentary groups are, in fact, indissoluble[50].

Damgaard adopts a "modification" of the minimum size principle: minimum winning coalitions are "those with the smallest number of members *under given distributions* of the total number of seats."[50] The word "members" refers to individual representatives (or, seats), but this time coalitions must consist of entire parliamentary groups. This definition of minimum winning coalitions as those with the smallest *weight* among all winning coalitions is identical with the definition of minimum size coalitions in the present study.

This time, Damgaard finds that all but four of the historical coalitions satisfied this criterion, the minimum size principle[51]. The four exceptions are Neergaard III, Hansen/Kampmann, Braunsgaard and, not mentioned by Damgaard, Krag I (1966).

The cabinet of Krag II (1971) was formed after Damgaard's article appeared. It consisted of Social Democrats only and was supported in parliament by the Left Socialists. The Social Demo-

DENMARK 1918 (Source for coalitions in this Table and the following:Damgaard, 1969)
MAJORITY LARGER THAN 70
```
ACTORS IN ASSEMBLY  SOCD   RAD   LIB   CONS
POLICY SCALE ORDER    1     2     3     4
SEATS IN ASSEMBLY    39    33    45    22
ZAHLE (1918)        MEMBERMEMBER

RESULTS OF THEORIES  WIN  MWIN  MSIZ  BRGP  MRAN  CLMR  CLCP  PDST  PD1N  PDCL
                     1;8  1;3   1;1   1;3   1;2   1;2   1;5   1;5   1;4   1;5
```


DENMARK 1920
MAJORITY LARGER THAN 70
```
ACTORS IN ASSEMBLY  SOCD   RAD   LIB   CONS
POLICY SCALE ORDER    1     2     3     4
SEATS IN ASSEMBLY    42    17    49    28
NEERGAARD (1920)                MEMBERMEMBER

RESULTS OF THEORIES  WIN  MWIN  MSIZ  BRGP  MRAN  CLMR  CLCP  PDST  PD1N  PDCL
                     1;7  1;3   1;1   1;2   1;3   1;2   1;4   1;2   1;2   1;2
```


DENMARK 1920
MAJORITY LARGER THAN 70
```
ACTORS IN ASSEMBLY  SOCD   RAD   LIB   CONS
POLICY SCALE ORDER    1     2     3     4
SEATS IN ASSEMBLY    42    16    52    26
NEERGAARD (1920)                MEMBERMEMBER

RESULTS OF THEORIES  WIN  MWIN  MSIZ  BRGP  MRAN  CLMR  CLCP  PDST  PD1N  PDCL
                     1;7  1;3   1;1   1;2   1;3   1;2   1;4   1;2   1;2   1;2
```


DENMARK 1920
MAJORITY LARGER THAN 74
```
ACTORS IN ASSEMBLY  SOCD   RAD   LIB   CONS
POLICY SCALE ORDER    1     2     3     4
SEATS IN ASSEMBLY    48    18    52    27
NEERGAARD (1920)                MEMBERMEMBER

RESULTS OF THEORIES  WIN  MWIN  MSIZ  BRGP  MRAN  CLMR  CLCP  PDST  PD1N  PDCL
                     1;8  1;3   0;1   1;3   1;3   1;2   1;4   1;2   1;2   1;2
```


DENMARK 1924
MAJORITY LARGER THAN 74
```
ACTORS IN ASSEMBLY  SOCD   RAD   LIB   CONS
POLICY SCALE ORDER    1     2     3     4
SEATS IN ASSEMBLY    55    20    45    28
STAUNING (1924)     MEMBERMEMBER

RESULTS OF THEORIES  WIN  MWIN  MSIZ  BRGP  MRAN  CLMR  CLCP  PDST  PD1N  PDCL
                     1;8  1;4   1;1   1;3   1;2   1;2   1;4   1;3   1;3   1;4
```

DENMARK 1926
MAJORITY LARGER THAN 74
ACTORS IN ASSEMBLY SOCD   RAD   LIB   CONS
POLICY SCALE ORDER   1   2   3   4
SEATS IN ASSEMBLY   53   16   47   30
MADSEN-MYGDAL (1926)   MEMBERMEMBER

RESULTS OF THEORIES WIN   MWIN   MSIZ   BRGP   MRAN   CLMR   CLCP   PDST   PD1N   PDCL
                     1;8   1;3   1;1   1;3   1;3   1;2   1;4   1;2   1;2   1;2

DENMARK 1929
MAJORITY LARGER THAN 74
ACTORS IN ASSEMBLY SOCD   RAD   LIB   CONS
POLICY SCALE ORDER   1   2   3   4
SEATS IN ASSEMBLY   61   16   44   24
STAUNING (1929)   MEMBERMEMBER

RESULTS OF THEORIES WIN   MWIN   MSIZ   BRGP   MRAN   CLMR   CLCP   PDST   PD1N   PDCL
                     1;8   1;4   1;1   1;3   1;2   1;2   1;4   1;4   1;3   1;4

DENMARK 1932
MAJORITY LARGER THAN 74
ACTORS IN ASSEMBLY SOCD   RAD   LIB   CONS
POLICY SCALE ORDER   1   2   3   4
SEATS IN ASSEMBLY   62   14   39   27
STAUNING (1932)   MEMBERMEMBER

RESULTS OF THEORIES WIN   MWIN   MSIZ   BRGP   MRAN   CLMR   CLCP   PDST   PD1N   PDCL
                     1;8   1;4   1;1   1;3   1;2   1;2   1;4   1;3   1;3   1;4

DENMARK 1935
MAJORITY LARGER THAN 74
ACTORS IN ASSEMBLY SOCD   RAD   LIB   CONS
POLICY SCALE ORDER   1   2   3   4
SEATS IN ASSEMBLY   68   14   29   26
STAUNING (1935)   MEMBERMEMBER

RESULTS OF THEORIES WIN   MWIN   MSIZ   BRGP   MRAN   CLMR   CLCP   PDST   PD1N   PDCL
                     1;7   1;3   1;1   1;3   1;1   1;1   1;3   1;2   1;2   1;3

DENMARK 1939
MAJORITY LARGER THAN 74
ACTORS IN ASSEMBLY SOCD   RAD   LIB   CONS
POLICY SCALE ORDER   1   2   3   4
SEATS IN ASSEMBLY   64   14   31   26
STAUNING (1939)   MEMBERMEMBER
BUEHL/SCAVENIUS   MEMBERMEMBERMEMBERMEMBER

RESULTS OF THEORIES WIN   MWIN   MSIZ   BRGP   MRAN   CLMR   CLCP   PDST   PD1N   PDCL
                     2;7   1;3   1;1   1;3   1;1   1;1   2;3   2;2   1;2   2;3

270

DENMARK 1945
MAJORITY LARGER THAN 74

ACTORS IN ASSEMBLY	COMM	SOCD	RAD	LIB	CONS
POLICY SCALE ORDER	1	2	3	4,5	4,5
SEATS IN ASSEMBLY	18	48	11	38	,26

KRISTENSEN (1945)   MEMBERMEMBERMEMBER

RESULTS OF THEORIES	WIN	MWIN	MSIZ	BRGP	MRAN	CLMR	CLCP	PDST	PD1N	PDCL
	1;15	1;6	1;1	0;1	1;2	1;2	1;8	1;5	1;5	1;8

DENMARK 1947
MAJORITY LARGER THAN 74

ACTORS IN ASSEMBLY	COMM	SOCD	RAD	LIB	CONS	JUST
POLICY SCALE ORDER	1	2	3	4,5	4,5	6
SEATS IN ASSEMBLY	9	58	10	49	17	6

Hedtoft (1947)   MEMBER

RESULTS OF THEORIES	WIN	MWIN	MSIZ	BRGP	MRAN	CLMR	CLCP	PDST	PD1N	PDCL
	0;32	0;5	0;2	0;2	0;2	0;2	0;11	0;8	0;8	0;11

DENMARK 1950
MAJORITY LARGER THAN 75

ACTORS IN ASSEMBLY	COMM	SOCD	RAD	LIB	CONS	JUST
POLICY SCALE ORDER	1	2	3	4,5	4,5	6
SEATS IN ASSEMBLY	7	60	12	33	27	12

Eriksen (1950)   MEMBERMEMBER

RESULTS OF THEORIES	WIN	MWIN	MSIZ	BRGP	MRAN	CLMR	CLCP	PDST	PD1N	PDCL
	0;32	0;8	0;4	0;2	0;8	0;5	0;10	0;5	0;5	0;10

DENMARK 1953
MAJORITY LARGER THAN 75

ACTORS IN ASSEMBLY	COMM	SOCD	RAD	LIB	CONS	JUST
POLICY SCALE ORDER	1	2	3	4,5	4,5	6
SEATS IN ASSEMBLY	7	62	13	34	26	9

Hedtoft   MEMBERMEMBER

RESULTS OF THEORIES	WIN	MWIN	MSIZ	BRGP	MRAN	CLMR	CLCP	PDST	PD1N	PDCL
	0;32	0;8	0;1	0;2	0;8	0;5	0;10	0;3	0;5	0;10

DENMARK 1953
MAJORITY LARGER THAN 88

ACTORS IN ASSEMBLY	COMM	SOCD	RAD	LIB	CONS
POLICY SCALE ORDER	1	2	3	4,5	4,5
SEATS IN ASSEMBLY	8	75	14	43	30

HEDTOFT/HANSEN   MEMBERMEMBER

RESULTS OF THEORIES	WIN	MWIN	MSIZ	BRGP	MRAN	CLMR	CLCP	PDST	PD1N	PDCL
	1;15	1;4	1;1	1;3	1;1	1;1	1;8	1;5	1;5	1;8

271

DENMARK 1957
MAJORITY LARGER THAN 87

ACTORS IN ASSEMBLY	SOCD	RAD	LIB	CONS	JUST
POLICY SCALE ORDER	1	2	3,5	3,5	5
SEATS IN ASSEMBLY	70	14	46	30	9
HANSEN/KAMPMANN	MEMBER	MEMBER		MEMBER	

RESULTS OF THEORIES	WIN	MWIN	MSIZ	BRGP	MRAN	CLMR	CLCP	PDST	PD1N	PDCL
	1;15	1;4	0;1	0;2	0;1	0;1	0;6	1;6	0;4	0;6

DENMARK 1960
MAJORITY LARGER THAN 88

ACTORS IN ASSEMBLY	LSOC	SOCD	RAD	LIB	CONS
POLICY SCALE ORDER	1	2	3	4,5	4,5
SEATS IN ASSEMBLY	11	78	11	39	32
KAMPMANN/KRAG		MEMBER	MEMBER		

RESULTS OF THEORIES	WIN	MWIN	MSIZ	BRGP	MRAN	CLMR	CLCP	PDST	PD1N	PDCL
	1;16	1;5	1;2	1;4	1;2	1;2	1;9	1;3	1;3	1;3

DENMARK 1964
MAJORITY LARGER THAN 88

ACTORS IN ASSEMBLY	LSOC	SOCD	RAD	LIB	CONS
POLICY SCALE ORDER	1	2	3	4,5	4,5
SEATS IN ASSEMBLY	10	77	10	38	36
KRAG (1964)		MEMBER			

RESULTS OF THEORIES	WIN	MWIN	MSIZ	BRGP	MRAN	CLMR	CLCP	PDST	PD1N	PDCL
	0;14	0;4	0;1	0;2	0;7	0;4	0;7	0;4	0;4	0;7

DENMARK 1966
MAJORITY LARGER THAN 88

ACTORS IN ASSEMBLY	LSOC	SOCD	RAD	LIB	CONS
POLICY SCALE ORDER	1	2	3	4,5	4,5
SEATS IN ASSEMBLY	20	70	13	35	34
KRAG (1966)	MEMBER	MEMBER			

RESULTS OF THEORIES	WIN	MWIN	MSIZ	BRGP	MRAN	CLMR	CLCP	PDST	PD1N	PDCL
	1;16	1;4	0;1	1;3	1;7	1;4	1;8	1;2	1;2	1;2

DENMARK 1968
MAJORITY LARGER THAN 88

ACTORS IN ASSEMBLY	LSOC	SOCD	RAD	LIB	CONS
POLICY SCALE ORDER	1	2	3	4,5	4,5
SEATS IN ASSEMBLY	11	63	27	34	37
BRAUNSGAARD (1968)			MEMBER	MEMBER	MEMBER

RESULTS OF THEORIES	WIN	MWIN	MSIZ	BRGP	MRAN	CLMR	CLCP	PDST	PD1N	PDCL
	1;16	1;4	0;1	0;3	1;2	1;2	1;9	1;5	1;5	1;9

```
DENMARK 1971
MAJORITY LARGER THAN 89
ACTORS IN ASSEMBLY  LSOC   SOCD    RAD    LIB   CONS
POLICY SCALE ORDER    1      2      3     4,5   4,5
SEATS IN ASSEMBLY    17     73     27     30     31
KRAG (1971)         MEMBERMEMBER

RESULTS OF THEORIES  WIN    MWIN   MSIZ   BRGP   MRAN   CLMR   CLCP   PDST   PD1N   PDCL
                     1;16   1;5    1;1    1;4    1;2    1;2    1;9    1;2    1;2    1;2
```

crats polled 71 votes but one of the Far Oer Representatives and the representative of Greenland joined them, thus giving the coalition the smallest possible majority[52]. The parliamentary coalition was a basic alternative and of minimum size, p.d. undominated in all three versions of the theory.

Damgaard introduces a third concept of "minimum winning coalitions": "When, as we have seen, highly cohesive parties are the real actors, it seems logical to define a minimum winning coalition as one which is made non-winning by the subtraction of any party." This is, of course, equivalent to the definition of the set W^m of Von Neumann and Morgenstern: the set of minimal winning coalitions, *i.e.* the set of coalitions without unnecessary actors. Indeed, all parliamentary majority coalitions under consideration are minimal winning!

In the face of this evidence, Damgaard rejects the minimum size principle with its four exceptions. This is ironical, since the minimum size principle, because it makes only one predicion at a time, scores much higher for the Danish case than does minimal winning theory which predicts up to six coalitions. The minimum size principle is significant at the 4.4% level; minimal winning theory is not significant at all (59.8%)!

After this analysis based on weights alone, Damgaard introduces an element of party affinity: there exists a party sequence, such that only coalitions have occurred in fact that consist of parties that are adjacent in this ranking, *i.e.* without skipping any party. Or, there exists a sequence of parties such that all historical coalitions may be described as closed coalitions in terms of the present study.

It should be borne in mind that Damgaard's purpose is not so much to propose an explanatory theory of coalition formation, but rather to present a parsimonious description of historical coalitions in Denmark. It is perfectly appropriate, therefore, that he should use information contained in the composition of historical coalitions to construct his "party sequence". The latter turns out to be

Left Socialists—Social Democrats—Radical Liberals—Liberals—Conservatives (Justice Party)

The treatment of the Justice Party is less elegant: "In 1957 the Justice Party in a way placed between SD and R" (*i.e.* Social Democrats and Radicals)[53]. With the exception of the Justice Party (JUST), which is placed at the extreme right in the present study on the basis of its program, Damgaard's observed party sequence agrees with the programmatic social economic policy scale in this study.

Damgaard speculates that his party sequence, based on observed coalition behavior, may be connected to "a normative idea in the minds of party actors and voters"[54]. Thus, a coalition that conflicts with the images of the parties involved might harm the party's interest because its voters may defect it because of such an alliance.

On the basis of his party sequence, Damgaard inspects the historical coalitions in order to assess which ones are minimal winning and conform to the party sequence. In terms of the present study, such coalitions would be closed, minimal winning coalitions and therefore also of minimal range: basic alternative coalitions, that is. Damgaard [55] finds, on the basis of his data and the party sequence, that one or two coalitions are minimal winning, conform the sequence in every situation and that the historical coalition is among them every time since 1906.

2.c Discussion

The results of the present study do not entirely match Damgaard's conclusions. The governments of Hedtoft and Kampmann in the Assembly of 1957—1960 included the Justice Party, rightmost on the policy scale, and were therefore open and not of minimal range. For these governments, Damgaard places the Justice Party *ad hoc* in the middle of his sequence; had he maintained that position for the Justice Party throughout, all his other coalitions would have conflicted with his party sequence. The Justice Party, however, is ignored by Damgaard in all other cases. Nevertheless, basic alternative theory, which corresponds to Damgaard's criterion that minimal winning coalitions conform to the party sequence, performed exceptionally well: significant at the 0.4% level.

274

Interestingly enough, policy distance theory also deals very well with the Danish case, predicting all historical coalitions; the 1,n permissibility version does the same, except for the non-1,n permissible Hansen/Kampmann coalition. As the predicted set of the p.d. theories is much larger than that of basic alternative or minimal winning theory, the scores do not reach a significant level.

Usually, minimal range theory, interval version, is not mentioned in the country by country discussion: the strong nature of its assumption is not justified by its statistical performance. However, in the Danish case it achieves the highest score, significant below the 0.1% level. It predicts one, at most two, coalitions in every situation; the historical coalition is always among them with the exception of the Hansen/Kampmann coalition with the Justice Party. Apparently, the underlying assumption that parties are not just ranked on the policy scale but that they are placed at equal distances from one another, on the whole agrees with Danish realities. Or, at least, there are no unbridgeable gaps between parties such as the chasm that separated Socialist parties during the years between the wars and Communist parties after 1945 from the other parliamentary actors in some other European countries.

The frequency of minority governments in Denmark may be explained by a related hypothesis: the presence of a potential all-party coalition in the Danish Assembly. Pedersen suggests: "the existence of minority governments — all other things being equal — makes it more probable that consensus will exist among the parties in the final division than would be the case with a majority government."[56] In other words, this relationship between parliamentary consensus and minority cabinets may indicate that minority cabinets are, in fact, supported by all-party coalitions in parliament. Such all-party coalitions were undominated throughout the period under study except in 1920, 1926 and 1966; they are, of course, by definition, 1,n non-permissible.

The relative success of the theories is an intriguing phenomenon and in a sense it is unfortunate since it does not allow the more and less satisfactory theories to be separated. Confidence in the formal empiricist method of explanation is, however, strenghtened by the fact that almost all historical coalitions may be explained when the basic data on the coalitional situation are known without ambiguity.

Even though all theories are very succesful in absolute terms, *i.e.* in the number of coalitions predicted correctly, the statistical scores allow separation of the chaff from the wheat in the Danish case. Basic alternative theory and minimal range theory, interval version, are extremely significant; closed minimal range theory (2.1%) and the minimum size principle (1.1%, its best performance) are well within the bounds of significance. Ordinal minimal range theory is on the borderline (5.3%) and the other theories are not clearly significant or insignificant. With so many good predictions, what counts for the Danish case is a parsimonious predicted set.

3. Norway

Norway has served various students of politics and history as a model of a stable and cohesive democratic community[57]. Yet the country also knows deep cleavages of territorial or cultural nature, cross-cut with divisions on "functional economic" issues[58]. The relative homogeneity of the Norwegian nation, a common religion and a readiness to compromise[59] have helped to maintain a political system without major upheaval except for the German invasion and occupation.

3.a The parliamentary system

The Norwegian parliament consists of a directly elected Assembly, the *Storting*, which elects from its midst a kind of Senate, the *Lagting* or, rather, the party leaders in the *Storting* appoint the 38 *Lagting* members in proportion to the distribution of seats in the entire *Storting*; the remaining 112 members meet as the *Odelsting*[60].

From a strictly formal point of view, laws enacted by the two Houses in separate sessions overrule resolutions adopted by the *Storting* in plenary session[61] but most business is transacted in the plenary sessions, among it all budgetary and financial matters[62]. The cabinet will resign after a defeat in the plenary *Storting* or in both the separate Houses but not after a defeat in only one House[63]. Since the *Lagting* is composed roughly in the same proportions as the *Storting*, and as a consequence the same is true for the *Lagting*, the relative strengths of the parties are more or less the same in the three bodies. It appears warranted to take only the *Storting* into account as the setting of coalitional politics in Norway.

Voting in the *Storting* occurs by simple majority, except for the two-thirds vote required for a decision in matters on which the two separate Houses took opposed action, or for the adoption of constitutional amendments in a second reading by a re-elected Storting[64].

The King has a purely formal right to veto the decisions of parliament but since 1905 this privilege has not been used[65]; "the King has not ventured to install a cabinet not acceptable to the Storting[66]. Parliamentary influence is further strengthened by the fact that the cabinet's "legislative proposals are normally organized and presented as a part of a general party plan...."[67].

There appear to be no organizations in the country whose influence is strong enough to qualify them as veto-groups in the sense of the theories.

Throughout the period under study, a strong Labor party has confronted a Liberal, an Agrarian and a Conservative party. Since the war, the Christian People's Party has acquired actor status. The Communist, but "insubordinate", Labor party split away from the Third International in 1927 and merged with a Social Democrat group to become, in one stroke, the largest actor in the Storting, growing until it achieved an absolute majority in 1945 which it was to retain until 1961[68]. A separate Communist party gained actor status for one legislative period in 1945 and a Left Socialist group achieved the same in 1961.

"Economic policy is the main area of dispute between the parties." Most important is "disagreement on the distribution of goods between various social groups and classes...."[69] The Labor party advocated public ownership of the key sectors of the economy; "But a long period of political responsibility has had the effect of forcing some compromise, if not with the objectives, at least with the timing of their implementation."[70]

On the subject of state control of business, Labor and the Conservatives represent the two extremes of Norwegian politics[71]. The Liberals are situated between these two parties in that they want some state control although they do not want to move as far as Labor[72].

The Agrarian Party (Center Party since 1959) draws its strength from the rural population; at its formation it "was politically situated between the Liberals and Conservatives"[73]. Since then, "It has been generally conservative on economic, social, and religious matters, but it has been radical in the demands on the state when agriculture has been in a depressed condition."[74] Thus, although the Agrarian or Center party apparently belongs to the right of the Liberals as far as general economic policy is concerned, whenever specific agricultural issues are at stake it accepts the desirability of government intervention; this will cause some problems for the theories that incorporate the policy scale.

The Christian People's Party (CHPP) is mainly concerned with problems of religion and education; "In economic matters they seem to come close to the Liberals."[75]

The postwar Communist and Left Socialist actors have pressed for complete and reinvigorated socialism[76]. Their place is to the left of the Labor party.

The preceding considerations suggest the following social economic policy scale.

Communists (Left Socialists)—Social Democrats—Liberals≠ Christian People—Center—Conservatives

This scale agrees with Groennings' diagram of Norwegian party positions on the economic axis[77] and it also conforms to the data on attitudes of "active" respondents towards Taxation and Control of the Economy (except restrictions on house building) presented by Rokkan[78]. The scale corresponds, moreover, to the main axis of a two-dimensional analysis of perceived party locations for 1965, by Converse and Valen. "The left—right axis does indeed dominate the solution....it currently enjoys the highest relative salience of any of these conflicts."[79]

It might be added that "the most important cleavage in Norwegian politics is between the Labor party on the one hand and the four non-Socialist parties on the other hand".[80]

3.b Historical coalitions

Coalition politics in Norway are characterized by a succession of Liberal and Conservative minority governments until 1935 and by Social Democrat governments with absolute majority from 1945 until 1961. Of interest for the present purpose are the coalition governments of Labor and Agrarians in the thirties and the all-bourgeois governments since 1965.

It is a puzzling question why minority cabinets succeeded one another in Norway until 1935 and why no more or less permanent majority coalitions can be ascertained in parliament for that period, somewhat similar to Sweden until 1932 (except for Edén and Branting). In Norway, also, the bourgeois parties controlled a majority all through the period between the world wars. "The non-existence of coalition governments is first of all explained by the Liberal party's attitude. The party has always turned down coalition suggestions from the Conservatives."[81] But it also refused to enter basic alternative coalitions with the Labor Party. The common explanations in terms of differences among parties on policies and personnel appear inadequate: in the Weimar Republic and the French Third and Fourth Republics, conflict was at least as intense and yet majority coalitions did come about. Perhaps further research will identify more or less permanent parliamentary majority coalitions and perhaps more than one at the time in the Norwegian *Storting* of the period, or in the Swedish *Riksdag* for that matter.

The coalitional situation for those years may be briefly summarized here. The all-bourgeois coalition was of minimal range and closed if the Agrarian party was an actor; the Agrarians were, however, unnecessary in the periods 1922–1927 and 1930–1933. From 1927 to 1930 and after 1933, the all-bourgeois coalition was a basic alternative; the coalition was p.d. undominated under $1,n$ permissibility throughout the period.

The coalition of Left Socialists, Social Democrats, Liberals and Agrarians was a p.d. undominated basic alternative from 1922 until 1927; after that, Social Democrats and Liberals alone constituted the basic alternative coalition. From 1933 until 1945, Social Democrats and Agrarians could have formed a minimal winning coalition which would have been open, however, given the present policy scale.

Whatever the reasons, only in 1935 did a government came about that was supported by a more or less permanent majority coalition in the *Storting*. After the elections of 1933, the Labor–Liberal coalition was one basic alternative and the all-bourgeois coalition (p.d. undominated) the other. This remained the same after the elections of 1936.

```
NORWAY 1933
MAJORITY LARGER THAN 75
ACTORS IN ASSEMBLY  SOCD    LIB   AGR  CONS
POLICY SCALE ORDER     1      2     3     4
SEATS IN ASSEMBLY     69     24    22    32
                    MEMBER
NYGARDSVOLD (1935)  MEMBER        MEMBER

RESULTS OF THEORIES  WIN  MWIN  MSIZ  BRGP  MRAN  CLMR  CLCP  PDST  PDIN  PDCL
                     1;8   1;4   0;1   1;3   0;2   0;2   0;4   0;2   0;2   0;4
```

279

The Social Democrats formed a cabinet, Nygardsvold (1935), and the Agrarian Party agreed to support it in parliament. [82] The Nygardsvold government lasted beyond the elections of 1936.

```
NORWAY 1936
MAJORITY LARGER THAN 75
ACTORS IN ASSEMBLY   SOCD    LIB    AGR  CONS
POLICY SCALE ORDER      1      2      3     4
SEATS IN ASSEMBLY      70     23     18    36
NYGARDSVOLD (1936) MEMBER           MEMBER
RESULTS OF THEORIES   WIN   MWIN   MSIZ  BRGP  MRAN  CLMR  CLCP  PDST  PD1N  PDCL
                      1;8    1;4    0;1   1;3   0;2   0;2   0;4   0;2   0;2   0;4
```

The coalition was based upon a program of budget increases to support depressed agriculture[83]. At this point, the Liberals were more conservative in economic matters than the Agrarians whose constituency was threatened by the great crisis. Nevertheless, the policy scale is left unchanged, with the Agrarians between Liberals and Conservatives, since no *ad hoc* changes are made and this seems to be the Agrarians' policy position in the long run. Nygardsvold's coalition was, therefore, open and not of minimal range, p.d. dominated in all three versions of the theory. The theories that ignore the actors's policy positions and take only weights into consideration do better this time: the coalition was minimal winning and conformed to the bargaining proposition.

The planned elections of 1940 were cancelled because of the German invasion[84]. The government went into exile and Nygardsvold (1940) contained Labor, the Liberals, the Agrarians and the Conservatives[85]. It is beyond the terms of the theories, however, since the parliamentary process was suspended while conditions of war prevailed.

In the elections of 1945, the Labor party gained an absolute majority; Gerhardsen governed with a one-party majority coalition until 1961, when Labor lost its majority.

A new actor appeared in the 1961 elections, the Socialist People's Party (SOCL). Every theory in the book predicts the coalition of the Socialist People's Party and Labor: a basic alternative, of minimum size, p.d. undominated in all three versions, conforming to the bargaining proposition. In fact, the Social Democrats governed with this Left Socialist support: Gerhardsen (1961)[86].

```
NORWAY 1961
MAJORITY LARGER THAN 75
ACTORS IN ASSEMBLY   SOCL   SOCD    LIB   CHPP   CENT   CONS
POLICY SCALE ORDER     1      2     3,5    3,5     5      6
SEATS IN ASSEMBLY      2     74     14     15     16     29
GERHARDSEN (1961)    MEMBERMEMBER
Lyng (1963)                           MEMBERMEMBERMEMBERMEMBER
GERHARDSEN (1963)    MEMBERMEMBER

RESULTS OF THEORIES   WIN   MWIN   MSIZ   BRGP   MRAN   CLMR   CLCP   PDST   PD1N   PDCL
                     1;32   1;6    1;2    1;5    1;4    1;4    1;11   1;1    1;1    1;1
```

The uneasy majority (a single vote) broke down when the Socialist People's Party supported a no-confidence vote initiated by the bourgeois parties. For four weeks, an all-bourgeois cabinet, Lyng (1963), existed. Two votes short of a majority, the bourgeois cabinet never obtained the confidence of the *Storting*. Gerhardsen resumed power with support from the Left Socialists.

Finally, in the 1965 elections, the four bourgeois parties gained a majority. Their coalition was a basic alternative, p.d. undominated and of minimum size. The Socialist People disappeared as an actor. The coalitions of the Social Democrats with the Liberals or with the Christian People's Party (CHPP) were also basic alternatives.

```
NORWAY 1965
MAJORITY LARGER THAN 75
ACTORS IN ASSEMBLY   SOCD    LIB   CHPP   CENT   CONS
POLICY SCALE ORDER     1     2,5    2,5     4      5
SEATS IN ASSEMBLY     68     18     13     18     31
BORTEN (1965)               MEMBERMEMBERMEMBERMEMBER

RESULTS OF THEORIES   WIN   MWIN   MSIZ   BRGP   MRAN   CLMR   CLCP   PDST   PD1N   PDCL
                     1;16   1;5    1;1    0;4    1;4    1;4    1;6    1;3    1;3    1;5
```

The four bourgeois parties entered government with the cabinet of Borten (1965). The elections of 1969 produced a situation with the same coalitional features and Borten continued on the same base, although with a majority of only a single vote.

```
NORWAY 1969
MAJORITY LARGER THAN 75
ACTORS IN ASSEMBLY   SOCD    LIB   CHPP   CENT   CONS
POLICY SCALE ORDER     1     2,5    2,5     4      5
SEATS IN ASSEMBLY     74     13     14     20     29
BORTEN (1969)               MEMBERMEMBERMEMBERMEMBER
Bratelli (1971)      MEMBER

RESULTS OF THEORIES   WIN   MWIN   MSIZ   BRGP   MRAN   CLMR   CLCP   PDST   PD1N   PDCL
                     1;16   1;5    1;1    0;4    1;4    1;4    1;6    1;3    1;3    1;5
```

The issue of Norway's membership in the European Economic Community (Common Market) raised intense conflict and premier Borten, an opponent of participation, resigned. Bratelli (1971) governed with the Social Democrats alone.

3.c Discussion

It is interesting to note the preferences of the various parties for different coalitions as described in Groennings' careful analysis of the maneuvering that prepared the ground for the all-bourgeois coalition. The Christian People's Party "favored the formation of an all-party government"[87]; in fact, according to policy distance theory, the five-party coalition had been its first preference up to 1969. "The strategically most attractive arrangement for the Liberal Party would be a five-party coalition of the four plus Labor. Beginning in 1953, it presented this option as its first choice at every election."[88] Again, according to policy distance theory, this had been its first preference since 1945 and for most of the time before 1940. Groennings presents arguments that agree with the basic assumption of policy distance theory: "The obvious strategic advantages were that such a government would be less conservative than the four-party option and would give the Liberals pivotal power."[88]

The position of the Center party was different: it would find itself, in terms of policy distance theory, in a pivotal position in the all-bourgeois coalition (as a matter of fact, with zero excess in 1965): "it favored the four-party alternative as a matter of principle"[89]. Lastly, the Conservatives, fearing to be left out of some minority government of the center parties, insisted on a four-party bourgeois majority coalition as its only chance of government. Whereas the Liberals and the Christian People procrastinated, the Conservatives were most emphatic about the desirability of an all-bourgeois coalition[90]. This, again, conforms to p.d. theory.

Once the formation of the coalition was agreed upon, "the parties quickly adopted the principle of equity in agreeing that they would distribute the number of cabinet posts in accordance with party size". This finding, too, agrees with the evidence collected by Browne and Franklin and with the assumptions of policy distance theory (and the Riker—Gamson minimum size principle, cf. Chapter 4).

It may be noted in this context that Ruin has found the Swedish Social Democrats to be the most opposed to all-party government and the Swedish Agrarians most positively disposed towards it; both Liberals and Agrarians repudiated a permanent two-block system in Sweden. The Swedish Conservatives would have preferred an all-bourgeois coalition most[91]. Given the analogous party system in Sweden and Norway, Ruin's conclusions seem to support those of Groennings and of policy distance theory.

Policy distance theory seems to account much better for the preferences of individual actors among various coalitions than for the actual outcome of the interplay of these preferences through the concept of domination and the core.

In conclusion, a summary of the theories' performance in the case of Norway is given. Three majority coalitions occurred in Norway (for eight cabinets) during the period under study: the "red—green" coalition of 1935, the Socialist coalition of 1961 and the bourgeois coalition of 1965. All three coalitions were minimal winning, the latter two were in the course of three legislative periods of minimum size, the former two conform to the bargaining proposition. The "red—green" coalition was open and not of minimal range because of the position assigned to the Agrarians on the policy scale. The other two coalitions were closed, of minimal range and p.d. undominated in all three versions of the theory.

It is hard to find significance in the results for Norway. Only the minimum size principle achieves a significant score: 2.3%. Surprisingly, policy distance theory, also under $1,n$ permissibility, achieves significance at the borderline: 5.7%.

CHAPTER 12

Conclusion

This study is at once premature and overdue. It comes too early to profit fully from the data-gathering efforts that are now underway in the field of European multi-party systems. This necessitated assumptions in anticipation of factual information that may become available at a later stage. On the other hand, several authors had already proposed theories on political coalition formation without these having been submitted to a systematic empirical test amounting to more than the cursory inspection of a small number of historical cases. As a result, it was unclear in which direction theory construction should continue and, at the same time, empirical investigators lacked clues as to what data would be most useful for the construction and validation of theories.

Though many doubts remain, a number of conclusions seem warranted at this point. They have a bearing, first, upon the explanation of parliamentary coalition formation proper; secondly, on the theory of democratic decision making; and, thirdly, on the validity for the investigation of political life of the formal empiricist method, especially if based on the rational decision model.

1. Parliamentary coalition formation

The evidence has clearly shown that parliamentary coalitions can not be explained satisfactorily in terms of the number of seats of the member actors alone: the actors' policy positions must also be taken into account. Theories that take into account the policy positions of the actors without exception, achieve better results than theories that ignore them. And, conversely, theories that achieve a significant outcome all incorporate the policy scale.

The evidence in its entirety strongly suggests that parliamentary majority coalitions in the countries and in the period under study tend to form from actors that are adjacent on the policy scale and, in times of normalcy, these closed coalitions tend to be of minimal range. Excepting situations of war or threatened war, closed minimal range theory achieves results that are significant at a level of 0.2%.

The very satisfactory performance of closed minimal range theory constitutes independent evidence against an approach to coalition formation in terms of maximization of portfolios per actor or per unit weight (vote): closed minimal range theory contradicts such theories since it requires, for a coalition to be stable, that it contains all actors within its range, that is including those actors that are unnecessary for the coalition to be winning. This implies that actors prefer to give up some portfolios to an unnecessary actor if that actor's membership closes the coalition, rather than to form a coalition of the same minimal range, exclude that unnecessary actor, divide his portfolios and accept the coalition being open.

Every theory that postulates a maximization relationship in terms of the coalition's spoils as distributed over the actors, fails decisively: whether it be the maximization of portfolios per number of votes (the minimum size principle), or per number of member actors (the bargaining proposition), or, much weaker, the attribution of portfolios only to those actors that are necessary to win (minimal winning theory). Apparently, there is something that matters at least as much as portfolios· policy.

Policy distance theory is based precisely on the primacy of policy: actors intend to use the coalition as an instrument to realize their own most preferred policies. Because of this, an actor will prefer to be in the coalition which he expects to adopt a policy as close as possible to his own most preferred policy position. To that end, the actor will attempt, if possible, to create a coalition in which he is pivotal. In such a coalition, the votes of the member actors on one side of the pivotal actor and of those on his other side are balanced closely enough for the pivotal actor to ensure acceptance of his proposal against every other by pitting his votes with one side of the coalition against the opposing proposal. The assumption, implicit in the policy scale, is, of course, that the two opposite wings of the coalition will not join forces against the pivotal actor. The more evenly balanced the coalition is around the pivotal actor, the more he will prefer it, regardless of the number of actors that must be included to achieve this balance and regardless, also, of the total weight of the coalition, as long as the excess towards either side is minimal. Obviously, the proportion of portfolios to actors, or actor's weights, is immaterial in policy distance theory: policy comes first. However, in this form, the theory has failed badly in its empirical predictions.

The purely numerical balancing act of minimizing the coalition's excess around the pivotal actor results in some coalitional oddities in which extreme parties are united in one coalition over a wide gap on the policy scale. The $1,n$ permissibility condition was introduced to eliminate such alliances. It caused considerable improvement in terms of chi-square scores but the $1,n$ permissibility version of policy distance theory still came nowhere near significance.

Policy distance theory depends as much upon the arithmetics of weights as does the minimum size principle except that it translates these numbers in expected policies of coalitions and in actors' preferences. But the actors in, for example, a seven-party system are still expected to calculate domination in a seven by sixty-four matrix after duly eliminating non-permissible coalitions. Clearly, the rationality postulate has become too demanding*.

It can be argued that without such "synoptic"[1] calculations from a complete matrix, real life actors may still come to reject unstable coalitions through incidental and pairwise comparisons with other coalitions. But in policy distance theory, unstable coalitions are often unstable because the corresponding preference vector is dominated by one that is itself unstable, and so forth... The chains of domination may number many links; only an overall view of the entire matrix, consisting of preferences that are based on quite complex calculations, makes it possible to determine which coalitions are stable.

In one word, policy distance theory is much too precise; a pseudo-precision, apparently, because the nature of the data does not allow such subtle numerical manipulations.

This constitutes an important negative finding. Weights alone do not explain coalition formation. But a theory based on policy preferences, which postulates quite intricate calculations in a matrix of the evaluations of all possible outcomes by all actors,

---

*Perhaps policy distance theory is right, but politicians are poor mathematicians!

286

also fails decisively. Apparently, both direct maximization in terms of portfolios and rationality in terms of policy distance calculations are inadequate tools of explanation in this case.

The theories that work well are formulated in terms of actors' weights and policy positions and they do not require actors to compare every coalition with all others; rather, they appear to be compatible with a wholly different view of decision making: *the incrementalist approach.* An actor will not survey all possible outcomes and calculate his own and every other actor's preferences for these states; the actor is much more likely to decide that, whatever the "best" coalition may be, his aspiration level will be satisfied if he is included in a winning coalition. As a consequence he will behave in a "satisficing", rather than in a maximizing manner[2]. His decision strategy will be incrementalist[3]: since he is not in a majority on his own, he will "remedy" this by searching for partners in a majority coalition. The actor is likely to enter the bargaining process in a "margin-dependent" manner by looking for that partner with whom policy differences are minimal and require only marginal adjustment: his neighbour on the scale. If the two do not control a majority together they will repeat the procedure with their respective neighbours, "step by step" until a majority has been achieved: such a majority would consist of a closed minimal range coalition.

Apparently, the rational decision model corresponds closely with a number of theories (policy distance theory, minimal winning theory, the minimum size principle and the bargaining proposition) which perform poorly in the empirical test and the model fits poorly to the theory that produces good predictions: closed minimal range theory. But this theory, in turn, conforms closely to an alternative approach to decision making: incrementalism.

It might be that, once a closed minimal range coalition has been achieved, the actors pause and find that some of their number are unnecessary to control a majority. They could then move to exclude these actors. If minimal winning theory were to hold, the necessary actors would certainly exclude their unnecessary partner: in a more ambiguous world, that of minimal range theory, they might or they might not. But the evidence shows that the odds are that the unnecessary actors will remain and that the coalition will stay closed. This is hard to reconcile with the rational decision model and fits more easily in the incrementalist view.

Axelrod has proposed the equivalent of closed minimal range theory and called the coalitions that satisfied it "minimal con-

287

nected winning coalitions". His theory was prompted by, rather than derived from, the measure of Conflict of Interest he developed*. This Conflict of Interest would be "comparatively low" in such coalitions[4]. However, for coalitional situations, no measure of conflict of interest was defined by Axelrod and rather than postulate once more a universal measure of preference, one might base closed minimal range theory upon a satisficing or incrementalist view of decision-making.

The evidence of the present study allows seven theories of coalition formation to be rejected with great confidence; one theory, with slightly significant results, is entertained until further evidence is available (policy distance theory, closed coalition version); two other theories are rejected, not so much on the basis of their independent performance, but because a related theory explains the same results at a higher level of significance; ordinal minimal range theory and basic alternative theory are superseded by the theory that achieves the best result of all: *closed minimal range theory*. The closed coalition proposition, rejected for times of normalcy, survives in the general conclusion: *parliamentary majority coalitions in the countries and in the period under study tend to form from actors that are adjacent on the policy scale and these closed coalitions are of minimal range in times of normalcy.*

It is also commendable on the basis of the evidence to abandon the model that hitherto served as the basis for theory construction and to replace it with a more adequate paradigm: the rational decision model is superseded by the incrementalist view of decision making.

Finally, the evidence in this study supports the notion of a social economic policy scale, a scale based on the parties' positions concerning the desired share of the national income to be redistributed by means of the national budget, defense and policy expenditures excepted. The notion of a left—right scale to convey

---

*See Chapter 4, Section 4. Closed minimal range theory was tested by this author in the light of the performance of minimal range theory and the closed coalition proposition separately before he knew of Axelrod's work. The fact that Axelrod proposed the same theory without knowing of the author's investigations allows the closed minimal range theory to be treated as a theory conceived independently of the data set against which it has been tested. The closed coalition proposition was conceived as a separate theory after the main body of data had been collected: the policy scale was constructed independently from the proposition. But the proposition is, for the same reasons, not independent of the present data set.

288

party space has been criticized as inadequate on several grounds*
and the objection of "built-in circularity" has been raised against
the policy scale[5]. The extensive discussion of the party system in
each country in Chapters 9—11 should provide a basis for the
policy scale that is independent of coalition behavior to a degree
that is acceptable for the study of social processes in which one-
way causation rarely, if ever, occurs: the policy scale is, of course,
not uncontaminated by past coalition behavior, but it appears to
be sufficiently anchored in both the structure of the party system
and the cognitive structure of ideology to be considered an independent variable in the context of social historical explanation.
From the present evidence, it emerges as a powerful explanatory
tool that, with its many hazards, deserves a more central role in
empirical political theory.

2. Coalition government and democratic theory

The second major finding of this study is negative: in multi-
party systems, there seems to be no simple and fixed connection
between the outcome of an election and the composition or policy
of the subsequent ruling coalition unless, of course, some party
has acquired a majority on its own. As a consequence, the voter in
such a system cannot calculate the effect of his vote, not even if
he knew how all citizens had voted, much less if he ignores their
choices as he does at the time of the elections[†].

Under these conditions, the value of the individual right to vote
as a means of influencing the composition and policy of the government is very dubious indeed[6]. An individual electoral vote can
be a rational decision only, if (1) its effect on the composition and
policy of the government is known and (2) this effect is independent of the votes of others. In a pure two-party system, both these
conditions are satisfied. A vote for one party increases its chances to
capture control of the government and diminishes the chances of its
opponent; where the policies of each party are known, and if the
parties can be trusted to carry them out when in power (!), the voter
is in a position to influence the probabilities of the policies of the

---

*Cf. section 7.4.
†Opinion polls may guide his expectations, of course, but if the present analysis
would prompt voters to change their decisions on the basis of such polls, then
the polls would become invalid as indicators of the results since many others
might change their minds too.

government to be elected by increasing the odds of his party coming to power. All this is independent of the choices of others.

The individual vote in a multi-party system lacks this rational character and exhibits some irrational and even paradoxical features: a vote for a given party does not necessarily increase its chances of entering the government; it may even diminish them. A voter's defection from an incumbent government party towards one that was hitherto in the opposition may contribute to the incumbent government party remaining in office and in a shift in the governing coalition's policy in a direction opposite to the shift in the voter's choice. This will be elucidated below.

The case that represents a borderline between a two-party system and a multi-party system is that of a system in which more than two parties exist, one of which stands a reasonable chance of gaining a majority on its own, *e.g.* because this "quasi-majority party" controls more than, say, 40%, of the votes. In such a system, a voter who hopes to see the quasi-majority party in office acts rationally by voting for it: there is a reasonable chance that it will gain a majority and the voter, by his vote, increases this chance. On the other hand, a voter who wishes to prevent the quasi-majority party from taking office is in a more difficult position. By withholding his vote from the party, he diminishes its chances of conquering a majority of its own but this is not enough to keep it out of office. The quasi-majority party may still enter a coalition with other actors. Depending on the coalition theory the voter subscribes to, and depending on the electoral outcome he expects, he may cast his vote so as to minimize the opportunities for the quasi-majority party to enter a governing coalition if it fails to conquer a majority. If the quasi-majority party is likely to remain in a pivotal position* as, for example, the Italian Christian Democrats, the voter has no way of preventing it from entering the government. Moreover, the voter has no way to influence the policy of the coming coalition, since the quasi-majority party in its

---

*The "pivotal actor" in this context is the actor that is pivotal for the coalition of all actors in the assembly, *i.e.* the actor that counts among its ranks the individual representative who is in the median position among all individual representatives in the assembly. Since no majority exists of votes on the left of this median individual representative, nor on his right, and since a closed coalition cannot omit the (pivotal) party to which he belongs, this median individual representative, and the pivotal actor to which he belongs, is included in every closed coalition that is winning.

pivotal position may seek its support from either side or from both sides.

If the quasi-majority party is not in a pivotal position, the voter can help keep it out of power by voting for a party at the opposite extreme of the scale: the evidence of this study suggests that coalitions between the parties on one side of the scale and a party on the opposite extreme are quite rare: they are ruled out under the terms of closed minimal range theory, the closed coalition proposition and policy distance theory in the $1,n$ permissibility version. But the voter should be careful to avoid a vote for a party adjacent to the quasi-majority party which he wishes to prevent from taking office: (closed) minimal range theory makes it quite likely that this will be the party that will help the quasi-majority party obtain its parliamentary majority if it failed to obtain it on its own. Thus, Swedes, Danes and Norwegians who wished to keep the Social Democratic party out of office did well to withhold their support from the Agrarian or Center party and give it to the Conservatives, even if they agreed with the Agrarian or Centrist policy position. Moreover, a vote for such a relatively small pivotal party will not increase its chances of entering the government (which according to the closed coalition theories are very high anyway) and the voter cannot influence the coalition's policy: the pivotal party is free to find its partners on either side of the scale. Thus, *the party that is most likely to gain office, is hardest to predict in its policies.*

When a quasi-majority party exists, in Sweden, Norway, Denmark, Israel (Social Democrats) or in Italy (Christian Democrats), the voter can use his vote to increase the odds of some outcomes but not of others. In the absence of such a quasi-majority party that serves to anchor the electoral calculations, the voting decision loses almost all rationality as a choice of a government.

In the light of the evidence in the present study, the best a voter can do is to rely on closed minimal range theory, even though it does not have the force of a behavioral law or of an (unwritten) constitutional principle. Moreover, apart from its finite validity, the theory is of little use to the individual voter who whishes to make a rational decision: closed minimal range theory does not guarantee at all that a party increases its odds of entering the government by gaining seats. The pivotal party will most likely be a member of the ruling coalition, but this is independent of the number of its seats, as long as it remains pivotal. The pivotal position is not bestowed upon it by its supporters alone, but equally by its opponents who support parties on either side of it in roughly the same numbers.

On the basis of closed minimal range theory, therefore, the voter can do little to influence the composition of government. He is almost equally helpless in determining the policies of the future government: closed minimal range theory allows coalitions to form over the entire width of the political spectrum, unless an actor unnecessarily adds to each coalition's range. Only a voter who supports a party that is to remain in a pivotal position may vote for it and thereby strengthen its importance in determining the coalition's expected policy (i.e. according to policy distance theory) and even though he cannot know at the time of his vote what coalition this pivotal party will enter. But a voter who disagrees with the policies of his party, hitherto included in the government, and deserts it for another party, say one on the left, may find to his surprise that the former government parties, after having lost the majority, make up for this defeat, not by adding the party of his choice, on their left, but a party on the other side which may not have won any votes at all or which may have lost votes. Only under certain specific numerical conditions can it happen that an extreme member of the coalition suffers defections from which its partners benefit, so that the first actor becomes unnecessary and is excluded from the coalition as adding to its range: this would result in a shift in the coalition's range that corresponded with the change of preferences of the defecting voters.

In conclusion, the theories, even if one were certainly true, offer little help to a voter who wishes to know what the effect of his vote would be on the composition or the policy of a government, and this independently of the votes of others. In this respect, the theories reflect some of the irrational qualities of a multi-party system as a means for the voters to influence the selection of the government. The most that the voters in such a system may do is elect an assembly that reflects their preferences and this more adequately than is the case in a two-party system where only two alternatives are open for the individual voter to choose from.

This state of affairs in multi-party systems has long been the object of critisicm. Recently, it has been proposed[7] to appoint the prime minister through direct elections. The prime minister, in turn, would appoint his cabinet, which would remain responsible to an assembly, also directly elected by universal suffrage. This arrangement would force the parties to join in coalitions, each nominating a candidate for the prime ministry and each having a reasonable chance of obtaining a majority. It is expected that the legislature would continue to be elected from a multiplicity of parties but that these parties would combine into something of a two-party system for the election of the executive head.

It would be necessary to find some solution for a situation in which the parties which together had won the prime ministry would lack a majority in the assembly. But a comparable situation occurs at times in the United States where the president's party may be in a minority in either or both the Houses of Congress.

If the system is to achieve its objective, it would force the pivotal party to take sides with one of the two coalitions competing for the prime ministry before the elections. This may, however, present a formidable obstacle to the acceptance of the reform proposal, precisely because the pivotal party would have to cooperate in giving up its present freedom of maneuver, unless the opponents on the social economic dimension voted together on the issue of institutional reform.

The subject of democratic reform leads naturally to the normative theory of democracy. The evidence from the present investigation suggests a vantage point for the discussion of some normative issues: the apparent validity of the policy scale for the explanation of coalition formation permits democratic politics to be reviewed as if all relevant issues could be placed on a single dimension, at least for the sake of the present argument. If this were the case, and admittedly it is not always true, certain policy proposals would be accepted against all others, if all proposals would be submitted to the vote in every combination of pairs: the proposal that would be most preferred by the median voter in the voting body would obtain a majority against any other proposal. This median proposal could be called "the verdict of the voting body".

A similar assumption of one-dimensional, scalable politics is made in the Hotelling—Downs model of two-party systems: both parties would gravitate towards the middle, towards the preference of the median individual voter in the electorate[8]. On the basis of policy distance theory, this view may be corrected*. It may be true that before and during elections both parties would formulate policies that would correspond with the preferences of the median

---

* Footnote see next page.

individual voter. But in the period between elections, either one of the parties would be in power and in a position to enforce its own policies which would be determined by the individual members of the party in the assembly (assuming a parliamentary democratic system): the expected policy of the (one-party) ruling coalition would correspond to the preferences of the median individual assembly member of that party. Hence, it would lie much further to the extreme than the median individual preference of the electorate or the assembly as a whole. Thus, even if the parties in a two-party system offer very similar programs to the electorate at the time of the elections, it certainly makes a difference which of the two wins, since they may well deviate in opposite ways from these programs. Moreover, the direction of this deviation is known to an informed voter at the time of his vote.

Once the assumption of a distribution of preferences on a single dimension is made, the preference of the median individual voter could be recommended as the verdict of the decision making body, for example on the basis of the definitional characteristics of polyarchy as advanced by Dahl[9], especially

> "4. Any member who perceives a set of alternatives, at least one of which he regards as preferable to any of the alternatives presently scheduled, can insert his preferred alternative(s) among those scheduled for voting."

This would ensure that all possible proposals would come up for voting. And

> "6. Alternatives (leaders or policies) with the greatest number of votes displace any alternatives (leaders or policies) with fewer votes."

This would ensure, on the assumption of one-dimensionality, adoption of the alternative preferred most by the median individual member of the voting body.

In a multi-party system where the assembly adequately reflects the preferences of the electorate, the median individual member of

---

*This section makes use of that part of policy distance theory in which the expected policy p_S of a coalition S is derived from the policy positions of its members; this is quite independent of the determination of actors' preferences among coalitions and the calculation of domination among preference vectors in p.d. theory. The first part of the theory, moreover, runs closely parallel to Black's Theory of Committees and Elections and is also a component of p.d. theory closed coalition version, which is still entertained on the basis of the present evidence.

the assembly represents the verdict of the electorate. He is, more-over, by definition a member of the pivotal party. Following the lines of the argument, his preferences ought to be government policy if polyarchy is the norm.

The coalition of all parties would adopt as its expected policy the preference of the median individual member of the assembly. Therefore, given a one-dimensional distribution of preferences, the coalition of all parties ought to govern. This, however, would con-tradict another major canon of democratic theory: those who are in government must be clearly identifiable, so that they can be held responsible by others in the assembly who, potentially, can vote them out of power and take over government themselves if they obtain a majority.

If the coincidental distribution of seats allows it, there may be another coalition, not including all parties, but balanced in such a way around the pivotal actor that it would adopt as its expected policy the most preferred policy of the median individual member of the assembly. If the indissolubility of parliamentary parties is maintained, however, such a distribution of seats would be purely coincidental.

Government could be entrusted to the pivotal party alone, since among its members it counts the median individual member of the assembly. Even if its expected policy would be the most preferred policy of the median individual member of the pivotal party rather than that of the median individual member of the assembly in its entirety, this would be a fair approximation. Theoretically, also, this one-party minority government would always be able to ob-tain a majority for its proposals. On the other hand, it would be hard to identify the actual supporters of the government and hold them responsible. Moreover, the pivotal party might remain in government on its own for an indefinite time*.

Finally, the execution of the decisions of the assembly might be left to professional civil servants, motivated only by monetary reward and professional, fiduciary, ethics. They would be ap-pointed by the assembly. The assembly would make its decisions by pairwise voting on proposals submitted by any party that wished to do so. If representatives voted their "true" preferences, this would result in the verdict of the assembly (and of the elec-

---

*One party has remained pivotal and has been in government for the entire period under study in Italy (Christian Democrats), the Netherlands (Catho-lics) and Israel (Mapai).

torate) being adopted and being executed by loyal, non-political officials. This idea runs entirely counter to the institutions and history of parliamentary democracy with its tradition of a more or less independent, be it responsible, executive. Also, some institutional device would have to prevent actors from forming coalitions and voting for the coalition's proposal rather than vote from their "true" preference, thereby falsifying, again, the "verdict of the assembly". One such device might be to allow the members of the party in the country to recall representatives who voted against the party's policy as determined by its membership. Thus responsibility would be enforced, not through the mechanisms of governing and opposition parties, but by the (activist part of the) electorate.

It appears that this last proposal could ensure adoption of the "verdict" of the electorate as government policy, while at the same time maintaining a measure of responsibility for those who collaborated in adopting that policy. The proposal is, however, based on the assumption of a one-dimensional distribution of preferences in the electorate. It might, therefore, be best suited for decision-making bodies that deal with a set of problems pertaining to a more limited territory or a smaller range of issues.

The normative approach based on the assumption of one-dimensionality singles out the preference of the median individual voter in the decision-making body as the "verdict" of that body. It allows the workings of multi-party systems to be criticized for the fact that the policy of the ruling coalition will often deviate from this verdict and, moreover, that the direction of this deviation is unpredictable, before the coalition has formed. It also produces a criticism of two-party systems, that is less often heard: the ruling (one-party) coalition will almost always adopt a policy that deviates from the verdict of the electorate, although in a direction that is predictable at the time of elections and even though at election time the party's professed policy will deviate the least from the "verdict" of the electorate.

Discussions of parliamentary systems from a formal point of view may easily acquire an unrealistic character. First of all, the preceding discussion is based on the assumption of one-dimensionality of preferences, which certainly does not describe political life exhaustively. Moreover, even if the one-dimensional character of basic party policies were a fact, this would not prevent politicians from practising their art of bringing other dimensions into play before the electorate. There are, however, more basic considerations that should be taken into account when discussing parliamentary reform.

Important realms of decision making are at present not under political control, *e.g.* the decisions governing economic investment. Since, as a consequence, major social processes are shaped outside the political system, or even against its manifest volition, any proposal that aims at translating individual preferences for social states into some sort of collective preference must take such a state of affairs into account.

Also, it may be that individual voters would have different preferences if they had been educated in forming and expressing their preferences and if they were motivated and capable of handling the necessary information. Moreover, the consciousness that one's choices would have a demonstrable and predictable consequence upon policy, might itself change individual preferences.

Finally, the impossibility of translating individual preferences into some collective policy according to an adequate decision rule may pertain to certain collectivities and not to others. For example, the assumption of one-dimensionality, which allows a "verdict" to be defined, might be valid if the present centralized national decision-making process were to be decomposed, at least in part, into smaller territorial and functional units. Other decisions, on the contrary, may be defined in a more meaningful sense only if their context were enlarged from the national setting to some supra-national entity.

These considerations very much complicate the problem of parliamentary reform. They imply political choices at many points. But they make it very clear that the subject of parliamentary reform cannot be dealt with within the narrow context of a theory of parliamentary behavior, much less within the constraints that a formal theory of the subject imposes. The reform of democratic institutions is a problem, or perhaps the problem, of a general theory of politics.

3. Formal empiricist method and the study of politics

In the opening sentence of this book, its purpose was defined as a test of the claim that formal theories can explain important processes of political life. This is the place to judge that claim in the light of the evidence bearing on parliamentary coalition formation in European multi-party systems after 1918, the subject of this inquiry.

No theory in this book can explain specific historical coalitions adequately. But such explanation of concrete historical events cannot be expected from parsimonious constructs such as the present theories and they were not intended for that purpose. What a theory of this kind should be able to explain are long-term tendencies that may be found to operate throughout the period and the systems under study. Closed minimal range theory does exactly that: with the aid of an underlying social economic policy scale and from an incrementalist viewpoint of decision making, it explains why parliamentary coalitions tend to be closed and, in normal times, of minimal range. The theory leaves it to the parliamentary historian to explain why one particular closed minimal range coalition formed rather than another. And also, since it furnishes a concept of what coalitions should be expected to form, it points at coalitions that are not of minimal range or open as requiring special historical explanation, perhaps with the aid of concepts from the other theories.

Moreover, the present approach has made it possible to abandon the model from which it started, the rational decision model, and replace it by another underlying model of decision making: incrementalism. In the process of verification, an explanatory tool, the social economic policy scale, was validated to a degree.

The formal empiricist method has allowed a half dozen theories to be rejected within a decade after their conception. Riker's minimum size theory was cast in a language that allowed criticism on logical grounds because the author did make an attempt at formal derivation. His theory could be refuted because its structure made operationalization possible after revision of the original terms. Similarly, the theories of Von Neumann and Morgenstern and of Leiserson (both the bargaining proposition and minimal range theory) were formulated in terms that allowed analytic reconstruction, operationalization and refutation. The same fate befell this author's own theory. It was refuted within two year's of its first publication. It is entertained only in the closed coalition version and, in a more limited sense, as a theory that describes the expected policy of a coalition on the basis of its members' policy preferences. Thus, if anyone has a reason to believe in the impersonal character of the formal empiricist method (and secretly bemoan it), it is the writer of these lines. And yet, the formal empiricist method should be recommended for precisely this reason. It forces the rejection of theories and, by implication, of the underlying paradigms of political life at the relatively low cost of analysis and

298

inquiry. Many theories survive, nevertheless, because the weakness of their structure or the strength of their adherents prevent any attempt at refutation. The purely empiricist approach, on the other hand, produces a great amount of factual knowledge which may be organized in the form of chronological narrative or, quantitatively, along the lines of statistical concepts without adding up to general statements connected within a logical structure. Thus, it will result in neither the rejection nor the support of underlying paradigms.

The formal empiricist method, however, is not indicated at every stage of inquiry and in many fields of research its time may come late, or perhaps never. For the subject at hand, it appears to be good heuristic strategy to follow the indications of the evidence in this study: policies matter more than portfolios. Such policies may be related to one another in a manner that is more structured than would appear from the clamor and vicissitudes of parliamentary politics. The policy positions of the parties may have been determined most of all by the problem of the redistribution of the national income by means of government measures, at least in the half century since 1918.

What is needed at this point is an analysis of party policy positions from two points of view. First, as determinants of the policy of the ruling coalition: what do these policy positions mean as proposals for government action, are they mutually compatible, internally consistent, where do they belong in a ranking of alternatives for government action and which alternatives are *not* represented by actors in the coalitional game?

The second form of inquiry into the policy positions that parties adopt should concentrate on the language parties use to propagate and justify their positions in order to raise support both inside and outside the assembly. Here, students of politics must squarely face a feature of political life that has been pushed aside too often because of an intellectualist bend of mind: the ambiguity of politics. Politicians must, of necessity, create at least the semblance of support from voters whose individual tastes may diverge widely among one another and from the policy proposed. Therefore policies must appear to be many things to many people and so must politicians. This necessitates an ambiguity of language that evokes multiple meanings with every statement. Political language eludes any simple-minded classification and must be understood on the basis of its function, the aggregation of divergent and perhaps inconsistent preferences that need not always be manifest or even conscious. That is the politician's art and its understanding requires skills of interpretation and analysis that cannot be laid down in operational rules. Yet, such interpretative inquiry is necessary, also, to provide formal empiricists with guidelines as to what sources to use and how to read them in order to determine a party's policy position. The traditional skills of the open interview, of observation in the field and of contextual interpretation are not all alternatives opposed to the formal empiricist method, but the source of insights that are indispensable for its progress.

In its present state, the formal empiricist method is poor in psychological, sociological, political and historical content. The distortions of reality imposed by the methodological requirements have been discussed at length in the Introduction, in Chapters 5 and 7 and in the Chapters dealing with conditions in specific countries. The actors in the theories have no memories and no expectations other than the outcomes of their calculations; their personal likes and dislikes are entirely ignored. Parties or coalitions have no social structure but are monolithic entities. Assemblies operate in a social and political void in which the electoral results play the solo part of destiny once every four years. Once the rules of the parliamentary game have been laid down, the theories know of no evolution right through a period of the great Crisis, the Second World War and the Cold War. Policies are reduced to positions on a single, narrow order. However, this need not be so in the formal empiricist method. To a great extent, it reflects the lack of systematic empirical knowledge in the field. There is no reason why organized information could not be incorporated in the structure of formal theories.

It may be true that the formal empirical method of its own warrants no conclusions on how political parties ought to act or how democratic systems ought to be organized. Yet, theories may be "loaded" a certain way. For example, the use of an ordinal policy scale may easily suggest that parties differ from one another only because they want more or less of the same and that their differences are a matter of degree only. But such a scale may contain, at some points, a transition that represents a huge leap, a true dichotomy, a rift as deep as that between Communism and Social Democracy or Conservatism and National Socialism. A rank-order, however, evokes an impression of a bland bargaining game where, in reality, irreconcilable opponents may have clashed. Are they not all "actors" playing the "coalitional game"? From a strictly formal point of view, there is nothing against using these terms to describe the rise of National Socialism in the Weimar

300

Republic or the downfall of the French Fourth Republic. But the theorist who uses those concepts should be permanently alert to the subtle manner in which such terms tend to creep out of their formal context and influence thinking about the historical situations beyond their initial definition. Thus, the policy scale may blind the eye to actual sources of conflict and suggest conciliatory and incremental strategies, not on formal but on psychological grounds.

An explicitly normative theory can greatly contribute to an understanding of the various evaluative stances towards the subject and it can help the investigator to distinguish between the suggestions and the implications of a theory. To offer an example from the present study: it was a vague, omnipresent democratic ethos that prompted the formulation of the problem of coalition formation as what coalition(s) would form, *given* the outcome of the elections. A systematic critique of democracy might have inspired the opposite, and much more pertinent, question: what coalitions can remain in power, *notwithstanding* the elections. But, then, this quality of governments to remain in power, to a high degree independently of the changing preferences of the citizenry, is called, in contemporary political, science "stability", whereas it would be equally objective, value-free and scientific to call it the "insensitivity", "inflexibility" or "immobilism" of the regime.

Formal theory may exist separately from political reality but formal theorists do not. They very much need both a theory on the psychological and social determinants of ideas and a normative theory of politics in order to disengage themselves of their environment and themselves. Thus, the formal empiricist method can only grow side by side with a method that employs the skills of observation and interpretation, with a psychological and sociological theory of ideas, and with a normative theory of political life.

Computer Programs

The calculation of the predicted sets of the theories in this book was done by COAL, a computer program in Fortran IV, conceived and written by the author.

The program is set up to deal with any formal theory of coalitions that contains the following variables: a set of actors, i, with a distribution of weights, w_i, over these actors and a majority criterion, m, defined in terms of these w_i; and, as the case may be, an ordered set of policy positions, p_i, corresponding to the actors, i, in which one pair of consecutive policy positions, p_i may be indeterminate in its ranking ("tying"). Moreover, a second distribution of weights, w_i', and an additional majority criterion, m', may be also included (e.g. when, in addition to the "assembly", there exists a "senate" which possesses a legislative veto).

For each historical situation, j, the data corresponding to these variables form the input to the program, together with the data on the composition (in terms of the actors, i) of the historical coalitions in that situation and with mnemonic codenames for the historical actors in situation, j.

At present, the program is equipped to deal with situations in which up to ten actors participate and in which, at most, eight historical coalitions have occurred. This is sufficient for European parliamentary history since 1918 but it can easily be extended.

A coalition is described in COAL by a binary code in which the nth digit characterizes the membership of the actor in the nth position (e.g. on the policy scale); "1" is "in", "0" is "out". The 2^n binary numbers represent all possible coalitions of n actors.

COAL first calculates which coalitions, S, satisfy the majority criterion, m (and m', as the case may be). The program next determines which is the pivotal actor, k, for every majority coalition, S, and what is the excess, e_S, of each coalition, S. This allows the preferences (in terms of policy distance theory) of each actor, i, over all majority coalitions, S, to be computed by first establishing the order of groups of coalitions with the same pivotal actor, $k(S)$, and, next, the order of coalitions, S, within each group, $k(S)$, on the basis of e_S. Preferences of an actor, j, between two coalitions which have different pivotal actors i and k on either side of j ($p_i < p_j < p_k$) are left indeterminate.

COAL then calculates which coalitions are closed and which are $1,n$ permissible, taking into account pairs of actors with tying policy positions. In a following phase, the program establishes which coalitions, S, are dominated, weakly dominated and undominated among the permissible coalitions; this is repeated for all versions of policy distance theory, taking into account tying policy positions and indeterminate preferences (*cf.* Chapter 5, Section 2).

From that point on, the calculation of the predicted sets of other theories is relatively straightforward since the weights, w_S, of coalitions S, the identity of the extreme members in the coalitions and the number of members have already been established, so that it is easy to calculate minimal winning theory, the minimum size principle and the two-thirds criterion on the one hand and the minimal range theories and the bargaining proposition on the other (*cf.* Chapter 4).

COAL prints out the preference matrices with domination and the composition of historical coalitions for all three versions of policy distance theory and also a list of thirteen theories (including the dummy "winning theory", which predicts *all* majority coalitions) with the size of their predicted set, r_{ij}, and the number of correct predictions, q_{ij}, for each theory, i in each situation, j.

This output is used in the statistical test programs RESULT and RENEE (*cf.* Appendix II) and in TABEL for the printing of tables with historical data and the results of the theories (*cf.* Chapters 9—11).

A Simple Model for Testing Coalition Theories

ROBERT J. MOKKEN

Our problem is to find a criterion against which we may measure the relative predictive success of a certain theory, i. A minimum criterion might be obtained with the introduction of a theory, $t_o^{(i)}$, against which the predictive performance of a theory, i, can be measured. It has the following features. Whereas a specific theory, i, predicts a set of specific winning coalitions, r_{ij}, the predicted set of theory $t_o^{(i)}$ is obtained by taking just a random selection of r_{ij} elements (*i.e.* a sample without replacement) from the set of n_j winning coalitions.

The predictive success of theory i in postulating a predicted set of r_{ij} elements will then be compared with that of theory $t_o^{(i)}$. We shall want theory i to predict very much better than theory $t_o^{(i)}$.

The criterion theory $t_o^{(i)}$, provides a null hypothesis against which the predictive success of a theory i can be tested as follows. In the set of n_j winning coalitions, the p_j observed coalitions may be labelled as the "historical coalitions"; the remaining n_j-p_j coalitions that were not observed are the "non-historical coalitions."

Under the operation of theroy $t_o^{(i)}$, some q from among the p_j observed or historical coalitions will be among the r_{ij} predicted coalitions, selected at random without replacement, from among the n_j winning coalitions. These q elements represent the predictive successes of theory $t_o^{(i)}$. We now have reduced the problem to that of a familiar and simple urn model: an urn that contains n_j

balls, p_j of which are labelled "historical coalition" and the rest, n_j-p_j, "non-historical coalition". If we draw a random sample without replacement of r_{ij} balls, what will be the probability of drawing q balls, labelled "historical coalitions", i.e. q "sucessful predictions"?

This probability for theory $t_o{}^{(i)}$, the null hypothesis, of producing q correct predictions is given by the hypergeometric distribution, well known in elementary probability theory[1].

This probability, Π_0, may be written as

$$\Pi_o(q;n_j;r_{ij};p_j) = \frac{\dbinom{p_j}{q}\dbinom{n_j-p_j}{r_{ij}-q}}{\dbinom{n_j}{r_{ij}}} \tag{1}$$

where

$$\max(0,r_{ij}+p_j-n_j) \leqslant q \leqslant \min(p_j,r_{ij}) \tag{2}$$

For a given theory i, we observe q_{ij} predictive successes. Since we want q_{ij} to have a much higher value than can be expected from the operation of theory $t_o{}^{(i)}$, we will have to calculate the right tail probabilities.

$$\Pi_o(q_{ij}) = \Pi_o\{q \geqslant q_{ij}\} = \sum_{q=q_{ij}}^{\min(p_j,r_{ij})} \Pi_o(q,n_j,r_{ij},p_j) \tag{3}$$

1. The statistical test criteria

Our criteria will be based on the right tail probabilities as defined in eqn. (3). We will use some results of the theory of combination of tests[2]. They are based on a result concerning the probability integral transformation for continuously distributed variables[3]. In its simplest form, the method amounts to the following procedure.

Let t_i ($i = 1,2,....,k$) denote the test statistics corresponding to k tests performed on k independent samples. Let p_i denote the one-sided (e.g. right tail) probability under a null distribution for an observed value t_i of test i. Fisher[4] proposed as an overall test statistic, which combines the results of the individual k tests

$$T = -2 \log \prod_{i=1}^{k} p_i = -2 \sum_{i=1}^{k} \log p_i \qquad (4)*$$

For continuously distributed t_i, $-2\log p_i$ is distributed as χ_2^2 (chi-square with two degrees of freedom). As a consequence, T is distributed as χ_{2k}^2 ($2k$ degrees of freedom), much as the hypergeometric distribution. For variates with discrete distributions, the chi-square test based on eqn. (4) is only a rough approximation.

1.a Test for a given level l

If we want to test a theory i for all situations j for a given nation or a given number of actors, we use a test that combines all right tail probabilities $\Pi_o(q_{ij})$ for all situations at level l. This is achieved through an immediate application of eqn. (4).

Let there be a total of J_l situations at level l, then the appropriate statistic for theory i is

$$T_{il} = 2 \sum_{j=1}^{J_l} \log \Pi_o(q_{ijl}) \qquad (5)$$

T_{il} is approximately distributed as $\chi_{2J_l}^2$ ($2J_l$ degrees of freedom)[+]

1.b Testing across levels

Having established tests for each level l, we may want to test theory i across all levels l (i.e. across nations or across numbers of actors). Let there be L levels in total, then the appropriate overall test is

$$T_i = \sum_{l=1}^{L} T_{li} = -2 \sum_{l=1}^{L} \sum_{j=1}^{J_l} \log \Pi_o(q_{ijl}) \qquad (6)$$

T_i is distributed as χ_{2J}^2 ($2J$ degrees of freedom), $J = \sum_{l=1}^{L} j_l$, that is, the total number of situations across levels.

---

*The symbol "log" refers to the natural logarithm.
[+]The index l should be added in eqns. (1), (2) and (3), in the manner it appears in eqn. (5) if we wish to restrict our attention to the situations at level l only.

By means of the two tests T_{il} and T_i, the predictive performance of a theory i may be tested against the null hypothesis provided by theory $t_o^{(i)}$, based on a random guess of r_{ij} winning coalitions in order to constitute a "predicted" set; the tests may be applied to each level, or across levels, respectively. Sufficiently high values of χ^2 may denote significant departures from this null hypothesis.

Some caution in interpreting these test scores is necessary. Theory $t_o^{(i)}$ provides a minimum criterion in terms of which the performance of a theory i is to be evaluated. The least that may be expected from a reasonably good theory with a predicted set of r_{ij} elements is that it performs significantly better than the null hypothesis with a predicted set composed by selecting r_j elements randomly from among the n_j winning coalitions in the given situation j. The finding that the results for a theory i depart significantly from those that are to be expected from the null hypothesis $t_o^{(i)}$, therefore, does not imply that the theory i is really adequate.

In this sense, a significant departure from the results of $t_o^{(i)}$ is a necessary but not a sufficient condition for an adequate theory. Or, it should not just be significant but it should deviate from $t_o^{(i)}$ in a rather extreme way. This implies that the significance levels should be evaluated at a much lower value than is usual in statistical practice.

1.c. Computations

The computational methods were programmed by Miss Renée Brandt*. The exact hypergeometric probabilities, as well as the exact probabilities of the χ_v^2 values from the χ^2 probability function for degrees of freedom ν up to 100, were computed by the program. For degrees of freedom $\nu \geqslant 100$ the Wilson-Hilforty approximation was used.

---

*Department of Methodology, Institute of Political Science of the University of Amsterdam.

Notes

Notes to Chapter 1

[1] For example, the list of "empirically testable propositions" (Downs, 1957, pp. 295—300). Richardson (1960) uses statistical data throughout his study for the estimation of parameter values. See also Simon (1957) and McPhee (1963).

[2] A partial test of coalition theories (Von Neumann and Morgenstern, Riker—Gamson, Leiserson, 1968) may be found in Browne (1971). See also Chapter 7.

[3] An early application of game theory (though, strictly speaking, not coalition theory) to political institutions is the analysis of the "distribution of power" in the U.S. Congress (Luce and Rogow, 1956). See also Riker (1959) (on defections in the French Assembly) and Mann and Shapley (1964) (on the U.S. electoral college). All these analyses make use of the Shapley—Shubik power index (cf. Shapley, 1953; Shapley and Shubik, 1954).

[4] See Ellsberg (1956), Koo (1959) and Rapoport (1964) p. 33.

Notes to Chapter 2

[1] Carlyle (1840) pp. 1—2.

[2] Sartre (1961) p. 54.

[3] Simon (1965) Chapters 4 and 5; Simon (1957) pp. 204—206 and Chapter 14.

[4] Braybrooke and Lindblom (1963) Chapter 5. For a brief exposition of these ideas see Lindblom (1968) pp. 24—27.

[5] Snyder et al. (1962) pp. 86—177. See also the comparative evaluation of this approach, general systems theory and field theory in the essay by Richard A. Brody in the same volume.

308

[6] Dahl (1961). The theoretical implications of this study have been spelled out, often in the polemics with other students of community power. by Polsby (1963). The debate that has arisen since then centers around two issues: (1) the alleged elitism of Dahl's views on democracy (Walker, 1966; Bachrach, 1967; Dahl, 1966), and (2) the problems in locating the true locus and subject of decision making through empirical studies of decision-making bodies in communities (Bachrach and Baratz, 1963; Gitlin, 1967).

[7] See Lindblom (1965) pp. 21—86.

[8] See, especially, pp. 64—88 and 523—538 on the components of the voter's decision. A critical discussion of these conclusions may be found in Daudt (1961). A recent attempt to establish the rationality of the voting decision on the basis of empirical evidence has been undertaken by Goldberg: "Despite all these qualms, the present study strongly suggests that there is a rational component to party identifications rooted in group norms" (Goldberg, 1969, p. 21).

[9] Downs (1957) Chapter 3, pp. 36—50; cf. also Davis and Hinich (1966, 1967).

[10] See, for example, the report on an experiment by Mosteller and Nogee (1967) in which the utilities of money bets were established over a range of 5 cents to 5 dollars, using students and guardsmen as subjects.

[11] Davis et al. (1960) p. 543: "as we have shown, the budgetary process can be described by very simple decision rules".

[12] Barber (1966) pp. 44—47, criteria for deciding on what items to spend the attention of the budgetary committee; and pp. 59—65, "informational strategies".

[13] The same approach is used by Riker and Leiserson, see Chapter IV in this book.

[14] Or: "the 'functionalist' approach to explanation — identified variously as 'functionalism', 'structural functionalism', 'systems analysis', or 'general systems theory". Meehan (1967) p. 111.

[15] Wiseman (1966) p. 2.

[16] Easton (1965) p. 257.

[17] Almond (1956) pp. 391—409; Almond and Powell (1966) p. 107.

[18] Kleerekoper (1956) Vol. I, p. 37 (quotation translated from the Dutch).

[19] Wiseman (1966) pp. 214—220; Harsanyi (1967) discusses "rational choice models vs. functionalistic and conformistic models of political behavior" in an unpublished paper with this title. "Finally, if it can be shown that a given social institution makes a significant contribution to the survival of the social system as a whole, this fact can 'explain' the existence of this social institution only in a very limited sense, unless the advocates of such 'collectivistic' functional explanations can specify the actual causal mechanisms by which the survival needs of the society are translated into individual behavior ensuring the existence of the required institutions. In actual fact, the advocates of such explanations have made no attempt to specify the nature of these causal mechanisms." (Harsanyi, 1967, p. 24, italics in the original).

[20] See Arrow (1963) p. 13; Luce and Raiffa (1957) p. 25, "connected" is used as equivalent to "complete"; Sen (1970) pp. 3, 8.

[21] Von Neumann and Morgenstern (1967) pp. 15—31.

[22] Thus, in the definition by Von Neumann and Morgenstern (1967), utility

may be measured along an "interval scale"; *cf.* Torgerson (1958) pp. 16 *et seq.*; or, an "ordered metric" scale; *cf.* Coombs (1953) p. 478. See also, Luce and Raiffa (1957) p. 33. Shapley and Shubik (1953) have shown that most conclusions in game theory can also be reached with ordinal utility scales, defined up to an order-preserving transformation. Such a utility scale will be used in the present book; *cf.* Howard (1972); see also Chapter 5, pp. 100—104.

23 Von Neumann and Morgenstern (1967) p. 16.
24 Von Neumann and Morgenstern (1967) p. 9.
25 Von Neumann and Morgenstern (1967) p. 30. Luce and Raiffa (1957, p.30) qualify the assumption as "a serious idealization".
26 Riker (1962) p. 23.

Notes to Chapter 3

1 This chapter contains a discussion of the work of Von Neumann and Morgenstern and of the literature that has grown around it. The presentation leans heavily on Luce and Raiffa (1957). For 2-person theory there are many introductions, that are accessible to the reader not trained in mathematics, *e.g.* Boulding (1962), Pen (1962), Rapoport (1960, 1964,1966), and J.D. Williams (1954). The literature in the field of *n*-person theory up to 1957 is discussed by Luce and Raiffa in a manner that demands basic knowledge of at least set theory. More recent contributions are only accessible in the original version, mostly as articles. Rapoport (1970) explains the indispensable mathematics for *n*-person theory and discusses many solution concepts developed since the theory was presented.

2 Von Neumann and Morgenstern (1967) p. 103.
3 Von Neumann and Morgenstern (1967) pp. 143—168.
4 *Cf.* Luce and Raiffa (1957) pp. 280—282.
5 Luce and Raiffa (1957) pp. 106—109.
6 Schelling (1963) pp. 115, 303; Luce and Raiffa (1957) pp. 97,101,110—112, 123—127.
7 Von Neumann and Morgenstern (1967) pp. 549—550; Luce and Raiffa (1957) pp. 124—137.
8 Schelling (1963) p. 113.
9 Luce and Raiffa (1957) p. 163.
10 Nash's proof; *cf.* Luce and Raiffa (1957) pp. 170—171.
11 Von Neumann and Morgenstern (1967) pp. 238—243; Luce and Raiffa (1957) pp. 182—185.
12 Luce and Raiffa (1957) p. 183.
13 Rapoport (1970) pp. 78—79.
14 Luce and Raiffa (1957) pp. 183—184.
15 Von Neumann and Morgenstern (1967) pp. 263—264; Luce and Raiffa (1957) p. 193.
16 Von Neumann and Morgenstern (1967) p 40, pp. 264 *et seq.*
17 See Von Neumann and Morgenstern (1967) pp. 282—290. Von Neumann and Morgenstern show that all three-person constant-sum games may be

described by a single characteristic function of the form (after 0,1 normalization): $v(S) = 1$ for any S with two or three members, $v(S) = 0$ for any S with no members or a single member.

[18] Von Neumann and Morgenstern (1967) p. 289, notation adapted.

[19] Gillies (1959) p.50.

[20] For the mathematical proof that the core of essential constant-sum games is empty, see Luce and Raiffa (1957) pp. 194—195. The authors say "these n-tuples (i.e. the undominated inputations constituting the core) should be included in any definition of equilibrium we propose."

[21] See Luce and Raiffa (1957) pp. 213—215.

[22] Luce and Raiffa (1957) p.168.

[23] Luce and Raiffa (1957) p. 222.

[24] The authors apply their ψ-stability notion to the results of the "RAND"-experiment without, however, arriving at a clear conclusion; Luce and Raiffa (1957) pp. 259—269.

[25] Aumann and Maschler (1964) p. 444. An existence proof for the bargaining set may be found in Davis and Maschler (1963a). An experiment testing the validity of its assumptions on gaming sessions with Israeli children is described in Maschler (1965).

[26] Aumann and Maschler (1964) p. 473.

[27] Aumann and Maschler (1964) p. 449.

[28] Aumann and Maschler (1964) p.445.

[29] Aumann and Maschler (1964) p. 471—472.

[30] Maschler (1965).

[31] Davis and Maschler (1963).

[32] Davis and Maschler (1963) p. 4, notation adapted.

[33] The game is 1,0 normalization and therefore $v(\{i\}) = 0$.

[34] See Freudenthal (1962) p. 34.

[35] For example Mann and Shapley (1964) on the U.S. electoral college and Luce and Rogow (1956) on a legislative model inspired by the U.S. congress and presidency. Both articles are also included in Shubik (1964).

Notes to Chapter 4

[1] Harsanyi (1961) p. 64.

[2] Von Neumann and Morgenstern (1967) p. 423.

[3] Von Neumann and Morgenstern (1967) p. 436.

[4] See, for example, p. 268.

[5] *The Randon House Dictionary*, 1966, p. 1419.

[6] Riker (1962) p. 32.

[7] Riker (1962) p. 32.

[8] Riker (1962) p.40.

[9] Riker (1962) pp. 43—45; *cf.* also p. 271.

[10] Southwold (1969) p.27.

[11] Riker (1962) p. 127.

[12] Riker (1962) p. 129.

[13] Riker (1962) pp. 129—130.

[14] Riker (1962) pp. 130—131.

[15] Riker (1962) p. 139.
[16] Riker (1966) pp. 173—174.
[17] Riker (1966) p. 172.
[18] See Kleerekoper (1956) Vol. I, pp. 387—472.
[19] Gamson (1961) p. 376.
[20] Riker (1962) pp. 88—89.
[21] Leiserson (1968) p. 775.
[22] Von Neumann and Morgenstern (1967) pp. 433—434, 457—473.
[23] Leiserson (1968) p. 774.
[24] Leiserson (1968) p. 775.
[25] Leiserson (1970) p. 90.
[26] Coombs (1953) pp. 66 *et seq*; Torgerson (1958) pp. 19—21.
[27] Leiserson (1966) pp. 333—414; *cf.* especially Table 7-2, p. 364, "De Gaulle", "Gouin", and "Bidault".
[28] Axelrod (1970) pp. 170 *et seq.*
[29] Axelrod (1970) pp. 32,150.
[30] Axelrod (1970) p.150.
[31] See also Taylor (1971) pp. 16—17 referring to an unpublished memorandum by Miller, University of California, 1971.

Notes to Chapter 5

[1] See, for example, Friedmann (1967) on the religious parties in Israel, pp. 217 *et seq.*
[2] For a careful investigation of cleavages in the Assembly of the French Fourth Republic, see MacRae (1967).
[3] Riker (1962) p. 81.
[4] Von Neumann and Morgenstern (1967) p. 423.
[5] See Luce and Raiffa (1957) pp. 193—194; there, however, utilities are defined so that their summation is meaningful and so that they are transferable.
[6] Riker (1962) pp. 108 *et seq.*
[7] Black (1958) pp. 18 *et seq.*

Notes to Chapter 6

[1] Von Neumann and Morgenstern (1967) p. 266.
[2] Von Neumann and Morgenstern (1967) p. 36.

Notes to Chapter 7

[1] Gamson (1962) p. 159.
[2] For a discussion on the relationships between cabinet and parliament in

small European democracies, see Daalder (1971).

[3] Browne and Franklin (1973); Browne (1973).
[4] Schumpeter (1950) p. 283.
[5] Schumpeter (1950) p. 282.
[6] Downs (1957) p. 28.
[7] Riker (1962) p. 21.
[8] Burke (1861) p. 372.
[9] Sjöblom (1968) p. 166; see also Sartori (1966) p. 158.
[10] Downs (1957) p. 112.
[11] Downs (1957) p. 122.
[12] Russett (1970) pp. 149—156. U.S. defense spending 1937—1967 corre-lates negatively with expenditures on education, health and welfare.
[13] Stokes (1963) p. 370.
[14] Stokes (1963) p. 373.
[15] Stokes (1963) p. 372.
[16] Stokes (1963) p. 375.
[17] Stokes (1963) p. 377.
[18] See, for example, Blondel (1967) pp. 12 *et seq.* and Daalder (1971) p. 292.
[19] Gregor (1969) p. 332.
[20] Romein (1938) p. 29 (translated from the Dutch).
[21] Nolte (1965) pp. 300—301.
[22] Saladino (1965) p. 257.
[23] Meynaud in Hoffmann (1951) p. xxi.
[24] Mannheim (1953) pp. 77—79.
[25] Rogger (1965) p. 578.
[26] Riker (1962) pp. 77 *et seq.*

Notes to Chapter 8

[1] Gregg and Simon (1967) p. 271. When a theory has not failed badly in comparison to stochastic theory as a null hypothesis but when the evi-dence is still inconclusive, the theory may be "entertained" until it can definitively be rejected or accepted.
[2] Browne (1970—1971) p. 406, independently made the same revision of the minimum size principle, setting the upper limit at 65% instead of at two thirds and found the same result.
[3] Leiserson (1966) pp. 347—356, 363—380, 387—397.
[4] Leiserson (1968) pp. 780—785.
[5] Axelrod (1970) pp. 178—183.
[6] Damgaard (1969) pp. 39—41, 43.
[7] Browne (1970-1971) p. 399.

Notes to Chapter 9

1 Sartori (1966) p. 153.
2 Sartori (1966) p. 160.
3 Halperin (1946) p. 156; *cf.* Eyck (1962) Vol. I, p. 105.
4 Halperin (1946) p. 158.
5 Halperin (1946) p. 136.
6 Milatz (1965) p. 99.
7 Hertzman (1963) p. 238.
8 Hertzman (1963) p. 199.
9 Neumann (1965) p. 40; *cf.* Flechtheim (1962) p. 125.
10 Halperin (1946) p. 127.
11 Neumann (1965) p. 44 *et seq.*; Milatz (1965) p. 95; Morsey (1962) p. 98.
12 Milatz (1965) p. 98.
13 Neumann (1965) pp. 54–59; *cf.* Milatz (1965) p. 99.
14 Milatz (1965) p. 106; *cf.* Neumann (1965) p. 63. For early economic programs and financial contributors, see Hertzmann (1963) pp. 80 *et seq.* and 64, respectively.
15 Milatz (1965) p. 102; Halperin (1946) p. 429.
16 Milatz (1965) p. 106.
17 Flechtheim (1962) p. 147.
18 Neumann (1965) p. 77.
19 For example, Gregor (1968) pp. 204–212.
20 Sartori (1966) pp. 153–155.
21 Eyck (1962) Vol. I, p. 92.
22 Eyck (1962) Vol. I, pp. 145–146.
23 Eyck (1962) Vol. I, p. 223.
24 Eyck (1962) Vol. I, pp. 353, 377.
25 Eyck (1962) Vol. I, p. 378.
26 Eyck (1962) Vol. I, pp. 408, 417, 425.
27 Eyck (1962) Vol. I, p. 427.
28 Eyck (1962) Vol. II, p. 37.
29 Eyck (1962) Vol. II, p. 208.
30 Eyck (1962) Vol. II, pp. 208–210.
31 Eyck (1962) Vol. II, p. 326.
32 Eyck (1962) Vol. II, pp. 367–368.
33 Eyck (1962) Vol. II, pp. 415–416.
34 Eyck (1962) Vol. II, p. 475; *cf.* also Carsten (1967) pp. 145 *et seq.*
35 MacRae (1967) p. 61, n. 1; Marichy (1969) pp. 173–181, 498, 525, 613.
36 Williams (1966) p. 239, n. 10: on average, 41 in the first Assembly.
37 Williams (1966) pp. 241 *et seq.*; *cf.* MacRae (1967) p. 67.
38 Leites (1959) p. 4.
39 Leites (1959) p. 11.
40 Goguel (1952) p. 141; *cf.* MacRae (1967) pp. 329 *et seq.*
41 Fauvet (1959) p. 358.
42 Converse and Dupeux (1969) p. 196.
43 Converse and Dupeux (1969) p. 190.
44 MacRae (1967) p. 211.
45 MacRae (1967) p. 214.
46 Duverger (1964) p. 261.

47 Sartori (1966) p. 156.
48 MacRae (1967) pp. 91 *et seq.*
49 Blondel and Drexer (1968) p. 108.
50 MacRae (1967) p. 117, Fig. 52.
51 Goguel (1952) p. 122.
52 Williams (1966) p. 62.
53 Goguel (1952) p. 62.
54 Williams (1966) pp. 184—186.
55 Blondel and Drexer (1968) p. 104; Micaud (1956) pp. 116, 118.
56 Blondel and Drexer (1968) p. 104.
57 Williams (1966) p. 161.
58 Williams (1966) p. 162.
59 MacRae (1967) p. 74.
60 Williams (1966) p. 145.
61 Williams (1966) p. 151; Henig and Pinder (1969) p. 122.
62 Henig and Pinder (1969) p. 122: "de Gaulle's determination to come to power legally probably prevented the RPF from developing further fascist characteristics." Other movements have come to power legally without being any less Fascist for it.
63 Blondel and Drexer (1968) p. 112; Williams (1966) p. 145.
64 Williams (1966) p. 154; Goguel (1952) p. 139.
65 Hoffmann (1951) pp. 349 *et seq.*
66 Hoffmann (1951) p. 372.
67 Hoffmann (1951) p. 237.
68 Henig and Pinder (1969) p. 181.
69 MacRae (1967) pp. 234—239.
70 Fox (1951) p. 124.
71 See Fauvet (1959) pp. 73, 78.
72 Fauvet (1959) pp. 106, 114—115.
73 Williams (1966) pp. 127, 146, 185.
74 Fauvet (1959) p. 166.
75 See Williams (1966) Appendix IV.
76 Williams (1966) p. 161.
77 MacRae (1967) p. 141, Fig. 5.1.
78 Leiserson (1966) pp. 362—363.
79 MacRae (1967) p. 117.
80 MacRae (1967) p. 119.
81 Fauvet (1959) p. 249, n. 2.
82 Fauvet (1959) p. 342; MacRae (1967) pp. 163—164.
83 Maranini (1969) p. 57; Carlyle (1965) p. 44.
84 Chassériaud (1965) pp. 183, 235, 242; Kogan (1966) pp. 34—53.
85 Kogan (1966) pp. 51—53, 77.
86 Kogan (1966) p. 77.
87 Chassériaud (1965) p. 80.
88 Barnes (1966) p. 304.
89 Barnes (1966) p. 316; *cf.* Adams and Barile (1966) p. 154.
90 Barnes (1966) pp. 304—305.
91 Sartori (1966) p. 140.
92 Adams and Barile (1966) p. 50; *cf.* Henig and Pinder (1969) pp. 238—239 and Barnes (1966) p. 321.

93 Kogan (1966) pp. 74—75.
94 Saladino (1965) pp. 254 *et seq.*; Gregor (1969) pp. 292—301; Carsten (1967) pp. 50, 76.
95 Spreafico and La Palombara (1963) pp. 244—245.
96 Godechot (1964) p. 244; Kogan (1966) p. 46.
97 Godechot (1964) p. 245.
98 Adams and Barile (1966) p. 87.
99 Kogan (1966) p. 85.
100 Kogan (1966) p. 122.
101 Godechot (1964) p. 272.
102 Kogan (1966) pp. 128—129.
103 Godechot (1964) p. 274.
104 Kogan (1966) p. 167.
105 Kogan (1966) p. 184; Godechot (1964) p. 275.
106 Kogan (1966) p. 198.
107 *Keesing's Historisch Archief*, December 30, 1968.

Notes to Chapter 10

1 Lijphart (1968) p. 84; *cf.* Goudsblom (1967) p. 94.
2 Daalder (1955) p. 1.
3 See Kruyt; Baehr (1969) p. 257; Goudsblom (1967) pp. 120 *et seq.*: Lijphart (1968) pp. 19 *et seq.*; Daalder (1966) pp. 213—220.
4 See Daalder (1966) pp. 221—222.
5 Van Raalte (1963) p. 90.
6 Van Raalte (1963) pp. 40—41; *cf.* Belinfante (1964) pp. 33—34.
7 Lijphart (1968) pp. 110—113; Scholten (1968) pp. 516—518, 525—530; Windmuller (1969) pp. 292, 296.
8 Duynstee (1966) pp. 16 *et seq.*
9 Baehr (1969) pp. 257—258; Goudsblom (1967) p. 89.
10 Lipschits (1969) pp. 104—105.
11 Lipschits (1969) p. 113.
12 Lipschits (1969) p. 115.
13 De Gruyter (1967) p. 5.
14 De Leeuw (1968—1969) p. 86.
15 Koomen and Willems (1968—1969) pp. 462—463.
16 Jacobs and Jacobs-Wessels (1968—1969) p. 46.
17 De Leeuw (1968—1969) pp. 87—88.
18 Stapel (1968—1969) p. 40.
19 Daalder and Rusk (1972) pp. 175—185.
20 Daalder and Rusk (1972) p. 54.
21 Daalder and Rusk (1972) p. 51.
22 Hazewindus and Mokken (1972) p. 8.
23 See Daalder (1955); Baehr (1969) pp. 256—268; Daalder (1957) pp. 217—232; Kirschen *et al.* (1964) p. 168; Weil (1970) pp. 84—92.
24 See Oud (1948) Vol. I pp. 22—36; De Jong (1969) Vol. I; Puchinger (1969) Vol. I.

[25] Van der Land (1962) pp. 25–46; 101, 117–118.
[26] Oud (1948) Vol. I p. 33.
[27] Oud (1948) Vol. I.
[28] Daalder (1957) pp. 220 *et seq.*; Lijphart (1968) p. 28; Weil (1970) pp. 88–90; Kirschen *et al.* (1964) p. 168 adopts the present order but reverses CHU and ARP which seems unwarranted.
[29] Nooij (1969) p. 205.
[30] Nooij (1969) pp. 43–45; *cf.* Baehr (1969) p. 257.
[31] Nooij (1969) p. 112.
[32] Daalder (1966a) p. 224; Daalder and Rusk (1972) p. 27. For a contrasting view, see Weil (1970) p. 217.
[33] Daalder (1966a) p. 222.
[34] See De Jong (1969) Vol. I, pp. 40 *et seq.*, 65 *et seq.*, 75.
[35] Daalder (1966a) Table 6.2, p. 419; *cf.* Oud (1948) Vol. III pp. 83–86, 99.
[36] See De Jong (1969) Vol. I, p. 599.
[37] De Jong (1969) p. 603.
[38] Duynstee (1966) p. 17.
[39] Duynstee (1966) p. 17; Lijphart (1966) pp. 111–122, 182.
[40] Duynstee (1966) pp. 200 *et seq.*
[41] Duynstee (1966) p. 246.
[42] Bernstein (1957) p. 41; Freudenheim (1967) pp. 163, 181.
[43] Bernstein (1957) p. 46.
[44] Freudenheim (1967) p. 148.
[45] Friedmann (1965) pp. 101 *et seq.*
[46] Arian (1966) pp. 271 *et seq.*
[47] Arian (1966) p. 267.
[48] Coombs (1953) p. 527.
[49] Arian (1966) p. 273.
[50] Arian (1966) p. 281.
[51] Arian (1966) p. 282.
[52] See Seligman (1964) pp. 32–37; Bernstein (1957) pp. 57–80; Badi (1963) pp. 43–61; Kraines (1961) pp. 56–79.
[53] Bernstein (1957) p. 70.
[54] Bernstein (1957) p. 71.
[55] Friedmann (1965) p. 258.
[56] Seligman (1964) pp. 42–43.
[57] Badi (1963) p. 98.
[58] Dr. I. Lipschits, University of Groningen, private communication.
[59] Etzioni (1963).
[60] Bernstein (1957) p. 126.
[61] Bernstein (1957) p. 126.
[62] Bernstein (1957) p. 116.
[63] *Keesing's Historisch Archief*, January 21, 1966.
[64] *Keesing's Historisch Archief*, August 27, 1970.
[65] Andrén (1964) pp. 73–75; Pesonen (1968) p. 3.
[66] Pesonen (1968) p. 3.
[67] Kastari (1969) pp. 152, 158.
[68] Andrén (1964) p. 76.
[69] Kastari (1969) p. 151.
[70] Pesonen (1968) p. 4.

71 Kastari (1969) p. 158.
72 Allardt and Pesonen (1967) p. 335.
73 Von Bonsdorff (1960) pp. 18—19; *cf.* Pesonen (1968) p. 13; Henig and Pinder (1969) pp. 326—327, Table I; Andrén (1964) pp. 193—194; Allardt and Pesonen (1967) p. 331.
74 Pesonen (1968) p. 14; Andrén (1964) p. 84.
75 See Hodgson (1967).
76 Andrén (1964) p. 83.
77 Andrén (1964) p. 86.
78 Andrén (1964) p. 87.
79 Rintala (1965) p. 440.
80 Rintala (1965) p. 437.
81 Borg (1966) p. 95.
82 Borg (1965) p. 103, Table 1.
83 See Nyholm (1972) pp. 36, 42.
84 See Törnudd (1969) pp. 59—60, Table I and pp. 68—69, Table V for the names, dates and composition of Finnish cabinets until 1970.
85 Wuorinen (1965) pp. 24 *et seq.*; Hodgson (1967) pp. 140—141.
86 Daalder (1971) p. 295.
87 Wuorinen (1965) p. 352 mentions two Conservative members of Ryti I; Törnudd (1969) pp. 60, 68 dates their entry to the government four months later, in Ryti II, after the conclusion of the Moscow peace treaty.
88 Wuorinen (1965) p. 364.
89 Wuorinen (1965) p. 237.
90 Wuorinen (1965) p. 431, note a.
91 See Wuorinen (1965) pp. 433, 440, 446—447 for specific instances of Soviet influence on the composition and resignation of Finnish cabinets.
92 The Progessives had constituted themselves at this time as the Finnish People's Party; Wuorinen (1965) p. 426.
93 Sänkiaho (1970) p. 122.
94 Borg (1966) p. 95.
95 *Keesing's Historisch Archief,* July 31, 1970.
96 *Keesing's Historisch Archief,* May 7, 1971.
97 *Keesing's Historisch Archief,* April 14, 1972.

Notes to Chapter 11

1 Andrén (1961) pp. 85 *et seq.*
2 Respectively "andra kammaren" (second chamber) and "första kammaren" (first chamber).
3 Only once, however, has a government resigned on an antagonistic vote in the Upper House: Branting II (10/'21). See Andrén (1961) p. 216.
4 Andrén (1964) p. 158.
5 Fusilier (1960) p. 93 (italics as in original book); *cf.* Stjernquist (1963) p. 117.
6 Andrén (1961) pp. 85—87.
7 Andrén (1964) p. 159.
8 Andrén (1961) p. 104.

9 See Fusilier (1965) pp. 198—204.
10 Fusilier (1965) p. 179.
11 Andrén (1961) p. 88; *cf.* Stjernquist (1963) p. 117.
12 Forsell (1971) p. 203.
13 Andrén (1961) p. 36.
14 Särlvik (1967) p. 168. Särlvik (1971) presents recent data on voters' perception of party positions that place the Center Party between Social Democrats and Liberals (see pp. 100—112).
15 Särlvik (1967) p. 170.
16 Andrén (1961) p. 31.
17 Andrén (1961) p. 24.
18 Stjernquist (1963) p. 123.
19 Andrén (1961) p. 27.
20 Andrén (1961) pp. 217—220.
21 Andrén (1961) p. 30.
22 Stjernquist (1963) p. 131.
23 Stjernquist (1963) p. 132.
24 Andrén (1961) p. 212.
25 Andrén (1961) p. 214.
26 Andrén (1961) p. 217.
27 Andrén (1961) p. 220. From 1922 onwards, data on the voting strength in the Lower House and in the Joint Division and on the dates, names and compositions of cabinets are taken from Stjernquist (1963) pp. 405—407.
28 Andrén (1961) p. 221.
29 Särlvik (1967) p. 193; Andrén (1961) p. 224.
30 Andrén (1961) p. 224; Sternquist (1963) p. 126.
31 *Keesing's Historisch Archief*, September 25, 1970.
32 Fusilier (1960) p. 312.
33 Damgaard (1969) p. 37.
34 Fusilier (1960) p. 328.
35 Miller (1968) p. 55; Fusilier (1960) p. 324; Andrén (1964) p. 40.
36 Miller (1968) p. 36.
37 Miller (1968) p. 138.
38 Miller (1968) p. 145.
39 Miller (1968) p. 61.
40 Miller (1968) p. 90.
41 Miller (1968) p. 84.
42 Miller (1968) p. 72.
43 Miller (1968) p. 80.
44 Miller (1968) p. 93.
45 Andrén (1964) p. 56.
46 Wasserman (1963) pp. 367, 375.
47 See also Pedersen (1967), especially pp. 153, 156—158.
48 Damgaard (1969) p. 36.
49 Damgaard (1969) p. 35.
50 Damgaard (1969) p. 36, italics added.
51 Damgaard (1969) p. 37.
52 *Keesing's Historisch Archief*, October 22, 1971.
53 Damgaard (1969) p. 42.
54 Damgaard (1969) p. 51.

[55] Damgaard (1969) Table IV, p. 43.
[56] Pedersen (1967) p. 161.
[57] See Eckstein (1964) p. 11; Rodnick (1955) pp. 145 *et seq.*
[58] See Rokkan (1966) pp. 74, 80; Rokkan (1967) p. 389 distinguishes territorial, sociocultural, religions, labor market and commodity market cleavages; *cf.* Converse and Valen (1971) pp. 109—112 and Eckstein (1964) pp. 51—52.
[59] Storing (1963) p. 8; Rodnick (1955) p. 122; Valen and Katz (1964) p. 329.
[60] Storing (1963) pp. 73, 78; *Norway Yearbook* (1954) p. 66.
[61] Storing (1963) p. 85.
[62] Storing (1963) p. 79; Valen and Katz (1964) p. 15.
[63] Storing (1963) p. 56.
[64] Storing (1963) pp. 86, 91.
[65] Storing (1963) p. 91.
[66] Storing (1963) p. 53.
[67] Storing (1963) p. 93.
[68] Rokkan (1966) p. 81.
[69] Valen and Katz (1964) p. 32.
[70] Storing (1963) p. 136.
[71] Valen and Katz (1964) p. 33; *cf.* Storing (1963) p. 137 and Rodnick pp. 124—129.
[72] Valen and Katz (1964) pp. 31—32; *cf.* Storing (1963) p. 138.
[73] Valen and Katz (1964) p. 27.
[74] Storing (1963) p. 140.
[75] Valen and Katz (1964) p. 34; *cf.* Eckstein (1964) p. 53.
[76] Storing (1963) pp. 142- 143.
[77] Groennings (1970) p. 61; *cf.* Kirschen *et al.* (1964) p. 168.
[78] Rokkan (1966) p. 102; see also the increasing percentages of "strong identifiers" or party members opposed to government intervention corresponding to the scale (Valen and Katz (1964) p. 260).
[79] Converse and Valen (1971) p. 134.
[80] Valen and Katz (1964) p. 34.
[81] Nyheim (1967) p. 257.
[82] Storing (1963) p. 35.
[83] Groennings (1970) p. 63.
[84] *The Norway Yearbook* (1954) p. 65.
[85] Friis (1950) p. 364.
[86] Nyheim (1967) p. 257.
[87] Groennings (1970).
[88] Groennings (1970) p. 71.
[89] Groennings (1970) p. 69.
[90] Groennings (1970) p. 66.
[91] Ruin (1969) pp. 78—80, 85.

Notes to Chapter 12

[1] Braybrooke and Lindblom (1963) pp. 51 *et seq.*
[2] Simon (1957) pp. 204—205.

320

[3] Braybrooke and Lindblom (1963) pp. 81—104.
[4] Axelrod (1970) p. 169.
[5] Brams (1972) pp. 237—238.
[6] See Downs (1957) pp. 160—163.
[7] The proposal was the subject of debate in the Netherlands. See Daudt (1968) pp. 299—300 for a summary in English.
[8] See Downs (1957) pp. 144 *et seq.* and Black (1958) pp. 14 *et seq.*
[9] Dahl (1956) p. 84.

Notes to Appendix II

[1] See Feller (1968) pp. 43—47.
[2] Oosterhoff (1969).
[3] Kendall and Stuart (1958) p. 394, ex. 16.4.
[4] Fisher (1932).

References

Adams, John C. and Barile, Paolo (1966). *The Government of Republican Italy* (2nd ed.). Boston: Houghton Mifflin.

Akzin, B. (1955). "The Role of Parties in Israeli Democracy", *Journal of Politics*, 17, pp. 507—545.

Allardt, Erik (1964). "Patterns of Conflict and Working Class Consciousness in Finnish Politics", in Allardt, E. and Littunen, Y. (eds.), *Cleavages, Ideologies and Party Systems; Contributions to comparative political sociology*, pp. 325—66. Helsinki: Transaction of the Westermarck Society.

Allardt, Erik and Pesonen, Pertti (1967). "Cleavages in Finnish Politics", in: Lipset, S.M. and Rokkan, S. (eds.), *Party Systems and Voting Alignments: Cross-national Perspectives*. New York: The Free Press.

Almond, Gabriel, A. (1956). "Comparative Political Systems", *Journal of Politics*, 18, pp. 391—409.

Almond, Gabriel A. and Powell, G. Bingham, Jr. (1966). *Comparative Politics; A developmental approach*. Boston, Toronto: Little, Brown and Co.

Andrén, Nils (1961). *Modern Swedish Government*. Stockholm: Almqvist and Wiksell.

Andrén, Nils (1964). *Government and Politics in the Nordic Countries; Denmark, Finland, Iceland, Norway, Sweden*. Stockholm: Almqvist and Wiksell.

Arian, Alan (1966). "Voting and Ideology in Israel", *Midwest Journal of Political Science*, 13, pp. 265—287.

Arrow, Kenneth J. (1963). *Social Choice and Individual Values* (1951) (2nd edn.). New York: Wiley.

Aumann, Robert J. and Maschler, Michael (1964). "The Bargaining Set for Cooperative Games", in: Dresher, M., Shapley, L.S. and Tucker, A.W. (eds.), *Advances in Game Theory; Annals of mathematics studies*, vol. 52, pp. 443—475. (Princeton, N.J.: Princeton U.P.

Axelrod, Robert (1970). *Conflict of Interest; A theory of divergent goals with applications to politics*. Chicago: Markham.

Bachrach, Peter (1967). *The Theory of Democratic Elitism; A critique*. Boston: Little, Brown and Co.

Bachrach, Peter and Baratz, Morton S. (1963). "Decisions and Nondecisions: An analytical framework", *American Political Science Review*, 57, pp. 632—642.

Badi, Joseph (1963). *The Government of the State of Israel; A critical account of its parliament, executive and judiciary.* New York: Twayne.

Baehr, Peter R. (1969). "The Netherlands", in: Henig, S. and Pinder, J. (eds.), *European Political Parties*, pp. 256—281. London: Allen and Unwin.

Barber, James D. (1966). *Power in Committees; An experiment in the governmental process.* Chicago: Rand McNally.

Barnes, Samuel H. (1966). "Italy: Oppositions on Left, Right, and Center", in: Dahl, R.A. (ed.), *Political Oppositions in Western Democracies*, pp. 303—331. New Haven and London: Yale U.P.

Belinfante, A.D. (1964). *Beginselen van Nederlands Staatsrecht (Hand- en Leerboek der Bestuurswetenschappen, 7).* Alphen aan de Rijn: Samsom.

Bernstein, Marver H. (1957). *The Politics of Israel; The first decade of statehood.* Princeton, N.J.: Princeton U.P.

Berting, J. (1968). *In het Brede Maatschappelijke Midden.* Meppel: Boom.

Black, Duncan (1958). *The Theory of Committees and Elections*, Cambridge: Cambridge U.P.

Blondel, Jean (1967). "Party Systems and Patterns of Government in Western Democracies", *International Political Science Association, Brussels, 1967.*

Blondel, Jean and Drexer, Godfrey, Jr. (1968). *The Government of France.* London: Methuen.

Borg, Olavi (1966). "Basic Dimensions in Finnish Party Ideologies: A factor analytical study", *Scandinavian Political Studies*, vol. 1, pp. 94—117. Helsinki, New York and London: The Academic Bookstore (Columbia U.P.).

Boulding, Kenneth E. (1962). *Conflict and Defense; A general theory.* New York: Harper and Row.

Brams, Steven J. (1972). "(Book review of) Groennings, S., Kelley, E.W. and Leiserson, M. (eds.), The Study of Coalition Behavior: Theoretical perspectives and cases from four continents, " *American Political Science Review*, 66, pp. 236—238.

Braybrooke, David and Lindblom, Charles E. (1963). *A Strategy of Decision; Policy evaluation as a social process.* New York: The Free Press.

Brody, Richard A. (1962). "Three Conceptual Schemes for the Study of International Relations", in: Snyder, R.C., Bruck, H.W. and Sapin, B. (eds.), *Foreign Policy Decision-Making.* New York: Free Press of Glencoe.

Browne, Eric C. (1970—1971). "Testing Theories of Coalition Formation in the European Context", *Comparative Political Studies*, 3, pp. 391—412.

Browne, Eric C. (1973). *Coalition Theories: A logical and empirical critique.* Sage Professional Papers in Comparative Politics, *forthcoming.*

Browne, Eric C. and Franklin, Mark N. (1973). "Aspects of Coalition Payoffs in European Parliamentary Democracies", *American Political Science Review*, 67, pp. 453—469.

Buchanan, James M. and Tullock, Gordon (1962). *The Calculus of Consent; Logical foundations of constitutional democracy.* Ann Arbor: University of Michigan Press.

Buchler, Ira R. and Nuttni, Hugo G. (eds.) (1969). *Game Theory in the Behavioral Sciences.* Pittsburgh: University of Pittsburgh Press.

Burke, Edmund (1861). *Thoughts on the Cause of the Present Discontents* (1770), *Works*, vol. 1. London: Bohn.

Butterworth, Robert L. (1971). "A Research Note on the Size of Winning Coalitions" and "Rejoinder to Riker's 'Comment'", *American Political Science Review*, 65, pp. 741—745 and pp. 747—748.

Campbell, Angus, Converse, Philip E., Miller, Warren E. and Stokes, D.E. (1960). *The American Voter*. New York: Wiley.

Carlyle, Margaret (1965). *Modern Italy* (rev. edn.). London: Hutchinson.

Carlyle, Thomas (1872). *On Heroes, Hero-Worship and the Heroic in History* (1840). London: Chapman and Hall.

Carsten, F.L. (1967). *The Rise of Fascism*. London: Batsford.

Chassériaud, Jean-Paul (1965). *Le Parti Démocrate Chrétien en Italie* (Cahiers de la Fondation Nationale des Sciences Politiques, 125). Paris: Colin.

Converse, Philip E. (1966). "The Problem of Party Distance in Models of Voting Change", in: Jennings, M.K. and Zeigler, H. (eds.), *The Electoral Process*, pp. 175—207. Englewood Cliffs, N.J.: Prentice-Hall.

Converse, Philip E. and Dupeux, Georges (1969). "Politicization of the Electorate in France and the United States", in: Lijphart, A. (ed.), *Politics in Europe; Comparisons and interpretations*, pp. 178—200. Englewood Cliffs, N.J.: Prentice-Hall. (Originally published in *Public Opinion Quarterly*, 1962, 26, pp. 1—23.)

Converse, Philip E. and Valen, Henry (1971). "Dimensions of Cleavage and Perceived Party Distances in Norwegian Voting", *Scandinavian Political Studies*, vol., pp. 107—152. Oslo, New York and London: Universitetsforlaget (Columbia U.P.).

Coombs, Clyde H. (1953). "Theory and Methods of Social Measurement", in: Festinger, L. and Katz, D. (eds.), *Research Methods in the Behavioral Sciences*, pp. 471—535. New York: Holt, Rinehart and Winston.

Czudnowski, Moshe M. (1970). "Legislative Recruitment under Proportional Representation; A model and a case study", *Midwest Journal of Political Science*, 14, pp. 216—248.

Daalder, Hans (1955). "Parties and Politics in the Netherlands", *Political Studies*, 3, pp. 1—16.

Daalder, Hans (1957). "Nationale Politieke Stelsels; Nederland", in: *Repertorium van de Sociale Wetenschappen; Politiek: begrippen, stromingen, stelsels*, pp. 213—238. Amsterdam, Brussel: Elsevier.

Daalder, Hans (1966a). "The Netherlands: Opposition in a Segmented Society", in: Dahl, R.A. (ed.), *Political Opposition in Western Democracies*. New Haven and London: Yale U.P.

Daalder, Hans (1966b). "Parties, Elites, and Political Developments in Western Europe", in: La Palombara, J. and Weiner, J. (eds.), *Political Parties and Political Development*, pp. 43—78. Princeton, N.J.: Princeton U.P.

Daalder, Hans (1971). "Cabinets and Party Systems in Ten Smaller European Democracies", *Acta Politica*, 6, pp. 282—303.

Daalder, Hans and Rusk, Jerrold G. (1972). "Perceptions of Party in the Dutch Parliament", in: Patterson, S.C. and Wahlke, J.C. (eds.), *Comparative Legislative Behavior: Frontiers of Research*, pp. 143—198. New York: Wiley.

Dahl, Robert A. (1956). *A Preface to Democratic Theory*. Chicago: University of Chicago Press.

Dahl, Robert A. (1961). *Who Governs? Democracy and power in an American city*. New Haven and London: Yale U.P.

324

Dahl, Robert A. (1966). "Further Reflections on 'The Elitist Theory of Democracy' ", *American Political Science Review*, 60, pp. 296–305.

Dahl, Robert A. (ed.) (1966). *Political Oppositions in Western Democracies.* New Haven and London: Yale U.P.

Damgaard, Erik (1969). "The Parliamentary Basis of Danish Governments: The patterns of coalition formation", *Scandinavian Political Studies*, vol. 4 pp. 31–57. Oslo, New York and London: Universitetsforlaget (Columbia U.P.).

Daudt, Hans (1961). *Floating Voters and the Floating Vote; A critical analysis of American and English election studies*, Dissertation, University of Amsterdam. Leiden: Stenfert Kroese.

Daudt, Hans (1968). "Party-System and Voters' Influence in the Netherlands", in: Stammer, O. (ed.), *Party Systems, Party Organizations, and the Politics of the New Masses (Parteiensysteme, Parteiorganisationen und die Neuen Politischen Bewegungen)*, pp. 291–304 (mimeographed). Berlin: Institut für politische Wissenschaft und der Freien Universität Berlin.

Davis, Morton and Maschler, Michael (1963a). "Existence of Stable Payoff Configurations for Cooperative Games", *Bulletin of the American Mathematical Society*, 49, pp. 106–108.

Davis, Morton and Maschler, Michael (1963b). *The Kernel of a Cooperative Game* (Econometric Research Program Research Memorandum, 58) (mimeographed). Princeton, N.J.: Princeton U.P.

Davis, Otto A. and Hinich, Melvin, J. (1966). "A Mathematical Model of Policy Formation in a Democratic Society", in: Bernd, J.L. (ed.), *Mathematical Applications in Political Science, II.* Dallas: Southern Methodist U.P.

Davis, Otto A. and Hinich, Melvin J. (1967). "Some Results Related to a Mathematical Model of Policy Formation in a Democratic Society", in: Bernd, J.L. (ed.), *Mathematical Applications in Political Science, III.* Charlottesville: Virginia U.P.

Davis, Otto A., Dempster, M.A.H. and Wildavsky, Aaron (1966). "A Theory of the Budgetary Process", *American Political Science Review*, 60, pp. 529–547.

De Gruyter, D.N.M. (1967). *The Cognitive Structure of Dutch Political Parties* (mimeographed). Leyden: Psychological Institute, Leyden Univeristy.

De Jong, L. (1969). *Het Koninkrijk der Nederlanden in de Tweede Wereldoorlog, Deel I: Voorspel.* 's-Gravenhage: Staatsuitgeverij.

De Leeuw, Jan (1968–1969). "Meerdimensionale Analyses van Politikologische Gegevens", *Hypothese, Tijdschrift voor Psychologie en Opvoedkunde.* 13, pp. 84–89.

De Swaan, Abraham, (1970). "An Empirical Model of Coalition Formation as an *N*-Person Game of Policy Distance Minimization", in: Groennings, S., Kelley, E.W. and Leiserson, M. (eds.), *The Study of Coalition Behavior; Theoretical perspectives and cases from four continents*, pp. 424–444. New York: Holt, Rinehardt and Winston.

Downs, Anthony (1957). *An Economic Theory of Democracy.* New York: Harper and Row.

Duverger, Maurice (1958). *The French Political System.* Chicago: University of Chicago Press. (Translated from the French.)

Duverger, Maurice (1964). *Political Parties; Their organization and activity in the modern state*, 3rd English edn. London: Methuen. (Translated from the French.)

Duynstee, F.J.F.M. (1966). *De Kabinetsformaties 1946-1965*. Deventer: Kluwer.

Easton, David (1965). *A Systems Analysis of Political Life*. New York: Wiley.

Eckstein, Harry (1964). "Party Systems in Scandinavia", in: Macridis, R.C. and Brown, B.E. (eds.), *Comparative Politics, Notes and Readings*, (pp. 213—219 (rev. edn.). Homewood, Ill.: Dorsey.

Elder, Neil (1964). "Party Systems in Scandinavia", in: Macridis, R.C. and Brown, B.E. (eds.), *Comparative Politics; Notes and Readings*, pp. 213—219. (rev. edn.). Homewood, Ill.: Dorsey.

Ellsberg, Daniel (1956). "Theory of the Reluctant Duellist", *American Economic Review*, 46, pp. 909—923.

Etzioni, Amitai (1963). "Alternative Ways to Democracy: The example of Israel", in: Eckstein, H. and Apter, D.E. (eds.), *Comparative Politics; A reader*, pp. 712—721. New York: Free Press of Glencoe.

Eyck, Erich (1962). *Geschichte der Weimarer Republik*, 2 Vols. (3rd edn.). Zurich: Erlenbach.

Fauvet, Jacques (1959). *La IVe République*. Paris: Fayard.

Feller, William (1968). *An Introduction to Probability Theory and its Applications*, Vol. I (3rd edn.). New York: Wiley.

Fisher, R.A. (1932). *Statistical Methods for Research Workers* (4th edn.). Edinburgh: Oliver and Boyd.

Flechtheim, Ossip K. (1962). "Die Rolle der KPD", in: *Der Weg in der Diktatur; 1981 bis 1933*. München: Piper.

Forsell, Harry (1971). "The Elections in Sweden in September 1970; Politics in a multi-level election", *Scandinavian Political Studies*, vol. 6, pp. 201—211. Oslo, New York and London: Universitetsforlaget (Columbia U.P.).

Fox, Edward Whiting (1951). "The Third Force", in: Earle, Edward Mead (ed.), *Modern France; Problems of the Third and Fourth Republic*, pp. 124—136. Princeton, N.J.: Princeton U.P.

Freudenheim, Yoshua (1967). *Government in Israel*. New York: Oceana. (Translated from Hebrew.)

Freudenthal, Hans (1962). *Waarschijnlijkheid en Statistiek*. Haarlem: Bohn.

Friedmann, Georges (1965). *Fin du Peuple Juif?* Gallimard.

Friis, Henning (1950). *Scandinavia between East and West*. Ithaca, N.Y.: Cornell U.P.

Fusilier, Raymond (1960). *Les Monarchies Parlementaires; Suède, Norvège, Danemark, Belgique, Pays-Bas, Luxembourg*. Paris: Eds. Ouvrières.

Fusilier, Raymond (1965). *Les Pays Nordiques; Danemark, Finlande, Norvège, Suède, Islande*. Paris: Pichon et Durand-Auzias.

Gamson, William A. (1962). "Coalition Formation at Presidential Nominating *Sociological Review*, 26, pp. 373—382.

Gamson, Willian A. (1962). "Coalition Formation at Presidential Nominating Conventions", *American Journal of Sociology*, 68, pp. 157—171.

Gillies, Donald B. (1959). "Solutions to General Non-Zero-Sum Games", in: Tucker, A.W. and Luce, R.D. (eds.), *Contributions to the Theory of Games*, vol. 4 (*Annals of Mathematics Studies*, No. 40), pp. 47—85.

Gitlin, Todd (1967). "Local Pluralism as Theory and Ideology", in: McCoy, C.A. and Playford, J. (eds.), *Apolitical Politics; A critique of behavioralism*. New York: Crowell.

Godechot, Thierry (1964). *Le Parti Démocrate-Chrétien Italien.* Paris: Pichon et Durand-Auzias.

Goguel, Francois (1952). *France under the Fourth Republic.* Ithaca, N.Y.: Cornell U.P.

Goldberg, Arthur S. (1969). "Social Determinism and Rationality as Bases of Party Identification", *American Political Science Review,* 63, pp. 5—25.

Goudsblom, Johan (1967). *Dutch Society.* New York: Random House.

Gregg, L.W. and Simon, H.A. (1967). "Process Models and Stochastic Theories of Simple Concept Formation", *Journal of Mathematical Psychology,* 4, pp. 246—276.

Gregor, James A. (1968). *Contemporary Radical Ideologies; Totalitarian thought in the twentieth century.* New York: Random House.

Gregor, James A. (1969). *The Ideology of Fascism; The rationale of totalitarianism.* New York: The Free Press.

Groennings, Sven (1970). "Patterns, Strategies, and Payoffs in Norwegian Coalition Formation", in: Groennings, S., Kelley, E.W. and Leiserson, M. (eds.), *The Study of Coalition Behavior; Theoretical perspectives and cases from four continents.* pp. 60—79. New York: Holt, Rinehardt and Winston.

Halperin, S. William (1946). *Germany Tried Democracy; A political history of the Reich from 1918 to 1933.* Hamden, Conn. and London: Archon.

Harsanyi, John C. (1961). "Theoretical Analysis in Social Science and the Model of Rational Behaviour", *Australian Journal of Politics and History,* 7, pp. 60—74.

Harsanyi, John C. (1967). "Rational Choice Models vs. Functionalistic and Conformistic Models of Political Behavior", *American Political Science Association,* Chicago, 1967 (mimeographed).

Hazewindus, W.G.A. and Mokken, R.J. (1972). "A Distance Analysis of Party Preferences" European Consortium for Political Research, *Workshop on European Cabinet Coalitions,* Helvoirt, The Netherlands, 1972 (mimeographed).

Henig, Stanley and Pinder, John (eds.) (1969). *European Political Parties* (PEP, Political and Economic Planning). London: Allen and Unwin.

Hertzmann, Lewis (1963). *DNVP; Right-wing opposition in the Weimar Republic, 1918—1924.* Lincoln: University of Nebraska Press.

Hinich, Melvin J. and Ordeshook, Peter C. (1970). "Plurality Maximization vs. Vote Maximization: A spatial analysis with variable participation", *American Political Science Review,* 64, pp. 772—791.

Hodgson, John (1967). *Communism in Finland: A history and interpretation.* Princeton, N.J.: Princeton U.P.

Hoffmann, Stanley (1951). *Le Mouvement Poujade* (Cahiers de la Fondation Nationale des Sciences Politiques, 81). Paris.

Hoogerwerf, A. (1964). *Protestantisme en Progessiviteit; Een politicologisch onderzoek naar opvattingen van Nederlandse protestanten over verandering en gelijkheid,* Dissertation Free Univeristy of Amsterdam. Meppel: Boom.

Hoogerwerf, A. (1965). "Latent Socio-Political Issues in the Netherlands," *Sociologia Neerlandica,* 2, pp. 161—179.

Jacobs, A.A.J. and Jacobs-Wessels, W. (1968-1969). " 'Duidelijkheid' in de Nederlandse Politiek", *Acta Politica* 4, pp. 41—54.

Kaplan, Abraham (1964). *The Conduct of Inquiry; Methodology for behavioral science*. San Francisco: Chandler.

Kaskimies, E. (1969). *The Finnish Parliament*. Helsinki: Söderstrom. (Translated from the Finnish.)

Kastari, Paavo (1969). "The Position of the President in the Finnish Political System", *Scandinavian Political Studies*, vol. 4, pp. 151—159. Oslo, New York and London: Universitetsforlaget (Columbia U.P.).

Keesings's Historisch Archief, Amsterdam (weekly publication since 1931).

Kendall, M.G. and Stuart, A. (1958). *The Advanced Theory of Statistics, Vol. I: Distribution Theory*. London: Griffin.

Kirschen, E.S. *et al.* (1964). *Economic Policy in Our Time, Vol. I: General Theory*. Amsterdam: North-Holland.

Kleerekoper, S. (1956). *Vergelijkend Leerboek der Bedrijfseconomie, I, II*. Groningen: Noordhoff.

Kogan, Norman (1966). *A Political History of Postwar Italy*. London: Crowell.

Koo, A.J. (1959). "Recurrent Objections to the Minimax Strategy", *Review of Economics and Statistics*, 41, pp. 36—43.

Koomen, W. and Willems, L.F.M. (1968-1969). "Waarneming van het Stelsel van Nederlandse Politieke Partijen", *Acta Politica*, pp. 460—465.

Kooy, G.A. (1964). *Het Echec van een 'Volkse' Beweging; Nazificatie en denazificatie in Nederland*. Assen: Van Gorcum.

Kraines, Oscar (1961). *Government and Politics in Israel*. Boston: Houghton Mifflin.

Kruyt, P.J. *Verzuiling*. Zaandijk: Heijnis.

La Palombara, Joseph and Weiner, Myron (1966). *Political Parties and Political Development*. Princeton N.J.: Princeton U.P.

Leiserson, Michael A. (1966). *Coalitions in Politics: A theoretical and empirical study* (mimeographed), Doctoral dissertation, Yale University, New Haven.

Leiserson, Michael A. (1968). "Factions and Coalitions in One-Party Japan: An interpretation based on the theory of games", *American Political Science Review*, 57, pp. 770—787.

Leiserson, Michael (1970). "Coalition Government in Japan", in: Groennings, S., Kelley, E.W. and Leiserson, M. (eds.), *The Study of Coalition Behavior; Theoretical perspectives and cases from four continents*. New York: Holt, Rinehart and Winston.

Leites, Nathan (1959). *On the Game of Politics in France*. Stanford, Calif.: Stanford U.P.

Lemberg, Magnus (1968). "Finland: Two Years of Left Wing Coalition", *Scandinavian Political Studies*, vol. 3, pp. 230—236. Oslo, New York and London: Universitetsforlaget (Columbia U.P.).

Lijphart, Arend (1966). *The Trauma of Decolonization: The Dutch and West New Guinea*. New Haven: Yale U.P.

Lijphart, Arend (1968). *Verzuiling, Pacificatie en Kentering in de Nederlandse Politiek*. Amsterdam: De Bussy.

Lijphart, Arend (ed.) (1969). *Politics in Europe: Comparisons and interpretations*. Englewood Cliffs, N.J.: Prentice-Hall.

Lindblom, Charles E. (1965). *The Intelligence of Democracy; Decision making through mutual adjustment*. New York, London: Free Press.

Lindblom, Charles E. (1968). *The Policy-Making Process.* Englewood Cliffs, N.J.: Prentice-Hall.

Lipschits, I. (1969). *Links en Rechts in de Politiek.* Meppel: Boom.

Lipset, Seymour M. (1960). *Political Man; The social bases of politics.* London: Heinemann.

Lipset, Seymour M. and Rokkan, Stein (eds.) (1967). *Party Systems and Voting Alignments; Cross-national perspectives.* New York and London: Free Press.

Luce, R. Duncan and Rogow, A.A. (1956). "A Game Theoretic Analysis of Congressional Power Distribution for a Stable Two-Party System", *Behavioral Science*, 1, pp. 83—95.

Luce, R. Duncan and Raiffa, Howard (1957). *Games and Decisions; Introduction and critical survey.* New York: Wiley.

McPhee, William (1963). *Formal Theories of Mass Behavior.* New York: Free Press of Glencoe.

MacRae, Duncan, Jr. (1958). *Dimensions of Congressional Voting; A statistical study of the House of Representatives in the eighty-first Congress* (with the collaboration of Fred H. Goldner). Berkeley and Los Angeles: University of California Press.

MacRae, Duncan, Jr. (1967). *Parliament, Parties, and Society in France 1946—1958.* New York: St. Martin's Press.

Mann, I. and Shapley, L.S. (1964). "The A Priori Voting Strength of the Electoral College", RAND RM 2651, Sept. 1960, in: Shubik, M. (ed.), *Game Theory and Related Approaches to Social Behavior; Selections.* New York: Wiley.

Mannheim, Karl (1953). "Structural Analysis in Sociology", *Essays on Sociology and Social Psychology*, Part. 1. London: Routledge and Kegan.

Maranini, G. (1961). *L'Italie (Comment ils sont gouvernés, 5).* Paris: Pichon.

Marichy, Jean-Pierre (1969). *La Deuxième Chambre dans la Vie Politique Française Depuis 1875.* Paris: Pichon et Durand-Auzias.

Maschler, Michael (1965). *Playing an N-person Game; An experiment* (Econometric Research Program, Research Memorandum, 73). Princeton, N.J.

Meehan, Eugene J. (1965). *The Theory and Method of Political Analysis.* Homewood, Ill.: Dorsey.

Meehan, Eugene (1967). *Contemporary Political Thought; A critical study.* Homewood, Ill.: Dorsey.

Micaud, Charles A. (1956). "French Political Parties: Ideological myths and social realities", in: Neumann, S. (ed.), *Modern Political Parties; Approaches to comparative politics*, pp. 106—154. Chicago: University of Chicago Press.

Milatz, Alfred (1965). *Wähler und Wahlen in der Weimarer Republik* (Schriftenreihe der Bundeszentrale für Politische Bildung, Heft 65). Bonn.

Miller, Kenneth E. (1968). *Government and Politics in Denmark.* Boston: Houghton Mifflin.

Miller, Nicholas (1971). *Memorandum* (unpublished, mimeographed). Berkeley: University of California.

Mokken, Robert J. (1972). "A Simple Model for Testing Coalition Theories" (mimeographed, unpublished). Institute for Political Science, University of Amsterdam.

Morsey, Rudolf (1962). "Das Zentrum Zwischen den Fronten", in: *Der Weg in der Diktatur; 1918 bis 1933*, pp. 95—120. München: Piper.

Mosteller, F. and Nogee, P. (1967). "An Experimental Measurement of Utility", in: Edwards, Ward and Tversky, Amos (eds.), *Decision Making*, pp. 124—169. Harmondsworth: Penguin Books.

Neumann, D. (1965). *Die Parteien der Weimarer Republik (1932: Die Politischen Parteien in Deutschland)*. Stuttgart: Kohlhammer.

Nolte, Ernst (1965). "Germany", in: Rogger, H. and Weber, E. (eds.), *The European Right; A historical profile*, pp. 261—307. Berkeley and Los Angeles: University of California Press.

Nooij, A.T.J. (1969). *De Boerenpartij; Desoriëntatie en radicalisme onder de boeren (The Farmers Party; Disorientation and radicalism among Dutch farmers)*, Dissertation University of Amsterdam (with a summary in English). Meppel: Boom.

Norway Yearbook, The (5th edn.) (1954). Mortensen, S. (ed.). Oslo: Tanum.

Nyheim, Jan Henrik (1967). "Norway: the Cooperation of Four Parties", *Scandinavian Political Studies*, vol. 2, pp. 257—262. Helsinki, New York and London: the Academic Bookstore (Columbia U.P.).

Nyholm, Pekka (1972). *Parliament, Government and Multi-Dimensional Party Relations in Finland* (Commentationes Scientiarium Socialium, 2). Helsinki and Helsingfors.

Oosterhoff, J. (1969). *Combination of One-sided Statistical Tests*, Doctoral dissertation, Univeristy of Leyden. Amsterdam: Mathematical Centre.

Oud, P.J. (1948). *Het Jongste Verleden; Parlementaire geschiedenis van Nederland, 1918-1940*, vol. 1, *1918-1922*. Assen: Van Gorcum.

Pedersen, Mogens N. (1967). "Consensus and Conflict in the Danish Folketing 1945-1965", *Scandinavian Political Studies*, vol. 2, pp. 143—166. Helsinki, New York and Londen: The Academic Bookstore (Columbia U.P.).

Pedersen, Mogens N., Damgaard, Erik and Olsen, P. Nannestad (1971). "Party Distances in the Danish Folketing 1945-1968", *Scandinavian Political Studies*, vol. 6, pp. 87-106. Oslo, New York and London: Universitetsforlaget (Columbia U.P.).

Pen, J. (1962). *Harmonie en Conflict*. Amsterdam: De Bezige Bij.

Pesonen, Pertti (1968). *An Election in Finland; Party activities and voter reactions*. New Haven: Yale U.P. (Translated from the Finnish by the author.).

Polsby, Nelson W. (1963). *Community Power and Political Theory*. New Haven: Yale U.P.

Puchinger, G. (1969). *Colijn en het Einde van de Coalitie, I: De Geschiedenis van de Kabinetsformaties 1918-1924*. Kampen: Kok.

Random House Dictionary of the English Language, The (1966). Stein, J. and Urdang, L. (eds.). New York: Random House.

Rapoport, Anatol (1960). *Fights Games and Debates*. Ann Arbor: University of Michigan Press.

Rapoport, Anatol (1964). *Strategy and Conscience*. New York: Harper and Row.

Rapoport, Anatol (1966). *Two-Person Game Theory; The essential ideas*. Ann Arbor: University of Michigan Press.

Rapoport, Anatol (1970). *N-Person Game Theory; Concepts and applications*. Ann Arbor: Univeristy of Michigan Press.

Richardson, Lewis F. (1960). In: Rashevsky, N. and Trucco, E. (eds.) *Arms and Insecurity; A mathematical study of the causes and origins of war*. Pittsburgh: Boxwood Press.

330

Riker, William H. (1962). *The Theory of Political Coalitions.* New Haven: Yale U.P.

Riker, William H. (1966). "A New Proof of the Size Principle", in: Bernd, J.L. (ed.), *Mathematical Applications in Political Science, vol. II*, pp. 167—174.

Riker, William H. (1971). "Comment on Butterworth, 'A Research Note on the Size of Winning Coalitions'", *American Political Science Review*, 65, pp. 745—747.

Riker, William H. and Ordeshook, Peter C. (1973). *An Introduction to Positive Political Theory*, Englewood Cliffs, N.J.: Prentice-Hall.

Rintala, Marvin (1965). "Finland", in: Rogger, H. and Weber, E. (eds.), *The European Right; A historical profile*, pp. 408—442. Berkeley and Los Angeles: University of California Press.

Rodnick, David (1965). *The Norwegians: A study in national culture.* Washington, D.C.: Public Affairs Press.

Rogger, Hans (1965). "Afterthoughts", in: Rogger, H. and Weber, E. (eds.), *The European Right; A historical profile*, pp. 575—589. Berkeley and Los Angeles: University of California Press.

Rokkan, Stein (1966). "Norway: Numerical Democracy and Corporate Pluralism", in: Dahl, R.A. (ed.), *Political Oppositions in Western Democracies*, pp. 70—115. New Haven: Yale U.P.

Rokkan, Stein (1967). "Geography, Religion, and Social Class: Crosscutting cleavages in Norwegian politics", in: Lipset, S.M. and Rokkan S. (eds.), *Party Systems and Voting Alignments; Cross-national perspectives*, pp. 325—366. New York and London: Free Press.

Rokkan, Stein and Hjellum, Torstein (1966). "Norway: the Storting Election of September 1965", *Scandinavian Political Studies*, pp. 237—246. Helsinki, New York and London: the Academic Bookstore (Columbia U.P.).

Rokkan, Stein and Valen, Henry (1970). "The Election to the Norwegian Storting in September 1969", *Scandinavian Political Studies*, vol. 5, pp. 287—300. Oslo, New York and London: Universitetsforlaget (Columbia U.P.).

Romein, Jan (1938). *De Sociale en Economische Grondslagen van het Fascisme* (Waakzaamheid, Tweede Reeks, 4). Assen.

Ruin, Olof (1969). "Patterns of Government Composition in Multi-Party Systems: The case of Sweden", *Scandinavian Political Studies*, vol. 4, pp. 71—87. Oslo, New York and London: Universitetsforlaget (Columbia U.P.).

Russett, Bruce M. (1970). *What Price Vigilance? The burdens of national defense.* New Haven: Yale U.P.

Rustow, Dankwart A. (1956). "Scandinavia: Working Multiparty Systems", in: Neumann, S. (ed.), *Modern Political Parties; Approaches to comparative politics.* Chicago: University of Chicago Press.

Saladino, Salvatore (1965). "Italy", in: Rogger, H. and Weber, E. (eds.), *The European Right; A historical profile*, pp. 208—260. Berkeley and Los Angeles: University of California Press.

Sänkiaho, Risto (1970). "Voting Strength in the Finnish Parliament 1951-1966", *Scandinavian Political Studies*, vol. 5, pp. 119—128. Oslo, New York and London: Universitetsforlaget (Columbia U.P.).

Sänkiaho, Risto (1971). "A Model of the Rise of Populism and the Support for the Finnish Rural Party", *Scandinavian Political Studies*, vol. 6, pp. 27—47. Oslo, New York and London: Universitetsforlaget (Columbia U.P.).

Sänkiaho, Risto and Laakso, Seppo (1971). "Results of the Parliamentary Election and the Formation of the Cabinets of Teuvo Aura and Ahti Karjalainen in 1970", *Scandinavian Political Studies*, vol. 6, pp. 212—215. Oslo, New York and London: Universiteitsforlaget (Columbia U.P.).

Särlvik, Bo (1967). "Party Politics and Electoral Opinion Formation: A study of issues in Swedish politics", *Scandinavian Political Studies*, vol. 2, pp. 167—202. Helsinki, New York and London: the Academic Bookstore (Columbia U.P.).

Särlvik, Bo (1969). "Voting Behavior in Shifting 'Election Winds'; An over-view of the Swedish elections 1964-1968", *Scandinavian Political Studies*, vol. 5. pp. 241—283. Oslo, New York and London: Universitetsforlaget (Columbia U.P.).

Särlvik, Bo (1971). *The Swedish Party System in a Developmental Perspective*. Institute of Political Science, University of Göteborg (mimeo-graphed).

Sartori, Giovanni (1966). "European Political Parties: The case of polarized pluralism", in: La Palombara, J. and Weiner, M. (eds.), *Political Parties and Political Development*, pp. 137—176. Princeton, N.J.: Princeton U.P.

Sartori, Giovanni (1968). "The Sociology of Parties; A critical review", in: Stammer, O. (ed.), *Party Systems, Party Organizations, and the Politics of the new Masses (Parteiensysteme, Parteiorganisationen und die Neuen Politischen Bewegungen)* (Beitrage zur 3. Internationalen Konferenz über Ver-gleichende Politische Soziologie, Berlin, 1968), pp. 1—25. Berlin: Institut für politische Wissenschaft an der Freien Universität Berlin.

Sartori, Giovanni (1970). "The Typology of Party Systems; Proposals for Improvement", in: Allardt, E. and Rokkan, S. (eds.), *Mass Politics; Studies in Political Sociology*, pp. 322—352. New York: Free Press.

Sartre, Jean-Paul (1961). *L'Existentialisme est un Humanisme*. Paris: Nagel.

Sawyer, Jack and MacRae, Duncan, Jr. (1962). "Game Theory and Cumulative Voting in Illinois: 1902-1954", *American Political Science Review*, 56, pp. 936—946.

Schelling, Thomas C. (1963). *The Strategy of Conflict*. New York: Oxford U.P.

Scholten, Gerard H. (1968). *De Sociaal-Economische Raad en de Ministeriële Verantwoordelijkheid*. Meppel: Boom.

Schumpeter, Joseph A. (1950). *Capitalism, Socialism and Democracy* (1943) (rev. 3rd edn.). London: Allen and Unwin.

Seligman, Lester G. (1964). *Leadership in a New Nation; Political development in Israel*. New York: Prentice Hall.

Sen, Amartya K. (1970). *Collective Choice and Social Welfare*. San Francisco: Holden-Day.

Shapley, L.S. (1953). "A Value for *N*-Person Games", in: Kuhn, A.W. and Tucker, H.W. (eds.), *Contributions to the Theory of Games, II, Annals of Mathematics Studies*, vol. 28, pp. 343—359. Princeton N.J.: Princeton U.P.

Shapley, L.S. and Shubik, Martin (1953). "Solutions of *N*-Person Games with Ordinal Utilities" (Report of the East Lansing Meeting of the Econometric Society, 1952), *Econometrica*, 21, pp. 348—349.

Shapley, L.S. and Shubik, Martin (1954). "A Method for Evaluating the Distribution of Power in a Committee System", *American Political Science Review*, 48, pp. 787—792.

Shubik, Martin (1952). "Information, Theories of Competition, and the Theory of Games", *Journal of Political Economy*, 60, pp. 145—150.

Simon, Herbert A. (1957*a*). *Administrative Behavior; A study of decision-making processes in administration organization*, (1945) (2nd edn.). New York: Free Press.

Simon, Herbert A. (1957*b*). *Models of Man Social and Rational; Mathematical essays on rational human behavior in a social setting*. New York; Wiley.

Sizoo, Jan (1971). *Inzake Rechts; Verkenning van een politieke gedachten-wereld*, Doctoral dissertation, Free University, Amsterdam. Meppel: Boom.

Sjöblom, Gunnar (1968). *Party Strategies in a Multiparty System*. Lund: Studentlitteratur.

Snyder, Richard C., Bruck, H.W. and Sapin, Burton (1962). "Decision-Making as an Approach to the Study of International Politics", in: Snyder, R.C., Bruck H.W. and Sapin B. (eds.), *Foreign Policy Decision-Making* pp. 14—185. New York: Free Press of Glencoe.

Southwold, Martin (1969). "A Games Model of African Tribal Politics", in: Buchler, I.R. and Nutini, H. (eds.), *Game Theory in the Behavioral Sciences*, pp. 23—44. Pittsburgh: University of Pittsburgh Press.

Spreafico, Alberto and La Palombara, Joseph (eds.) (1963). *Elezioni e Comportamento Politico in Italia*. Cremona: Communita.

Stapel, J. (1968-1969). "Wie en Wat Staan Waar Tussen Links en Rechts?", *Acta Politica*, 4, pp. 32—40.

Stateman's Yearbook, The; Statistical and historical annual of the states of the world. London: Macmillan (yearly publ. since 1865).

Stehouwer, Jan (1967). "Long Term Ecological Analysis of Electoral Statistics in Denmark", *Scandinavian Political Studies*, vol. 2, pp. 94—116. Helsinki, New York and London: The Academic Bookstore (Columbia U.P.).

Stjernquist, Nils and Bjurulf, Bo (1970). "Party Cohesion and Party Cooperation in the Swedish Parliament in 1964 and 1966", *Scandinavian Political Studies*, vol. 5, pp. 129—164. Oslo, New York and London: Universitetsforlaget (Columbia U.P.).

Stokes, Donald E. (1963). "Spatial Models of Party Competition", *American Political Science Review*, 57, pp. 368—377.

Stone, I.F. (1969). "Nixon and the Arms Race: How much is 'sufficiency'?", *The New York Review of Books*, 12 (6), March 27, pp. 6—18.

Storing, James A. (1963). *Norwegian Democracy*. London: Allen and Unwin.

Taylor, Michael (1971). "On the Theory of Government Coalition Formation" (unpublished, mimeographed). University of Essex.

Torgerson, Warren S. (1958). *Theory and Methods of Scaling*. New York: Wiley.

Törnudd, Klaus (1969). "Composition of Cabinets in Finland 1917-1968", *Scandinavian Political Studies*, vol. 4, pp. 58—70. Oslo, New York and London: Universitetsforlaget (Columbia U.P.).

Valen, Henry and Katz, Daniel (1964). *Political Parties in Norway; A community study*. Oslo: Universitetsforlaget.

Van der Land, Lucas (1962). *Het Ontstaan van de Pacifistisch Socialistische Partij*. Amsterdam: De Bezige Bij.

Van Raalte, E. (1963). *Het Nederlandse Parlement* (3rd rev. edn.). 's-Gravenhage: Staatsdrukkerij.

Von Bonsdorff, Göran (1960). "The Party Situation in Finland", in: *Democracy in Finland (Studies in Politics and Government)*, pp. 18—27. Helsinki: Finnish Political Science Association.

Von Neumann, John and Morgenstern, Oskar (1967). *Theory of Games and Economic Behavior.* New York: Wiley.

Waelès, Raoul (1969). *Israël (Comment Ils Sont Gouvernés, 18).* Paris: Pichon et Durand-Auzias.

Walker, Jack (1966). "A Critique of the Elitist Theory of Democracy", *American Political Science Review*, 60, pp. 285—295.

Wasserman, Louis (1963). "Denmark: Land, Politics and Single Tax Sentiment", *American Journal of Economics and Sociology*, 22, pp. 363—377.

Weg in der Diktatur, Der (1962). Munchen: Piper.

Weil, Gordon L. (1970). *The Benelux Nations; The politics of small-country democracy.* New York: Holt, Rinehardt and Winston.

Williams, J.D. (1954). *The Compleat Strategyst; Being a primer on the theory of games of strategy.* New York: McGraw-Hill.

Williams, Philip M. (1966). *Crises and Compromise; Politics in the Fourth Republic* (1954) (rev. edn.). Garden City, N.Y.: Doubleday.

Windmuller, John P. (1969). *Labor Relations in the Netherlands.* Ithaca, N.Y.: Cornell U.P.

Wiseman, H.V. (1966). *Political Systems; Some sociological approaches.* New York: Praeger.

Wiskemann, Elisabeth (1969). *Fascism in Italy; Its development and influence.* London and New York: MacMillan.

Wiskemann, Elisabeth (1971). *Italy since 1945.* London: MacMillan.

Wuorinen, John H. (1965). *A History of Finland.* New York and London: Columbia U.P.

Index of Names

Names of Prime Minsters are printed in italics and without initials, as they refer to the cabinet of the premier rather than to the person.

Almond, G.A., 16
Andreotti, 204
Antonovsky, L., 228
Arian, A., 227, 228
Arrow, K.J., 103
Aumann, R., 40
Aura, 252
Axelrod, R., 4, 8, 75, 76, 83, 156, 287, 288

Barber, J.D., 15
Barnes, S.H., 194
Bauer, 167, 173
Beel, 218
Ben Gurion, 231-235
Bidault, 182
Biesheuvel, 224
Black, D., 113, 114, 294
Borten, 281, 282
Bourgès-Mannoury, 191
Branting, 258, 259, 264, 278
Bratelli, 282
Braunsgaard, 268, 272
Braybrooke, D., 14
Browne, E.C., 128, 156, 157, 282
Brüning, 171-173
Buchanan, J.M., 3
Bühl, 270
Burke, E., 133

Cajander, 244, 246
Cals, 223
Campbell, A., 15
Carlyle, T., 12
Castrén, 245
Colijn, 214, 216, 217
Colombo, 203
Converse, P.E., 175, 278
Cuno, 173

Daalder, H., 210
Dahl, R.A., 3, 14, 294
Damgaard, E., 156, 157, 265, 267, 268, 273
Davis, M., 42, 43, 94
Davis, O.A., 3, 15
Dayan, 235
De Gasperi, 196-198
De Gaulle, 179, 180, 181, 183
De Geer, P.J., 215, 217
De Gruyter, D.N.M., 208, 209
De Jong, 223
De Leeuw, J., 208, 209
De Quay, 222
De Swaan, A., 4
Den Uyl, 225
Downs, A., 2, 3, 15, 133, 134, 293
Drees, 219-221
Dupeux, G., 175

Duverger, M., 176

Easton, D., 16
Edén, 258, 264, 278
Ekman, 85, 257, 259, 260
Erich, 241
Eriksen, 271
Erlander, 261-264
Eshkol, 234, 236
Eyck, E., 162

Fagerholm, 247-249, 252
Fanfani, 198-200
Fehrenbach, 168, 173
Fox, E.W., 180
Franklin, M.N., 128, 282

Gaillard, F., 191
Gamson, W.A., 3, 8, 52, 63, 71, 128, 156, 282
George, H., 266
Gerbrandy, P.S., 217
Gerhardsen, 280, 281
Geszler, J., 169
Gouin, 181
Gregor, J.A., 140
Groennings, S., 278, 282, 283
Guttman, L., 228

Hackzell, 245
Hansen, 268, 271, 272, 275
Hansson, 260, 261, 264
Hazewindus, W.G.A., 76, 210
Hedtoft, 271, 274
Hinich, M.J., 3
Hitler, A., 172, 173
Hotelling, H., 2, 293

Ingman, 242

Jacobs, A.A.J., 209
Jacobs-Wessels, W., 209

Kallio, 242, 244
Kampmann, 268, 272, 274, 275
Kaplan, A., 2
Karjalainen, 249, 251
Kastari, P., 238
Kekkonen, 247, 248
Kivimäki, 243, 244
Kleerekoper, S., 17

Koivisto, 250
Koomen, W., 209
Krag, 268, 272, 273
Kristensen, 271

Laniel, 189
Larsen, A., 266
Lehto, 249
Leiserson, M.A., 4, 8, 65, 71, 83, 156, 298
Leites, N., 175, 176
Leone, 201, 202
Lijphart, A., 3
Lindblom, C.E., 14, 15, 23
Linkomies, 245
Lipschits, I., 135, 210, 211
Lipset, S.M., 3
Luce, R.D., 35
Luther, 169, 170, 173
Lyng, 281

MacRae, D., Jr., 4, 132, 176, 177, 178, 188
Madsen-Mygdal, 270
Mantere, 242
Marie, 184
Marijnen, 222, 223
Marx, 168-170, 173
Maschler, M., 40, 42, 43, 94
Mayer, 188, 192
Meehan, E.J., 2
Meir, 236
Mendès-France, 189
Meynaud, J., 141
Micaud, C.A., 175
Miettunen, 248
Mokken, R.J., 9, 10, 76, 210
Mollet, 191
Morgenstern, O., 3, 8, 21, 26, 28, 33, 35, 49, 50, 60, 65, 157, 273, 298
Moro, 200-202
Müller, 167, 171

Neergaard, 268, 269
Nenni, P., 196, 201, 202
Nygardsvold, 280

Ombre, E.L., xii

Paasio, 250, 252
Paasiviki, 245

336

Palme, 263, 264
Pehrsson-Bramstorp, 260, 261
Pekkala, 246
Pella, 198
Pflimlin, P., 191
Poujade, P., 180, 190

Raiffa, H., 35
Ramadier, 182
Rangell, 245
Rapoport, A., 35
Richardson, L.F., 3
Riker, W.H., 3, 8, 24, 52-54, 56-62,
  64, 84, 113, 133, 144, 156, 176,
  268, 282, 298
Rogger, H., 141
Rokkan, S., 3, 278
Romein, J., 140
Ruin, O., 282, 283
Rumor, 202, 203
Rusk, J.G., 210
Ruys de Beerenbrouck, 213-215
Ryti, 244, 245

Saladino, S., 141
Sänkiaho, R., 250
Sarragat, G., 196, 202, 203
Sartori, G., 10, 131, 160, 161, 177,
  192, 194
Sawyer, J., 4
Scavenius, 270
Scelba, 199
Scheidemann, 85, 165
Schelling, T.C., 29
Schuman, 183
Schumpeter, J.A., 132, 133
Segni, 199
Selten, H., 158
Sen, A.K., 103

Shapley, L.S., 44-46
Sharett, 232
Shubik, M., 24
Simon, H.A., 14, 15, 23
Sizoo, J., 135
Sjöblom, G., 133
Snyder, R.C., 14
Stapel, J., 209
Stauning, 269, 270
Stokes, D.E., 136-138
Stresemann, 168, 173
Sukselainen, 248
Sunila, 242, 243
Svinhufvud, 242, 243

Tambroni, 200
Tanner, 242
Törngren, 248
Tullenheimo, 242
Tullock, G., 3
Tuomioja, 247, 248

Valen, H., 278
Vennamo, R., 250
Vickrey, W., 37, 38
Virolainen, 249
Von Hindenburg, P., 170, 172
Von Neumann, J., 3, 8, 21, 26, 28,
  33, 35, 49, 50, 60, 65, 157, 273,
  298
Von Papen, F., 172, 173
Von Schleicher, K., 172, 173

Willems, L.F.M., 209
Williams, P.M., 132
Wirth, 168

Zahle, 269
Zijlstra, 223

Index of Subjects

Action Paysanne (France), 179, 188
Action Républicaine (France), 179
Actor, as a unitary entity, 81, 84
  defined, 131
Agrarian League (Finland), see
  Agrarian Party (Finland)
Agrarian Party (Denmark), 266
Agrarian Party (Finland), 239, 241-
  249
Agrarian Party (Norway), 266-281,
  283; see also Center Party
  (Norway)
Agrarian Party (Sweden), 85, 258-
  262; see also Center Party
  (Sweden)
Agrarians (Sweden), see Agrarian
  Party (Sweden)
Agudat Israel, 131, 229, 231-234,
  236
Ahdut Ha'Avoda (Israel), 228, 232-
  236
Algérie Française (France), 191
All-bourgeois coalition (France),
  186-190
All-bourgeois coalition (Netherlands),
  221-224
All-bourgeois coalition (Norway),
  111, 112
All-bourgeois coalition (Weimar),
  169, 170
All-party coalition, 83, 87, 88, 111,
  117

Anti Revolutionary Party (Nether-
  lands), 207, 208, 212-225
Antier-faction (France), 178
Assembly, 9, 127, 130, 302
Assembly (Denmark), see *Folketing*
Assembly (Finland), see *Eduskunta*
Assembly (France), 174
Assembly (Israel), see *Knesset*
Assembly (Italy), 192
Assembly (Netherlands), 206
Assembly (Norway), see *Storting*
Assembly (Sweden), see *Riksdag*
Assembly (Weimar), see *Reichsrat*

Bargaining proposition, 8, 65, 67,
  112, 285, 287, 298, 303
  statistical results, 148, 150, 152,
  156, 158
Bargaining set, 39, 42-44
Basic alternative, 10, 111, 112
Basic alternative theory, 10, 78
  statistical results, 149, 151, 154,
  158
Basic Ideological Ordinal Scale, 240
Bayerische Volkspartei (Weimar),
  163-172
Bicameral parliament, 84, 130, 255
Blocking coalition, 49
Boerenpartij (Netherlands), 208
Boomerang effect, 92

Cabinet, 9, 143, 144

Cardinality, 20, 21, 31, 75
Catholic Party (Netherlands), 207, 208, 212-225, 295
Catholics (Weimar), see *Zentrum* party (Weimar)
Center Party, 109
Center Party (Finland), 239, 249-253; see also Agrarian Party (Finland)
Center Party (Norway), 109, 112, 277, 282
Center Party (Sweden), 256, 257, 262-264
Characteristic function, 27, 74, 101 defined, 30
Cheapest winning coalition, 3, 63
Christian Democracy, 139
Christian Democratic Party (France), 175, 177
Christian Democratic Party (Italy), 290, 291, 295
Christian Historical Party (Netherlands), 207, 208, 212-225
Christian People's Party (Norway), 109, 112, 277, 278, 282
Classical theory of parties, 133
Clericalism (France), 176
Clericalism (Italy), 195
Closed coalition, 74, 75, 159, 303 defined, 70 of minimal range, 9
Closed coalition condition in policy distance theory, 117
Closed coalition proposition, 10, 118, 288 statistical results, 149, 151, 153-156, 158
Closed coalition version of policy distance theory, 117, 288, 294 statistical results, 148-153
Closed minimal range theory, 159, 285, 287, 288, 291, 292, 298 statistical results, 149, 151, 154-158
Closed minimal winning coalition, 111
Closed-system viewpoint, 81
COAL, 4, 10, 302, 303
Coalition, ad hoc, 81, 85 all-bourgeois, see All-bourgeois coalition all-party, 83, 87, 88, 117; see also

All-party coalition
    basic alternative, 10, 111, 112
    blocking, 49
    cheapest winning, 3, 63
    closed, 74, 75, 159, 303
    closed and of minimal range, 9
    closed, defined, 70
    closed minimal range, 76
    closed minimal winning, 111
    closed, proposition, 10, 118, 288
    defined, 30
    excess of, 89, 90, 94, 104, 106, 111
    expected policy of, 88-95, 113, 128
    expected policy of, defined, 91
    governing, 1
    grand national, 80; see also All-party coalition
    group rational, 90
    large, 64, 83, 129
    legislative, 6
    losing, 50
    majority, 6, 83, 129-132
    membership in, 84, 143, 144
    minimal connected winning, 75, 288
    minimal range, 73
    minimal winning, 50, 51, 54, 60, 62, 111
    minimal winning, minimal range, 78
    minimum size, 52, 53, 56, 60, 62, 63, 87, 111
    non-minimal, 80-87
    non-permissible, 115
    one-man, 89, 90, 92
    open, defined, 70
    1-n permissible, 115
    range of, 8, 88, 159
    realizable, 61
    undominated, 111
    uniquely preferable winning, 56, 57, 59, 62
    virtual, 145
    weakly dominated, 111
    winning, 81, 83
    winning, defined, 49
Coalition-bargaining potential, 131
Coalition formation in multi-party systems, 2, 289-297

Communism, 138, 142
Communist Party (Denmark), 143,
  266, 267
Communist Party (France), 175, 177,
  181-192
Communist Party (Israel), 228, 230-
  236
Communist Party (Italy), 193
Communist Party (Netherlands), 207,
  208, 212-225
Communist Party (Norway), 277, 278
Communist Party (Sweden), 256,
  258-264
Communist Party (Weimar), 163,
  165-172
Communists (Finland), see Finnish
  People's Democratic League
Compensation principle, 103
Complete connected order, 89
Complete defeat, 49, 50, 98
Complete information, 14, 22, 27, 64
  defined, 23
Completeness, of policy scale, 68
Concord, 81, 87
Condition, constant-sum, 74
  limiting, 82
  modifying, 82
Confindustria, 195, 197
Conflict of interest, 8, 75-77, 83, 288
Connected order, complete, 89
Connectedness, 20, 91
Consensus, 81, 83, 87, 196, 254
Conservatism, social economic, 9, 135
Conservative Party (Denmark), 266,
  267, 274
Conservative Party (Finland), 239,
  241-251
Conservative Party (Norway), 277-
  283
Conservative Party (Sweden), 256-
  264
Conservatives, 139
Conservatives (France), 175, 178,
  181-192
Conservatives (Norway), 109
Conservatives (Sweden), 85
Constituent Assembly (Italy), 195
Constitutional amendment, 83, 129,
  130
Constitutional amendments
  (Denmark), 265

Constitutional amendments
  (Finland), 238
Constitutional amendments (France),
  182
Constitutional amendments (Israel),
  227
Constitutional amendments (Italy),
  193, 196
Constitutional amendments (Nether-
  lands), 218, 219, 222
Constitutional amendments
  (Sweden), 255
Constitutional amendments
  (Weimar), 162, 166
Constitutional requirement, 81
Context of the game, 48, 101
Core, 90, 104
  defined, 36

Decision-making analysis, 12
Decision-making approach, 12
Deductive theory, 2
Democratic Party (Weimar), 131
Democratic Socialists '70 (Nether-
  lands), 223, 224
Democrats (Netherlands), 223
Democrats (Weimar), 85
Democrats '66 (Netherlands), 22, 224
Democrazia Cristiana (Italy), 193
Denmark, 10, 265-276
  statistical results of theories, 148,
  275, 276
Desétatisation, 180
Determination of government policy,
  87, 88
Determination of major government
  policy, 128, 245
Deutsche Demokratische Partei
  (Weimar), 163-172
Deutsche Volkspartei (Weimar), 163-
  172
Deutschnationale Volkspartei
  (Weimar), 163-172
Distance, 92
  along policy scale, 68
Domination, 107, 303
  defined, 33
  statistical results, 152
  weak, 108, 111

Eduskunta (Finland), 237, 238, 245

Equilibrium, 121, 122, 124, 145
Equilibrium set, 122
Equilibrium strategy, 26
Event, 147
  defined, 123
Excess, in theory of the kernel, 43
Excess of the coalition, 89, 90, 94,
  104, 106, 111, 303
Exclusion from winning coalition, 98
Existentialism, 13
Expected policy of the coalition, 88-
  95, 113, 128, 294, 298
  defined, 91
Extreme polarization, 160

Faction, 84, 132
Factual assumption, 125
Fascism, 140-142
Fascists (Italy), 193, 195
Federalism (Weimar), 166
Finland, 10, 237-253
  statistical results of theories, 148,
    252, 253
Finnish Conservative Party (Finland),
  239
Finnish Patriotic Movement
  (Finland), 239
Finnish People's Democratic League
  (Finland), 239, 245
Finnish People's Party (Finland),
  239, 248, 249; see also Progressive
  Party (Finland)
Focal point, 29
Folketing (Denmark), 265
Foreign influence, 145, 146, 166,
  183, 193, 197, 207, 217, 245, 246
Formal empirical theory, 2
Formal empiricist method, 136, 138,
  297-301
Formal theory, 1
  of voting, 3
France, 174-192
  statistical results of theories, 148,
    149, 192
French Fourth Republic, 10, 279;
  see also France
French Third Republic, 279
Function, characteristic, 74
Functional analysis, see Structural
  functional analysis

Gachal (Israel), 234-236
Gain, pro rata, 63
Game, constant-sum, 27, 51, 74
  constant-sum, three-person,
    example, 34
  cooperative, 27, 29
  cooperative *n*-person, 29
  iterated, 28
  non-constant-sum, 27-29, 55
  non-cooperative, 27, 28
  non-simple, 55, 60, 62
  n-person, 27
  quota, 35
  simple, 35, 49-51, 56, 62, 63
  simple, constant-sum, 90
  strictly determined, 28
  strong simple, 66
  symmetric, 54
  symmetric simple, 52
  weighted majority, 35, 53
  zero-sum, 27, 51
Game context, 48, 101, 144-146
Game setting, defined, 127
Game theory, 4, 13, 26, 88, 90
  n-person, 3, 26-46
Gaullists (France), 175, 179, 181-192
General Zionist Party (Israel), 228-
  236
Germany, see Weimar Republic
Governing coalition, 1
Government intervention, 135
Government policy, determination of,
  87, 88
  major, determination of, 128
Grand coalition, 87, 115, 245, 261
Grand coalition (Netherlands), 217
Grand coalition (Weimar), 167-169,
  171, 173
Grand Committee (Finland), 237
Group rational coalition, 90, 103

Heretic set, 38
Herut (Israel), 228, 230-236
Hierarchical theory, 2
Histadrut (Israel), 227-229
Historic romanticism, 13
Homo economicus, 17
Homogeneity of the coalition, 74, 83
Homogeneous weights, 66, 67
Hotelling-Downs model, 2, 293

341

Hypergeometric distribution, 305

Ideological diversity, 8, 71, 74, 75, 83
Imputation, defined, 33
  undominated, 90
Incomplete information, 85
Incrementalism, 14, 287, 288, 298
Independent Liberal Party (Israel),
  234-236
Independent Socialists (Weimar), 163,
  165-172
Independents (France), 178; see also
  Conservatives (France)
Individual rationality, 102
Influence, outside, see Foreign
  influence
Information, complete, 14, 22, 27, 64
  incomplete, 85
  perfect, 64
Information effect, 64, 84, 144
Intensity of preference, 114, 115, 117
Interest group, 130
Interpersonal comparison of utilities,
  76
Interval minimal range theory, 75
  statistical results, 148, 149, 158
Intransigence, 132
Israel, 10, 226-237
  statistical results of theories, 148,
  236, 237
Israel Labor Party, 235
Italian Republic, 10; see also Italy
Italy, 192-204
  statistical results of theories, 148,
  204

Joint Division (Sweden), 130, 255,
  258
Justice Party (Denmark), 266, 267,
  274

Kernel, 39, 42-44, 94
King, 130
King (Denmark), 265
King (Netherlands), 206
King (Norway), 277
King (Sweden), 255
Knesset (Israel), 227, 229, 233, 235

Labor Party (Norway), 277-283
Lagting (Norway), 276

Länder (Weimar), 161
Landsting (Denmark), 265
Landvolk (Weimar), 164-172
Large coalition, 64, 129, 148, 152
League of Nations Assembly, 82
Left Socialist Party (Denmark), 274
Left Socialist Party (Norway), 278,
  279; see also Socialist People's
  Party (Norway)
Left Socialists (Italy), see Proletarian
  Socialist Party (Italy)
Left Socialists (Weimar), see
  Independent Socialists (Weimar)
Leftness, 135, 209
Left-right comparison, 69, 96, 97
Legislative coalition, 6, 143, 144
Liberal League (Finland), 239
Liberal Party (Denmark), 266, 267,
  274
Liberal Party (Israel), 233
Liberal Party (Italy), 131, 193, 195
Liberal Party (Netherlands), 207, 208,
  212-225
Liberal Party (Norway), 277-283
Liberal Party (Sweden), see People's
  Party (Sweden)
Liberal People's Party (Finland), 249-
  253
Liberals, 139
Liberals (Norway), 109, 112
Liberals (Sweden), 85
Limiting condition, 87
Logrolling arrangement, 84
Losing coalition, 50
Lower House (Sweden), see Riksdag
  (Sweden)

Mafdal, see National Religious Party
  (Israel)
Major government policy,
  determination of, 245
Majority, qualified, 81
  simple, 129
Majority coalition, 6, 83
Majority criterion, 48, 126, 302
Majority requirement, 129
Mapai (Israel), 228-236, 295
Mapam (Israel), 228-236
Maximization, payoff, 81
Membership, 81
  defined, 143

in the coalition, 83, 84, 143
Minimal connected winning coalition, 75, 288
Minimal range coalition, 73
Minimal range theory, 8, 10, 73-75, 89, 128, 298, 303
  closed, see Closed minimal range theory
  interval version, 75
  ordinal version, 75
  ordinal version, statistical results, 153
  statistical results, 148, 153, 156
Minimal winning coalition, 50, 51, 54, 60, 62, 111
Minimal winning, minimal range coalition, 78
Minimal winning set, 8, 52
Minimal winning theory, 52, 285, 287, 303
  statistical results, 148, 150, 151, 154, 157, 158
Minimum size coalition, 52, 53, 56, 60, 62, 63, 87, 111, 144
Minimum size principle, 4, 8, 60, 62, 64, 128, 267, 268, 285-287, 298, 303
  statistical results, 148, 150-152, 156, 158
Minority cabinet, 81, 85
Minority government, 127, 144
Mizrachi Labor Party (Israel), 229, 231, 232
Mizrachi Workers' Party (Israel), 231
Moderates (France), see Conservatives (France)
Modifying condition, 86
Monarchists (Italy), 193, 195
Move, dominated, 29
M-stability, 41
Multi-party system, 1, 88, 289, 290, 292, 294, 296, 297
  coalition formation in, 2, 289-297
Musjawara, 82

National Progressive Party (Finland), 239
National Religious Front (Israel), 230, 231
National Religious Party (Israel), 229-236

National Socialism, 140-142
National Socialist Movement (Netherlands), 212, 216
National Socialist Party (Denmark), 266
National Socialist Party (Weimar), 163, 165-172
National Union Party (Finland), 245; see also Conservative Party (Finland)
Nationalism, 141
Nationalism (Weimar), 165-172
Nationalism dimension, 163
Netherlands, 10, 205-226
  statistical results of theories, 148, 225, 226
Non-minimal coalition, 80-84, 86, 87
Non-permissible coalition, 115
Non-utilitarian strategy preference, 71
Normalcy, period of, 80
  times of, 145, 156, 159, 162, 285
-1,0 normalization, 63
0,1 normalization, 31, 50, 62, 63
1,0 normalization, 56
Norway, 10, 109, 276-283
  statistical results of theories, 148, 282, 283
n-person game theory, 3, 26-46
Null hypothesis, 305, 307

Odelsting (Norway), 276
One-dimensionality, 134, 136, 294, 297
  of policy scale, 68
One-man coalition, 89, 90, 92
Ordered-metric scale, 69, 75
Ordinal minimal range theory, statistical results, 149, 151, 158
Ordinal policy scale, 75, 76, 90
Ordinality, 20, 21, 31, 93, 96, 97, 134
  of policy scale, 68
Outside influence, 166
Overlapping range, 97, 113

Pacifist Socialist Party (Netherlands), 208, 211, 212, 222, 223
Pareto-optimality, 32, 36, 102, 103
Parliament, bicameral, see Bicameral parliament

Parliamentary group, 5, 84, 131
Parliamentary system, 6, 9, 81, 130, 144, 145
Partisan mutual adjustment, 15
Party cohesion index, 238
Patriotic People's Movement (Finland), 244-246
Patronat (France), 180
Payoff, 127, 128
  in policy distance theory, 101
Payoff configuration, 40
Payoff maximization, 81
Peasant Party, see also Agrarian Party
Peasant Party (Finland), see Vennamo Peasant Party
Peasant Party (Netherlands), 208, 212, 223
Peasant Party (Weimar), see *Landvolk*
Peasants (France), 178; see also Poujadist Party (France)
People's Party (Sweden), 256-264
Perceptions of parties (Netherlands), 208, 211
Permissibility, statistical results, 152
Permissibility condition, 115-119
$1,n$ permissibility, 115; see also Policy distance theory, $1,n$ permissibility version
$1,n$ permissibility condition, 115, 117, 286
$1,n$ permissible coalition, 115, 303
Pivotal actor, 89, 93, 95, 104, 106, 111, 285, 286, 290-293, 295
  defined, 94
Poalei Agudat Israel, 131, 229, 234
Polarized pluralism, 10, 192
Policy distance theory, 9, 77, 82, 83, 87, 88, 90-92, 128, 285-288, 294, 303
  closed coalition condition in, 117
  closed coalition version, 118, 288, 294
  closed coalition version, statistical results, 151, 153, 158
  payoff in, 101
  $1,n$ permissibility version, 116
  $1,n$ permissibility version, statistical results, 149, 151, 152, 158

pure core version, 99, 116
pure core version, statistical results, 149, 151, 152, 158
  side-payment in, 101
  statistical results, 149, 151, 153
Policy position, 68, 88-93, 95, 117, 132
Policy preference, 4, 5, 68
Policy scale, 9, 10, 89, 90, 92, 132, 134, 135, 288, 289, 298
Political Radical Party (Netherlands), 224
Political Reformed Party (Netherlands), 208, 212, 215
Political requirement, 81
Polyarchy, 294, 295
Positivism, 123
Poujadist Party (France), 250
Poujadists (France), 179, 180, 190
Predicted set, 98, 121, 123, 124, 303, 307
Predictive performance of a theory, 147-159, 304, 307
Preference, intensity of, 114, 115
  non-utilitarian strategy, 71
Preference curve, single peaked, 113
Preference indeterminate, 99
Preference matrix, 98, 101, 107
Preference order, 100, 101, 106, 294
Presidency (Weimar), 162
President, 130
President (Finland), 238
President (Italy), 193
President (United States), 293
Presidential Council (Finland), 238
Presidential veto, 86
Principle, minimum size, 60, 62, 64, 285-287, 298, 303
Progressive Party (Finland), 239, 241-248
Progressive Party (Israel), 228-236
Progressive Three (Netherlands), 224, 225
Progressivism, social economic, 9, 135
Proletarian Socialist Party (Italy), 201, 202
Proportionality rule, 128
Proposition, bargaining, see Bargaining proposition
  closed coalition, see Closed

344

coalition proposition
Pro rata gain, 63
Proto-coalition, 56-59
Pseudo-precision, 286
Ψ-stability, 39, 44

Quasi-majority party, 290, 291

Radical Democracy, 138
Radical Democratic Party (Netherlands), 208, 212-225
Radical Liberal Party (Denmark), see Radical Party (Denmark)
Radical Party (Denmark), 266, 267, 274
Radicals (France), 175, 177, 178, 181-192
Radikale Venstre (Denmark), see Radical Party (Denmark)
Rafi (Israel), 234-236
Range, of the coalition, 8, 69, 88, 159
overlapping, 97
Rassemblement du Peuple Français (France), see Gaullists (France)
Rational actor, 4
Rational decision model, 2, 4, 10, 12-23, 87, 88, 287, 288, 298
Rationality, 5, 286
bounded, 14
defined, 18
individual, 32
limited, 14
Realizable coalition, 61
Red-green coalition (Norway), 279
Red-green coalition (Sweden), 85, 260
Reichsrat (Weimar), 161
Reichstag (Weimar), 161, 162, 165-172
Religious party, 84
RENEE, 303
Republic of Salo, 195
Républicains Sociaux (France), 190
Republican Party (Italy), 131, 193, 194, 196-202
Requirement, constitutional, 81
political, 81
RESULT, 303
Rightness, 135, 209

Riksdag (Sweden), 255, 256, 258-264, 279
Rules of the game, 27

Saddle point, 28
Satisficing, 14, 287
Scalogram method, 228
Second Chamber (Netherlands), see Assembly (Netherlands)
Self-policing equilibrium, 37
Senate, 127, 130, 302
Senate (Denmark), see *Landsting* (Denmark)
Senate (France), 174
Senate (Italy), 130, 192
Senate (Netherlands), 206
Senate (Norway), see *Lagting* (Norway)
Senate (Sweden), 258
Senate (Weimar), see *Reichsrat* (Weimar)
Sephardic Party (Israel), 231
Setting of the game, defined, 127
Shapley value, 44-46
Side-payment in policy distance theory, 101
Single-interest party, 130
Single Tax Party (Denmark), see Justice Party (Denmark)
Situation, 123
defined, 121
Size principle, 54, 57, 74
Small party, 131
Social Democracy, 138
Social Democratic League of Workers and Small Farmers (Finland), 248-253
Social Democratic Opposition (Finland), see Social Democratic League of Workers and Small Farmers (Finland)
Social Democratic Party (Denmark), 266, 267, 274, 291
Social Democratic Party (Finland), 241-252
Social Democratic Party (France), 175, 177
Social Democratic Party (Israel), 291
Social Democratic Party (Italy) (Sarragat), 143, 193, 195-203

Social Democratic Party (Nether-
lands), 207, 208, 212-225
Social Democratic Party (Norway),
109, 112, 282, 291; see also Labor
Party (Norway)
Social Democratic Party (Sweden),
85, 256-264, 291
Social Democrats (Weimar), 85, 167-
172
Social Economic Council
(Netherlands), 207
Social economic dimension, 135
Social economic progressivism,
defined, 135
Socialism, 138
Socialist Party (Italy), 193
Socialist Party (Italy) (Nenni), 143,
193-203
Socialist People's Party (Norway),
280, 281
Solution, main simple, 50
strong (Vickrey), 38
V, 33, 34, 38
Von Neumann-Morgenstern, 38
Sozialistische Partei Deutschland
(Weimar), 85, 163-172
Stampede point, 126
State Party (Israel), 236
Statistical results of theories, per
country, 148, 173, 192, 204, 225,
226, 236, 237, 252, 253, 264,
274-276, 283
per number of actors, 150
Stochastic model, 124
Storting (Norway), 109, 276, 279,
281
Strategy, maximin, 28; see also
Strategy, minimax
minimax, 27-30
mixed, 28
Structural functional analysis, 12, 16,
17
Structural functional theory, see
Structural functional analysis
Superadditivity, 30, 32, 74, 101
Supercoalition, 81, 86, 221, 226
Suspensive veto, 130
Swede-Finns, see Swedish People's
Party (Finland)
Sweden, 10, 85, 254-264
statistical results of theories, 148,
264

Swedish People's Party (Finland),
239, 241-252
Symmetric-ordinal scale, 97
Synoptic decision making, 14
Systems analysis, see Structural
functional analysis

TABEL, 303
Technical terms, defined, 126-146
Theoretical prediction, 121-124
Theory, basic alternative, 78
classical, of parties, 133
closed minimal range, 10, 77, 285,
287, 288, 291, 292, 298
deductive, 2
formal, 1
formal empirical, 2
formal, of voting, 3
hierarchical, 2
minimal range, 8, 10, 73-75, 89,
128, 298, 303
minimal range, interval version, 75
minimal range, ordinal version, 75
minimal winning, 52, 285, 287,
303
of committees and elections, 113,
294
of games, 4, 13, 88, 90
of games and economic behavior,
49
of political coalitions, 53, 56
policy distance, 9, 77, 82, 83, 87,
88, 90-92, 285-288, 294, 303
policy distance, closed coalition
version, 117, 288, 294
policy distance, payoff in, 101
policy distance, $1,n$ permissibility
version, 116
policy distance, pure core version,
99, 116
policy distance, side-payment in,
101
predictive performance of, 304,
307
Threat of civil war, 82, 146, 166, 174,
190, 196
Threat of war, 82, 146, 166, 174,
217, 226, 228, 235, 236, 245,
261, 280, 285
Torah Religious Front (Israel), 229
Trade Party (Denmark), 266
Traincars on a single track, 69

Transactivity, 21, 91
  of policy scale, 68
Transferable utility, 103
Two-party system, 1, 289, 292, 294, 296
Two-third criterion, 303
  defined, 64, 65
  statistical results, 148, 150-152, 158
Tying actor, 78, 89, 302
  as pivotal actor, 111

Undominated coalition, 111
Unidimensionality, 228
Unit of analysis, 147
Unitarian Socialist Party (Italy), 202
United Nations Security Council, 84, 130
Unnecessary actor, 51, 58, 60, 74, 88, 129, 159
Uomo Qualunque, 196
Upper House (Sweden), 255; see also Senate (Sweden)
Utilities, interpersonal comparison of, 76
Utility, 19, 21, 22
  defined, 20
Utility function, 20, 21
  cardinal, 20, 21
  ordinal, 20, 21

Valence issue, 137
Vennamo Peasant Party (Finland), 250

Venstre (Denmark), see Liberal Party (Denmark)
Verdict of the electorate, 1
Verdict of the voting body, 293-297
Versailles treaty (Weimar), 162, 166, 167
Veto, 130
Veto power, 81, 84
Virtual coalition, 145
Virtual existence, 123
Votes, weighted, 48
Voting studies, 15
Vrijzinnige Democratische Bond (Netherlands), 217

Wartime situations, 155
Weak domination, 103, 108, 111
Weakly dominated coalition, 111
Weight, 88, 93, 104, 131
  defined, 131
Weighted votes, 48
Weimar, statistical results of theories, 148, 173
Weimar coalition, 85, 165-167, 173
Weimar Republic, 10, 161-173, 279
Winning coalition, 83, 129-131
Winning theory, statistical results, 148
Wirtschaftspartei (Weimar), 164-172
Workers' and Smallholders' Social Democratic League (Finland), 239
Working majority, 127

Zentrum party (Weimar), 85, 163-172